JOHANNES VAN DEN BERG

RELIGIOUS CURRENTS AND CROSS-CURRENTS

STUDIES IN THE HISTORY OF CHRISTIAN THOUGHT

VOLUME XCV

JAN DE BRUIJN PIETER HOLTROP
ERNESTINE VAN DER WALL (EDS.)

JOHANNES VAN DEN BERG

RELIGIOUS CURRENTS
AND CROSS-CURRENTS

JOHANNES VAN DEN BERG

RELIGIOUS CURRENTS AND CROSS-CURRENTS

ESSAYS ON EARLY MODERN PROTESTANTISM AND THE PROTESTANT ENLIGHTENMENT

EDITED BY

JAN DE BRUIJN
PIETER HOLTROP
ERNESTINE VAN DER WALL

BRILL
LEIDEN · BOSTON · KÖLN
1999

This book is printed on acid-free paper.

Library of Congress Cataloging-in-Publication Data

Berg, Johannes van den, 1922-
Religious currents and cross-currents : essays on early modern Protestantism and the Protestant enlightenment / Johannes van den Berg ; edited by Jan de Bruijn, Pieter Holtrop, Ernestine van der Wall.
p. cm. — (Studies in the history of Christian thought, ISSN 0081-8607 ; v. 95)
Includes bibliographical references and indexes.
ISBN 9004114742 (cloth : alk. paper)
1. Protestantism—History—17th century. 2. Netherlands—Church history—17th century. 3. England—Church history—17th century. 4. Protestantism—History—18th century. 5. Netherlands—Church history—18th century. 6. England—Church history—18th century. I. Bruijn, Jan de. II. Holtrop, Pieter. III. Wall, Ernestine G. E. van der. IV. Title. V. Series.
BX4805.2.B47 1999
280'.4'09409032—dc21
99-31253
CIP

Die Deutsche Bibliothek - CIP-Einheitsaufnahme

Johannes van den Berg : religious currents and cross-currents ; essays on early modern protestantism and the protestant enlightenment / ed. by Jan de Bruijn ... – Leiden ; Boston ; Köln : Brill, 1999
(Studies in the history of Christian thought ; Vol. 95)
ISBN 90-04-11474-2

ISSN 0081-8607
ISBN 90 04 11474 2

PRINTED IN THE NETHERLANDS

CONTENTS

PLACES OF ORIGINAL PUBLICATION

Chapter 1 in *Nederlands Archief voor Kerkgeschiedenis* 69 (1989), 176-194.

Chapter 2 in *Sir Thomas Browne M.D. and the Anatomy of Man*, Leiden 1982, 19-24.

Chapter 3 (translation of: "De Engelse Puritein Francis Rous (1579-1658) en de vertaling van enkele van zijn geschriften in het Nederlands") in *De zeventiende eeuw* 1 (1985), 48-66.

Chapter 4 in J. van den Berg and Ernestine G.E. van der Wall, *Jewish-Christian Relations in the Seventeenth Century*, Dordrecht etc., 1988, 33-50. Appendix: John Covel's Letter on the Karaites (1677) in *Jewish-Christian Relations in the Seventeenth Century*, 135-144.

Chapter 5 in Y. Kaplan, H. Méchoulan and R.H. Popkin (eds.), *Menasseh Ben Israel and his World*, Leiden etc., 1989, 98-116.

Chapter 6 in *Pietismus und Neuzeit*, 14 (Chiliasmus in Deutschland und England im 17. Jahrhundert), Göttingen 1988, 185-202 (title slightly altered).

Chapter 7 in H.J.M. Nellen and E. Rabbie (eds.), *Hugo Grotius Theologian. Essays in Honour of G.H.M. Posthumus Meyjes*, Leiden etc. 1994, 169-183.

Chapter 8 in R. Buick Knox (ed.), *Reformation, Conformity and Dissent. Essays in Honour of Geoffrey Nuttall*, London 1977, 180-198..

Chapter 9 in *Nederlands Archief voor Kerkgeschiedenis* 68 (1988), 164-179.

Chapter 10 in J. van den Berg and P.G. Hoftijzer (eds.), *Church, Change and Revolution*, Leiden etc. 1991, 130-144.

Chapter 11 in S. Groenveld and M. Wintle (eds.), *The Exchange of Ideas. Religion, Scholarship and Art in the 17th Century* (*Britain and the Netherlands* II), Zutphen 1994, 84-99.

Chapter 12 in J.W. van Henten, H.J. de Jonge, P.T. van Rooden and J.W. Wesselius (eds.), *Tradition and Reinterpretation in Jewish and Early Christian Literature. Essays in Honour of Jürgen C. Lebram*, Leiden 1986, 284-295.

Chapter 13 in D.S. Katz and J.I. Israel (eds.), *Sceptics, Millenarians and Jews*, Leiden etc. 1990, 256-274.

Chapter 14 in D. Baker (ed.), *Sanctity and Secularity: The Church and the World* (*Studies in Church History* X), Oxford 1973, 173-192 (title slightly altered).

Chapter 15 in *Durham University Journal* 75 (1982), 1-14.

Chapter 16, translation of: "Theologiebeoefening in Franeker en Leiden in de achttiende eeuw" in *It Beaken* 47 (1985) 181-194.

PREFACE

As colleagues and students of Jan van den Berg, we would like to show our high esteem for his work as specialist in seventeenth- and eighteenth-century international religious history with this volume of his collected essays. It is a great honour that Jan van den Berg has been willing to accept our invitation to make a selection of a number of his articles which show his expertise in the history of early modern Protestantism and the Protestant Enlightenment. This collection is a most valuable contribution to religious history in general and Anglo-Dutch relations in particular.

We wish to acknowledge the Dr. C. Louise Thijssen-Schoute Foundation grant and the Hendrik Muller's Vaderlandsch Fund grant which have made the publication of this volume possible.

We also extend our gratitude to Professor Heiko A. Oberman for his willingness to include this book in his prestigious series "Studies in the History of Christian Thought".

January 1999

Jan de Bruijn / Amsterdam
Pieter Holtrop / Kampen
Ernestine van der Wall / Leiden

INTRODUCTION: RELIGIOUS CURRENTS AND CROSS-CURRENTS IN SEVENTEENTH AND EIGHTEENTH CENTURY EUROPE

The religious history of seventeenth and eighteenth century Protestantism was marked by a twofold movement. On the one hand there were attempts to consolidate and, if necessary, to reaffirm the heritage of the Reformation; on the other hand, we meet a growing critical evaluation of the legacy of mainstream orthodox thought, which could lead to a process of gradual renewal and reorientation, but also to forms of more radical and controversial criticism. Conservative as well as critical tendencies can be discerned in the religious landscape on both sides of the North Sea. In spite of differences in the historical framework and spiritual culture, the developments in Great-Britain and on the Continent often present remarkable parallels, and the water of the North Sea was not too deep for creative interaction.

In England, the moderate Calvinism of the Anglican establishment of the first decades of the seventeenth century was replaced by a rising current of Latitudinarian thinking which less than a century later turned into the so-called "Protestant Enlightenment". In the course of time, through their works, British Latitudinarians and their enlightened successors were instrumental in the rise of a more enlightened theology within the circle of continental Protestantism. Next to this, however, there were other, more or less contrasting currents. Not all England bade John Calvin farewell. English Puritanism, in its own way heir to the Genevan tradition and related to Scottish Calvinism, became a driving force behind the movement of the "Further Reformation" in the Netherlands. It also strengthened Pietist tendencies in Germany; in particular, though not exclusively, in the circle of Reformed German Protestantism. Related to Latitudinarianism as well as to Puritanism and Pietism were the millenarian expectations and speculations which, from the seventeenth till halfway through the nineteenth century, were rife on both sides of the North Sea. Often they were accompanied by a keen interest in the supposed rôle of the Jewish people in the eschatological process.

In the eighteenth century more radically than in the seventeenth century, the theological framework of the Reformation period was subjected to attempts at a critical reinterpretation. The new theological orientation, "biblical" rather than "confessional" or dogmatic and averse to the "scholastic" approach of seventeenth-century orthodoxy, somehow influenced religious perceptions and attitudes at the base of church life, though it is difficult to assess to what extent. In the English-speaking world, the theologically conservative Evangelical movement partly stemmed the tide of the Protestant Enlightenment. In some respects, continental Pietism played a similar part. And below the often turbulent surface of religious currents and counter-currents, there existed hidden cross-currents which could form a connection between seemingly contrasting streams.

The articles collected in this volume reflect my various fields of interest. From the beginning of my studies in church history I was fascinated by eighteenth-century Evangelicalism as it manifested itself in the rise of the missionary movement in Great Britain. It was the subject of my doctoral dissertation, *Constrained by Jesus' Love* (1956). Later my interest turned more and more to the influence of the Enlightenment upon Protestant life and thought. The change of emphasis in my studies did not detract, however, from my primary interest: two of my more recent studies deal with "Pietistic" tendencies in the Netherlands (see the bibliography in this volume under 1993 and 1995). My eighteenth-century studies quite naturally led me to the seventeenth century: to the period which contains the early roots of the Evangelical revival and the Protestant Enlightenment. Furthermore, the vexed problem of the attitudes of Christian theology to the spiritual heritage of the Jewish people led to a number of studies in this field, partly connected with my studies on Millenarianism. Another field of interest was (and still is) the nineteenth century Dutch "Réveil"-movement and its ramifications. This part of my studies, however, falls outside the scope of this volume.

I refrained as much as possible from making changes in the articles, published in this volume; they contain my views at the time in which they were written. Perhaps they are dated in both senses of the word, but I am afraid that attempts to bring them "up to date" would scarcely have led to real improvements and could even cause confusion. Because some articles deal with related subjects a certain amount of overlap is unavoidable. Attempts to eliminate this could only be made at the cost of the unity and completeness of the articles in which the overlap occurs. I have corrected some mistakes, and in a few articles I have mentioned literature which appeared after the date of their publication, but for obvious reasons I have not tried to complete the bibliographical data.

There were and are many people to whom I owe thanks: teachers, friends, colleagues who have stimulated me in my studies. It is impossible to mention all of them; in the context of this volume, however, I would like to make two exceptions. For my studies in the field of English church history my contacts with dr. Geoffrey F. Nuttall were most stimulating. I consider it a privilege that he let me profit from his impressive knowledge of the world of Puritanism and Dissent, and it was a pleasure to cooperate with him in our joint study on Philip Doddridge (1987). Our contacts turned into a friendship which is kept alive by a continuing correspondence. In the fields of Millenarianism, Latitudinarianism and Jewish-Christian relations Professor Richard H. Popkin was an indefatigable guide whose interest in my work and whose personal friendship I highly value. A word of special thanks to dr. Norma E. Emerton, together with her husband, Professor John A. Emerton, a friend of many years, who was ever willing to correct the English of my publications, as she did for most of the articles in this volume.

I much appreciate the exertions of the editors of this volume. The cooperation of Professor Jan de Bruijn, director of the "Historisch Documentatiecentrum voor het Nederlands Protestantisme (1800-heden)"[1] at the "Vrije Universiteit",[2] Amsterdam, reminds me of the time (between 1959 and 1976) when I taught at the Free University. During eight years of this period Professor Pieter N. Holtrop worked with me as an assistant and lecturer; now he is Professor of Missiology at the Theological University of the Reformed Churches at Kampen, where I studied and where I received my doctorate. Likewise for a period of eight years, Ernestine G.E. van der Wall, now Professor of Church History in the Theological Faculty of Leiden University, cooperated with me first as assistant, then as lecturer in Leiden, where I taught from 1976 till 1987. It is to me as if, symbolically, they represent the three phases of my life as a church historian. Furthermore, I thank Mr. Hans Seijlhouwer for his accurate handling of the technical aspects of this publication.

My last and most deeply felt words of thanks are for my wife, whose warm interest in my work always was and still is such an invaluable stimulus.

J. van den Berg
December 1998
Leiden

[1] Centre for the Documentation of the History of Dutch Protestantism from 1800 onward.

[2] Free University: a University which as an institution on a religious, *i.c.* Protestant foundation is formally free from the State and which, apart from one exception (the Theological Faculty), has no institutional links with one of the Protestant Churches in the Netherlands.

CHAPTER ONE

THE SYNOD OF DORT IN THE BALANCE

In this farewell lecture[1] I intend to bring together some threads of the research I had the opportunity to do during my Leiden period. I chose as my subject a number of critical reactions to the doctrinal resolutions of the General Synod of the Reformed Church in the Netherlands which met in the town of Dort (Dutch: Dordrecht or Dordt) from November 1618 till May 1619. To the historian, these reactions are especially interesting because they are a mirror of the theological trends and developments in seventeenth and eighteenth-century Protestantism: the decisions of Dort were much debated and often led to a parting of the ways between conservative and more latitudinarian forms of theological thinking.

Thanks to the participation of a comparatively large number of foreign delegates, to a certain extent the Synod was a muster of the forces of Calvinism in Western Europe; it was an assembly of an ecclesiastical nature with, unmistakably, political aspects and effects as well. Central in the discussions stood the doctrine of predestination, which in the preceding decades had given rise to vehement conflicts in the Netherlands—the more virulent, because they were closely bound up with the political divisions in the young Republic. It all started in this town, this university, these buildings.[2] In a public disputation, held on 7 February 1604, the Leiden professor of theology Jacobus Arminius defended a number of theses on the doctrine of predestination which were carefully and unpolemically formulated, but whose angle of approach was different from that of Calvin and Beza. His colleague Franciscus Gomarus, who right from the beginning had been suspicious with regard to the doctrinal purity of Arminius, held a disputation on 31 October, in which he defended the Calvinist doctrine of predestination with all its logical conclusions. One thing and another led to a chain-reaction which did not end with the dead of Arminius in 1609 and the departure of Gomarus from Leiden in 1610. Inside

---

[1] This article is the slightly revised text of my "farewell lecture", given in the "Great Auditorium" of Leiden University on 18 December 1987. It first appeared in januari 1989 in a "house edition" under the title *Dordt in de weegschaal. Kritische reacties op de synode van Dordrecht (1618-1619)* and was dedicated to the memory of Prof. Dr. J.N. Bakhuizen van den Brink (1896-1987).

[2] For what the Remonstrant historian Gerard Brandt calls "the birth of the wrangle", see his *Historie der Reformatie* II, Amsterdam 1674, 53ff.; cf. C. Bangs, *Arminius*, Nashville and New York 1971, 262ff. A dogmatic examination of the conflict from a Calvinist point of view is given by C. Graafland in his *Van Calvijn tot Barth. Oorsprong en ontwikkeling van de leer der verkiezing in het Gereformeerd Protestantisme*, 's-Gravenhage 1987.

and outside the province of Holland a heavy confrontation took place between the followers of Arminius, the Remonstrants, and their opponents, the Contra-Remonstrants. At last Prince Maurits threw (as the poet Vondel says) his "blade of steel" into the balance. The subsequent fall of the Pensionary Oldenbarneveldt, the most influential politician in the Republic, with whose fortunes those of the followers of Arminius were almost indissolubly connected, sealed the fate of the Remonstrants: their doctrine was condemned, and they were banned from the Synod in a dramatic way. The orthodox doctrine and the condemnation of the Remonstrants were laid down in the "Canons of Dort", which henceforth together with the Belgic Confession and the Catechism of Heidelberg constituted the three so-called "Forms of Unity" of the Reformed Church in the Netherlands.

What was in theological respect the core of the conflict? The discussions on the doctrine of predestination were determined by the question how man can reach his ultimate goal, eternal salvation. Common to most seventeenth century believers was the idea of a future eternal bipartition of mankind. Universalism in the sense of a belief that ultimately all men would be saved was still very rare at that time. When in seventeenth-century discussions the word "universalism" was used, its meaning was that in the fulness of his universal love God wanted all men to attain salvation, but it was implicitly supposed that many would reject the offer of salvation and thus be eternally lost. The "decline of hell" had scarcely set in.[3] Heaven and hell were still full realities. This gave to the discussions on this matter an existential tension which helps to explain why a doctrinal conflict such as that between Arminius and Gomarus could draw such deep furrows in the field of the church.

In their doctrine of salvation the Reformers had strongly emphasized the factor of God's free grace. For Calvin (as indeed for the younger Luther)[4] this implied that for his eternal salvation man was totally dependent on a God who according to his free will elects the one while passing by and thus rejecting the other. In his *Institutes* Calvin had given a strongly worded formulation of the doctrine: for some, eternal life has been determined in advance; for others, eternal damnation.[5] This implies an image of God in which his stern majesty is heavily emphasized; an image of man which is marked by man's total

---

[3] For this, see D.P. Walker, *The Decline of Hell. Seventeenth-century discussions of eternal torment*, London 1964.

[4] Over against Calvin and the younger Luther the Remonstrants appealed to Melanchthon, and sometimes also to the later Luther; see G. Brandt, *Historie* I (1677), 98ff.; II, 55 (here somewhat more cautiously). Cf. B. Lohse's remark in C. Andresen (ed.), *Handbuch der Dogmen- und Theologiegeschichte* II, Gottingen 1980, 135: "Auf jeden Fall hat Luthers nicht ganz einheitliche Behandlung der Prädestinationslehre mit zu den späteren Differenzen beigetragen".

[5] *Inst.* III, 21,5: "Non enim pari conditione creantur omnes: sed aliis vita aeterna, aliis damnatio aeterna praeordinatur".

impotence to pave for himself the road to salvation. It would be unfair to consider Calvin exclusively under this aspect. We find in his works also a different line: less speculative, more concentrated upon God's offer of grace in and through Christ.[6] In this context we might perhaps even speak of a certain duality in his world of thought.[7] But all this does not detract from the fact that until the last edition of the *Institutes* the doctrine of a "double predestination", grounded in an "absolute decree" was not less unequivocally formulated by Calvin than by the theologians of Dort.

In a meeting of the States of Holland on 31 October 1608, shortly before his death, Arminius summarized his objections to Calvin's doctrine (though without mentioning Calvin's name) in a "Declaration" which according to his biographer Carl Bangs represents his mature views.[8] Arminius considered the doctrine of double predestination to be incompatible with the nature of God: "for this doctrine says that he wishes to damn ... Truly this differs much from the goodness of God". Of course in this context Arminius' view of the nature of God demanded the complement of another image of man: for Arminius, reprobation primarily is not a matter of God rejecting man but of man rejecting God. The doctrine, attacked by Arminius, "is inconsistent with the freedom of the will, in which and with which man has been created by God; for it prevents the use of freedom".[9] All this was attended by a different view of the church. While the Calvinists advocated a strict maintenance of pure doctrine (if necessary by means of a vigorous exercise of ecclesiastical discipline), Arminius and his followers pleaded for a larger measure of doctrinal latitude and mobility. A confession should be short and elementary, and above all it should be formulated in biblical terms: that would result in fewer errors and less strife. "Let us follow in this the example of the old church", the church of the first centuries.[10]

Arminius' followers considered themselves Christians who wanted to maintain the catholicity of the church as well as the heritage of the Reformation. In 1613 Grotius remarked with regard to those magistrates who inclined towards the Remonstrants: "Christiani sunt, Catholici manent, Reformati esse non

---

[6] Over against the views of Alexander Schweizer and others, in more recent Calvin studies this line receives a strong emphasis; *cf.* W. Niesel, *Die Theologie Calvins*, München 1957, 161ff. But we should beware of wishful thinking on this point: though the doctrine of "double predestination" does not take such a central place with Calvin as Calvin studies, especially in the nineteenth century, would lead us to believe, yet they were right in calling attention to the undeniable presence of a strict predestinarian element in Calvin's theology.

[7] For this, see also: W.J. Bouwsma, *John Calvin. A Sixteenth Century Portrait*, New York-Oxford 1988, esp. 180.

[8] Bangs, 307.

[9] I quote from G.J. Hoenderdaal's annotated edition of the text of the "Declaration", *Verklaring van Jacobus Arminius*, Lochem 1960, 78f.

[10] *Verklaring*, 134.

desinunt"—a terse summary, indeed, of the Remonstrant position.[11] But the Synod of Dort did not agree with the latter point: it refused to accept the Remonstrants as truly Reformed Christians. A complex of theological and political factors led to the defeat of the Remonstrant party. Within the national as well as (at least to all appearance) within the international context consistent Calvinism had triumphed. The foreign delegates, too, signed the decisions of the Synod, and, thanks in part to the moderating influence of some foreigners—in particular the English theologians[12]—they were formulated in a not too extreme spirit.

After some time, however, feelings of discontent manifested themselves outside the Netherlands, indeed, particularly in England. In a copy in our University Library of a work on the Synod of Dort by the German church historian Mosheim to which we shall return later we read on the front page in the handwriting of the nineteenth-century Leiden professor of church history N.C. Kist:

> Les théologiens anglais, peu satisfaits de leur mission, caracterisèrent, à leur retour, le fameux Synode de Dordrecht, dans ce bizarre distique: Dordrechti synodus, nodus; chorus integer, aeger; conventus, ventus; sessio stramen: amen![13]

With a slightly different punctuation (no doubt the original one) it becomes an echo-poem which can be translated as follows: Synod of Dort? a knot; a sound company? no, sick; a gathering? wind; a session? straw—Amen. It is not exactly what might be called lofty poetry, and it is of course quite impossible that it is the creation of the English delegates or of one of them: in a letter of 1622 it is attributed to a Jesuit source, which is more probable than the attribution to an Anglican source.[14] The Jesuits belonged to the most vehement

---

[11] Hugo Grotius, *Ordinum Hollandiae ac Westfrisiae pietas*, Lugd. Bat. 1613, 126.

[12] For this, see among others: G.J. Hoenderdaal, "The debate about Arminius outside the Netherlands", in Th.H. Lunsingh Scheurleer and G. H.M. Posthumus Meyjes, *Leiden University in the Seventeenth Century*, Leiden 1975, 153f.; J. Platt, "Eirenical Anglicans at the Synod of Dort", in D. Baker (ed.), *Reform and Reformation in England and the Continent c.1500-c. 1750*, Oxford 1979, 221-243.

[13] J.L. Moshemius, *Johannis Halesii Historia Concilii Dordraceni*, Hamburg 1724 (Un. Libr. Leiden 598 G 2; from the collection of Professor Kist).

[14] I thank Dr. N. Tyacke, London for his kind assistance in tracing the provenance of the epigram. As an echo-poem (with a very free seventeenth century English translation) it occurs on the first page of the manuscript of a play by Thomas Randolph, possibly written about 1620, but published as late as 1930: *The Drinking Academy*. A Play by Thomas Randolph, Cambridge 1930. It is quoted in a letter from James Howell to his brother, April 16, 1622: "The Jesuits have put out a geering libell against it [the Synod of Dort], and these two verses I remember in 't ...", *Epistolae Ho-Elianae*, London 1645, 54 (the date of the letter in the later editions, from 1650 onward). Howell's letters were translated into Dutch by W. Sewell: J. Howell, *Gemeenzame Brieven* (the distichon in Volume I, Amsterdam 1697, 205); but Kist must have used a different source (cf. the punctuation, the mentioning of the English delegates and the use of the French language).

opponents of the Calvinist doctrine of predestination; more than sixty years after the Synod of Dort the Jesuit Louis Maimbourg wrote that this doctrine "détruit absolument toute l'idée qu'on doit avoir de Dieu, et ensuite conduit tout droit a l'Athéisme".[15]

In England, discontent about Dort did not immediately emerge. Initially, the decisions of Dort met with a fairly large response, though the English Church did not go as far as to endow them with binding authority.[16] After 1620, however, an anti-calvinist reaction set in, determined by various factors, partly of a political, partly of an ecclesiastical or theological nature. The attitude of Charles I towards Calvinist doctrine differed much from that of his father James I. William Laud, influential already before he became Archbishop of Canterbury in 1633, was a protagonist of a High Church ecclesiology which was incompatible with the Calvinist ideal, and as early as 1623 Richard Montagu, later successively Bishop of Chichester and of Norwich, explicitly dissociated himself from the Canons of Dort. The new orientation was not just Arminian in the strict sense of the word—there was, *e.g.*, in many respects a world of difference between the High Church Archbishop Laud and the Low Church Remonstrants—, but in the controversies of those times the term "Arminianism" was used to denote an anti-Puritan and anti-Calvinist attitude. Of course, the two attitudes should not be identified: before 1620, many leading Anglicans combined a Calvinist theology with an anti-puritan bias, but more and more anti-Puritanism and anti-Calvinism went together. The Commonwealth period saw a short revival of Calvinism, but here again we should beware of the danger of identification. Not all leading Puritans were consistent and outspoken Calvinists; I remind here of the leading Puritan Richard Baxter, who stood for a moderate approach of the issues with regard to the doctrine of predestination, so much that his opponents (though unjustly) accused him of Arminianism.[17]

After the Restoration of 1660 Calvinist views lived on in the circle of the Dissenters, who now could recur to a product of their own soil, the "Westminster Confession" of 1647,[18] in which the doctrine of double predestination is unequivocally formulated: "By the decree of God, for the manifestation of his glory, some men and angels are predestinated unto everlasting life, and others foreordained to everlasting death" (Ch. III, 3). After 1689 it became the uncon-

---

[15] L. Maimbourg, *Histoire du Calvinisme*, Paris 1682, 73.

[16] For this and the following, see N. Tyacke, *Anti-Calvinists. The Rise of English Arminianism c. 1590-1640*, Oxford 1987 (esp. 105, 152, 176f., 179).

[17] M.R. Watts, *The Dissenters from the Reformation to the French Revolution*, Oxford 1978, 294.

[18] By Patrick Collinson described as "the climax of English Calvinism": "England and international Calvinism 1558-1640", in Menna Prestwich (ed.), *International Calvinism 1541-1715*, Oxford 1985, 222,

tested rule of faith of the restored Church of Scotland. For the Scots, the doctrine of predestination either as a cherished heritage or as an odious stumbling-block was not primarily embodied in "Dort", but in "Westminster". But the formal authority of the Confession could not prevent the world of thought of the eighteenth-century Scottish moderates gradually moving away from the Calvinism of Westminster, and we know at least of one candidate for the ministry who in 1766 was accepted by the Presbytery while he signed the Confession with the formula "erroribus exceptis".[19] No doubt he was one of a fairly large group of ministers and theologians who felt more at home in the climate of the Enlightenment than in that of a stern and unrelenting Calvinism.[20]

In the Church of England of the post-Restoration period Calvinist influence was extremely weak. The line of the later twenties was taken up again, and with respect to doctrine Arminian tendencies became dominant. Again, the political factor should not be underestimated: the Puritan-Calvinist attitude as it had manifested itself in the period of the Commonwealth was seen as politically disruptive. But in addition to this, the religious factor had its own momentum. When we consider the course of life of some leading seventeenth-century Anglican theologians it strikes us that they came from solidly Calvinist stock, but that they took leave of the Calvinism in which they had been reared because of theological and emotional objections to the dark side of predestinarian thinking: the doctrine of reprobation. John Hales, observer at the Synod of Dort on behalf of the English ambassador, arrived as a Calvinist, but returned as an Arminian: "there, I bid John Calvin good night".[21] The Cambridge Platonist Henry More could not "swallow down that hard doctrine concerning Fate" or "Calvinistick Predestination", from which already at an early age he had a deep aversion.[22] His colleague at Christ's College, Cambridge, Ralph Cudworth, abandoned his earlier Calvinism because he could not stand the thought that God would damn men, women and children by an arbitrary decree of predestination.[23] And for Simon Patrick, to whom the doctrine of "absolute

---

[19] A.L. Drummond and J. Bulloch, *The Scottish Church 1688-1843*, Edinburgh 1973, 110.

[20] *Cf.* J.K. Cameron, "Theological Controversy: A Factor in the Origins of the Scottish Enlightenment", in R.H. Campbell and A.S. Skinner, *The Origins and Nature of the Scottish Enlightenment*, Edinburgh 1982, 116-130.

[21] *Golden Remains of the ever memorable Mr. John Hales*, London 1659, letter of Anthony Farindon (following on "To the Reader"). The second edition of the *Golden Remains* (1673) gives the date of 17 Sept. 1657. J.L. Mosheim, who mentioned the story in his *Johannis Halesii Historia*, 149ff., was critical with regard to the reliability of Farindon's letter. There is no compelling reason, however, to doubt the authenticity of Hales' famous utterance; at any rate it is a succinct expression of his change of mind at the time of the Synod. On Hales and Dort also: R. Peters, "John Hales and the Council of Dort", in: *Councils and Assemblies* (Studies in Church History VII), Cambridge 1971, 277-288.

[22] Rosalie L. Colie, *Light and Enlightenment. A Study of the Cambridge Platonists and the Dutch Arminians*, Cambridge 1957, 37.

[23] Colie, 38ff.

predestination" had always been "very hard", it was a great relief when his teacher John Smith laughed at his scruples, "and made such a representation of the nature of God to me, and of his goodwill to men in Christ Jesus, as quite altered my opinion".[24]

The Cambridge Platonists, in some respects the precursors of a more enlightened generation of theologians, shared with the Dutch Arminians an image of God and man and a view of the church which counterbalanced the Calvinist conceptions with regard to these points. Henry More in particular sharply criticized the image of God which stood behind the doctrine of double predestination. "The Design of the Gospel is the Manifestation of the exceeding superabundant Loving-Kindness of God to the World"; but the "sad opinion of the *Predestinatours* does confront this Design at the very first Sight, making the Goodness of God such an halffaced thing, nay I may say of a more thin and sparing Aspect than the sharpest new Moon ...".[25] More declared he wanted to take a middle course between Calvinism and Arminianism, but it is clear that in fact he had already gone over to the Arminian camp. We meet an uncalvinistical image of man in Simon Patrick's *Parable of the Pilgrim* of 1665, which formally bears a slight resemblance to Bunyan's *Pilgrim's Progress* of 1678. But Patrick has a different image of man from Bunyan's: less dramatic, more optimistic, with greater emphasis on man's capacity of walking in the way of salvation and of reaching his heavenly destination. Patrick's road is less arduous than that of Bunyan, and thus his pilgrim travels more light-footedly to the New Jerusalem: "Do not measure your Drink, nor weigh your Meat, nor confine your Divertisements to a minute, but enjoy them freely ... And as the old saying is, soft and fair, goes far".[26] And all this is attended with a different image of the church: she is not a stern disciplinarian, but "an indulgent Mother", with a large heart—a moderate and tolerant church. The "Latitudinarians" (with whom Patrick reckoned himself) did not derive their wisdom from "the Spinose school-men or Dutch systematicks, neither from Rome or Geneva" but from the writings of the apostles and evangelists.[27]

Latitude was also considered a positive quality of the church (*i.c.* of the Church of England) by Gilbert Burnet, Bishop of Salisbury, one of the advisers

---

[24] *Autobiography of Simon Patrick, Bishop of Ely*, Oxford 1839, 18f. For Patrick, see J. van den Berg, "Between Platonism and Enlightenment: Simon Patrick (1625-1707) and his place in the Latitudinarian Movement", this volume Ch. 9.

[25] H. More, "An Explanation of the Grand Mystery of Godliness", X, 4, *The Theological Works*, London 1708, 350f. More even goes as far as to pose that the idea of a God (or: "that great Idol ... for it is no God") who "wills merely because he wills" can lead into "most desperate Atheism", 353. The work "Grand Mystery" was first published in 1660, more than twenty years before Maimbourg made his remark which we quoted above.

[26] S. Patrick, *The Parable of the Pilgrim*, London 1665, 222f.

[27] *A Brief Account of the New Sect of Latitude-Men* (1662; facs. ed. Los Angeles 1963), 11f.

of William III in the period of the Glorious Revolution. In his exposition of the Thirty-Nine Articles, which first appeared in 1699 and which was dedicated to the King, Burnet argued that Art. 17 (on "Predestination and Election"), though formulated in a way which seemed to be more favourable to the Calvinists than to the Remonstrants, did not explicitly exclude the Arminian views, to which he himself inclined. According to Burnet, the Church of England had not been peremptory, but had left "a Latitude to different Opinions"; therefore he could end his exposition of Art. 17 by remarking: "I leave the Choice as free to my Reader, as the Church has done".[28]

One of the leading Latitudinarians was Archbishop John Tillotson, a broad-minded and moderate orthodox (as Anglican archbishops usually are and probably should be), whose published sermons had a great influence inside and outside England. He, too, was an opponent of the Calvinist doctrine of predestination;[29] in his sermons he rarely touched upon the subject, but when he spoke of it he was critical or aloof. Among the "false and mistaken principles in Religion" he reckoned the idea "that God does not sincerely desire the Salvation of Man, but hath from all eternity effectually barr'd the greatest part of mankind from all possibility of attaining that happiness which he offers to them ... This were a melancholy consideration indeed, if it were true ...".[30] Among eighteenth-century Anglicans views like those of Tillotson were dominant. In Dissenting circles, too, we meet with a growing uncertainty with regard to the traditional doctrine of predestination,[31] and the Methodist leader John Wesley was such a convinced anti-predestinarian that he abhorred the Synod of Dort even more than the Council of Trent.[32] The distance between England and Dort had indeed become very large!

In France the situation was different. As a result of political complications the French Reformed Church had not been able to send representatives to the Synod of Dort, but the French had followed the events in the Netherlands with anxious attention. As a loyal partaker in Calvin's theological heritage the French Church wholeheartedly agreed with the decisions of Dort. At a session

---

[28] G. Burnet, *An Exposition of the Thirty-Nine Articles of the Church of England* (The Second Edition Corrected), London 1700, 170.

[29] See L.G. Locke, *Tillotson. A Study in Seventeenth-Century Literature* (Anglistica IV), Copenhagen 1954, 95f.

[30] From a sermon on Ps. 119: 65, *The Works of the Most Reverend Dr. John Tillotson*, London 1707, 138; cf. a remark in a sermon on I John 3: 10, 166f.

[31] See J. van den Berg and G.F. Nuttall, *Philip Doddridge (1702-1751) and the Netherlands*, Leiden 1987, 12.

[32] John Wesley, *Journal* II (ed. Curnock), 473. His judgement on the image of God, implied in the doctrine of predestination, is not less radical than that of Henry More (above, note 25); Watts, *The Dissenters* I, 430; cf. E. Gordon Rupp, *Religion in England 1688-1791*, Oxford 1986, 370f. Wesley's remark is reminiscent of a similar expression in Milton's "On the New Forcers of Conscience under the Long Parliament" (the Presbyterians): "But we do hope to find out all your tricks, Your plots and packing worse than those of Trent".

of the Synod which met in 1620 in Alès the members took the oath on the doctrine of Dort, and they promised "qu'ils la défendront de tout leur Pouvoir, jusqu'au dernier Soupir de leur Vie".[33] Ten years later the Synod of Charenton decided in relation to those who (even in private conversation) propagated the doctrines of Arminius, "que tout ces Dogmatiseurs seroient poursuivis par les Censures de l'Eglise".[34] But these stern measures themselves are an indication that in French Protestant circles there still was a measure of sympathy for the views of Arminius. In some publications the French theologian Daniel Tilenus—in the winter of 1618-19 deposed from his function as professor at the Academy of Sedan[35]—sharply criticised the "Fathers of Dort", who had taken the easiest way of dealing with their opponents: "Aussi est-il plus court, de proscrire, que d'enseigner ... de tourmenter, que d'argumenter"; they had treated their brethren according to the methods of the Turks.[36] The judgement passed on the Remonstrants by the Synod of Alès, was "fausseté" and "calomnie"; Arminius was not a Pelagian, but had only protested against Manicheism.[37] The accusation of Manicheism as a distinguishing mark of the Calvinist doctrines of predestination and original sin (often combined with the accusation of Stoicism) dates back to the sixteenth century[38] and would be voiced till the late eighteenth century.[39] The idea of a God who in absolute freedom elects one, rejects another would postulate a duality between light and darkness in the essence of God, and the Calvinist views on the doctrine of original sin would make the propagation of evil an almost physical necessity.[40]

For theologians who thought like Tilenus the French Church had no more place than the Church in the Netherlands. But in spite of the loyalty of the French Reformed Church to Dort the problems which surrounded the doctrine

---

33 J. Aymon, *Tous les synodes nationaux des Eglises Réformées de France* II, La Haye 1710, 183.

34 Aymon II, 278.

35 E. et E. Haag, *La France Protestante* VIII (1858), 383-387.

36 [D. Tilenus], *Traicté de la cause et de l'origine du péché*, Paris 1621, 88.

37 [D. Tilenus], *Considerations sur les canon et serment des Eglises Réformées, conclu et arresté au Synode National d'Alez ... pour l'approbation des Canons du Synode tenu a Dordrecht ...*, s.l. 1622. For Arminius in connection with the accusation of Manicheism, see Hoenderdaal, *Verklaring*, 95.

38 See O. Ritschl, *Dogmengeschichte des Protestantismus* II, Göttingen 1912, 450.

39 *E.g.* by the Remonstrant theologian Paulus van Hemert, *De rede en haar gezag in den godsdienst* I, Utrecht 1784, 7f.

40 See the broad exposition on this point in P. Bayle, *Dictionnaire Historique et Critique* III, ^{5}1740, s.v. "Pauliciens". In a dialectical disquisition (629, note F) Bayle introduces a Manichean who remarks with reference to Jurieu's *Jugement* (see below, note 64): ... si vous examinez votre Système avec attention, vous reconnoîtrez qu'aussi bien que moi vous admettez deux principes, l'un du bien, l'autre du mal; mais au lieu de les placer, comme je fais, dans deux sujets, vous les combinez ensemble dans une seule et même substance, ce qui est monstrueux et impossible"; cf. 631, note I: "... lorsqu'une Secte Chrétienne accuse les autres de faire Dieu auteur du péché, elle ne manque jamais de leur imputer a cet égard le Manichéisme".

of predestination continued to cause trouble. At the Synod of Alençon (1637) a complaint was lodged against Moyse Amyraut, a professor of the Academy of Saumur. Amyraut's theology was an attempt to meet certain objections against the doctrine of predestination without abandoning the idea as such. His theology contained a universalist element: behind the double decree of election and reprobation stood a single decree of predestination which was an expression of God's will to save the whole of mankind. This "hypothetical universalism" implied a mitigation of the harsh image of the God of double predestination, but it was an effort to reconcile the irreconcilable: Amyraut satisfied neither the strict Calvinists nor the Arminians.[41] In his *Unpartheyische Kirchen- und Ketzer Historie* the Pietist theologian and historian Gottfried Arnold remarks that Amyraut intended to soften the "gar zu greuliche expressiones" of Calvin and others, "gleichwol eben in der sache selbst mit der einen Hand wider nahm, was er mit der andern zugegeben hat, und also im grund mit den andern eins blieb".[42] The latter also appears from his declaration, given at the Synod of Alençon, that he agreed with those resolutions of the French Church which had ratified the Canons of Dort and that he was prepared to seal them with his own blood.[43] In France, the authority of the Synod of Dort to all appearances remained unimpaired. But it was not easy to convince the opponents of Amyraut that in his theology "les ombres d'Arminius"[44] dit not somehow manifest themselves. The emphasis on the universality of God's love which we meet with Amyraut could be seen as potential dynamite under the seemingly massive foundations of Dort.

By sending delegates the Swiss churches and the Genevan church had actively participated in the Synod of Dort and like the French Calvinists they had fully endorsed its decisions. As late as 1708 the Zürich theologian Johann Jacob Hottinger sharply criticized the theology of Arminius, which he traced to the views of Erasmus. He also saw a danger in the theology of Amyraut. In this context he mentioned the *Formula Consensus*, partly directed against the

---

[41] For the theology of Saumur, see Alexander Schweizer, *Die protestantischen Centraldogmen in ihrer Entwicklung innerhalb der reformirten Kirche* II, Zürich 1856, 225-438, and B.G. Armstrong, *Calvinism and the Amyraut Heresy*, Madison etc. 1969. Both authors maintain the essential orthodoxy of Amyraut, but while Schweizer interprets Amyraut within the context of seventeenth-century scholastic theology, Armstrong pays special attention to the affinity between Calvin and Amyraut. The conflicts engendered by Amyraut's theological concept are clearly treated by F.P. van Stam, in his *The Controversy over the Theology of Saumur, 1635-1650*, Amsterdam and Maarssen 1988.

[42] G. Arnold, *Unpartheyische Kirchen- und Ketzerhistorie* I-II, Franckfurt am Mayn 1729, 981, A similar remark was already made by Grotius in a letter to Samson Johnson, 30 Sept. 1638 *Briefwisseling van Hugo Grotius* 9, R.G.P. CXLII, 599, see also Van Stam, 429.

[43] Aymon I, 58.

[44] The title of one of the first publications directed against Amyraut (see Aymon II, 58). It appeared anonymously and can no longer be located; possibly written by Gabriel Bouquet: R. Nicole, *Moyse Amyraut. A Bibliography*, New York-London 1981, 165.

doctrines of Arminius and Amyraut, which in 1675 by the "Evangelical Confederates" in Switzerland was accepted as "ein Zaun und Vormaur um die Eidgenössische Glaubensbekanntnuss";[45] one year later, Geneva joined the Swiss churches in its acceptance of the *Formula*. It implied an unequivocal confirmation of Dort, but when Hottinger wrote appreciatively about the *Formula*, its authority was already on the wane: in most Swiss Protestant towns it soon lost its binding character. Perhaps it was the strictest, no doubt it was the most ephemeral of all Reformed confessions. The rather drastic change of attitude towards the *Formula* was partly the result of the rise of a new theological climate, sometimes described as "orthodoxie libérale",[46] which clearly had an affinity with that of the English Latitudinarians. There were indeed a number of mutual contacts. When, in 1718, in Switzerland there still was a rather sharp controversy with regard to the question whether the binding character of the *Formula* should be abolished, the Anglican Archbishop William Wake wrote to the Genevan theologian Jean-Alphonse Turrettini (the son of one of the authors of the *Formula*): "I heartily wish it may come to a peaceable end; which in my opinion such affairs can never do, unless more libertie be allowed in point of subscription of such sort of formularies than most churches seem willing to consent unto. The moderation of the Church of England has been very exemplary in this respect ...".[47]

Among the more progressive theologians Jean-Frédéric Ostervald (of Neuchâtel) and Jean-Alphonse Turrettini took an important place. They did not intend to be unorthodox and never presented themselves as Arminians (which in the context of the Swiss situation anyhow would have been asking for trouble), but their theology broke through the confines of seventeenth-century scholastic theology. It rather breathes something of the early Enlightenment. Their image of God is different from that of an older generation. The universal character of the love of God takes a central place: nothing occurs more often in Scripture, Turrettini remarks, and is more certain in religion, than that God is good, not for some, but for all.[48] Complementary with this image of God is an image of man which leaves ample scope for human freedom and responsibility. In his exposition of the first eleven chapters of the Epistle to the Romans Turrettini makes "reprobation" as mentioned in Rom. 9 (the great stumbling-block in the discussions around the idea of predestination) dependent on the

[45] J.J. Hottinger, *Helvetische Kirchengeschichte* III, Zurich 1708, 1000ff., 1086f.

[46] So H. Vuilleumier, *Histoire de l'Eglise Réformée du Pays de Vaud* III, Lausanne 1930, 4ff.

[47] N. Sykes, *William Wake, Archbishop of Canterbury 1650-1737* I, Cambridge 1957, 32.

[48] J.A. Turrettini, *De Sacrae Scripturae interpretandae methodus tractatus bipartitus*, Trajecti Thuriorum (= Dordrecht) 1728, 221; an edition of lectures given by Turrettini, published without his knowledge, though we do not need to doubt the factual correctness of the rendering of his lectures. See the introduction to the *Tractatus* in Turrettini's *Opera Omnia* II, Leovardiae et Franequerae 1775 (where the quoted passage occurs on 91).

free decision of the human will.[49] Referring to this commentary P. Wernle remarks: "So ungefähr hatte auch Erasmus den Paulus erklären können".[50] Turrettini was indeed an admirer of Erasmus,[51] though he could not without difficulty forgive him for not choosing the Protestant side.[52] Furthermore, the new theology strongly emphasized the ethical aspect of the Christian faith; in this context I mention Ostervald's *Traité des sources de la corruption qui règne aujourd'hui parmi les Chrétiens*[53] and his influential Catechism, which first appeared in 1702.[54] Some reproached Ostervald for not having dealt with predestination in his Catechism. To Turrettini he wrote: "Il faut avoir de plaisantes idées d'un Catéchisme pour vouloir que cette matière y entre".[55] As such this did not prove that he was a critic of the doctrine of predestination—he indeed appealed to the warning of Dort against an imprudent use of this doctrine—, but still "c'est le ton qui fait la musique"!

With regard to the church Ostervald, Turrettini and their friends advocated a broad margin of toleration. Turrettini in particular devoted himself to this cause. His *Nubes Testium* of 1719, in which he called "a cloud of witnesses" (among whom, of course, was Erasmus)[56] in favour of the idea of toleration was of great influence on the spread of a more tolerant attitude. In view of this it was not to be wondered at that in his compendium of the history of the church Turrettini dealt with the Synod of Dort in a rather off-hand way. According to Turrettini, the schism could have been prevented or at least quickly have come to an end if the Christians had left the hidden things to God and had contented themselves with fulfilling in practice what has been revealed.[57]

In Germany, too, the decision of Dort evoked opposition. Of course here the situation was different from that in the Reformed world in that the majority of the German Protestants stood in another confessional and theological tradition; following the line of Erasmus seventeenth-century Lutheranism decidedly rejected the doctrine of double predestination. We find this in the orthodox circle: in his popular dogmatic manual *Epitome Credendorum* (1625) the orthodox theologian Nikolaus Hunnius argued that the doctrine of reprobation was not consonant with the philanthropy of a God who does not will that any

---

[49] *In Pauli Apostoli ad Romanos Epistolae Cap. XI Praelectiones, Opera* II, 388f.

[50] P. Wernle, *Der schweizerische Protestantismus im XVIII. Jahrhundert* I, Tübingen 1923, 495.

[51] "Oratio de variis christianae doctrinae fatis", *Opera* III (1776), 509.

[52] "Oratio inauguralis de theologo veritatis et pacis studioso", *Opera* III, 373.

[53] See, *e.g.*, *Traité*, Amsterdam ^{3}1700, 81.

[54] For a clear analysis of Ostervald's theology, see P. Barthel, "La "Religion de Neuchâtel"" au petit matin du XVIIIe siécle. Un phénoméne unique en Europe", *Musée Neuchâtelois* 1987, 41-80.

[55] E. de Budé, *Lettres inédites adressées ... à J.A. Turrettini* III, Paris et Genève 1887, 7.

[56] "Nubes Testium", *Opera* III, 62f.

[57] "Compendium Historiae Ecclesiasticae", *Opera* III, 286.

should perish.[58] Similar objections are to be found in the Pietist circle: Gottfried Arnold saw a clear parallel between Lutheran and Arminian doctrine, while moreover he criticized the "tyrannische *Proceduren*" of the Synod of Dort.[59]

When partly under the influence of the emergence of enlightened views the tendency towards unity between the two large Protestant confessions gained strength, in Lutheran circles the doctrine of predestination as formulated in the Canons of Dort and the *Formula Consensus* was more and more seen as a stumbling-block on the road to union. This was unequivocally voiced by the Tübingen theologian Christoph Matthaeus Pfaff in a publication on the *Formula Consensus* (1723); he considered the doctrine of absolute predestination "obsolete", and the doctrinal constraint of the *Formula* reminded him of the "rigor Romaniensium". With Ostervald and Turrettini he advocated a practical Christianity, reduced to its essential elements.[60]

Two years later, in a similar way Johann Lorenz von Mosheim turned against the Synod of Dort in his edition of the letters of John Hales. Mosheim was a moderate, fairly orthodox representative of the Protestant Enlightenment. He did not take all too strongly to Calvin. In a publication on Servet he had even averred that the way Calvin had fought against Servet in defence of the abused truth had made him a "Todschläger", a judgement which he later (though not very handsomely) retracted, for the sake of peace with the Reformed, for that still mattered to him.[61] But in condemning the doctrine of the Arminians, Dort had also condemned that of the Lutherans: "concordia" would only be possible, if the authority of the decisions of Dort could be put aside.[62] In the light of all this it is little wonder that a Danish theologian, Søren Lintrup, rejoiced at the fact that at least the English church no longer adhered to Dort; not without a burst of orthodox-Lutheran triumphalism he declared that thanks to its disregard of the Synod of Dort England was on the way to "lutheranizing".[63]

---

[58] I used the Dutch translation: *Kort Begrijp*, Amsterdam 1692, 151. For Hunnius and the doctrine of predestination, see O. Ritschl, *Dogmengeschichte* IV, 1927, 313f.; H. Leube, *Kalvinismus und Luthertum* I, Leipzig 1928, 138-163.

[59] *Kirchen- und Ketzerhistorie* I-II, 973a.

[60] C.M. Pfaff, *Schediasma theologicum de Formula Consensus Helvetica*, Tubingae 1723, 42, 48.

[61] J.L. von Mosheim, *Neue Nachrichten von dem berühmten spanischen Arzte Michael Serveto*, Helmstedt 1750, 85f.

[62] *Joannis Halesii Historia Concilii Dordraceni*, 8f.

[63] Severinus Lintropius, *Anglia plurimis modis Lutheranizans, sive de contemtu Concilii Dordraceni in Anglia, schediasma theologicum*, s.l. 1710 (reprint of his theological dissertation, defended in or before 1695; for Lintrup, see *Dansk Biografisk Leksikon* IX, 1981, s.v.) He saw the aversion from an "absolute decree" which he observed with a number of English theologians as the main, though not the only mark of a lutheranizing tendency; in this context he spoke of an Anglo-Arminian harmony.

More than once Reformed theologians appealed to the Lutherans to change their attitude with regard to Dort. One of them was Pierre Jurieu, who in 1686—one year after the Revocation of the Edict of Nantes—published a work which explicitly aimed at a reconciliation between Reformed and Lutherans. It must have scandalized Jurieu that a Lutheran theologian saw the persecution of the French Protestants as partly a judgement on their adherence to the idea of "particularisme", in fact the orthodox doctrine of predestination. The stress of those bad times led Jurieu to a strong plea for peace between the Protestants, who together should resist the common enemy. Together with many Reformed authors Jurieu drew attention to the moderate character of the Canons of the Synod of Dort, which indeed had not adopted the extreme formulations of the "Supralapsarians", but rather had followed the "infralapsarian" line. Contrary to the majority of Reformed theologians the Supralapsarians maintained that in the order of God's decrees the decree of election and reprobation precedes the decree to allow the fall; because of this they were reproached with making God the author of sin. The infralapsarian theory tried to avoid this misunderstanding by placing the double decree subsequent to the fall.[64] But the Remonstrants thought the difference unreal; in the same year 1686 the leading Remonstrant theologian Philippus van Limborch pointed out that there was no essential difference between the two points of view, both of which supposed indeed an absolute decree of reprobation.[65] And entering from quite a different side into the discussion—his views should not be identified with those of the Remonstrants—Pierre Bayle wrote in an ironical outburst against Jurieu's argument that the Synod had not agreed with the approach of the Supralapsarians: "quand tout est bien compté et pesé, il se trouve que ceux-ci et ceux qu'on nomme Infralapsaires, soutiennent an fond la même chose ...".[66]

With Jurieu and Bayle, both living in Rotterdam, and the Amsterdam theologian Philippus van Limborch we are home again, in the country of the Synod of Dort. There, since 1619 the discussions on the doctrine of predestination had gone on without new arguments being added. For enlightened spirits it was all very far removed from their actual world of thought. According to the Remonstrant Jean le Clerc (a friend of Turrettini, though more radical in his theology) posterity would find difficulty in believing that an otherwise rather sedate people such as the Dutch had become so heated over speculative dog-

---

[64] [P. Jurieu], *Jugement sur les methodes rigides et relachées d'expliquer la providence et la grace*, Rotterdam 1686, 2, 85f. The theologian in question was Daniel Severin Schultze (Scultetus); see F.R.J. Knetsch, *Pierre Jurieu. Theoloog en politicus der refuge*, Kampen 1967, 248.

[65] P. a Limborch, *Theologia Christiana*, Amstelodami 1686, 315f.

[66] *Dict.* III (1740), 633.

mas, full of difficulties and therefore incomprehensible to most of those who took sides in this matter.[67]

But in the first half of the eighteenth century most Reformed theologians still took sides, though not as heatedly as the generations before them. Even into the second half of the century the majority of the Reformed in the Netherlands strictly kept within the boundaries set out by Dort, and unlike the Swiss the Dutch also formally maintained the authority of the Canons. At the centenary of the Synod in 1719, the Leiden professors of theology (putting aside their petty differences) sounded the praises of Dort in a common publication.[68] In 1725 (shortly after the publication of Mosheim's edition of Hales) the later professor Johan van den Honert defended the doctrine of Dort against Mosheim. He tried to demonstrate that those Lutherans who agreed with the Arminians themselves deviated "ab ipso Megalandro suo Luthero et ab Antiqua Lutherana Ecclesia".[69] In the second half of the century some Orangist theologians—Johannes Barueth, Petrus Hofstede, Didericus van der Kemp—entered the list on behalf of the Synod of Dort. Their struggle had not only a theological and an ecclesiastical, but also a political component: for them, the confessional order as fixed by Dort, the position of the Reformed Church and the dominant place of the House of Orange formed a closely-knit unity.[70] Furthermore, for a long time church assemblies (in particular provincial synods) remained vigilant in guarding the church against the Arminians, as the Frisian Synod expressed it in 1768.[71] This vigilance—renewed from time to time—was connected with the fact that behind the façade of Dort a process of gradual erosion was taking place. The works of English Latitudinarians, Swiss "liberal-orthodox" theologians and German opponents of Dort were also read in the Netherlands, often in Dutch translation.[72] Something of the milder image

---

[67] [J.] le Clerc, *Histoire des Provinces Unies des Pays Bas* I, Amsterdam 1723, 329. For the rest Le Clerc adopted a reserved position in this discussion: "J'ai tâché d'inspirer la douceur sur les Controverses de Dordrecht, en toute mon histoire"; Le Clerc to J.A. Turrettini, 15 May 1725, J. Collen, *Etude biographique sur Jean le Clerc* (1657-1736), Genève 1884, 69.

[68] "Festivitas Secularis" (in B. de Moor, *Commentarius perpetuus in J. Marckii Compendium* V, Lugd.Bat. 1768, 777-825).

[69] *De gratia Dei, non universali sed particulari, nec non de essentia et existentia Dei dissertationes*, Lugd.Bat. 1725, **3.

[70] For this, see J. van den Berg, "Hervormden, dissenters en de patriottenbeweging", in Th.S.M. van der Zee and others (eds.), *1787 De Nederlandse Revolutie?*, Amsterdam 1988, 122-133.

[71] N.C. Kist, "Handelingen der Synode van Friesland betreffende de zaak en leer der Remonstranten", *Archief voor Kerkelijke Geschiedenis* VIII (1837), 437.

[72] For the English influence, see J. van den Berg, "Eighteenth century Dutch translations of the works of some British latitudinarian and enlightened theologians", *Nederlands Archief voor Kerkgeschiedenis* 59 (1978-79), 194-212; for that of the Swiss: idem, "Theologiebeoefening te Franeker en te Leiden in de achttiende eeuw", English translation: this volume Ch. 16. Pfaff's work on the *Formula Consensus* (1723) appeared already in the same year in Dutch translation, while Mosheim's edition of Hales was published in Dutch translation in 1733.

of God and the more optimistic view of man irresistibly penetrated into the Low Countries. In 1776 the Leiden professor Jan Jacob Schultens in a private letter expressed his expectation that in the generation after him Remonstrantism would take the upper hand in the Reformed Church.[73] That was a too optimistic thought: when in 1797 the Remonstrants made a proposal for the reunion of all Protestants in the Netherlands the reactions in the Reformed circle were eventually negative. Yet it was significant that quite a number of Reformed ministers sympathized with the proposal.[74] It was also significant that in 1827 A. Ypey and I.J. Dermout (the latter was then Secretary of the General Synod!) in their authoritative work on the history of the Reformed Church criticized the Synod of Dort and sang the praises of the Remonstrant theologians of their own time, "who proceeded with stately tread in the advancement of christian religious knowledge and virtue".[75] It seemed as if even in the Netherlands the authority of the Synod of Dort was going to belong to the past.

But the development of history is not as linear as that. At the second centenary of the Synod the theological faculty of Leiden was silent, but in the Leiden "Marekerk" the conservative minister Nicolaas Schotsman erected (at least figuratively) a "column of honour" for the Synod of Dort[76]—it was the subject of the paper I wrote for my doctoral examination: Dort has been pursuing me for quite a long time! Between 1830 and 1833 one of the leading figures of the Dutch evangelical revival (the "Réveil"), C.M. van der Kemp, published a work in three volumes in which he defended the honour of the Reformed Church (for him: the church, founded on the doctrine of Dort) against Ypey and Dermout.[77] The historian and politician Guillaume Groen van Prinsterer, though more moderate than Van der Kemp,[78] saw in the events of 1618-19 the salvation of the Reformed Church.[79] In the circle of the Dutch Seceders of 1834

---

[73] In a letter to R.M. van Goens of 25 March 1776, J. Wille, *De literator R.M. van Goens* I, Zutphen 1937, 319.

[74] See A. Stolker, *Onontbeerlijke bijlage tot de geschiedenis der Christelijke Kerk in de achttiende eeuw van A. Ypey*, Leyden 1810, 203.

[75] A. Ypey and I.J. Dermout, *Geschiedenis der Nederlandsche Hervormde Kerk* II, Breda 1822, 232; III (1827), 283.

[76] N. Schotsman, *Eere-zuil, ter gedachienis van de voor twee honderd jaren te Dordrecht gehouden Nationale Synode*, Leyden 1819 (contains two sermons, preached on 9 and 16 May 1819).

[77] C.M. van der Kemp, *De eere der Nederlandsche Hervomde Kerk gehandhaafd tegen Ypey en Dermout*, 3 vls., Rotterdam 1830-1833.

[78] For Groen van Prinsterer and the doctrine of predestination, see G.C. Berkouwer, *De Verkiezing Gods*, Kampen 1955, 7ff.

[79] G. Groen van Prinsterer, *Handboek der geschiedenis van het vaderland*, Amsterdam [5]1876, 218; a critical remark on scholastic and confessionalist developments in the period after Dort occurs on 228.

loyalty to the heritage of Dort played a large part.[80] And even in the beginning of this century the Calvinist (or "Neocalvinist") theologian Abraham Kuyper eloquently expressed his veneration for the doctrine of Dort in the preface to his *E Voto Dordraceno*.[81]

Perhaps there were some who dreamt that the ecclesiastical clock could be put back to 1619. But history is not as cyclical as that. It is not so easy to put aside the critical reflections of a number of generations. Also in the circle of nineteenth century orthodoxy penetrating questions were put forward with regard to the doctrine of Dort. In 1871 Daniel Chantepie de la Saussaye—one of the profoundest theologians whom the Netherlands have ever produced—wrote about a dualism in the Canons of Dort between metaphysical understanding and religious experience: a dualism between the metaphysical concept of the absoluteness of God which understands the predestination to eternal salvation and eternal damnation as an absolute decree, and the reality of the christian life, experienced in faith and rooted in Christ.[82]

A statement such as this makes us aware of the fact that behind the "petite histoire" of various ecclesiastical and theological conflicts stands the "grande histoire" of man's search, through the ages, for an answer to the great existential questions of religious life. Who is God in his relation to man, what is man in his relation to God, and in this context: what should be the shape of the church in which men in their communal life try to experience and to express something of this mutual relation? With these questions church and theology are never finished: no pronouncement of the church is definitive, no human formulation has eternal value. But the great questions remain on the agenda—they simply cannot be repressed.

His discipline does not enable the church historian to answer these questions (if they can be answered at all). But perhaps the mirror of the past, which he holds up, can also be meaningful for today's discussions. Therefore it is his proper task to go on seeking and groping for an answer to the historical question "wie es eigentlich"—a word with a special depth dimension[83]—"gewesen": and thus also, even in the first place, to the question how men have thought about God, about their own existence, about the shape of the church. It is a task which is endlessly fascinating; but also a task which makes us inexorably conscious of the boundaries of our knowledge and our understanding.

---

80 See P.N. Holtrop, "De Afscheiding breekpunt en kristallisatiepunt", in W. Bakker and others (eds.), *De Afscheiding van 1834 en haar geschiedenis*, Kampen 1984, 69ff.

81 *E Voto Dordraceno* I, Amsterdam etc. 1904, the unpaginated preface in which Kuyper states that in his time "through the faithfulness of our God the love for what our forefathers confessed in Dordrecht has again become more general".

82 "Confessionalisme en Modernisme", *Protestantsche Bijdragen* 2 (1871), 18.

83 For the background of the word "eigentlich" with Ludwig von Ranke, see K. Scholder, "Ferdinand Christian Baur als Historiker", *Evangelische Theologie* 21 (1961), in particular 440ff.

CHAPTER TWO

SIR THOMAS BROWNE AND THE SYNOD OF DORT

The Synod of the Reformed Church in the Netherlands, which met in the town of Dort (Dordrecht) in the years 1618-19, won fame with some, but fell into disrepute with others because of the maintenance of the Calvinist doctrine of predestination and its consequent action against the Arminians or Remonstrants. I am afraid it is somewhat difficult to find a place for a paper on "Sir Thomas Browne and the Synod of Dort" within the framework of a symposium dedicated to "Sir Thomas Browne and Anatomy". It might be possible to consider the Synod of Dort as a kind of *theatrum anatomicum*, where serious divines were engaged in dissecting the deepest secrets of theology with the scalpel of sharp scholastic distinctions. We shall, however, quickly dismiss this image, which does not occur in Sir Thomas Browne's works, in order to listen to what he himself in his *Religio Medici* remarks on the Synod of Dort.

Of course, he must have been acquainted with its principal decisions. In England, the doctrinal pronouncements of Dort, to which also the English delegation to the Synod had given its assent, became well known and played a part in the theological discussions of the ensuing years. Furthermore, Browne undoubtedly received information about the Synod during his stay in Leiden—perhaps from Polyander, who had attended its meetings. Browne mentions the Synod in a passage in which he attests to this attachment to the Church of England and his agreement with its "articles, constitutions, and customes", which seemed to him to be "consonant unto reason, and as it were framed to my particular devotion". As a Protestant he considered the voice of the church and that of reason subordinate to the voice of Scripture:

> where the Scripture is silent, the Church is my Text; where that speakes, "tis but my Comment; where there is a joynt silence of both, I borrow not the rules of my Religion from *Rome* or *Geneva*, but the dictates of my owne reason (I. 5).

Indeed, "Rome" and "Geneva" had already been mentioned, when he remarked: "I condemne not all things in the Councell of *Trent*, nor approve all in the Synod of *Dort*"(I. 5). With regard to Dort, this sentence makes us wonder how far Browne could agree with the Calvinist doctrine of predestination as it had been formulated by the Synod of Dort in an uncompromising way, and with the Synod's condemnation of the Remonstrant point of view.

Though the Remonstrants did not oppose the term "predestination" as such, they strongly objected to the idea of a "double predestination", which was considered to be a hall-mark of strict Calvinism. This idea implied that God in His inscrutable wisdom had decided to elect a number of people to eternal life, and to reject the others, whose fate would be eternal damnation. Contrary to this, Arminius and his followers taught that the fact that some people would not attain salvation did not result from an eternal "decree of reprobation", but from their own unbelief. God, according to the Remonstrants, had decided to elect those who in faith would entrust themselves to His grace; those who would not believe would place themselves outside the boundaries of salvation; in His "praescientia" God saw beforehand who would accept the offer of His grace and thus belong to the elect, who would reject this offer and thus exclude themselves from salvation. Perhaps from a logical point of view the Remonstrant position was less satisfactory than the monolithic doctrine of Dort, but in attempting to divest the idea of predestination of its harsh offensiveness the Arminians left scope for a milder image of God and for a more humane theological approach.

The XXXIX Articles of the Church of England, while using the terms "predestination" and "election" (Art. XVII), do not contain the idea of a "double predestination" or the concomitant notion of "reprobation", and thus on this point left room for a more latitudinarian interpretation. Still, in England the strict doctrine of predestination, though it was not always carried to the extreme, was dominant until the second quarter of the seventeenth century. But then the tide began to turn: in the course of time, various English theologians and ecclesiastical leaders became critical of the Calvinist position and expressed their sympathy with the doctrine of Arminius. One of them was John Hales, who, commissioned by the English ambassador in the Netherlands, had attended the meetings of the Synod as an observer. He had gone to Dort as a Calvinist; during the meetings of the Synod, however, he was so much impressed by the Remonstrant point of view, that he could declare at a later stage: "There, I bid John Calvin good night".[1] Next to him, the Cambridge Platonists should be mentioned, some of whom entertained good relations with the Dutch Remonstrants. Ralph Cudworth belonged to this group; in 1668 he wrote a revealing letter to the Remonstrant professor Philippus van Limborch in which he decried the doctrine of reprobation as "horrenda ista decreta".[2] These words remind one of a similar term, used by Calvin in the context of his exposition of the doctrine of predestination in his *Institutes*: "decretum horri-

---

[1] Anthony Farindon mention this in a letter which precedes his edition of the *Golden Remains of the ever Memorable Mr John Hales*, London 1659. For this, see this volume p.6, n.21.

[2] "... non poteram Deo adscribere horrenda ista decreta, quibus ex mere beneplacito homines insontes vel ad culpas et peccata aeternis cruciatibus luenda inevitabiliter damnaret" (quoted in G.F. von Hertling, *John Locke und die Schule von Cambridge*, Freiburg im Breisgau 1892, 164, n. 2).

bile", a decree which makes man shudder at God's majesty.[3] But while the two expressions have a remarkable similarity, their connotation is fundamentally different: what Calvin accepts in fear and trembling, Cudworth rejects as unworthy of the nature of God.

Leaving aside for a moment the doctrine of predestination, it is obvious that in general the ideas expressed in Browne's *Religio Medici* present many parallels to those of John Hales and the Cambridge Platonists.[4] Therefore it would seem to be only natural if we were to find in Browne a criticism of the doctrine of double predestination similar to that which was voiced by kindred spirits in his own time and culture. Moreover, in his younger years Browne had sympathized with Origen's doctrine that ultimately all people would attain salvation (the idea of "apokatastasis"). At a later stage his sympathy for these views had faded away; still, his initial affinity with Origen's views testifies to a certain sensitivity with regard to the problems posed by the doctrine of predestination (I. 7).

However, contrary to what could be expected, when Browne speaks of "that terrible term, *Predestination*," (I. 11) he stands closer to Calvin than to Cudworth: he is prepared to accept the idea of predestination with its full consequences as an awe-inspiring mystery. Some are elected, others are rejected. Who belong to the first category, and who to the latter, is hidden from our observation: "I beleeve many are saved who to man seeme reprobated, and many reprobated who in the opinion and sentence of man, stand elected"(I. 57). But this does not detract from the absolute and ultimate character of predestination, "the reprobates in the flame, and the blessed in *Abrahams* bosome"(I, ll). I must add that with Browne "heaven" and "hell" do not function in a completely literal sense: "... where the soule hath the full measure, and complement of happinesse ... I thinke is truely Heaven"; "... I feele somtimes a hell within my selfe ..."(I. 49, 51). But, however this may be, man's eternal fate is destined by God's eternal counsel, in one place described by Browne as "Synod": "the decree of that Synod held from all Eternity"(I. 59).

Sir Thomas Browne tries to support and elucidate the doctrine of predestination, "which hath troubled so many weake heads to conceive, and the wisest to explaine" (I. 11), with a platonizing argument which reminds one of certain passages in Augustine.[5] Predestination:

[3] Inst. III.23.7.

[4] For parallels between Browne and Hales, see L. Nathanson, *The Strategy of Truth: A Study of Sir Thomas Browne*, Chicago and London 1967, esp. 136ff.; for Browne and the Cambridge Platonists, 168ff.

[5] See the quotations from Augustine in E.P. Meijering, *Augustin über Schöpfung, Ewigkeit und Zeit*, Leiden 1979, 34; and also *Confessiones* 11.8.

> is in respect to God no prescious[6] determination of our estates to come, but a definitive placet[7] of his will already fulfilled, and at the instant that he first decreed it; for to his eternitie which is indivisible, and altogether, the last Trumpe is already sounded.

In eternity there is no distinction of tenses:

> for to speake like a Philosopher, those continued instants of time which flow into a thousand years, make not to him one moment; what to us is to come, to his Eternitie is present, his whole duration being but one permanent point without succession, parts, flux, or division (I. 11).

Predestination is lifted up above the level of human history with its sequence of causes and results: because it is indissolubly connected with God's eternity, it is itself eternal, immovable, unchangeable. In a commentary on this passage Joan Bennett remarks that by means of this formula Browne hoped to by-pass the fearful doctrine of "Predestination".[8] Perhaps in this context the term "to by-pass" is not quite felicitous; I would rather say that with the help of a platonizing construction Browne tried to incorporate this difficult and debated doctrine into the whole of his world of thought.

Why did he think fit to uphold the doctrine of predestination in its stricter form, inclusive of that great stumbling-block for so many Anglicans, the idea of reprobation? We could see it as a remnant of his education in a period in which Arminianism had not yet affected Anglican theology, and—in connection with this—as an expression of loyalty towards the older, more Calvinistic tradition of his church.[9] We could also think of Dutch influences; especially Polyander may have influenced him on this point.[10] But these hypotheses, though not quite ungrounded, cannot be verified from the little we know about Browne's spiritual development. One motive, however, clearly manifests itself in his *Religio Medici*. It is indeed a religious one: he receives comfort and strength from the knowledge that his salvation is not dependent on the vicissitudes of human history, but is anchored in God's eternal counsel. "That

[6] If the reading of G. Keynes (whose edition of 1964 I followed) is right, the use of the term "prescious" (others read: "previous") might imply an indirect attack on the Remonstrant position with regard to the connection between predestination and "*praescientia*".

[7] The word "*placet*" perhaps corresponds with the "*beneplacite*" of I.59; others, however, read "blast".

[8] Joan Bennett, *Sir Thomas Browne*, Cambridge 1962, 59,

[9] Cf. Cudworth's remarks on his own Calvinistic upbringing which with him, however, had no lasting influence: "Quod meipsum attinet, fateor me aliena (Calvinistica) dogmata fere cum materno lacte suxisse, iisque in primoribus adolescentiae annis penitus imbutum fuisse"(see n. 2).

[10] For the relations between Browne and Polyander, see C.W. Schoneveld, "Sir Thomas Browne and Leiden University in 1633", *English Language Notes* 19 (1981-82), 335-359.

which is the cause of my election, I hold to be the cause of my salvation, which was the mercy and beneplacit of God, before I was, or the foundation of the World". Though he knew what it meant to "worke out your Salvation with feare and trembling", and though his soul was assailed by "many doubts", still this knowledge could raise him above the flux of time and the threat of destruction: "though my grave be *England*, my dying place was Paradise ..." (I. 59). In his religious experience, the doctrine of predestination functioned as an anchorage for the notion of God's saving grace, as it was expressed on the frontispiece of several editions of *Religio Medici*: man, falling into the abyss, helpless and powerless, is saved by a hand from above—"a coelo Salus".

We heard Sir Thomas Browne remark that he did not approve of everything in the Synod of Dort. In fact, in many ways the trend of his thought was alien to the spirit of Dort. Let me just mention his plea for toleration, his irenical attitude towards the Roman Catholic Church, his critical remarks with regard to ecclesiastical points of difference, his method of explaining (in a more or less spiritualizing way) biblical notions like that of heaven and hell which within the Calvinist tradition primarily had a literal sense, and (last but not least) his openly avowed predilection for the Hermetic tradition. Because of all this, it is not astonishing that the reception of *Religio Medici* in Dutch Calvinist circles does not appear to have been undividedly favourable.[11] Undeniably, he was a predestinarian; but does this make him a Calvinist in the sense of the Synod of Dort?

Almost a century after the appearance of *Religio Medici*, in 1741, John Wesley, working in the Bodleian Library, came across the story of the Synod of Dort, which filled him with deep indignation. He, too, put Trent and Dort into juxtaposition; but unlike the passage quoted from Sir Thomas Browne, his remark has bitter overtones:

> What a pity it is that the *holy Synod* of Trent and that of Dort did not sit at the same time: nearly allied as they were not only as to the purity of doctrine, which each of them established, but also to the spirit wherewith they were executed. If the latter did not exceed![12]

To him the doctrine of predestination as it was formulated by Dort was no more than a species of fatalism, "true Turkish doctrine". Yet he, too, maintained—indeed, like the Remonstrants and the Cambridge Platonists—that man could only find salvation in and through the grace of God at it was revealed in Christ.

---

[11] For this, see the "Voor-Reden" (by A. van Berkel) to the Dutch translation of *Religio Medici*, Leiden 1665.

[12] John Wesley, *Journal*, Curnock ed., II, 473f. (6 July, 1741).

The opponents of Dort, however, refused to believe that trust in God's grace would be strengthened by the extra-doctrinal guarantee of the idea of double predestination. This doctrine, they were afraid, would darken rather than enlighten the mystery of God's love towards fallen man.

In 1784 a young Anglican clergyman, who was known as a Calvinist, the future Evangelical leader Charles Simeon, visited John Wesley, called by him "the great and venerable leader of the Arminians in this kingdom". When Simeon started a discussion on the differences between Arminianism and Calvinism, Wesley gave a personal testimony of his belief in God's saving grace, which so deeply moved the young Calvinist that he could only answer; "Then, Sir, with your leave I will put up my dagger again; for this is all my Calvinism".[13] With Simeon, the doctrine of predestination, though part of his tradition, was only an auxiliary line, marginal to the centre of his religious experience. Therefore, he could recognize a kindred spirit in one who, while rejecting the doctrine of predestination, shared his belief in the centrality of the notion of God's saving grace. This centrality is also a distinguishing mark of *Religio Medici.* Sir Thomas Browne's thoughts on this point were couched in predestinarian categories which were part of his spiritual heritage and which only derived their importance from the connection he believed existed between them and the doctrine of grace. "A coelo salus" was the heart and core of his belief. Perhaps we may even say that this is all Sir Thomas Browne's Calvinism.

---

[13] H.C.G. Moule, *Charles Simeon*, London [2]1948, 79f.

CHAPTER THREE

THE ENGLISH PURITAN FRANCIS ROUS AND THE INFLUENCE OF HIS WORKS IN THE NETHERLANDS

In the seventeenth century Netherlands those in particular who sympathized with the movement of the "Further Reformation" (in more than one respect a parallel to English Puritanism) were interested in the writings of English Puritan authors.[1] One of the leaders of the movement, the right-wing orthodox theologian Gisbertus Voetius, felt a close bond with the Puritans: they advocated a pure form of church discipline, they opposed "useless ceremonies" and fought against doctrinal errors such as those of the Remonstrants, and they pleaded for a return to the simplicity of the apostolic church. We should, Voetius remarked, no more be ashamed of our fellowship with these pious spirits as we are of that with Luther, Zwingli and Calvin and furthermore with all other Reformed theologians.[2] Among those Puritans who became more widely known in the Netherlands, Francis Rous (1579-1659), though not the most prominent one, certainly takes a place of some importance. More clearly than with many others, various seemingly disparate aspects of the Puritan movement are reflected in his person as we know him from his activities and his publications. On the one hand we are struck by the almost agressive fierceness with which he combated what he considered the decline of church and society; on the other hand by the mystical introspection which was a precondition for answering the great question of the relation between "God and the soul". The extraverted as well as the introverted traits of Puritanism can be recognized in the life and work of this man, who is described by C.E. Mallet, in his description of the history of the University of Oxford, as "theologian, mystic, politician, pamphleteer".[3] In this essay I shall first pay attention to his career and to some of his works; then to those writings which have been translated into Dutch. This naturally leads to the question to what extent it is possible to detect in the Netherlands some influences or effects of his writings.

---

[1] See the bibliography of translations of—mostly—Puritan authors in: J. van der Haar, *From Abbadie to Young*, Veenendaal 1980; cf. also what C.W. Schoneveld remarks about the "trend of religious translation" in the Netherlands of the seventeenth century in his *Intertraffic of the Mind*, Leiden 1984, 124f. (with bibliography, 167-245).

[2] G. Voetius, *Politica Ecclesiastica* I,2, Amstelodami 1666, 340.

[3] C.E. Mallet, *A History of the University of Oxford* II (1924), New York and London 1968, 282.

Francis Rous[4] was born in the circle of the gentry, in which Puritanism was not without influence. His birthplace was Dittingham in Devon. The family had its roots in Cornwall; with reference to (among others) Francis Rous, G.F. Nuttall remarks that the presence of the Celtic element in radical Puritanism is very noticeable. He studied in Oxford, in "Broadgates Hall", known as Pembroke College from 1624, which later would be endowed by Rous with a number of scholarships.[5] In 1597 he became Bachelor of Arts; two years later he matriculated at Leiden University as "studiosus artium liberalium",[6] together with Richard Rous, who was one year his elder. At that time he had already some poems to his name, among which was *Thule, or Virtue's History*, a poem from 1598 after the manner of Spenser. In 1601 we meet him again in England, in the "Middle Temple" in London, from which we may conclude that he aspired to a career in the law. Soon, however, he retired to Cornwall, where he occupied himself with theological studies. It is possible that this turn in his career originated in a change in his personal life. In the preface to the translation of one of his writings, to which we shall return below, the Dutch theologian Jacobus Koelman remarked that the author "in a specific way had been taught by God, though ... according to our common usage he was not a theologian, as in his youth he had only studied Law"; he prepared himself "to have at heart above all the work of the Soul" and described in the dedication of his works to his father "how the Lord had touched him and driven to these Studies".[7] Anthony Wood, who in his *Athenae Oxonienses* devoted a very biased passage to Rous, mentions that according to some he "took Holy Orders, and became Minister of Saltash in his own Country",[8] but this communication (of which apparently Wood himself was not certain) is doubtless wrong.[9]

Rous used the quiet time in Cornwall to write a number of works which breathe a Puritan and mystical spirit. In 1616 appeared his *Meditations of Instruction, of Exhortation, of Reprofe*, followed by *The Arte of Happiness* (1619), *Diseases of the Time* (1622) and *Oile of Scorpions* (1623).[10] Some

---

[4] See *Dictionary of National Biography*, s.v.; R.L. Greaves and R. Zaller, *Biographical Dictionary of British Radicals in the Seventeenth Century* III, Brighton 1984, s.v.; N. Tyacke, *Anti-Calvinists. The Rise of English Arminianism c. 1590-1640* (1987), Oxford [2]1990, *sparsim*. Sometimes he is confused with his son Francis Rous (1615-1643?), author of *Archaeologiae Atticae Libri Tres*, Oxford 1637, 1645; thus C.G. Jöcher, *Allgemeines Gelehrtenlexicon* III, Leipzig 1751, c. 2259; C. Saxe, *Onomasticum Literarium*, Traj. ad Rhenum 1782, 426f.

[5] G.F. Nuttall, *The Holy Spirit in Puritan Faith and Experience*, Oxford 1946, 148.

[6] *Album Studiosorum Academiae Lugduno Batavae MDLXXV-MDCCCLXXV*, Hagae Comitum 1885, c.54.

[7] F. Rous, *Het binnenste van Godts Koninkrijk*, Amsterdam 1678, f. * 2[ro].

[8] A. Wood, *Athenae Oxonienses* II, London [2]1721, c. 231ff.

[9] Cf., below, his function in the Westminster Assembly.

[10] The edition of 1656 has as title: *Oyl of Scorpions*.

quotations may serve to indicate the tenor of these works. In *The Arte of Happiness* he wrote, in a passage which in its tone reminds of the medieval mystics:

> ... the very substance of the Spirit in us, is a kinde of heavenly oyl, which makes glad, not so much the face as the very heart of Man. It has in it a taste and relish of the Deity, and therefore above all other, this is the true oyl of gladness. The heart anointed herewith, as it finds a light to guide it, and a vertue moving it to good, and freeing it from the slavery of sin, so also feeleth in itself a blessed Rest, and heavenly Sabbath, a joy glorious and unspeakable, an harmony with God, which passeth all understanding. Hence come those vehement pangs and expressions of love and joy, uttered by the Spouse of Christ, and penned by the wisest of men, which flesh knoweth not how to understand but by the flesh; but the spiritual Man that discerneth all things, fully discerneth and rellisheth them as spiritual truths. From the sound of this harmony come those dancings and exultations of many of the Sons of God, who for this joy of heart have danced before him, who hath filled them with joy.[11]

Various marks of mystical experience are here present: the emphasis on the work of the Spirit in the heart, the tasting and enjoying of the Deity, the inner light by which man is guided, the unspeakable joy which is attended by the inner experience of the "sabbath-rest", the pain of love which the "bride of Christ" experiences and the almost ecstatic character of the joy which flows from harmony with God.

In some Puritans a mystic was hidden, in almost all a moralist. The two can indeed very well go together; think only of Savonarola, one of Rous's most beloved late-medieval authors. We meet the stern, moralizing Puritan in *Oyl of Scorpions*, which has as subtitle: "The Miseries of these Times, Turned into Medicines and curing themselves". By way of example I mention an ironical outburst against the fashion of his time:

> ... by following the Tide of Fashion, men fall both into the great and little deformity; for some time both men and women swell in Ruffs, and Puffs, and Gowns, and Garments; yea, Beards and Curles; and sometimes they ebb away into nothing, and are in all these like a tree whose branches are newly polled, even a stump and no more.

It is no wonder that this man had a gloomy view of the situation of his country:

> ... though this Land be an Iland, bounded by the Sea, yet even in this Iland our Sins are a Continent. For a limit of their extent will hardly be found. I wish we might at length find them bounded with a Sea of penitent tears.[12]

---

[11] Quoted from a collection of Rous's theological and devotional works: *Treatises and Meditations*. Dedicated to the Saints, and to the Excellent throughout the three Nations, London 1657, 35.

[12] *Treatises and Meditations*, 253f. The spelling is that of the 1656 ed.

In doctrinal respect Rous was a convinced adherent of the doctrine of predestination. Until the third decade of the seventeenth century that was indeed the dominant doctrine within the Church of England, which in 1619 by the mouth of her official representatives had agreed with the doctrinal position of the Synod of Dort.[13] But soon with regard to this point the climate would change. Typical of a new approach were two publications by Richard Montagu, then Canon of Windsor, which gave evidence of a predilection for the Arminian position.[14] Rous turned against the second work, *Appello Caesarem* (1625) in his *Testis Veritatis* (1626), in which he showed that the late King James I was a supporter of the doctrine of predestination. Rous's publication is fiercely anti-Arminian. A main line in his discourse is that Arminianism should be seen as a bridge to Rome, and therefore dangerous from an ecclesiastical as well as from a political point of view:

> ... Arminianisme being a kind of twilight, and a double-faced thing that lookes to two Religions at once, *Protestantism* and *Popery*, he that is in it, is like him that stands in the borders of two adioyning Kingdomes, who is ready to dwell in either, as either serves his turne best. So that an *Arminian* is like a flying fish—if preferment bee among the birds, he is ready to fly after it with the birds, and if it bee among the fishes, then among the fishes he will swimme after it.

Only Spain benefits by a victory of Arminianism: "there is not a *Policy* more advantageable to the *Spaniard*, than to bring in Division into a Land, by bringing in *Arminianisme*".[15]

But was it still possible to turn the tide? Charles I was on the side of the Arminians, as appeared from the fact that in 1628 Montagu was appointed Bishop of Chichester. Rous offered strong resistance. Perhaps the knowledge that church and state were threatened by serious dangers made him decide to take to the stormy field of politics: from 1625 to 1626, and then again from 1628 to 1629, he was a member of Parliament, in which with regard to the controversial points he made his voice very clearly heard. So on 26 January 1629 (O.S.) he delivered a sharply anti-Arminian discourse, which, as we shall see, shortly afterwards was translated into Dutch; a discourse in which he depicted the Arminians as the Trojan horse which would bring England under the power of the Pope and of the Spanish king: "I desire that we may look into the very belly and bowels of this Trojan horse to see if there be not men in it ready to open the gates to Roman tyranny and Spanish monarchy ..."[16] Of

---

[13] For the transition from Calvinism to Arminianism in the Church of England, see N. Tyacke, "Puritanism, Arminianism and Counter-Revolution", in C. Russell (ed.), *The Origins of the English Civil War*, London 1973, 119-143, and Tyacke, *Anti-Calvinists*.

[14] See Tyacke, *Anti-Calvinists*, 103-105, 125-128.

[15] *Treatises and Meditations*, 105f.

[16] In England the discourse was published in 1641: *A religious and worthy Speech spoken by*

course we have to see this discourse within the context of the opposition against Charles I in the House of Commons of that time. But while some opponents attacked in particular the King's taxation policy (the levying of "tonnage" and "poundage"), others, among whom were Rous and his brother-in-law John Pym,[17] mainly emphasized the religious factor, in particular the danger of Arminianism. However this may be, the opposition in which Rous took such an important part can be seen as a prelude to the events of the Civil War.[18]

In spite of all his activities on the political front Rous the mystic was not submerged in the politician. Between 1629 and 1640 he published two of his most important mystical writings: *The Mysticall Marriage: Or Experimental Discourses of the Heavenly Marriage between the Soule and her Saviour* (1635) and *The Heavenly Academie* (1638); both would later be translated into Dutch. The first work describes the communion between Christ and the soul in terms of traditional bridal mysticism, largely borrowed from the Song of Songs. The soul seeks and finds in Christ her spouse, who gives her true and full felicity. She learns to know the joys and the obligations which go with marriage to the heavenly bridegroom. Rous concludes *The Mysticall Marriage* with these words:

> The fountain of joy shall flow continually into the mouth of the soul; the new wine of the Kingdom shall still overcome her, and set her up in a continual trance, and extasie of joy ... O! Honey and sweetness it self to the soul that loveth. Her beloved comes quickly, her consummate marriage comes quickly.[19]

Apart from quotations from the Bible *The Mysticall Marriage* contains no references, but from *The Heavenly Academie* it appears that he was acquainted with Bernard of Clairvaux's sermons on the Song of Songs.[20] In the Puritan

---

Mr. Rouse in Parliament; in the same year in *A True Relation* (the debates, held in the Commons in 1629); furthermore in J. Rushworth, *Historical Collections* I, London 1659, 645f. I quote from *A True Relation* as it was edited by W. Notestein and F.H. Relf in *Common Debates for 1629*, Minneapolis 1921, 12f.; this text deviates on some minor points from the text as it was rendered by Rushworth.

[17] For Rous's intellectual affinity to Pym, see Tyacke, *Anti-Calvinists*, 138.

[18] For the historical context of Rous's discourse see Tyacke, "Puritanism", 134f.; C, Russell, *Parliaments and English Politics 1621-1629*, Oxford 1979, 404f.; R. Ashton, *Reformation and Revolution 1558-1660*, London ²1985, 263f.

[19] *Treatises and Meditations*, 739. For *The Mysticall Marriage*, see among others G. Rupp, "A Devotion of Rapture in English Puritanism", in R. Buick Knox (ed.), *Reformation, Conformity and Dissent.* Essays in honour of Geoffrey F. Nuttall, London 1977, 184, with reference to E.I. Watkin, who points out the parallels between *The Mysticall Marriage* and the Writings of St. John of the Cross.

[20] In the fourth chapter (in which medieval-mystical concepts take a large place) he quotes Bernard's 85th sermon on the Song of Songs, in connection with the idea of the mystical marriage; furthermore the tract *De natura et dignitate amoris divinae*, cap. 8, formerly attributed to Bernard, now to Guillaume de Saint-Thierry (*Dictionnaire de Spiritualité* I, c. 1501).

circle he was not an exception in the use he made of the terms of medieval bridal mysticism. In this context G.F. Nuttall remarks: ... "from the constant output of Puritan sermons and commentaries on the *Song of Songs*, the idea of such a "marriage" was before men's minds, and the use of erotic terms in description of the soul's state when enjoying "the life of the Spirit" is not infrequent."[21]

Rous's most interesting writing is perhaps *The Heavenly Academie*, written for young people who were studying and because of this—in contrast to other works of a devotional character—provided with lengthy quotations and references. The gist of the discourse becomes clear from the motto on the title-page, a quotation from Augustine, with "Cathedram in Coelo habet, qui corda docet"[22] as its central message. God is the teacher of teachers. From Him and unto Him are the heavenly gifts. Christians have the advantage over all other people, that they are taught by Christ himself, the best and infallible teacher. Rous does not despise the wisdom of the "lower Academies".[23] The heathen teachers of logic and philosophy are compared with the Gibeonites, who carried wood and water for the building of the Temple. Furthermore the study of Scripture, the external Word, is an important matter. But the two schools have to be connected; he who studies at the lower Academy should strive to move at the same time in the higher Academy, where experimental theology is being taught as it was once to Paul's pupil Timothy. Along this way the student will penetrate ever deeper into the true spiritual knowledge, which is granted in man's inner life, where it spreads its lustre, where it is revealed by God who is the internal teacher.

Once more, this writing is not directed against the "lower Academies", the schools, the universities, theological education with its philosophical substructure. Rous was a man of study; at least with regard to his knowledge of the Early Church he far surpassed the average of his Puritan contemporaries, and in the last phase of his life he would even take an active part in the affairs of the "lower Academie". But at the same time, as a mystic who emphasized religion as a matter of the "interior man", he was deeply conscious of the insufficiency of all that he denoted as "external knowledge". Religous knowledge proceeds from inner enlightenment, so that through the working of the Spirit the heart becomes aware of what no human knowledge can embrace.

---

[21] Nuttall, *Holy Spirit, loc. cit.* 148.

[22] *In Epistolam Johannis ad Parthos Tractatus decem*, III, 13.

[23] An "Advertisement to the Reader" placed before a later edition, mentions that the work was written "to Retrieve a most necessary *Evangelical Doctrine*, which had been too much (at least) neglected, if not almost exploded, among Protestants, for being thought perhaps too favorable to Popery. And it was writ by an Academical Person, and one who was in no wise averse to that common Learning, which is Profess'd and Taught in our Universities ...": *Academia Coelestis: The Heavenly University*, 3d ed., revised and compared with the Latin, London 1702, f. A 2 ro.

With a certain predelection Rous uses for this the image of "tasting":

> ... even in natural fruits there are certain relishes, and, as I may call them, Idaea's and characters of taste, which nothing but the taste it self can truly represent and shew unto us. The West-Indian Piney cannot be so expressed in words, even by him that hath tasted it, that he can deliver over the true shape and character of that taste to another that hath not tasted it.[24]

It is interesting to see to whom this Puritan, so strictly Calvinist in doctrine, appeals. Practically none of the authorities whom he quotes belongs to the circle of the Reformation; a quotation from Luther's *De Servo Arbitrio* is the one exception. Repeatedly, however, he quotes the Fathers: Clement of Alexandria, Origen, Gregory of Nazianzus, Gregory of Nyssa, Chrysostom, Irenaeus, Tertullian, Cyprian and above all Augustine, while also "Dionysius the Areopagite", the source for so many mystical authors, is often quoted, even with a certain predilection.

For the Fathers Rous had a great admiration. In his *Diseases of the Time* he wrote:

> And that Divinity is not a shallow knowledge, fit to be waded through by dwarfish ignorance, the experience of the Fathers may confirm. For the chiefest of them were men of admirable wisdom, great learning, and unwearied study, and yet they found in Divinity Wisdom beyond their understanding, Learning above their Learning, and Work beyond their Time.[25]

In 1650 he published (probably first of all on behalf of students) his *Mella Patrum*, an anthology from the Fathers of the first centuries, according to J.M. Rigg an "inaccurate compilation",[26] but yet a testimony of the importance he attached to the knowledge of the thought-world of the Fathers.

Next to this, in *The Heavenly Academie* we meet many quotations from medieval authors such as Anselm, Bernard of Clairvaux, Thomas Aquinas, Thomas à Kempis and Savonarola. In particular the quotations from Savonarola are crucial for the understanding of Rous's thinking: from him he derives the idea that, just as the blind cannot distinguish colours, those who have not received internal enlightenment are not able to penetrate into the secrets of God.[27] But also ideas of Bernard and of Thomas à Kempis play an important part. The whole work of Rous is permeated by the spirit of medieval mysticism, though in its mild, not in its more extreme form. In his mystical approach he certainly was not alone among the Puritans; but G.F. Nuttall

---

[24] *Treatises and Meditations*, 622f.
[25] *Treatises and Meditations*, 111f.
[26] *DNB*, s.v. Rous.
[27] See in particular Savonarola's *De simplicitate vitae christianae* (1496), lib. V, concl. XVI.

remarks in regard to Rous, that with him we find "a consciousness of mystical tradition greater than that of other Puritan writers."[28] One may wonder whether for Rous the medieval authors in particular whom he quoted were the source of his mystical views, or whether they rather served *a posteriori* in corroboration of his mystical inclinations. I think the first supposition goes too far. We also meet views similar to his in authors who had no demonstrable knowledge of medieval mysticism. But on the other hand we underestimate the function of the medieval mystics in Rous's thought-world when we see them only as useful corroborators of a position which had been adopted altogether independently. They indeed gave a typical colour and timbre to the way Rous formulated his experiential-Puritan views. In Rous's form of Puritanism, the Calvinist tradition allied itself with elements from the medieval mystical tradition, just as in a similar way in German Pietism a connection came into being between medieval spirituality and Reformation thought.[29]

One passage from *The Heavenly Academie* however, makes us look ahead to a development which took place after Rous's time. There is a striking similarity between the way the image of the tasting of the pineapple (the "West-Indian Piney") functions with Rous and with John Locke. In Locke's *Essay on the Human Understanding* we read:

> For words, being sounds, can produce in us no other simple *ideas* than of those very sounds ... He that thinks otherwise, let him try if any words can give him the taste of a pineapple and make him have the true *idea* of the relish of that celebrated delicious fruit.[30]

G.F. Nuttall, who was the first to observe the similarity, speaks of the naive realism which prevailed in the epistemology of Locke's century.[31] It strikes us with Rous as well as with Locke. Of course there is a world of difference between Rous and Locke. Rous started from the idea of an immediate experience of God, while Locke, on the contrary, suspected "all these pretenses to supernatural illumination" of being "nearly the effect and operation of the phansy".[32] Yet it is quite possible that Locke borrowed the image as such from Rous; it would even be rather improbable if in the period he was a student in Puritan Oxford his attention had not been called to *The Heavenly Academie*.

---

[28] Nuttall, *Holy Spirit, loc. cit.*

[29] This is the element of truth in Albrecht Ritschl's thesis (in other respects one-sided and rather partial) that Pietism harks back beyond the Reformation to the Middle Ages. For Ritschl's view of Pietism, see among others M. Schmidt, "Epochen der Pietismusforschung", in J. van den Berg and J.P. van Dooren (eds.), *Pietismus und Réveil*, Leiden 1978, 40f.

[30] *An Essay Concerning Human Understanding*, III, IV, 11.

[31] *Holy Spirit*, 179, cf. 139.

[32] From Locke's "Journal" for 19 February 1682: R.I. Aaron and Jocelyn Gibb, *An Early Draft of Locke's Essay*, Oxford 1936, 120.

However this may be, in Locke's epistemology we meet with a secular reflection of an image, used by Rous in a mystical-religious context. Conversely, Locke's empirical epistomology could function in a new way in the context of eighteenth-century revivalist theology, in which the idea of experience was so prominent. Jonathan Edwards, the father and most important theologian of the American "Great Awakening", read the *Essay* with much sympathy and admiration precisely because of its emphasis on "sensation" and "experience",[33] and the religious-empirical approach of John Wesley, the leader of English Methodism, was linked with the images which he encountered in the *Essay*.[34]

After *The Heavenly Academie* still more theological works from the hand of Rous were published. In 1641, on the eve of the Civil War, appeared *Catholick Charity*, a work in which (as the subtitle indicates) he tried to show "that Rome is uncharitable to sundry eminent parts of the Catholick Church, and especially to Protestants, and is therefore Uncatholick". In this work, the mystical tones are not less clearly recognizable than in Rous's other works. At the same time we may observe a glimpse of those millenarian expectations which were so common with many Puritans in the turbulent middle years of the seventeenth century: "... we will hope that the kingdom of grace shall be speedily changed into the kingdom of glory".[35] With Rous, however, this is only an isolated utterance, an "aside", not determinative for the whole of his thinking. Furthermore, from his other works I mention a Latin translation of *The Mysticall Marriage* and *The Heavenly Academie*, apparently prepared by himself.[36] It appeared in 1655 under the title *Interiora Regni Dei*, with addition of an anti-Arminian treatise, entitled "Grande Oraculum".[37] *The Balme of Love to Heal Divisions* (1648) also deserves to be mentioned, which was no doubt written in view of the dissensions in the Puritan world.[38] In wider circles his name became known through a metrical translation of the Psalms, destined for congregational use (1643), which found acceptance not only in England (with Presbyterians and Independents), but also in Scotland. It received the appro-

---

[33] Perry Miller, *Jonathan Edwards* (1949), New York 1959, 55.

[34] M. Schmidt, *John Wesley* II, Frankfurt a. Main 1966, 295; cf. G.R. Cragg in his edition of Wesley's *The Appeals to Men of Reason and Religion* (The Works of John Wesley II), Oxford 1975, 57 n.1.

[35] *Treatises and Meditations*, 486.

[36] Thus in the preface before the 1702 edition of *Academia Coelestis* (cf. n. 23).

[37] In this tract Rous argues that the salvation of men is not dependent on man's free will, but only on God's special and efficacious grace.

[38] On the strength of this publication G. Yule considers Rous a defender of toleration: "Presbyterians and Independents: some comments", *Past and Present* 47 (1970), 131 n.3; B. Worden, however, observes with Rous only "a tolerant disposition": *The Rump Parliament 1648-1653*, Cambridge 1974, 127 n.1. Perhaps we may state that Rous was tolerant with regard to the "lesser differences" within the Calvinist-Puritan circle, intolerant over against what lay outside this circle.

bation of the "Westminster Assembly" and was appreciated because it remained "close to the text".[39]

When the metrical Psalms appeared, Rous had again been a member of Parliament for a few years. There he played an increasingly important part; we receive the impression that he was more and more seen as "an elder statesman", to whom momentous tasks could be entrusted. Writing on Parliament as it was in 1641 A. Fletcher depicts him as the leader of "a solid phalanx of Puritan gentry".[40] With regard to that time he can be reckoned with the Presbyterians.[41]

His attitude towards the High Church, Arminian and, politically speaking, Royalist part of the Anglican clergy, becomes clear from a rather demagogic discourse, pronounced in Parliament in 1641: "... for certainly this Army of Priests does many ways advance the Design and Plot of Popery".[42] In 1643 he became a "lay assessor" of the Westminster Assembly. At the beginning of 1643 he received the honourable appointment of Provost of Eton. In 1649 he went over to the Independents; according to some, in the preceding period his theological symathies were still with the Presbyterians, and as such he stood near to the Scottish Presbyterian leader Robert Baillie, but for political reasons he was already at that time more or less sympathetic towards the Independents.[43] After the "purging" of Parliament by Cromwell in 1648 ("Pride's Purge") he remained a member of the Rump Parliament, because he feared that otherwise a situation of anarchy would come about.[44] In his transition to the Independents he followed in fact the swiftly developing course of events.[45] His role remained important. He was Speaker of Barebone's Parliament, which dissolved itself in 1653 for fear that otherwise the "Fifth Monarchy Men" would take over. Rous led the procession of moderates, which marched to Whitehall to put the power into Cromwell's hands.[46]

---

[39] Thus the ministers of Worcestershire (among whom was Richard Baxter) in a letter of 1654: G.F. Nuttall, *Richard Baxter*, London and Edinburgh 1965, 52.

[40] A. Fletcher, *The Outbreak of the English Civil War*, London 1981, 311.

[41] In a discourse, pronounced in the Commons in December 1641, Rous's utterances with regard to the episcopal office were not explicitly anti-episcopalian (see W. Cobbett, *Parliamentary History of England* II, London 1807, c. 998-1001). That he was a Presbyterian until 1649 (though the *terminus a quo* is not quite clear) seems to be borne out by the fact that in 1649 appeared an anonymous tract which is attributed to Rous: *The Lawfulness of Obeying the Present Government*. Proposed by one that loves all Presbyterian lovers of truth and peace, and is of their communion.

[42] Rushworth, *Historical Collections* II, 2, 1362f.

[43] Thus R. Ashton (in accordance with V. Pearl), *The English Civil War*, London 1978, 250.

[44] See D. Underdown, *Pride's Purge*, Oxford 1971, 264; Worden, 65f.

[45] Thus R.F. Jones, *Spiritual Reformers in the Sixteenth and Seventeenth Centuries*, London 1914, 268.

[46] Tai Liu, *Discord in Zion: the Puritan Divines and the Puritan Revolution 1640-1660*, The Hague 1973, 114f.

On 16 December 1653 he was sworn in as a member of the Council of State, an important function which brought him near to Cromwell. Another momentous function was that of Chairman of the Commission of Triers, which (even retrospectively) had to judge all new appointments of church ministers. How far, we wonder, will he have been able to realize in this function the ideals laid down in *The Heavenly Academie*? In 1655, as a member of the Council he was involved in the matter of the persecution of the Waldensians. Surely at that time he will have had contacts with Milton, who drafted the Latin letters on this matter which were sent to a number of European States; it inspired Milton to his moving sonnet: "Avenge, O Lord, thy slaughtered saints ...".[47]

In 1657 he became a member of the House of Lords, but he did not bear the title of "Lord" for long; in 1659 he died at the age of 80 at his ancestral home in Cornwall. Within the leading circles of the Commonwealth he was "a grand old man"; he was hated, however, by his royalist opponents, as appears from the invectives they used against him.[48]

Particularly when we survey the latter years of his life we may wonder how his mystical inclinations could go together with his political activities. He certainly was a mystic, with an affinity to the Quakers on some points.[49] According to Ritschl, Rous's *Interiora Regni Dei* proves that in the circle of English Independent Calvinism there was a return to the medieval pattern of mysticism, though he adds that still on various points the work keeps within the horizon of the Reformation.[50] We may think the combination between mysticism and politics strange, as we meet it with Rous in a very striking form—but then, perhaps, we are projecting our sense of contradiction upon a time in which other contrasts prevailed. According to some, was not the greatest English politician of that time, Cromwell, equally "in essence a mystic"?[51]

As we saw already, more than once Rous was translated into Dutch. The first time this happened was in 1629, the year in which Rous pronounced his anti-Arminian discourse in Parliament. The situation in England differed from that in the Netherlands: while in England Arminianism was in the ascendant, in the Netherlands it was a small, defeated minority, without any possibility for new expansion. But the leaders of the Reformed Church were still not quite at ease. The stadtholdership of the tolerant Frederick Henry seemed to open up new possibilities for the Remonstrants. It is true, the edicts against the Remonstrants remained in force, and for reasons of state the Stadtholder was not

---

[47] D. Masson, *The Life of John Milton* V (1877), Gloucester (Mass.) 1965, 183-192.
[48] See Wood, *loc.cit.*
[49] Jones, 269; cf. Nuttall, *Holy Spirit*, 42.
[50] A. Ritschl, *Geschichte des Pietismus in der reformirten Kirche* II, Bonn 1880, 129f. According to L. Bouyer, for Rous traditional Christian mysticism is the fulfilment of the "sola gratia" in the believing soul: Rupp, *loc.cit.*
[51] Nuttall, borrowing a characterization by John Buchan: *Holy Spirit*, 115.

prepared to make official concessions to them, but unofficially in some places they received more freedom: in various towns the meetings of the Remonstrants were connived at. That was also the case in Amsterdam, where in spite of a strong opposition from the side of the Church the magistrates took a more of less tolerant course towards the Remonstrants. The matter reached a climax in 1628. Personal mediation by Frederick Henry had not availed; feelings ran very high, and at the end of the year there even was the threat of a revolt from a number of soldiers of the town militia who refused to serve under officers with Remonstrant sympathies.[52]

From the anti-Arminian side in 1628 five petitions had been delivered to the local authorities or to the Stadtholder, in which the maintenance of the edicts against the Remonstrants was insisted on. Against these petitions the Remonstrant leader Johannes Wtenbogaert (or Uytenbogaert) protested in a dignified and well-reasoned discourse, which appeared anonymously under the title *Ondersoeck der Amsterdamsche Requesten tot verdedigingh der onschuldige ende onder-rechtingh der misleyde* (Examination of the Amsterdam petitions, to defend the innocent and to instruct those who are misled).[53] Also in 1628 appeared an answer to Wtenbogaert from the side of the Church, equally anonymously: *Ondersoeck van de Wettelijckheydt der Remonstrantsche Conventiculen* (Examination of the legality of the Remonstrant conventicles), which hit out very fiercely at the Remonstrants: the "Remonstrant religion" was depicted as worse in this country for the true Reformed religion and the Republic than any other religion; "for never in this country has any sect done such a great evil to the Church ... as the sect and faction of the Remonstrants".[54] This "sect" and "faction" was dangerous to the state: the activities of the Remonstrants could even lead to a civil war or to an invasion by enemies to whom a bridge had been presented. Whatsoever might be tolerated, never should the meetings of the Remonstrants be permitted.

A second edition of this anti-Remonstrant pamphlet appeared in 1629, to which was now added, with continuing pagination, "the Proposition made by Mr. Rouse in the House of Commons"; it was also published separately. That

---

[52] See J.E. Elias, *Geschiedenis van het Amsterdamsche Regentenpatriciaat*, 's-Gravenhage 1923, 95f.; J.G. van Dillen, "Documenten betreffende de politieke en kerkelijke twisten te Amsterdam (1614-1630)" in *Bijdragen en Mededeelingen Historisch Genootschap* 49 (1938), 191-249; H. Brugmans, *Geschiedenis van Amsterdam* III, Utrecht-Antwerpen ^{2}1973, 39f.; J.J. Poelhekke, *Frederik Hendrik*, Zutphen 1978, 206-212; for the broader political context, see also J.I. Israel, *The Dutch Republic and the Hispanic World 1606-1661*, Oxford 1982, 200f., 228.

[53] For this, see H.C. Rogge, *Johannes Wtenbogaert en zijn tijd* III, Leiden-Amsterdam 1876, 172f.

[54] The tract *Ondersoeck van de Wettelijckheydt* ... appeared in first and second edition in Haarlem with A. Rooman; the separate edition of the *Propositie* (with different spelling) in The Hague with A. Meuris. The translation is based on the text as given by Notestein and Relf (see n. 16).

Rous's discourse, which was still unpublished in England, appeared so speedily in Dutch translation indicates that there existed not only a feeling of affinity, but also a direct contact between English Puritans and Dutch church leaders of the character of Adriaan Smout and Jacobus Trigland, fierce opponents of everything that tended towards any form of tolerance with regard to the Remonstrants.[55] Just as later the Dutch Remonstrants would look upon the English Arminians as their theological allies, so now some Dutch anti-Remonstrants tried to strengthen their case by the authority of one of the leading English Puritans. How much Rous's discourse linked up with their arguments, so that it could be applied immediately to the Dutch situation, appears from the following passage from the anti-Remonstrant pamphlet:

> For the Arminians are the brood of the Papists; and if you let shine your favour upon them, you will see they will change into the Frogs that come up from the Abyss. And if you well observe it, you will see that an Arminian extends his hand to the Papist, a Papist to the Jesuit, and a Jesuit extends one hand to the Pope while he extends the other hand to the King of Spain ...[56]

But all this sound and fury was of no avail: in the following year the newly built spacious Remonstrant church on the Keizersgracht in Amsterdam was officially taken into use.

In the "Proposition" we hear the voice of Rous as a militant Calvinist controversialist. The mystical aspect of Rous would in due time also become known in the Netherlands. In 1656 appeared a Dutch translation of *The Mysticall Marriage*,[57] by "P.H.", "a learned and godly young man".[58] This translation had been made at the request of Georgius Hornius, professor of history at Leiden university, who in his youth had visited England as tutor of the sons of an English nobleman.[59] Jöcher mentions that there he sympathized with the "Presbyterians", by whom surely the Puritans are meant;[60] also at a

---

[55] For the activities of the militant Contra-Remonstrant ministers, see J. Wagenaar, *Amsterdam in zijne opkomst, aanwas, geschiedenisse ... en regeeringe* IV, Amsterdam 1763, 425-434, 454-459; R.B. Evenhuis, *Ook dat was Amsterdam* I, Amsterdam 1965, 311-314.

[56] f. C 3 ro,vo

[57] *Het verborgen houwelik of ondervonde ontdekkinghe van het hemelsche houwelik tusschen de Siele ende haren Saligmaker*, Rotterdam (J. Vishoeck), 1656.

[58] Probably Petrus Hering(h)a, who matriculated into Leiden University in 1644, and later became minister in the village of Oost-Graftdijk (North-Holland); he translated several works from the English. See *Biographisch Woordenboek van Protestantsche Godgeleerden in Nederland* III s.v.; Van der Haar, 154; *Album Studiosorum*, 355.

[59] For Hornius, see *BWPGN* IV, 304-310; J.J. Prins, "Georgius Hornius en zijne "Kerckelijcke Historie"" (with postscript by H.C. Rogge) in *Archief voor Nederlandsche Kerkgeschiedenis* 6 (1897), 321-342. His life ended, early, in tragic darkness.

[60] Jöcher II, c. 1708f.

later stage he was very well disposed towards the Puritans.[61] In a short preface to the translation Hornius wrote:

> This little book has been forwarded to me from England with the purpose to have it translated into the Dutch language or to translate it myself as something which would be very useful to the churches beyond the sea ... The contents of this book are Christian and lovely.[62]

The translator declared that he kept as much as possible to the author's own words, so that the readers also in the Dutch translation would be able to observe "the sweet English style of the Author".[63] The work linked on to a number of publications from the circle of the "Further Reformation", the puritanically-minded Voetian reform movement, writings in which in a mystical way the relation between Christ and the soul was rendered in terms derived from the Song of Songs and which show how highly Bernard's bridal mysticism was valued in this circle.[64] In 1678 a new edition appeared, now joined with a translation of *The Heavenly Academie* under the title *Het binnenste van Godts Koninkrijk* (a translation of *Interiora Regni Dei*).[65] The "Grande Oraculum" was left out; it was indeed somewhat out of tune with the rest of the work. The work was edited by Jacobus Koelman, who himself translated *The Heavenly Academie*, while for *The Mysticall Marriage* he used the existing translation.

In Koelman we meet a conspicuous, even extreme representative of the "Further Reformation".[66] He was a pupil of Voetius, though ultimately his radical stand in ecclesiastical affairs estranged him from his more established teacher.[67] In his first congregation (the little town of Sluis in Zeeland) his strict maintenance of ecclesiastical discipline, his resistance against the celebration of the ecclesiastical festival days and his protests against the use of fixed formularies and set prayers in church services brought him into conflict with the magistrates, by whom in 1675 he was dismissed from his office and even banished. He was not a separatist such as the Labadists whom he opposed; as

---

[61] See especially his eulogy of the early Puritans (and by implication of those later Puritans who had maintained the original ideals): "Viri, omnino vita *sanctissimi*, doctrina *purissimi*, zelo Religionis *ferventissimi*": *Historia Ecclesiastica et Politica*, Lugd. Bat. ^{3}1671, 232; a clear parallel to Voetius' view of the Puritans.

[62] f. (*) 2ro.

[63] f. (*)4ro.

[64] I. Boot, *De allegorische uitlegging van het Hooglied voornamelijk in Nederland*, Woerden 1971, 189f.

[65] The full title is *Het binnenste van Godts Koninkrijk, vertoont in 2 tractaten, genaamt: Het verborgen houwlijk en: De hemelsche Academie*. In het Engels beschreven door den Heer Franciscus Rous. Amsterdam (J. Wasteliers) 1678. "De hemelsche Academie" has a separate titlepage, but a continued pagination.

[66] For him, see A.F. Krull, *Jacobus Koelman*, Sneek 1901; on 352-357 a survey of translations from the English by Koelman; cf. also Van der Haar, s.v. Koelman.

[67] A.C. Duker, *Gisbertus Voetius* III, Leiden 1914, 225-229.

a minister, dismissed by the secular authorities but not suspended by the Church, he continued to function as "minister of the Word" by preaching in various places in conventicles. Furthermore he wrote various theological works, often of a polemical nature, and he translated a number of English and Scottish authors to whose theology, spirituality, and stand in ecclesiastical affairs he felt closely related.[68]

It is small wonder that this man in his situation, after his dismissal through which he felt expelled from the ecclesiastical and scholarly "establishment" that refused to stand up for him over against the authorities, was attracted to *The Heavenly Academie* and thought it important to translate it into Dutch. To the translation he added a circumstantial "address" to "the Students of Holy Theology in the Lower Academies". In this "address" he fiercely attacked the church of his own days, and in particular the ministerial order:

> This is the miserable situation of the Church in these days, especially in our Low Countries, that therein so many have been appointed Watchmen and Pastors and Teachers, who have not received more than a part of brain knowledge about the general truths; and being bloated through this, they have no ear for salutary warnings ... in particular to consider the Reformation in themselves and in others. This will lead the Church to destruction ...

He saw the church as a dying church because of her carnality, her lukewarmness and the daily round of her formality in the way she confesses and practises Christianity. There was all the more reason to warn the students against a great evil,

> namely, that you are not satisfied with seeking a little Academic scholarship, as if you would have well studied when you had filled your head with some Scholastic knowledge as well of Philosophy and Philology as of Theology: yet this is the practice and custom of most students in the Academies.

Koelman declared emphatically that he did not despise academic scholarship: he only wanted to warn against "knowledge which puffeth up". Those who have little reading are often infected by the plague of pride. The dangers are all the more threatening because of the influence of "the Popish, but in fact Atheistic Philosopher" Descartes, whose philosophy has "seduced and debauched the students to a prodigious wantonness and audacious boldness in speaking of God and Divine matters." Koelman exhorts the students not to keep to the letter only, but to strive after spiritual knowledge and so to come to the heavenly academy:

---

[68] Van der Haar, 154, mentions 12 authors.

> sit down at the feet of Jesus, and learn from him immediately, before you undertake to teach others; he will deliver you from your natural Phrenesy ...[69]

It is all Rous, transposed into the Dutch situation of the late seventies as Koelman saw it. The "address" is more fierce, more polemical, more explicit in its criticism of the "lower Acadmies" than the work of Rous as such. Yet Koelman did not use Rous's writing to legitimate his own position, as in 1696 the German minister Samuel Nethenus did. He was a younger contemporary of Koelman, and to a certain extent of Koelman's way of thinking; when he was dismissed from the ministerial office because of his Labadist inclinations he appealed to Rous and defended himself over against the theologians of Marburg, by saying that he was a servant of God, who had been taught in "the heavenly academy".[70]

One may doubt whether Rous's mystical works were really popular in the Netherlands. There was one reprint, as late as 1731,[71] which makes us surmise that (compared with the many editions of other devotional works) the interest was not very high. To a broad public in the Netherlands the name of Rous will not have been well known, and possibly Koelman's warm recommendation will not have been conducive to the interest outside the circle of Koelman's sympathizers. There is a curious, somewhat abridged reprint of the translation of *The Heavenly Academie* (with Koelman's "address") which appeared in the second half of the nineteenth century.[72] It was edited by Wouterus Bekker, a lay preacher, who, separate from the Reformed Church, on his own authority held services in a chapel in the old town centre of Amsterdam.[73] This edition, which will not have reached a broad public, will partly have been meant to serve as a legitimation of Bekker's anomalous ecclesiastical position.

In an indirect way, however, Rous's views have had a not unimportant influence in the Netherlands. With several authors we meet the idea, which had been formulated by him in particular with reference to Savonarola, that just as one who has been born blind cannot distinguish colours, a "natural man" has no knowledge of spiritual matters: they can only be known through experience.[74] One of these was the Utrecht minister Jodocus van Lodensteyn, one of the most beloved authors from the circle of the "Further Reformation", whose *Beschouwinge van Zion* (Observation of Zion, first published in 1674), con-

---

[69] f.*3vo, 4^{ro,vo}.

[70] Ritschl II, 395f.

[71] In Rotterdam with N. Topijn (Van der Haar, no. 1608).

[72] Without date; Van der Haar (no 1609) has as year of publication: 1878.

[73] The building "Nazareth" in the Barndesteeg. Bekker could preach as fiercely and demagogically as Smout, who was one of his examples: Evenhuis V, 232.

[74] On this more extensively J. van den Berg, "'Letterkennis' en 'geestelijke kennis'", in *Nederlands Archief voor Kerkgeschiedenis* 60 (1980), 236-263.

tains various passages which are reminiscent of Rous; at that time, Koelman's translation had not yet appeared, but Van Lodensteyn may have consulted *The Heavenly Academie* in *Interiora Regni Dei.*[75] Furthermore we find the bridal mysticism from *The Mysticall Marriage* (with reference to Rous) with Herman Witsius, an irenic theologian who taught from 1680 to 1698 at the University of Utrecht, and after that till his death in 1708 at Leiden University.[76] From posthumously published lecture notes it appears that he called on his students to try to be admitted "to the inner sanctuary of the heavenly Academy, where we shall be taught about God through seeing and tasting".[77] Finally I mention Wilhelmus Schortinghuis, minister of Midwolda (Province of Groningen), who in 1740 published *Het innige Christendom* (Inner Christianity), a work on which he was heavily attacked because of its mystical tendencies, but which for the same reasons became very popular in "experiential", pietistically-coloured circles.[78] With him, too, the idea takes a central place that true theology can only be known by means of supernatural enlightenment. For this, he appeals to Lodensteyn and Witsius, and—through Rous—to Savonarola:

> But in order to know the things of God an understanding should be given by God, a spiritual understanding, to distinguish spiritual things. These are the meaningful words of F. Rous in his *Hemelsche Academie*, p. 37. Qui sine lumine supernaturali scripturas se intelligere arbitratur sine alis et pennis volare contendit ... There is *a peace of God which passeth all understanding*, which, though the mind of him who possesses this peace cannot fully embrace it, yet he understands and knows it in some measure through tasting that *peace of God in his soul*, Phil. 4.7, and the more he tastes it, the more he will know it, says the aforenamed F. Rous ibid., p. 252.[79]

Partly thanks to Rous, views from later medieval mysticism have had influence in the pietistic sector of Dutch Protestant culture.

Rous was not a great theologian, though his mediating role between medieval mysticism and Reformed Pietism was not without importance. Neither was he a great politician, though in his political activities he was a typical representative of English Puritanism in the Commonwealth period. We know him as a fierce anti-Catholic, but he found his sources rather in the writings of the Fathers and the medieval theologians than in those of the Reformers. In essence he was a conservative, but perhaps in spite of himself he helped to

---

[75] For the image of the blind and the colours: *Beschouwinge van Zion*, Amsterdam [4]1718, 26; for Lodensteyn's estimation of "mystical theology" 39f.

[76] J. van Genderen, *Herman Witsius*, The Hague 1953, 175f.; Boot, 203.

[77] *Practicale Godgeleerdheid*, Rotterdam [2]1732 (translation of *Schediasma Theologiae Practicae*, 1729), 13.

[78] For Schortinghuis, see J.C. Kromsigt, *Wilhelmus Schortinghuis*, Groningen 1904; for his influence M.J.A. de Vrijer, *Schortinghuis en zijn analogieën*, Amsterdam 1942.

[79] *Het innige Christendom*, Groningen, [4]1752, 14

prepare the way for new developments, and precisely those elements in his writings which harked back to the Middle Ages could form a point of departure for Pietists as well as for empiricists. His opponents in Royalist circles sometimes called him a "Proteus"[80]—unfairly, for his life and thought are ultimately marked by continuity and consistency. But he was indeed a man of widely diverging interests and activities: a mystic who in the tranquillity of Cornwall concentrated on the "inner life"; a politician who in the midst of the turbulence of London life devoted himself to the immediate interests of Church and State, and who in all this makes something visible of the complex character of mid-seventeenth century English culture.

---

[80] Wood, *loc.cit.*

CHAPTER FOUR

PROTO-PROTESTANTS? THE IMAGE OF THE KARAITES AS A MIRROR OF THE CATHOLIC-PROTESTANT CONTROVERSY IN THE SEVENTEENTH CENTURY

In the seventeenth century and at the beginning of the eighteenth century the Karaites, a Jewish group which had its origins in the eighth century and which was marked by a rejection of the authoritative character of the post-biblical Jewish tradition,[1] enjoyed a large amount of interest in Christian circles. This interest was not of a purely historical or scholarly nature: it was bound up with the Catholic-Protestant controversy as it expressed itself in discussions and expositions which to a large degree were determined by more or less overtly formulated polemical arguments. The great confessional cleavage within Christianity was projected upon the cleavage between the traditional Jews (the "Rabbinists") and the Karaites, and consequently, as we shall see, somehow the image of the Karaites was coloured by the confessional views of the various Christian authors who occupied themselves with this subject.

The first discussion on the Karaites had its beginning in a scholarly controversy with confessional overtones on another group, the Essenes, to which I only refer in brief; it has been dealt with extensively by J.C.H. Lebram in an article "De Hasidaeis ...".[2] In 1583, the orientalist Johannes Drusius, then professor at the University of Leiden, published his *Quaestionum ac responsionum liber*, in which he dealt with the "Asidaioi", mentioned in the Books of the Maccabees.[3] Drusius saw in the "Asidaioi" (according to him a transcription of "chasidim") the Pharisees, but on this point he was attacked by the Jesuit scholar Nicolaus Serarius, professor at the University of Mainz. In his commentary on the Books of the Maccabees (1590) Serarius averred that the "Asidaioi" were to be identified with the Essenes, whom he considered an "adumbration" of the present-day monks.[4] In this context, he opposed the

---

[1] For the Karaites, see J. Fürst, *Geschichte des Karäerthums*, 3 volumes, Leipzig 1862-69 (repr. Hildesheim 1975); Zvi Ankori, *Karaites in Byzantium. The Formative Years, 970-1100*, New York and Jerusalem 1959; N. Wieder, *The Judean Scrolls and Karaism*, London 1962; S. Szysman, *Le Karaïsme*, Lausanne 1980. It was Professor P.A.H. de Boer, Leiden (†) who drew my attention to these titles.

[2] J.C.H. Lebram, "De Hasidaeis. Over Joodse studiën in het oude Leiden", *Voordrachten Faculteitendag 1980,* Leiden 1980, 21-31.

[3] *Quaestionum ac responsionum liber* [I], In Ac. Lugdunensi 1583, 37.

[4] *Commentarii in Sacros Bibliorum libros Iosuae, Iudicum, Ruth, Tobiae, Iudith, Esther, Maccabaeorum*, Lutetia Parisiorum 1611, 733: "Insignis Monachorum, religiosorumque nostrorum adumbratio in piis istis priscae legis Asidaeis et Essenis notari potest".

famous linguist Joseph Justus Scaliger, later professor at Leiden University, who had denied the Christian character of that group of Essenes which lived in Egypt in Philo's times: according to Serarius, who referred to Baronius, they were Christians because they believed in the coming Christ.[5]

Drusius replied in 1603 in a little work *De Hasidaeis.* His attitude towards Serarius appeared to be somewhat ambivalent. In a letter to Johannes Wtenbogaert (or Uytenbogaert), later one of the leaders of the Remonstrant party, which formed the preface to the first edition, Drusius evinced a certain measure of appreciation for Serarius as a fellow Hebraist. On the whole, however, the tone of his rejoinder was rather sharp. Drusius' irritation was caused by the fact that Serarius had treated him as a heretic. On this point, Drusius remarked that two factors are required to qualify someone as a heretic: first of all, that he errs in the fundamental truths of the faith, and secondly, that he obstinately perseveres in his error. Thus, Serarius' accusation was quite off the mark: "All my little knowledge moves around Grammar and History. I leave the dogma's of faith to others. In History is no heresy, much less in Grammar". But "if a heretic is someone who loves truth, then I certainly confess to be a heretic".[6] Straight from the beginning the discussion was overshadowed by the Catholic-Protestant controversy, which also influenced the attitude towards the Essenes. Serarius saw in them a prototype of the Christian monastic orders; for Drusius, however, they were no more than a relatively unimportant side-branch on the tree of Judaism.[7]

Serarius, in his turn shocked by Drusius' attack,[8] replied in his work *Trihaeresium seu de celeberrimis tribus, apud Judaeos, Pharisaeorum, Sadducaeorum et Essenorum sectis* (1604). In his discussion of the Pharisees, the Catholic-Protestant controversy became quite explicit. He had noticed, that by heretics the Catholics were sometimes injuriously described as "Pharisees".[9] To this, he reacted by remarking that as far as the Pharisees were representatives of the Jewish religion, they were no heretics, and thus the

---

[5] "Ii certe nostri, qui, cum Iuda, religionem viribus omnibus tuebantur, Christiani fuerunt ... quia in venturum Christum credebant ...", *loc. cit.*; cf. what Caesar Baronius (though somewhat more cautiously) remarks in his *Annales Ecclesiastici* I (first cd. 1588), Coloniae Agrippinae 1624, c. 689ff. For Scaliger's opinion, see his famous work *De emendatione temporum* (first ed. 1583), Francofurti 1593, 251f.

[6] *De Hasidaeis quorum mentio in libris Machabaeorum libellus ad Johan. Utenbogardum*, Franekerae 1603, 22, 35. *De Hasidaeis* was also published (though without the introductory letter) in a work, edited by the Leiden professor J. Trigland: *Trium Scriptorum illustrium de tribus Judaeorum sectis Syntagma*, Delphis 1703, in two parts. For this work see below, 52f.

[7] Lebram, "De Hasidaeis", 25.

[8] According to Sixtinus Amama, Serarius saw himself "misere flagellatum" by Drusius: Amama to John Prideaux, 30 July 1619, *Syntagma* I, ††† (1)vo.

[9] In this context, Serarius quotes Theodorus Beza on Matth. 4 (without mentioning the source of the quotation): "Nec enim ovum ovo similius, quam vos Theologi et Canonistae veteribus illis Pharisaeis".

Catholics could in a good sense be compared with the Pharisees. On the other hand, among those who participated in the faults of the Pharisees such as hypocrisy, superstition etc., there were Lutherans, Calvinists and other heretics as well as Catholics; in this respect, the heretics were worse than the bad Catholics, because with the moral faults of the Pharisees they joined perfidy and heresy.[10]

Dealing with the Sadducees, Serarius remarked that in his own time there still existed adherents of that sect in the form of the Karaites, whom Leo Africanus had mentioned in his description of Africa.[11] Now, the Karaites began to take a place in the discussion. Drusius had already mentioned them in 1583 in his *Quaestionum ac responsionum liber*. There, he had stated that the Sadducees, who strongly adhered to the written law and rejected the orally transmitted doctrine, were called Karaites.[12] This could be explained as an identification between Sadducees and Karaites, such as was to be found with Serarius. In his answer to Serarius, given in his *De tribus sectis Judaeorum* (1605), Drusius made it clear, however, that this was not his intention. He would not deny that in early times the Sadducees were called Karaites, but they were different from the present-day Karaites, who unlike the Sadducees believed in the resurrection. He distinguished between three groups of Jews in the Orient: the Talmudists, the Karaites and the Samaritans. His sympathy was with the Karaites. Quoting the sixteenth century scholar and traveller Guillaume Postel, he explained the name "Karaites" as "Lecturarii" ("if it is allowed to invent a word"), who, rejecting all documents of men, embraced and observed the sacred documents alone.[13]

Drusius strongly emphasized the purely historical character of his scholarly work, as appears from his reiterated rejection of the accusation that his work was marked by his heretical views: "Ubi nuda historia, ibi nulla haeresis est".[14] But in spite of this, the confessional rupture does not remain invisible if (which is probable) by using the quotation from Postel in this context Drusius implicitly referred to the Catholic-Protestant controversy which had already played its part in the discussion around the Essenes.

Another opponent of Serarius was Scaliger, who in a little work, *Elenchus Trihaeresii* (1605), angrily attacked the expositions of the Jesuit scholar. He

---

[10] *Syntagma* I, "Serrarii Trihaeresium" 74f.

[11] *Syntagma* I, "Serrarii Trihaeresium" 99; cf. Ioannes Leo Africanus, *Africae descriptio IX lib. absoluta* (first ed., Italian, 1550), Lugd. Bat. 1632, 127. L. Massignon sees in the Karaites, mentioned by, Leo, "pseudo-Karaïtes, juifs non talmudistes", *Le Maroc dans les premières années du XVIe siècle,* Alger 1906, 157.

[12] *Quaest.*, 34f. The same passage is to be found in *Quaestionum Ebraicarum libri tres*, Franekerae 1599, I, 34f.; in essence the same work, but with notes. Here, Drusius refers in a note to Leo Africanus.

[13] *Syntagma* I, "De tribus Judaeorum sectis" 296; cf. G.Postellus, *Linguarum duodecim characteribus differentium alphabetum introductio*, Parisiis s.a. [1538], CII^{vo}.

[14] *Syntagma* I, "De tribus Juadeorum sectis" 348.

had to concede that at one time (as Serarius had observed) he had indeed identified the Karaites with the Sadducees, on the authority of Jewish scholars. But this pronouncement had to be changed. From Philippus Ferdinandus,[15] "a Christian from the Jews", who had come to know the Karaites intimately during his stay in Constantinople and had often visited their synagogues, he had learned that the Karaites only differed from the other Jews in their rejection of the secondary authorities.[16] They believed, together with the other Jews, in the resurrection, in the compensation of merits and the eternal punishment of sins, in paradise and hell. Hence the Karaites could not be identical with the Sadducees. A passage on the hatred of the "Rabbanists" against the Karaites contains a scarcely hidden reference to the Catholic-Protestant controversy: "... just as the zealots of today hate those who are better than they themselves are, so are the Karaites hated by the rabbinic Jews because of the integrity of their life as well as their neglect of the traditions".[17]

For Scaliger, an irascible man who was much vexed because of the *Trihaeresium*,[18] it was sufficient to have vented his anger against Serarius in his *Elenchus*. According to Sixtinus Amama, he did not even deign to read Serarius' reply: *Minerval Josepho Scaligero et Johanni Drusio Depensum*, which appeared in 1605.[19] In this work, Serarius declared that he doubted the reliability of Philippus Ferdinandus as a witness. As regards the relation between the Sadducees and the Karaites he averred that even in case there were differences there could be an amount of continuity: the present day Lutherans and Calvinists do not follow Luther or Calvin in every respect.[20] He explained the sympathy of the Protestants (the "Novatores") for the Karaites from their rejection of the good and apostolic traditions of the Catholic Church; on this point there was a formal parallel. Scaliger had also praised the Karaites for their moral life and their probity in traffic. That, however, Serarius considered too much praise. He was willing to concede that the "Novatores" were Karaites, but with him this was no positive qualification: in commercial life, Calvinists and Karaites seemed to be almost equally cunning and fraudulent. Lastly, he remarked that Scaliger had passed lightly over the Karaites' acceptance of the idea of the compensation of merits: is there anyone who is ignorant of the opinion of Lutherans and Calvinists alike with regard to this doctrine?[21]

---

[15] The text (of the *Syntagma* as well as of the earlier editions) has Philippus Fredericus—manifestly a misprint. See H.F. Wijnman, "Philippus Ferdinandus, Professor in het Arabisch aan de Leidse Universiteit ...", in *Jaarbericht van het Vooraziatisch-Egyptisch Genootschap Ex Oriente Lux* VI (1967), 558-580. 1 thank Dr. H.J. de Jonge, Leiden, for this reference.

[16] The "δευτερώτα".

[17] *Syntagma* I, 376f.

[18] "Bilis mota est Generosi Seni": Amama in his letter to Prideaux (see note 8).

[19] *Syntagma* I, ††† 2ro.

[20] "Quemadmodum anni tempestates, sic et haereseon dogmata immutantur".

[21] *Syntagma* II, "Minerval" 71-75.

At that time, Serarius was not the only Catholic to see a parallel between Karaites and Protestants. The French Friar Jean Boucher, who travelled widely in the Orient, even noticed a resemblance between the Paschal rite of the Karaites and the way the Huguenots celebrated the Lord's Supper: the ceremony of these good people "n'est guère éloignée de celle qu'observent nos Messieurs de la Prétenduë en leur Cène ...".[22]

The discussion between Drusius and Serarius went on, though the Karaites receded into the background. The arguments became repetitive, the tone more and more bitter. While much scholarly material was brought forward it is easy to perceive that the struggle between both scholars was ultimately determined by the tensions of the confessional controversy.[23]

With Protestant theologians, the Karaites remained in favour, though initially their knowledge of the Karaites was not as great as the sympathy they evinced for them. In the West, the works of the Karaites were practically unknown, and there were few who had personal contacts in the Karaite circle. The first to acquaint the world of Western Christian scholarship with the Karaites was Postel, of whom Richard Simon wrote: "Il nous a ... fait connoître la Secte des Caraites parmi les Juifs".[24] As we saw Scaliger changed his mind with regard to the Karaites under the influence of the communications of Philippus Ferdinandus. The orientalist Johann Heinrich Hottinger mentioned the Karaites in his *Thesaurus Philologiae* (1649), in which he quoted a letter from the Genevan professor Antoine Léger, who between 1628 and 1636 acted as chaplain to the Dutch ambassador in Constantinople.[25] Léger described the Karaites as people who, disregarding the Talmudic phantasies and the rabbinic traditions, had only the inspired books as the norm of their faith; they read the Scriptures in Greek (their vernacular language) and imbued their children with biblical knowledge.[26] Again, the parallel with the Protestants is evident. In the Netherlands the Leiden professor of law Petrus Cunaeus, a scholar whose world of thought had close affinities to that of Drusius and Scaliger, had given a sympathetic (though very elementary) pic-

---

[22] J. Boucher, *Bouquet sacré* ..., 1613 (?; the year is mentioned in handwriting in a copy of the British Library of which the title-page is missing), 462.

[23] In 1606, Drusius published his *Responsio ad Minerval Serarii,* in which again he complained of the accusation of heresy: "Abraham haereticus erat Sabiis, Moses idololatris, Christus Pharisaeis: sic ego haereticus sum Serario. Non est discipulus supra magistrum", *Syntagma* II, "Responsio ad Minerval" 226. In his turn, in his *Rabbini* (which appeared together with his *Herodes* in 1607), Serarius complained of the arrogance of his opponents, their lightheartedness in introducing innovations, their temerity and their impudence towards the Fathers: *Syntagma* II, "Rabbini" 367.

[24] R. Simon, *Lettres choisies* (nouv. éd.), Amsterdam 1730, 1, 214; cf. R.H. Popkin, "Les Caraïtes et l'émancipation des Juifs", *Dix-huitième siècle* 13(1981), 138.

[25] For Léger, see J. Aymon, *Monumens authentiques de la religion des Grecs,* La Haye 1708, 10f.

[26] J.H. Hottinger, *Thesaurus Philologiae,* ed. sec. 1659, 42f.

ture of the Karaites in his famous work *De Republica Hebraeorum (1617).*[27] Another Leiden professor, the theologian Johannes Hoornbeeck, continued the line of Drusius and Scaliger in his apologetic work *Tesjubat Jehudah* (1655). He extolled the Karaites above the other Jews: the better the "Scripturarii" were, the more they were hated and wronged by the others.[28]

In his description of the hatred of the "rabbinic Jews" against the Karaites, Hoornbeeck referred to the German orientalist Johann Stephan Rittangel, who had a deep interest in the Jews.[29] According to Mordecai ben Nisan, a Karaite who lived near Lemberg, "a certain German scholar, named Rittangelius, who applied himself to the study of the doctrine of the Karaites, went to all the places in Lithuania where Karaites lived, and accurately, inspected their books in the synagogue of Trahai near Wilna".[30] This happened, Mordecai says, "in the year 5401" (*i.e.* A.D. 1641); it is the more strange that in the *Liber Jezirah,* which appeared one year later, Rittangel confuses the Karaites with the Samaritans![31]

Of course it is possible, that the *Liber Jezirah,* which gives only scanty and defective information about the Karaites, was written before Rittangel visited them in Lithuania. At any rate, the information on the Karaites he personally gave to the Protestant irenicist John Dury was more detailed and elaborate. In a letter Dury wrote for the first edition of Thomas Thorowgood, *Jewes in America* (1650), he paid ample attention to the Karaites.[32] The Protestant emphasis is explicit; speaking of the Pharisees and the Karaites he remarks:

---

[27] F. Cunaeus, *De Republica Hebraeorum libri tres,* Lugd.Bat. 1703, 472.

[28] *Tesjubat Jehudah, sive pro convincendis et convertendis Judaeis libri octo,* Lugd.Bat. 1655, 71ff.

[29] For Rittangel, see P.T. van Rooden and J.W. Wesselius, "J.S. Rittangel in Amsterdam", *Nederlands Archief voor Kerkgeschiedenis* 65 (1985), 131-152; Ernestine G.E. van der Wall, "Johann Stephan Rittangel's Stay in the Dutch Republic (1641-1642)", in J. van den Berg and E.G.E. van der Wall (eds.), *Jewish-Christian relations in the seventeenth century, Studies and Documents*, Dordrecht/Boston/London 1988, 119-134. Fürst [III] 47, writes about Rittangel: "... durch seine kabbalistische Schwärmerei missleitet hatte er weder für das literarische, noch fur das geschichtliche Leben der Karäer einen richtigen Blick ...".

[30] J.C. Wolfius, *Notitia Karaeorum ex Mardochaei, Karaei recentioris, tractatu haurienda*, Hamb. et Lipsiae 1714, 54 (a second ed., with a slightly different title-page, appeared in Hamburg in 1721). For Mordecai, see below, n. 57.

[31] *Liber Jezirah*, Amstelodami 1 2, 33.

[32] "An Epistolicall Discourse of Mr. John Dury to Mr. Thorowgood", in: Tho. Thorowgood, *Jews in America, or, Probabilities that the Americans are of that Race* ..., London 1650. The expressions: "... as Mr Ritangle (of whom I have all the information which I know concerning the Caraits) tells me ...", and "Mr Ritangle ... told me ..." make it clear that with regard to this point there had been direct contacts between Dury and Rittangel: *Jewes* [e 2ro, 3vo]. See also Van der Wall, "Johann Stephan Rittangel's Stay", 120f. For Dury and the Caraites, see also R.H. Popkin, "The Lost Tribes, the Caraites and the English Millenarians", *Journal of Jewish Studies* 37 (1986), 213-227.

> ... they differ from each other as the Protestants doe from Papists; for the Pharisees, as the Papists, attribute more to the Authoritie and traditions of their Rabbis and Fathers, than to the Word of God; but the Caraits will receive nothing for a rule of faith and obedience but what is delivered from the Word of God immediately. These two sects are irreconcilably opposite to each other, and as the Papists deale with Protestants, so do the Pharisees with the Caraits, they persecute and suppress them and their profession by all the meanes they can possibly make use of.

To Dury, the Karaites were not only "proto-Protestants", but to a certain extent even "proto-Puritans":

> ... the Caraits have true grounds of spirituall and raised thoughts concerning the Messiah and his Kingdom, little different from what the better sort of Christians truly believe, and professe of these misteries. The Pharisees in their Sermons insist upon nothing but their traditions and ceremonies, and foolish curiosities; but the Caraits insist only upon necessary and profitable duties, teaching the way of Godlinesse and honesty, to bring men from the outward forme to the inward power and spirituall performance of divine worship.

Dury had such a high regard for the Karaites, that he saw them as taking a leading place in the events which would introduce the coming of the millennium: when the ten tribes will march towards the place of their inheritance, "the Caraits their brethren will be leaders of them in their way ...". And when "the great bataille of Harmageddon" should be fought,

> then shall the sword of the Spirit, the word of God, prevaile mightily over the spirits of all men ... and when this sword shall be thus powerfull in the hand of his Saints, (the true Protestants with the one troope, and the true Caraits with the other) then shall be fulfilled the Prophecie of the Psalmist, that vengeance shall be executed upon the Heathen ...[33]

Perhaps influenced by the high opinion Dury had of the Karaites, his friend Samuel Hartlib wrote to John Worthington that he hoped "that the Caraites might be invited hither and encouraged, being such as begin to look to their engraffing again".[34]

Another English Protestant who was interested in the Karaites was the Cambridge Platonist Henry More, as appears from a request for information he sent to the English ambassador in Constantinople. The request was passed on to the chaplain, John Covel, who answered in a long letter (11 March 1677) in which, though the Protestant emphasis is not as explicit as with others, in

---

[33] *Jewes, loc. cit.* For the chiliastic aspect, see esp. Popkin, "Caraïtes", and Popkin, "The Lost Tribes".

[34] Hartlib to Worthington, 12 Dec. 1655: D.S. Katz, *Philo-Semitism and the Readmission of the Jews to England 1603-1655*, Oxford 1982, 216 (quoting from *The Diary and Correspondence of Dr. John Worthington* I, 1847, 78).

general he gives a favourable account of the Karaites.[35]

Interest in the Karaites seems to have spread all over Europe. In 1690, the Swedish King sent the Uppsala orientalist Gustav Peringer to Lithuania in order to study the Karaites.[36] I know no published records of Peringer's journey, apart from one letter he sent in 1691 to J. Ludolf; it was published by W.E. Tentzel in his *Monatliche Unterredungen.*[37] Peringer's letter will not have added much to the existing knowledge of the Karaites. He recognized—as all others did at that time—that the Karaites accepted as canonical all the books of the Old Testament. They used the system of punctuation of the vowels which they traced back to Moses; as regards their attitude to tradition, they did not reject such traditions as agreed with Scripture and sound reason—an approach, analogous to that of many late seventeenth century Protestants. In general, Peringer's observations were not coloured by his confessional views; they were apt to satisfy the curiosity of the "Liebhaber der Curiositäten" to whom the *Unterredungen* were dedicated. In his commentary on the letter, given in the form of a "dialogue", the editor[38] dealt in particular with the views of two Catholic authors who had written on the Karaites: Jean Morin and Richard Simon. From Morin, a Huguenot who after his study in Leiden was converted to Catholicism and who became well known through his exegetical works, he quoted some passages from an interesting letter Morin sent to Johannes Buxtorf (the son) in November 1646.[39] Unlike Serarius, who saw the Karaite movement as a continuation of that of the Sadducees, Morin put the beginnings of the Karaite schism in the middle of the eighth century;[40] now this is the accepted opinion of all modern scholars on the subject.[41] He saw as the distinguishing mark of the Karaites, that they did not accept the Talmud and

---

[35] See this volume 57-63, J. van den Berg, "John Covel's letter on the Caraites (1677)".

[36] Fürst (III), 48.

[37] [W.E. Tentzel], *Monatliche Unterredungen einiger guten Freunde von allerhand Büchern und andern annemlicher Geschichten*, Leipzig Juli 1691, 572-574. According to Fürst, it was a shortened version of an originally Latin letter.

[38] Tentzel was not a professional orientalist or Hebraist, but a scholar with a broad historical interest; a "Polyhistor", according to the *Allgemeine Deutsche Biographie* XXXVII, 571f.

[39] The full letter in *Antiquitates Ecclesiae Orientalis ... quibus praefixa est Jo. Morini ... Vita*, Londini 1682, 349-396.

[40] Cf. his *Exercitationum Biblicarum de Hebraei Graecique textus sinceritate libri duo*, Parisiis 1660, 307: "Anas igitur et Saül se se Talmudi et Talmudicis opposuerunt circiter annum Christi 740 aut 750 ortaque est illo tempore celebris Karaitarum haeresis atque eodem tempore coeptum est a Judaeis Talmud explicari, et commentariis illustrari".

[41] See the article "Karaites" in *Encyclopaedia Judaica* X (1971), 761-786 (by J.E. Heller and Leon Nemoy). Yet it must be added, that opinions differ with regard to the background of the movement in earlier history. According to Wieder (*Judaean Scrolls*, 256), Anan ben David, the eighth-century founder of the movement, canalized existing anti-traditional currents into a major focus of resistance to the hegemony of the rabbinic authorities, while Szyszman (*Caraïtisme*, 24), in the same way, sees in Anan the person who reorganized all those movements which were the precursors of Karaitism.

the Mishna as "regula fidei". Because of this he, too, drew a parallel between the Protestants and the Karaites: "they have the same controversy with the other Jews, whom they call Rabbanists, on Scripture and tradition, as the Catholics have with the Lutherans".[42] This does not lead him, however, to take a negative view of the Karaites such as we meet with Serarius.

Deeper than Morin's interest in the Karaites was that of Richard Simon, a Catholic with more or less enlightened views. Simon wrote about them at length in his *Histoire critique du Vieux Testament* (first ed. 1678). In the context of his work, he pays special attention to their use of the Old Testament. He refutes the opinion of those who think their copies of the Bible are different from those of the other Jews: everyone who has read their books knows that, just like the others, they use the Masoretic text. With Morin, Simon asserts that the Karaite movement had its origins in the eighth century, after the compilation of the Talmud and after the Masorites had introduced their system of punctuation. As regards their acceptance of tradition, Simon opposed the opinion of the English Hebraist John Selden, who in his work on the marriage laws among the Jews had stated that the Karaites received no traditions at all, apart from the explications of their fathers if these had reached them in uninterrupted continuity.[43] But, Simon remarked,

> ... cela me paroît trop subtil; car il est constant que les Caraïtes ne rejettent les Traditions des autres Juifs, que parce qu'ils ne les croyent pas de véritables Traditions ...
>
> On peut dire plutôt qu'ils reçoivent l'Ecriture et la Tradition, aussi bien que les autres Juifs; mais qu'ils font toûjours venir au secours leur raison, qui juge si les consequences qu'on tire de l'Ecriture suivent necessairement et immédiatement, et si ce qu'on nommé [sic] Tradition est tel en effet, et s'il n'a jamais été interrompu. C'est ce qu'ils nomment une Tradition constante, et en quelque façon hereditaire.[44]

In the same way, Simon wrote about the Karaites in a supplement to the French translation of the work of the Jewish scholar Leo of Modena on Jewish ceremonies and customs. In his preface to the French edition Simon indicated that for his knowledge of Karaite doctrine he drew on a work of a Karaite ("un des plus sçavans et plus renommez de sa Secte") which had been broüght to Paris by the French ambassador in Turkey; the same work had also been used by Morin.[45] Leo had presented the Karaites as "des Saducéens reformez", who in

---

[42] *Antiquitates*, 364.

[43] "Praeter Scripturam autem atque Argumentationem, Haereditaria interpretationum (licet non traditionum, qua traditionum) Transmissione, id est avitis explicationibus ... utuntur ...", J. Seldenus, *Uxor Ebraica,* ed. nova, Francofurti ad Oderam 1673, 8.

[44] [R. Simon], *Histoire critique du vieux Testament,* [Paris 1678], 199f.

[45] Léon de Modène, *Cérémonies et coûtumes qui s'observent aujourd'hui parmi les Juifs. Traduit de l'Italien ... Avec un Supplement touchant les Sectes des Caraites et des Samaritaines*

order to make themselves tolerable in the eyes of the other Jews had adopted the doctrines of Jewish mainstream thinking. In the supplement, Simon criticized and corrected this image:

> L'origine de cette Secte, vient de ce que les Juifs les plus eclairez de ce siècle-là, s'opposèrent à une infinité de réveries qu'on debitait sous les noms specieux de traditions de Moyse ... Or comme les Juifs qui ne vouloient pas recevoir ces vaines traditions, se servoient pour les détruire de l'Ecriture sainte, qu'ils nomment *Micra,* ils en furent surnommez *Caraim,* comme l'on a vû de nos jours des Protestants se nommer *Evangeliques*, à cause qu'ils pretendoient qu'on ne doit s'appuyer que sur l'Evangile, en rejettant les traditions.[46]

Here, we meet again with the usual parallel between Protestants and Catholics. With Simon, however, the parallel is not as obvious as with earlier Catholic authors. His attitude with regard to the Karaites was ambivalent. As a Catholic who was more or less influenced by the spirit of the early Enlightenment he sympathized with those whom he saw as enlightened Jews. In his view, the Karaites could be good or bad: good, compared with the traditional Jews, bad compared with the Catholics, in the same way as the Protestants were bad, compared with their Catholic fellow Christians.[47]

Simon recognized a certain form of respect for tradition in the Karaite circle. To him, they were not simply proto-Protestants. In a discussion with a learned Jew, Simon took the part of the Karaites; and when his opponent remarked that among the Christians it was the Catholics who attached as much value to the traditions in their disputes with the Protestants as the rabbinic Jews did over against the Karaites, Simon replied

> que les Caraites ne rejettoient pas toutes sortes de Traditions, mais seulement celles qui leur paroissoient n'avoir aucun fondement, qu'il en etoit de même des Catholiques qui ne recoivent pas indifferement toutes sortes de Traditions, mais seulement cellé qui étoient appuiées sur de bons Actes.[48]

Still, it remains remarkable, and perhaps indicative for the ambivalence of his attitude, that in his correspondence with "un Gentilhomme Huguenot" (De Frémont d'Ablancourt) he addressed his Protestant friend as "mon cher Caraite", while he himself signed "le rabbaniste"—a playful echo of the harsh tones of the discussion between Serarius, Drusius and Scaliger.[49]

In 1703, that discussion was republished as a whole by the Leiden professor

---

de notre temps, sec. éd. augmentée d'une seconde Partie par le Sieur de Simonville, Paris 1681, "Preface" e IIII$^{ro, vo}$.

46 *Cérémonies*, 157f.

47 Cf. Popkin, "Caraïtes", 141: "... l'utilisation des Caraïtes par Simon était ambigue".

48 *Lettres choisies* III (2), 10. The name of the learned Jew is not mentioned.

49 *Lettres choisies* I, 190 note 1.

Jacobus Trigland ("the younger"), together with a learned tract of his own hand "Diatribe de secta Karaeorum", in his *Trium scriptorum illustrium de tribus Judaeorum sectis Syntagma*.[50] It seems that Trigland was incited to study the Karaite movement when he read a short treatise "de fide Karaeorum" from the hand of the seventeenth century Dutch orientalist and collector of Eastern manuscripts Levinus Warner.[51] The treatise was among the manuscripts which Warner bequeathed to the University of Leiden.[52] Johann Christoph Wolf, who studied the manuscripts, edited the treatise in his *Bibliotheca Hebraea*.[53] During his stay in Constantinople Warner may have had direct contact with the Karaites, but his treatise is silent on this point. It gives quotations from Karaite sources with short commentaries. In the first quotation, "Jezus Nazarenus" is described as a great wise man, righteous and good, who never thought or prescribed anything outside the written law of the Lord. The source is not indicated and the authenticity of the quotation seems to be dubious, but it may have made the study of the Karaites the more attractive to Trigland.

Trigland's work is a solid and elaborate study of a conservative nature. Going back behind Morin and Simon, he considered the Karaite movement, which he clearly distinguished from that of the Sadducees, to be of an early date. Of course he was aware of the activities of Anan in the eighth century; Anan, however, was not the founder of the movement, but a reformer who after a period of decline put the movement upon a more solid foundation.[54] In the image of the Karaite movement as given by Trigland the parallel with the Reformation again is obvious: the main cause of the schism is the "doctrina Karaeorum de Sufficientia Scripturae semoto Traditionum choragio".[55] As an orthodox Calvinist, Trigland was afraid of textual criticism as practised by "plurimi Romanenses, Isacus Vossius et alii Bibliomastiges", who held that the text of the Bible was corrupted. In this context, study of the Karaite writings could be helpful; apparently, Trigland expected that this could strengthen the conservative attitude towards the text of the Old Testament. Furthermore, the Karaites could be helpful in disputes with the Jews, because they rejected a number of errors to which the "Rabbanites" obstinately held.[56] In 1713, J.C. Wolf republished Trigland's work in his *Notitia Karaeorum,* which also contained the edition of a Karaite author in Hebrew and Latin and a largely bib-

[50] See above, note 6. In the same year, the "Diatribe" was also separately published.
[51] Thus J.C. Wolfius, *Bibliotheca Hebraea* IV, Hamburgi 1733, 1086.
[52] For Warner, see *Levinus Warner and his legacy* ... Catalogue of the commemorative exhibition ... 1970, Leiden 1970.
[53] IV, 1086-1115; see Levinus Warner, 49f.
[54] *Syntagma* II, 101.
[55] *Syntagma* II, 10.
[56] *Syntagma* II, † 3vo, [4ro].

liographical survey of the Karaite movement.[57] Wolf's appreciation of the Karaites was essentially the same as that of Trigland, for whose work he had a great admiration.

A similar approach, though perhaps a bit more coloured by early Enlightenment appreciation of reason, is to be met with in Jacques Basnage's *Histoire des Juifs* (first ed. 1706-07). Basnage pays much attention to the Karaites for whom, in line with most preceding Protestant authors on the subject, he evinces a warm sympathy:

> En effet, la Religion des Caraïtes est beaucoup plus pure que celle de tous les autres Juifs; parce qu'ils sont plus scrupuleusement attachés au texte de l'Ecriture Sainte ... Ils n'expliquent donc point l'Ecriture par la Tradition; mais seulement, par la Lumière de la Raison, qui leur sert à entendre les Paroles de l'Ecriture et à tirer de la Loi les Conséquences naturelles et necessaires.

In this context, he combated the views of Simon, who in order to be able to give a more positive appreciation of the Karaites from the Catholic side had somewhat softened the idea of their rejection of tradition. Basnage conceded that on some small points they were indeed prepared to accept the Jewish tradition.

> Mais, ce ne sont là que des Minuties, semblables à celle que les Catholiques Romains objectent aux Protestans, lors qu'il traitent la même Controverse ...
>
> Comme les Réformez sont Ennemis de la Tradition; parce qu'il rejettent les Dogmes qu'on a cousus à ceux de Jesus Christ, et qu'ils ne veulent pas se soumettre aveuglément à son Autorité on doit reconnoître la même chose des Caraïtes anciens et modernes, qui ont précisément la même Répugnance pour les Traditions. Comme on ne peut pas dire que les Protestans admettent la Tradition, parce qu'ils expliquent un Passage comme St. Jérôme l'a expliqué, ou parce qu'ils se mettent à Genoux en recitant l'Oraison Dominicale, quoi que Jesus Christ ne l'ait pas ordonné, Mr. Simon ne doit pas soutenir que les Caraïtes suivent la Tradition, par ce qu'ils recoivent les Points inventez par les Masorethes; car, cela n'a aucune influence sur les Dogmes de la Religion.[58]

As far as I can see, Basnage is the last one who wrote about the Karaites in the context of the Catholic-Protestant controversy. In 1759 the Venetian scholar Blasius Ugalinus, possibly himself a convert from Judaism to Catholicism, published a number of works on the Karaites and other Jewish sects (among which were Trigland's work and Warner's treatise) in his *Thesaurus Antiqui-*

---

[57] For full title, see above, note 30. The Hebrew tract ("Dod Mordecai"), written by Mordecai ben Nisan in answer to a letter by Trigland of 1698 (see Fürst, [III 58f., 88-93]), contained an exposition of the history and doctrine of the Karaite movement, which largely concurred with the traditional Protestant view : Mordecai "defends the antiquity of Karaism ... and its independence from Sadduceeism", *Enc. Jud.* 12, c. 314f.

[58] J. Basnage, *Histoire des Juifs* (nouv. éd.) II, La Haye 1716, 380f., 384f.

tatum Sacrarum. In the preface he remarked that the Karaites, who could rightly be called "Textuales" and "Scripturarii", had become very well known through the fame of their doctrine and judgment, but much more still through the hatred of the "Rabbanites", caused by the fact that they ridiculed their traditions.[59]

The clouds of the old controversy had lifted. In "the age of Enlightenment" the intellectual interest shifted from the antithesis between Catholicism and Protestantism to that between conservative and enlightened thinking. At the end of the eighteenth century, as R.H. Popkin has shown, the French enlightened abbot Henri Grégoire saw in the Karaites the forerunners of Jewish emancipation.[60] To a certain extent, this approach had been prepared by Simon and Basnage, who both of them had emphasized the rational element in Karaite thinking. But they still wrote within the context of the great confessional controversy, which was projected upon the controversy between the mainstream Jews, well-known in the West, and the far-away, mysterious Karaites. Catholics looked at them with mixed feelings; for Protestants they were the embodiment of the presence of the "Sola Scriptura" principle within Judaism and thus an external confirmation of the legitimacy of the Protestant rejection of the authority of tradition as it was to be found in traditional Judaism as well as in the Catholic Church.

---

[59] B. Ugolinus, *Thesaurus Antiquitatum Sacrarum* XXII, Venetiis 1759, "Lectori" (not paginated). For Ugolinus (Biagio Ugolini), see *Die Religion in Geschichte und Gegenwart*[3] VI, c. 1106.

[60] See Popkin, "Caraïtes", 141f.

CHAPTER FOUR—APPENDIX

JOHN COVEL'S LETTER ON THE KARAITES (1677)

The author

On 11 March 1677 John Covel, then English chaplain in Constantinople,[1] sent a long letter to the Cambridge scholar Henry More, in which he provided him with extensive information about the Karaites.[2] Apparently, More had asked the English Ambassador for information on this point. In his turn, the Ambassador had passed on More's request to his chaplain, then already a scholar of some renown. It remains obscure why More was interested in the Karaites; perhaps (as was the case with quite a number of seventeenth-century Protestants) because the Karaites, who in their own way adhered to the "sola Scriptura" principle, were considered to be more "pure" than the other Jews.[3] However this may be, Covel was certainly the right man to answer the letter of his former Cambridge teacher. Born in 1638, Covel had studied at Christ's College (the college of Henry More) from 1654-1661. After that, he was elected to a fellowship of his college and took Holy Orders. In 1670 he went out as a chaplain to the English Ambassador in Constantinople, where he stayed till 1677. Via Italy, where he stayed for some time, he returned to England in 1679.

In a letter to George Davies, the English consul at Naples, of 5 July 1678, written from Rome, Covel gave an account of the motives which prompted him to go out to the Levant.[4] He wrote this letter because, as Covel had learned from Davies, the Jesuits at Naples had reported that there was "an English minister now in Rome"—and the only English clergyman who was there at that time was Covel—"which was turn'd Papist or Roman Catholick". The

[1] For Covel, see *DNB* s.v.; J.T. Bent (ed.), *Early Voyages and Travels in the Levant* (Works Hakluyt Society LXXXVII), London 1893, XXVI-XXXIII (101-287 contain extracts from Covel's Diary).

[2] J. Covel to H . More, Constantinople, 11 March 1677, Christ's College Cambridge, MS 21, f.28; published with the permission of the Master and Fellows of Christ's College, Cambridge. Covel's draught notes for this letter are in the British Library, *Additional* 22.911, f.373: "Some account of the Jewes Karaims and Rabanaims" (undated). That More addressed his request to the Ambassador, Sir John Finch, can be explained from the fact that John Finch, a brother of More's friend Lady Conway, had been a pupil of More; see Marjorie H. Nicolson, *The Conway Letters,* revised edition , ed. by Sarah Hutton, Oxford 1992, 44.

[3] For this, see J. van den Berg, "Proto-Protestants? The image of the Karaites as a mirror of the Catholic-Protestant controversy in the seventeenth century" (this work, Ch. 4).

[4] British Library, *Additional* 22.910, f. 164-167.

rumours were founded in the fact that Covel had been observed attending a service in a Catholic church. With reference to these rumours Covel wrote:

> It was my design when I first left England to see and understand and take an account with mine own eyes (and not to be beholden to the fallible relations of others) of what was acted and believed by all people abroad, where I went in my travailes. And therefore I have been in the Turkish Mosche's at Constantinople many and many times at their hours of prayer ... Next I have been often and often in the Synagogues of the Jewes and converst with them and their bookes as well with those who are cal'd the Rabanaims as the Karaims, which are counted schismaticks by the others, and I met with them only at a town by Constant[ino]ple, where are about 60 familyes of them ... Now these Father's Machiavels ... may with the same charity and as much reason say that J. Covel is in his heart, A Turk, A Jew, A Greek, an Armenian, or the like ...

Furthermore, Covel wrote to James Crawford, chaplain to the English Ambassador at Venice: "Meer curiosity of learning some things abroad, whereof I thought we had but a slight account at home, was one of those motives which brought me hither ...".[5]

From this letter to Davies as well as from that to More it appears, that Covel had personal contacts with a Karaite community near Constantinople. His interest in the Karaites was not, as far as we can see, prompted by theological motives: it was his almost insatiable curiosity, which drove him to build up contacts with them and to study their life and manners. The value of his letter (which alas is incomplete, because the corners of some of the pages have been cut off) lies in the fact that it is based on personal observation; it confirms and adds to what we know about the differences in practice and in ritual between the Karaites and the rabbinic Jews. Its lack of theological depth is compensated by the mass of detailed information which it provides. One just wonders whether for such a man as Henry More this was sufficient. If not, perhaps the books Covel sent him made him understand at a deeper level the world of ideas of the Karaites.

Covel was only incidentally interested in the Jews, for whom, it seems, he had no real sympathy.[6] The main object of his studies during his stay in the Levant was the Greek Church. For the Greeks, too, he had but slight sympathy (according to Sir Steven Runciman he even disliked them),[7] but here he could not avoid paying full attention to the theological background. In France, there had been a Catholic-Protestant discussion on the question whether or not the Greeks believed in the doctrine of transubstantiation; a question important in

---

[5] Quoted in: J. Covel, *Some Account of the Present Greek Church*, Cambridge 1722, "The Preface".

[6] Cf. the remarks in his Diary on the Jews in Adrianople: Bent, *Early Voyages*, 189f.

[7] S. Runciman, *The Great Church in Captivity*, Cambridge 1968, 293.

connection with "the Protestant cause".[8] Some English theologians, who wanted to give support to the Protestant thesis that the Greek Church did not hold the doctrine of transubstantiation, had asked Covel to make a study of the question *in loco*.[9] Covel collected much material, which however he only published at a later stage, in 1722 (the year of his death), when interest in the question had faded away. The conclusion of his work, entitled *Some Account of the Present Greek Church*, is somewhat ambiguous. Covel could not deny, that most contemporary Greek theologians adhered to the idea of the "real presence", but he attributed this to the fact that the Greeks, whose ignorance in theological matters he loudly proclaimed, were taken in by the Jesuits.

Shortly after his stay in the East, Covel became chaplain to Princess Mary, the wife of the Dutch Stadtholder William III. An unhappy incident made an end to his stay in the Netherlands.[10] A letter from Covel, partly written in cipher and addressed to the British Ambassador at the Hague, Bevin Skelton, was intercepted and decoded at the court of the Prince. In this letter, Covel had written (probably referring to William's relation with Elizabeth Villiers): "... the Princesse's heart is ready to break ... the Prince treats her as His absolute slave ... None but Pimps and Bawds must expect any tollerable usage here"[11] The Prince, of course, was very indignant. Covel was immediately dismissed; William wrote to the Earl of Rochester: "Vous serez, sans doute, surpris qu'un homme de cette profession peut être un si grand fripon ... La princesse et moy n'avons fait autre chose que la chasse de la maison, en laissant le chastiment à l'Evesque sous lequel il est".[12]

It did not hinder Covel in his further career. In 1688 he succeeded the famous Cambridge Platonist Ralph Cudworth as master of Christ's College, Cambridge. In 1689 he was Vice-Chancellor of the University; in that capacity, he had to receive William, now King of England, who made a formal visit to Cambridge. It seems Covel was rather nervous about the occasion, but the

---

[8] The main protagonists in the discussion were on the Catholic side the Jansenists Antoine Arnauld and Pierre Nicole, on the Protestant side the Reformed minister Jean Claude. For this discussion, see Covel, *Some Account*, "The Preface".

[9] The theologians, mentioned in Covel, *Some Account*, "The Preface", III, are: Peter Gunning, John Pearson and the later Archbishop of Canterbury, William Sancroft.

[10] A somewhat coloured version of the whole affair in: Hester W. Chapman, *Mary II, Queen of England*, London 1953, 121ff.; she describes Covel as a poor intriguer, elderly, gossiping and ill-bred.

[11] A copy of the letter (decoded) in British Library, *Additional* 15.892, f.264; quoted in S.W. Singer (ed.), *The Correspondence of Henry Hyde, Earl of Clarendon and of his brother Laurence Hyde, Earl of Rochester* I, London 1828, 165 (with some discrepancies in spelling).

[12] Singer, *The Correspondence of Henry and Laurence Hyde*, 163f.; cf. Hans Willem Bentinck's letter to Henry Sidney, 22 October 1685, in R. W. Blencowe (ed.), *Diary of the Times of Charles the Second by the Honourable Henry Sidney* II, London 1843, 253; here, Covel is mentioned as "le malicieux espion de la maison, qui a rapporté beaucoup de choses forgées pour nuire".

King is reported to have intimated that he knew to distinguish between Dr. Covel and the Vice-Chancellor of the University. In his turn, Covel made an exuberant speech: "Give us then leave ... to prostrate ourselves at your Royal Feet ... He [God] raised up in You ... a Speedy and Mighty Deliverer, under whose Shadow all our Fears and Dangers immediately vanish't ...".[13]

Covel was no man of great scholarly activity. His *Account* is his only major publication—a work of some value, but quite definitely not a masterpiece. Still, he was known and to a certain extent respected in the intellectual world of his time, as appears from his correspondence with some learned contemporaries, among whom was Newton.[14] That he was a keen and intelligent observer appears from his Journals (only partially published) and also from his letter on the Karaites.

The letter[15]

I should have been very glad, as I even was very ambitious ... holding a commerce of letters with a person of soe much reall worth ... publick esteem in the world as your self, but really I knew my own want ... ment, and besides that, I could not lay hold of any opportunity to begin ... correspondence till just now when I am thinking of returning from ... place. My Ld [Lord] Ambassador was pleased to communicate part of a letter ... which you wrote to him, wherein I was acqainted with a desire you had to know what private opinion there were amongst our Karraims here, different from the rest of the Common Jewes, or Rabbanims: as likewise what bookes they had amongst them of any antiquity or Curiosity; whereupon I have here given you some small account of what I have observed in my converse with them. In a place cal'd Hasmi (just opposite to Stambole on the other side the freshwater river) there are amongst many other Jewes, about 200 familyes of these Karraims; and I never heard of any, anywhere else here abouts, but they tell me there are many in Poland, in Jhena (or Georgia) upon the border of Armenia, as likewise some few in Cairo, and Capha upon the Black (or Euxine) sea; in all places, they are very much despised and hated by the other Jewes, and where they are much exceeded by the others in number, they often suffer by them, and dare not stick close to their own rites, for fear of the others bringing some *Avania* or false pretence upon them. These here have but one little Synagogue, made much after the fashion of the others, and their devotions and reading of the law every Sabbath are

[13] British Library, *Additional* 22.910, f.373-376.

[14] In particular, he was considered an authority on the Greek Church; cf. Archbishop Thomas Tenison's letters to Covel, written on the occasion of the visit of the Metropolitan of Philippopolis to Cambridge in 1701: G. Williams, *The Orthodox Church of the East in the Eighteenth Century,* Oxford and Cambridge 1868, LIX.

[15] In the transcription of the letter (as also in the quotations in the introduction) I resolved the usual abbreviations, while in the letter I indicated the missing passages by three dots.

perform'd much after the same manner; Though these beside the law written in great scroles and rowl'd up (like our maps) have three or four Manuscripts very large and fair without pricks, bound up like our bookes, which they use upon their feast dayes. The first grand difference betwixt them is this. These own nothing of tradition, but stick close to the bare text; and therefore make no account of the Misnah, Gemara, or any other comment whatever. Yet I find a great error in Lewis Modena's account of the Karraim, or else these differ extreamly from those which he convers't with, for these own beside the Pentateuch, all the rest of the Old Testament (except the Apocrypha) as well as we to be dictated by the Spirit of God, and to be of infallible truth; and therefore they count it their rule as much as we, or the other Jewes doe, whereas he saith, they own none, but the Pentateuch; and in the next place he maketh them to be an upstart heresy out of Sadducisme, whereas they count themselves the ofspring of Kohen, and of the family of Levi, and not onely firmely beleive both angels, and spirits and the Immortality of the soul, but pray alsoe for the dead not that they can now ease them, but their opinion is this, that the soules of the departed are in a middle state some thing suitable to their merits here, and that God respit'd ... till the generall day, and their prayers are onely mediatory to... he should now ease or releave them, but then in that day ... sentence in their favour. The next thing that sets them ... is their purifying of their women after their monthly infi[rmity] six dayes after they are clean, wash all over head and eares in a Bango o... ceremonyes of poring of nailes, cleaning of rings, ear[r]ings poure 40 dishes of water upon their head so soon as they are ... be it the 2^{d}, 3^{d}, 4th or what day they please after; upon this scruple ... mix one with other in mariage. The Kar. are not scrupulous in their eating and drinking with Christians provided they be free from being discover'd to other Jewes; whereas all our Brokers at all our Merchant houses refrain most peremptorily from touching anything of meat or drink with us, except onely Coffe and a pipe of tobacco. Again the Kar. scruple not to eat many meals without the ceremonyes practised by the other; as for example they will eat cheese and flesh both together at the same meal, whereas the other after flesh clear the table and wash before they will touch cheese; these and the like sup[er]stitions in their food, hinder them from ever eating and drinking together; yet when ever any of the Kar.dye they hire the Rab.to bury them here; for the Kar.after the dead is laid forth and put in the coffin never ... touch or come near the bier, and none but near relations come near the dead as far as purifyed themselves; upon necessity (as sometimes the Rab. out of peevishnesse will not asist them) they performe this office of carying out their dead themselves. They alwayes accompany the dead at some distance to the grave, and have their service or songs much like the others. The Kar. are most strict observers of the Sabbath. They suffer no fire at all in their houses, besides a lamp or two which are hang'd up out of reach and lighted at Friday sunset. They will not suffer any

Christian slave or other of their servants to touch any fire whatever, which amongst the other Jewes here is common. They will not led blood or make broth to save a mans life that day themselves, but if absolute necessity requires admit of strangers to do it. The Rab. have a way to order their year so as their day of Expiation (the 10 Tizri) never falls on Friday or Sunday, but with these it sometimes so fall out, and they observe it and the adjoyning Sabbath with like striktnesse, you must understand once for all that these Kar. count the first day of their Moon from it's appearance as the Turkes every where do; the Rab.reckon as we do from the reall conjunction; this makes a difference of a day at least in all their feasts, of which briefly this account. The Pascha is kept in by the Rab. 8 dayes, by the Kar. but 7 dayes. They both begin on the 15th of Nisan, but the 15th according to the Rab.account, bring but the 14th according to the Kar.account ... no[t] that they alwayes end together; so that the Rab. begin one day before ... yet here in this place the Kar. dare not publickly open shop, not much ... road, or doe any kind of Merchandize the first day of the Rab's Pascha [or an]y other day which is in controversy between them, as you will see in ... for fear they (the Rab.) should traduce them to the Turkes and cause them to ... mey, yet this first day, of the Rab.Pascha is no wayes else observed by, [the K]ar.or kept as their feast. So the Rab.keep Pentecost 2 dayes; the ... e day; but about the time of keeping of it there is very great difference, and the oc[casion o]f immortall [?] quarrels betwixt them. The Rab. always reckon their 49 [da]yes (sanctifying the 50th) from the evening of the Pascha, as if they begin their Pascha on Saturday night reckoning it and Sunday, their feast, Sunday night and Monday they reckon their first day. So alwayes reckoning from the Evening and day following their Pascha let it fall on what day it will, but the Kar. reckon their Pentecost from the Sabbath Evening following their feast. As if it falls on a Sabbath, that evening they begin their account; if it falls on Sunday, they begin their account not till the Sabbath Evening following; so that their Pentecost alwayes fall on a Sunday, and by consequence not alwayes upon the 6th of Sivan as with the others, but many times severall dayes distant from the dayes observed by the Rabanim's. Rosch haschanah or their Caput Anni (New Years day) is held holy for two dayes by the Rab. but for onely one by the Kar. Likewise the Kar. have no respect unto any lent or pennance from the beginning of Elul to the 10th of Tizri; or Jiom hachipur, which both observe solemnly. The feast of Tabernacles is observed ... 9 dayes by the Rab. 8 by the Kar. They both observe the same ceremonyes, and make baths in the same manner and dresse them up with Palm branches etc. which here are brought at that time of the year from several places of Anatolia on purpose. The Karaim's observe not Chanucàh in the least, yet the Rab. here keep it 8 dayes from 25th of Kiliev Purim (when leap year) is kept by the Rab. in Veadar, but the Kar. in Adar, and the Kar.call not the intercalated month Veadar, but Venisan. The Kar.fast the 9th of Tamuz, the

Rab. the 17th in remembrance of Moses' breaking the Tables. They keep the 10th of Ab a fast the Rab. keep the 9th (still remembering their difference in the counting the dayes of the month). Tzom Gedaliah is kept by ... 3 Tizri. The Karaim keep not the Eve to their Purim as a fast. The Kar. make extraordinary prayers from the beginning of Shebeth till the 10th but keep their fast on the fifth. The Kar. think they are strickt observers of the Sabbath, yet they have not the superstitions of the others, in not handling or carying money about them, touching things of weight, as rings, jewells, ornaments, etc. The Kar.are kept up their way by meer devotion, for they dare not exercise the least severe censure, for fear the party suffering should embrogle them with the Turkes. These Kar.here seem to have the same dread for the name Jehovah, that the other Jewes have, yet one of them my particular acquaintance told me, that they do refrain to speak it not so much out of religious fear, as fear of the other Jewes, who should they hear such a thing from any one of them, would certainly contrive his ruine; I have heard this man pronounce it severall times, but for the rest I have only his word. I have been among ... their Sabbath and they would not be persuaded to write the least letter ... to do it. They are very free from many conceits which the Rab. fall into ... possest, of the spirits of dead men, speaking in the body of others etc. I have ... that there are severall profest Samaritans now in Cairo, but it never ... meet with any one of them or any ... those parts that could give me ... of them I have thus given you in brief many of their differen[t] trifling ceremonyes which are very various amongst them, in their ... But the cheifest thing which you see and to dep ... bookes, which here I have sent you enclosed. I beleive they a[re re]lating more particularly to the controversies between them ... if there be any of these which you desire to have if you signify ... Emb.and desire him to Employ Old Moyse (an old Rabanim that use to come after thither) he knowes where to go to procure you what you desire. I must beg your pardon heartily for scribbling over that account thus confusedly; I was in hast by ... of the ships departure; but at my returne I shall be ready with all my heart to give you what other satisfaction I am able. My hearty and humble respects to Dr Cudworth, and the rest of our Society. I hope by God's blessing in one yeare more to bee amongst you. Till then I commit you to God and with my hearty respects rest

... Rev.S,
Your reall and ready freind to serve you,

Joh.Covel

CHAPTER FIVE

MENASSEH BEN ISRAEL, HENRY MORE AND JOHANNES HOORNBEECK ON THE PRE-EXISTENCE OF THE SOUL

In the thought of the leading Cambridge Platonist Henry More (1614-1687) as well as in that of two of his friends and admirers, George Rust (d. 1670) and Joseph Glanvill (1636-1680), the idea of the pre-existence of the soul took an important place. The same holds true for Menasseh ben Israel, who expounded his views on this point in several of his publications. When, between September 1655 and October 1657, Menasseh was in London, he discussed these views with the author of the "Annotations" on two tracts by Glanvill and Rust, which appeared in the second edition of the tracts in 1682.[1] There can be no doubt about the attribution of the "Annotations" to More: his biographer Richard Ward, who had known More personally and who was well informed, mentions "his excellent *Annotations on Lux Orientalis*" in the (unpublished) sequel to *The Life of the Learned and Pious Dr More* (1710).[2] Speaking of the idea of pre-existence (the main topic of the two tracts) More wrote in the "Annotations":

> That this was the common opinion of the wiser men amongst the Jews, R. *Menasse Ben Israel* himself told me at *London* with great freedom and assurance, and that there was a constant tradition thereof; which he said in some sense was also true concerning the Trinity, but that more obscure. But this of Preexistence is manifest up and down in the Writings of that very ancient and learned Jew *Philo Judaeus*, as also something toward a Trinity, if I remember right.[3]

---

[1] *Two choice and useful Treatises: the one Lux Orientalis or an Enquiry into the Opinion of the Eastern Sages concerning the Praeexistence of Souls. Being a Key to unlock the Grand Mysteries of Providence. In relation to Mans Sin and Misery. The other, a discourse of Truth, by the late Reverend Dr. Rust Lord Bishop of Dromore in Ireland. With Annotations on them both*, London 1682. The first tract, by Glanvill, first appeared in 1662; the tract by Rust was first published in 1677.

[2] R. Ward, "Some Account of Dr. More's Works", Christ's College, Cambridge, MS 20, f. 129 (quoted with the permission of the Master and Fellows of Christ's College); *cf. DNB* s.v. Glanvill and More. I thank Dr. Alan Gabbey, Belfast, for his kind assistance in this matter. In the More correspondence I have found one place where the "Annotations" are mentioned. More had drawn the attention of Henry Hallywell (who some years later edited Rust's *Remains*, see n.41) to the "Annotations", as appears from Hallywell's letter to More of 14 May 1683: "... I thank you for giving me notice of the annotations upon Lux Orientalis, the Author of which seemes to be of a very gay, pleasant and airy temper, and as he sayes of himself a Person not unexercised in those speculations": Christ's College, Cambridge, MS 21, f.33. Probably this sentence contains a hidden compliment to More, though of course it is also possible that Hallywell really was unaware of the identity of the author.

[3] *Two choice and useful Treatises*, "Annotations", 27.

Apart from this passage, nothing is known about a possible personal contact between Menasseh and More—but from the "Annotations" we know that More, like his friend and fellow Platonist Ralph Cudworth,[4] met Menasseh during the latter's stay in London. That at this meeting Menasseh and More discussed the idea of pre-existence in a spirit of mutual understanding is quite feasible, as they had a common interest in this matter, which resulted from partly similar motives.

Menasseh mentions the idea in passing in his *Conciliador* (1632), when in a passage on Gen. 1.26 ("and God said: let us make man"), he referred to a rabbinic opinion, to be found in *Bereshit Rabbah* (cap. 3),[5] that God had consulted with the souls before uniting them with a body, because he did not want to join them with matter against their will. In this context he remarks that according to most of the Hebrews the souls had been created on the first day.[6]

Starting from this belief, Menasseh gives a broad exposition of the idea of pre-existence in his *De Creatione Problemata XXX* (1635).[7] In his answer to the question (Probl. XV) whether the souls have been created in the beginning of the world or together with the body, he states again that according to all Hebrews the souls of men were created before the body. This opinion was also held by Hermes Trismegistos, Pythagoras, Plato and several others from the gentiles; Menasseh points out that it had certainly reached them from the Hebrews and that, apart from all other testimonies, it can very well be proved from some places of Holy Scripture.

The first text quoted by Menasseh is Deut. 29.14, 15, of which he gives the following translation: "Neque vobiscum solis ego pango foedus meum ... sed cum eo qui adstat hic nobiscum hodie ... et cum illo qui non est hic nobiscum hodie". He adds a commentary of the "ancients", a quotation from Tanhuma:[8] "All the souls which existed from Adam onward, and which will exist until the end of the world, all these were created in the six days of creation, and they were all in the garden of Eden ... Thus can be said: with him who is with us today, and with him who is not with us today". All the souls, says Menasseh, which at one time will come into the light, were present when God gave his law, and with all of them he entered into a covenant.

Another proof-text is Isaiah 57.16—"animas ego feci", which God says in the past tense, "ad significandum omnes in principio mundi conditas fuisse".

---

[4] See David S. Katz, *Philo-Semitism and the Readmission of the Jews to England 1603-1655*, Oxford 1982, 234.

[5] An old midrash on Genesis: *Encyclopaedia Judaica* VII, c. 399ff.

[6] I used the Latin ed. of 1633, *Conciliator, sive De convenientia Locorum S. Scripturae, quae pugnare inter se videntur* ..., Francofurti [?], 1633, 12.

[7] *De Creatione Problemata XXX* ..., Amstelodami, 1635, 61-68 (Probl. XV), 68-69 (Probl. XXI).

[8] A midrash on the Pentateuch: *Encyclopaedia Judaica*, c. 794 f.

Furthermore, the words in which the vocation of Jeremiah is described—Jer. 1.5: "Antequam te formassem in ventre, indidi tibi sapientiam"—lead Menasseh to a long exposition in which he avers that virtue, wisdom, knowledge, holiness and heavenly warmth had been given to the soul of the prophet before his body was formed in his mother's womb. In this context, he refers to the opinion of the Kabbalists and to Plato's doctrine of anamnesis. The passage ends with a sentence which has a true Platonic ring: "From these words can also be confirmed, it seems, the opinion of those who hold that the soul is the totality of man ("hominis totum") and the body only an instrument which is subservient to the soul". Other texts which Menasseh adduces as proofs of the pre-existence of souls are Eccl. 4.2, 3 (how can those who have not yet been born be praised above the living if they do not exist?) and Job 38.21 ("... noveris te iam tunc natum fuisse": "tunc" or "tum" refers to the "principium mundi").

After the appeal to Holy Scripture, Menasseh turns to Jewish tradition. He devotes much attention to the morning prayer of the great synagogue in the times of Ezra: "Mi Deus, anima quam mihi dedisti, munda est, illam tu creasti, formasti, eamque mihi inspirasti, nec non servas eam in me, hanc accepturus es cum ex me evolaverit". He points out that the soul is pure, which means that it is a "substantia subtilis et spiritualis", formed from "pura et munda materia"; a "corpus spirituale, natura caelesti praeditum". Plato thinks of this body, when he calls it a heavenly vehicle, while the Kabbalists teach that in this body the soul enjoys in paradise the reward of its works, or conversely is punished in hell. At the end of this exposition, he quotes Rabbi Johanan, who says in *Midrash ha-Ne'lam*[9] that there are two seats and domiciles of the soul: one of those souls who have not yet descended into the world, the other of those who have left this world and have returned to their source and origin. Menasseh concludes by remarking that because after the six days of creation God makes nothing "ex nihilo", but "aliud ex alio", all souls have been created at the beginning of the world, all together and all at one moment. Thus it is most certain that the idea of pre-existence is not only Scriptural, but also reasonable: "hoc ita esse ... etiam ex ratione certissimum est".

In Problema XVI Menasseh answers the question on which day the souls of men were created. He states that without any doubt they were created on the first day, together with light. This provides him with the occasion to expatiate on the Kabbalistic doctrine of the ten superior lights or 14 "sephirot". The souls are the third light: so they precede the fourth light, the angels, and the fifth light, the light which lightened the earth during the first three days of creation. Menasseh realizes that according to at least one authority, Rabbi

---

[9] A Kabbalistic midrash, the earliest part of the *Zohar: Encyclopaedia Judaica* X, c. 533; XVI, c. 1196f.

Eleazar (*Bereshit Rabbah*, VII), the soul of Adam was created on the sixth day, but he brushes this aside by remarking that Eleazar did not speak about the soul as such, but about the "anima vitalis".

While in *De Creatione* Menasseh dealt with the idea of pre-existence as if it were an abstract problem, in a work which appeared only a short time afterwards, *De Resurrectione Mortuorum*, the same idea was used by Menasseh as a strong argument in his defense of the doctrine of the resurrection of the dead. As the subtitle indicates, the work was directed against the "Sadducees", who denied the immortality of the soul and the resurrection of the body.[10] No doubt the word "Sadducees" primarily refers to Uriel da Costa (1585-1640), though Menasseh does not mention him explicitly. Because of his denial of the immortality of the soul, Da Costa had been attacked by Samuel da Silva in his *Tratado da Immortalidade* (1623). The conflict between Uriel da Costa and the Amsterdam Jewish community had revived in the period after 1633, in which Da Costa became the target of heavy attacks from the side of the synagogue.[11] Against the background of this conflict, Menasseh wrote his work on the resurrection.

To Menasseh, in this context the idea of the pre-existence of the soul was of supreme importance: once it has been ascertained that the souls were happy and blessed in a glorious state before being united with a body, it is clear that they can exist without a body, and that thus they can return to the same blessed state after the body has died.[12] This is the reason why in this work again he devotes so much attention to the many questions with regard to the human soul. The greatness of the soul as a spiritual substance of divine origin is taught by the ancient philosophers, among them Zoroaster, Hermes, Orpheus, Pythagoras, Porphyrius "atque divinus Plato". And although, says Menasseh, it is certain that we cannot know what is the nature of this substance, the opinion of Heraclitus seems to be probable, who stated that the soul was light; according to the ancients, the creation of the soul was contained in the creation of light on the first day.[13]

The soul as "anima rationalis" is infused into the children who are in the mother's womb. In this connection, Menasseh mentions the old story (*Bereshit Rabbah* XXIV), according to which there burns a candle above the

---

[10] *De Resurrectione Mortuorum Libri III.* Quibus animae immortalitas et corporis resurrectio contra Zaducaeos comprobatur; caussae item miraculosae resurrectionis exponuntur: deque iudicio extremo, et mundi instauratione agitur: Ex Sacris Literis, et veteribus Rabbinis, Amstelodami 1636.

[11] For this, see C. Gebhardt, *Die Schriften des Uriel da Costa*, Amsterdam etc., 1922, esp. XXIXff. and 188, n. 279 (where Gebhardt remarks that Menasseh recapitulates the arguments of Da Costa); furthermore C. Roth, *A Life of Menasseh ben Israel—Rabbi, Printer, and Diplomat*, Philadelphia, 1934, 71.

[12] *De Res.*, 221ff.

[13] *De Res.*, 52ff.

head of the unborn children, but as soon as the child has been born, an angel extinguishes the light. He sees as the meaning of this story, that before birth the souls of men are very wise, and provided with knowledge of all things, but they are deprived of this knowledge when they are brought into a body. Still, their knowledge is not lost; here, Menasseh ben Israel makes a comparison with those who because of a perturbation of their brains have become phrenetic: when they recover their knowledge, it is nothing else but the memory of that which they have known. "Quae Platonis sententia quoque fuit, plane contraria opinioni Aristotelis".[14]

The doctrine of the pre-existence of souls was part and parcel of the Platonist-Pythagorean tradition, though it was not adopted by the Renaissance Platonists any more than the related doctrine of "metempsychosis". In the context of his exposition of the idea of pre-existence, Menasseh ben Israel refers more than once to the "ancient philosophers", among whom of course Plato holds pride of place. This does not detract from his conviction that the idea of pre-existence is essentially of Hebrew origin. The authorities he directly quotes are all Jewish: Biblical texts, the Jewish morning prayer, some of the older midrashim, such as *Tanhuma* and *Bereshit Rabbah*, and also Kabbalistic writings such as *Midrash ha-Ne'lam.* His main thesis—that of the formation of all human souls on the first day of creation—is traditionally Jewish, but it is coloured by his dependence on the Kabbalistic world of thought. Here, we are reminded of the idea, mentioned before, that the soul is one of the ten supreme lights, "quas Cabalistae vocant sephirot"; furthermore I mention the notion of the paired creation of the male and the female soul and that of the transmigration of souls, in which he follows "magnus et insignis Cabalista R. Isaak Luriensis". Lastly: while in *De Creatione* he dealt with the idea of pre-existence without an explicit purpose, in *De Resurrectione*, as we saw, the same idea received a special function in his struggle against the "Sadducees" of his own days.

In his conversation with Menasseh on this subject Henry More, we may assume, will have recognized in the Amsterdam rabbi a kindred spirit, who shared his interest in a problem which lay outside the horizon of most of his fellow philosophers and theologians in England. More's first utterances on the idea of the pre-existence of the human soul are to be found in a number of poems which he wrote as a young man deeply committed to the Neo-Platonist world of thought. When, almost forty years later, he looked back upon that period, he spoke with a somewhat critical undertone about "that so ardent desire of Philosophizing, which seized me when I was very young".[15] In the

---

[14] *De Res.*, 174ff.

[15] From the autobiographical preface of his theological works (first ed. 1679): *The Theological Works of the Most Pious and Learned Henry More* ..., London 1708, I.

first poem of the series, *Psychozoia or the life of the Soul* (1642), written in "rhythmes which from Platonic rage do powerfully flow forth",[16] More paid homage to the "ancient philosophers" in the following words:

> So if what's consonant to Plato's school
> (Which well agrees with learned Pythagore,
> Egyptian Trismegist, and th'antique roll
> Of Chaldee wisdome, all which time hath tore
> But Plato and deep Plotin do restore)
> Which is my scope, I sing out lustily:
> If any twitten me for such strange lore,
> And me all blamelesse brand with infamy,
> God purge that man from fault of foul malignity.[17]

Psychozoia is an eloquent testimony of More's belief in "the Souls excellence ... her radiant life and lovely hue",[18] which, of course, implies the belief in its immortality:

> But souls that of his [God's] own good life partake
> He loves as his own self; dear as his eye
> they are to him: He'll never them forsake;
> When they shall dye, then God himself shall die ...[19]

The idea of pre-existence is implicitly present throughout the poem,[20] but the term as such does not yet occur. It is used for the first time in a second poem, *Psychathanasia or The Immortality of the Soul*, which appeared together with *Psychozoia*; there, More speaks of "the souls pre-existencie, before into this outward world she glides".[21] The subject became the special theme of a poem which appeared in the 1647 edition of the *Philosophicall Poems*: "The Prae-existency of the Soul", in which the idea of pre-existence functions as an extra argument for the belief in "the Souls future subsistency after death". From the

---

[16] *Psychozoia* Cant. I, 2: *The Complete Poems of Dr. Henry More* ... ed. by A.B. Grosart, New York 1967; (first published 1878), 13; *Philosophical Poems of Henry More*, ed. by G. Bullough, Manchester 1931, 11.

[17] Cant. I, 4: *loc. cit.; Phil. Poems*, 12.

[18] Cant. I, 12: *Compl. Poems*, 14; *Phil. Poems*, 15.

[19] Cant. II, 19: Compl. *Poems*, 21; *Phil. Poems*, 38.

[20] For the presence of the idea of pre-existence in the world of thought of More's authorities at that time, the "ancient philosophers", see D.P. Walker, *The Ancient Theology*, Ithaca, New York 1972, 6, 10. One may wonder whether in this poem More reacts against Sir John Davies' "creationist" poem *Nosce Teipsum* (1599), where we read: "Then neither from eternity before, / Nor from the time when Time's first point begun, / Made He all souls, which now He keeps in store ... / But as God's handmaid, Nature, doth create, / Bodies in time distinct and order due, / So God gives souls the like successive date, / Which Himself makes, in bodies formed new ...". See G. Bullett (ed.), *Silver Poems of the Sixteenth Century*, London, 1941, 362f. I thank this reference to Dr. N.E. Emerton.

[21] Book III, Cant. 22, 1, cf. 4: *Compl. Poems*, 70 (not in *Phil. Poems).*

beginning to the end, the poem is couched in Neo-Platonic language. Plotinus is More's guide:

> For I would sing the Praeexistency
> Of humane souls, and live once ore again
> By recollection and quick memory
> All what is past since first we all began.
> But all too shallow be my wits to scan
> So deep a point and mind too dull to clear
> So dark a matter: but Thou, O more than man!
> Aread thou sacred Soul of *Plotin* deare
> Tell what we mortalls are, tell what of old we were.[22]

From "The Preface to the Reader" it appears that More was aware of the "heavie prejudice" with regard to "the opinion of the Praeexistency of the Soul"; because of this, he remarked, "That which I have taken the pains and boldnesse to present to the free judgment of others, hath been already judged of old, very sound and orthodox, by the wisest and most learned of preceding ages. Which *R. Menasseh Ben-Israel,* doth abundantly attest in his 15. *Problem. De Creatione;* avouching that it is the common Opinion of all the Hebrews, and that it was never called into controversie, but approved of, by the common consent and suffrage of all wise men". But though More agreed with the rabbi's appeal to the Old Testament, he added that Menasseh "might ... have been more fitly furnished, could his Religion have reached into the New". As "proof-texts" from the New Testament, More mentioned Phil. 2.6, 7, 8; John 9.1, 2, 3; John 17.4, 5 and Mark 8.27, 28: "all those places do seem so naturally to favour this Probability, that if it had pleased the Church to have concluded it for a standing Truth; He that would not have been fully convinced upon the evidence of these passages of Scripture, would undoubtedly, have been held a man of a very timorous and Scepticall constitution, if not something worse".[23] It is interesting to note that (apart from John 9.1, 2, 3) within the context of More's metaphysical way of thinking these texts could be used as "proofs" for the pre-existence of the soul of Jesus, but not, or at least not directly for that of the human soul in general; apparently, for More the probability of the one implied that of the other.

One other point should be noted. While Menasseh did not contrast the idea of emanation (which he used in connection with the "Sephirot") with that of the creation of the souls on the first day, More (loyal to his "guide" Plotinus) explicitly uses the term "emanation" with rejection of the term "creation":

[22] St. 2, *Compl. Poems*, 119.
[23] *Compl. Poems*, 118.

Wherefore man's soul's not by Creation,
Nor is it generate, as I proved before.
Wherefore let't be by emanation
(If fully it did not praeexist of yore)
By flowing forth from that eternall store
Of Lives and souls ycleep'd [named] the World of life,
Which was, and shall endure for evermore.[24]

In 1653, More published his *Conjectura Cabbalistica*,[25] which (otherwise than the title might make us surmise) is not a Kabbalistic work in the strict sense of the word. At this stage of his development More's knowledge of the Kabbalah was slight and indirect,[26] and indeed in the *Conjectura Cabbalistica* he laid no claim of being at home in the field of Jewish Kabbalistic thought. From the "Preface to the Reader" it becomes clear that More used the word "Cabbala" to denote a certain method of explaining the Scriptures, *in casu* the Book of Genesis. His "Cabbala" is not identical with, but analogous to the "Jewish Cabbala". In accordance with what he took for the Jewish method, he tried to combine a more literal exegesis with an interpretation of the more "mysterious" or "mystical" meaning of the text.[27]

In *The Defence of the Threefold Cabbala*, an apology for the "Cabbalistic" method which was published together with the *Conjectura*, More mentions the names of many authorities, Christian as well as pagan. With regard to the latter, he says in the preface: "As for citing the *Heathen Writers* so frequently; you are to consider that they are the Wisest and the most Vertuous of them, and either such as the Fathers say had their philosophy from *Moses* and the Prophets, as *Pythagoras* and *Plato*, or else the Disciples or Friends of these Philosophers". Next to them and the "Fathers", More also mentions (which he declares to conceive as valid in this case) "the *Jewish Rabbins*, who, in things where prejudice need not blinde them, I should think as fit as any to confirm a *Cabbalistical* sense, especially if there be a general consent of them, and that

[24] St. 95, *Compl. Poems*, 128. Menasseh speaks of "emanationes" in *De Creat.*, 105f.: "... dicimus illas Scephirot ... esse ... tantum emanationes quasdam essentiae conjunctas, perinde uti radii solares cum sole ...".

[25] *Conjectura Cabbalistica*, or a Conjectural Essay of Interpreting the mind of Moses, in the Three first Chapters of Genesis, according to a Threefold Cabbala: Viz. Literal, Philosophical, Mystical, or Divinely Moral; reprinted (in the 1662 ed.) in: H. More, *A Collection of Several Philosophical Writings* II, New York and London 1978.

[26] For More and the Kabbalah, see R.J. Zwi Werblowsky, "Milton and the *Conjectura Cabbalistica*", *Journal of the Warburg and Courtauld Institutes* XVIII (1955), esp. 22, and A. Coudert, "A Cambridge Platonist's Kabbalist Nightmare", *Journal of the History of Ideas* 36 (1975), esp. 646; also W. Schulze, "Der Einfluss der Kabbala auf die Cambridger Platoniker Cudworth und More", *Judaica* 23 (1965), 75-126, 193-240. Schulze, however, does not distinguish as clearly as Allison Coudert does between More's knowledge of the Kabbalah before and after he came into contact with F.M. van Helmont and C. Knorr von Rosenroth.

[27] *Conjectura*, 1.

they do not write their private fancy, but the minde of their whole Church".[28] One of them is Menasseh ben Israel, whom again he quotes in support of the idea of pre-existence. That the souls of men were from the beginning of the world, "is the general opinion of the Learned Jews, as well as of the *Pythagoreans* and *Platonists* ...".[29] Adam was "created amongst the *Angelical* Orders part of the First Day's Creation, when God made *Heaven* or *Light*". This "appears from what *Menasseh Ben Israel* cites out of *Gemara Haguigae:* In caelo Empyreo esse domicilia vitae, et pacis, et animarum justorum et Spiritum, atque etiam animarum istarum quae in Mundum venturae sunt". Furthermore, it is confirmed by *Bereshit Rabbah*, on the strength of which Menasseh says "that the wise men of his Nation interpret that of the Psalms, *Post et ante me formasti* Ps. 139.4, of the creating *Adam*, that is, mankind, *first* in the *First* day, and *after* in the *Sixth*".[30] It is to be noted that here (unlike what he wrote in the earlier poem on pre-existence) More does not speak of emanation, but (in accordance with Menasseh) of the creation of the soul.

Shortly after More's meeting with Menasseh, in 1659, appeared his *The Immortality of the Soul*; a subject which, as we saw, had been dealt with at great length by Menasseh in his *De Resurrectione Mortuorum*. The two works differ in scope and character. Though with Menasseh philosophical arguments are not quite absent, they are brought forward within the context of traditional Jewish theology; More's work, on the contrary, has a predominantly philosophical character. And while Menasseh mainly deals with the immortality of the soul as such, More's defense of the immortality of the soul is indissolubly connected with his belief in the existence of a world of spirits and demons. How crucial this belief was to his thinking, appears from the closing lines of his *An Antidote against Atheisme* (1652): "For assuredly that Saying is not more true in Politicks, *No Bishop, no King*, than this is in Metaphysics, *No Spirit, no God*".[31] Moreover, there is no indication whatever that More had taken cognizance of Menasseh's work on the subject.

Still, there are some parallels between both works. Menasseh had written his work as an attack against the "Sadducees" of his own days, whom he saw represented in Uriel da Costa; in similar vein, More opposed the "materialists", whose main representative at that time was Hobbes. In his *The Immortality of the Soul* he did not yet dub them "Sadducees"—his language with regard to Hobbes is rather restrained[32]—but that ultimately More and his

---

[28] *Defence* (1662 ed., repr. 1978), 43f. (continuous pagination with *Conjectura).*
[29] *Defence*, 87.
[30] *Defence*, 147.
[31] *Antidote* (ed. 1662, repr. in *A Collection* ..., I), 142.
[32] For this, see J.Tulloch, *Rational Theology and Christian Philosophy in England in the Seventeenth Century* II, Edinburgh and London 1874, 364ff.

friends saw the "materialists" as "Sadducees" appears already from the title of Joseph Glanvill's work *Saducismus Triumphatus ... Or, A full and plain evidence concerning Witches and Apparitions* (1681).[33] In a letter to Glanvill, written in 1678 and included in *Saducismus*, More spoke of "such coarse grain'd Philosophers as those *Hobbians* and *Spinozians*, and the rest of that Rabble", who "slight Religion and the Scriptures, because there is such express Mention of Spirits and Angels in them, things that their dull Souls are so inclinable to conceit to be impossible ...".[34]

Furthermore, in his *The Immortality of the Soul* More sees, again in accordance with Menasseh's views, a direct connection between the doctrine of the soul's immortality and the belief in pre-existence; a belief which "has been received by the most learned Philosophers of all Ages, there being scarce any of them that held the Soul of man Immortal upon the mere light of Nature and reason, but asserted also her Praeexistence ...". To the many testimonies of the ancient world "you may adde the abstruse Philosophy of the Jews, which they call their *Cabbala*, of which *the Soul's Praeexistence* makes a considerable part, as all the learned of the Jews do confess".[35]

In 1660 appeared More's most important theological work: *An Explanation of the Grand Mystery of Godliness*, a work which marks the fact that somehow in his thinking the centre of gravity had shifted from philosophical speculation to a more theological approach.[36] In this work, the idea of pre-existence functions within the context of More's attack on the doctrines of the "Psychopannychites", who taught that the soul "sleeps" from the moment of man's death till that of his bodily resurrection.[37] The background of More's objections against "this sinister conceit" is clear: it makes the active life of the soul dependent on that of the body and thus in fact denies the primacy of the soul, a notion fundamental to Platonic thinking. In his opposition, More links the idea of "the souls living and subsisting after Death" with that of her preexistence. He deplores the fact that "the ancient Fathers", in spite of their being

[33] The work, full of ghost stories, is a new ed. of *A Blow at modern Sadducism* (1668), which in its turn is a new ed. of *Philosophical Considerations concerning Witches and Witchcraft* (1666). It contains a letter from More to Glanvill (1678) and a translation from More's *Enchiridion Metaphysicum* (1671); see *DNB*, sv. Glanvill, and J.I. Cope, *Joseph Glanvill, Anglican Apologist*, St. Louis 1956, 91-103.

[34] *Saducismus*, London, 1726, "Dr. More's Letter", 9.

[35] *The Immortality of the Soul* (ed. 1662, repr. in *A Collection* ... II), 111, 113.

[36] See F.J. Powicke, *The Cambridge Platonists*, Hamden, Connecticut 1971; repr. of 1926 ed., 157.

[37] In the period of the Reformation, the doctrine of the sleep of the soul was held within the Anabaptist circle, and attacked by Calvin in one of his earliest publications, the *Psychopannychia* of 1534. More referred to Calvin, "that solid interpreter of Scripture", but his way of arguing is totally different from that of the Genevan reformer; it is certainly an understatement when More in this context speaks of some "slight" differences between him and Calvin: *Grand Mystery*, in *The Theological Works*, London 1708, 17.

so conversant with Plato's writings, had omitted the idea of pre-existence, probably because of its supposed "Uncompliableness with Scripture"; it would not have been difficult for them to make their cause plausible out of Scripture itself. "The Jews would have contributed something out of the Old Testament". Here More turns again to the arguments brought forward by Menasseh ben Israel in his *De Creatione* (though here he does not mention its title); this time without the just slightly superior tone he assumed in the preface to his poem on pre-existence. As a complement to the proof-texts from the Old Testament, More mentions (as he did before) a number of texts from the New Testament, now with a broad exposition of his belief in the pre-existence of "the Soul of the Messiah". In passing we note that he remarks in his exposition of 1 John 4.2: "Here St. John seems to cabbalize, as in several places of the Apocalypse, that is, to speak in the language of the Learned of the Jews ...".[38]

In the year after the appearance of More's *An Explanation of the Grand Mystery of Godliness*, in June 1661, an anonymous work was published under the title: *A Letter of Resolution concerning Origen and the chief of his Opinions*.[39] On 14 September More wrote to his friend Lady Conway: "I can not imagine who should be the Authour of it, it is a pretty odd Book, but has some thinges very consyderable in it ...".[40] The work is attributed to one of More's Cambridge friends and pupils, George Rust, who in May 1661 had been made Dean of Connor; in 1667 he was consecrated Bishop of Dromore.[41] From this pamphlet, it appears how much the author admired Origen, whom he even calls "the *Holy Father*". The doctrine of the soul receives much attention: "... you will finde many things concerning the Nature of the Soul and her Operations, her Union with Matter, with many other speculations, not prov'd by me, but supposed, because they are fully and excellently discussed in the Writings

---

[38] *Grand Mystery*, 15ff.; More had mentioned in passing the idea of the pre-existence of the soul of the Messiah as "the opinion of the *Jewes*" in his *Conjectura Cabbalistica*, 95.

[39] It appeared in London, and was reprinted in *The Phenix*, 1 (1707); again in *A Collection of Choice, scarce and valuable tracts* (1727); lastly in a reprint with a biographical note by Marjorie Hope Nicolson, New York 1933.

[40] Marjorie Hope Nicolson, *Conway Letters. The Correspondence of Anne, Viscountess Conway, Henry More, and their Friends, 1642-1684*, revised edition ed. by Sarah Hutton, Oxford 1992, 192 (Letter 118).

[41] *DNB*, s.v. Rust. Marjorie Nicolson takes Rust's authorship for granted, but J.I. Cope (*Joseph Glanvill*, 10, n. 32) rightly remarks: "The evidence of authorship is not complete. More never knew it, if Rust wrote the book (*Conway Letters*, 173), and Glanvill ... does not mention it among Rust's works in the manuscript *Bensalem*". See also Charles F. Mullett, "A Letter by Joseph Glanvill on the Future State", *The Huntington Library Quarterly* 1 (1937-1938), 447-456, who with regard to the question of the authorship does not come further than a "perhaps". If Glanvill's letter of 20 Jan. 1661/62, published by Mullett, was indeed directed to Rust, then it is certain that Rust was an adherent of the doctrine of pre-existence. At any rate, Rust was a Platonist with much interest in "Cabbalistical or Traditional Learning", known for his "Reading and Skill in the Jewish Writers", as Henry Hallywell writes in the "Preface to the Reader" in: *The Remains of that Reverend and Learned Prelate, Dr George Rust* ..., London, 1686.

of that learned Gentleman Mr *More* of *Cambridge* …".[42] The author is firmly convinced of the truth of the idea of pre-existence, which he defends throughout his work, and which in accordance with More he connects with the doctrine of the pre-existence of the soul of Christ. But he differs from More in this, that apart from a few scattered utterances[43] there are no references to Jewish opinion on this point.

From another letter More wrote to Lady Conway it appears that in Cambridge the book (which, according to More, had "witt and learning") was considered dangerous. The Vice-Chancellor had censured it, "and one of the unsound opinions of Origen was the Praeexistence of the soule, which was conceiv'd to be repugnant with the incarnation of Christ. A flaw in the opinion that the short sighted Rabbins could not spy out who were in more speciall manner earnest for the pre-existence of the soule of the Messias above all other soules, and yett their expectation was that he should come in the flesh …".[44]

Another defense of the idea of the pre-existence of the soul was published in 1662 under the significant title *Lux Orientalis*.[45] It was written by a friend of More and Rust, the Anglican clergyman Joseph Glanvill, whom we met before as the author of *Saducismus Triumphatus*. No doubt the author reflected upon the way the doctrine of pre-existence as formulated in *A Letter of Resolution* had been censured in Cambridge, when he wrote: "As for the opinion of praeexistence, the subject of the following Papers, it was never determined against by ours, nor any other Church that I know of; And therefore I conceive is left as a matter of *School Speculation*, which without danger may be *problematically* argued on either hand. And I have so great confidence in all true Sons of our common Mother to think, that they will not fix any harsh and severe censures, upon the innocent *Speculations* of those, though possibly they may be Errours, who own the *Authority, Articles, Canons, and Constitutions* of that Church which they are so deservedly zealous for"[46] He realized that the subject had already been dealt with by *"the learned D. More"* (though not in a special treatise)[47] and by the author of "the Account of Origen". But because the latter had confined himself to Origen and his opponents (and thus perhaps in the eyes of Glanvill had made himself more vulnerable to criticism), Glanvill remarked that the author had "not so fully stated and cleared

---

[42] *Letter* (ed. 1933), 22.

[43] *E.g.*, on 41: "… the opinion of Praeexistence, but in a special manner of the Soul of the *Messiah*, was the common doctrine of their Nation …".

[44] *Conway Letters*, 194 (Letter 119, 26 Oct. 1661).

[45] *Lux Orientalis, or an Enquiry into the Opinion of the Eastern Sages, Concerning the Praeexistence of Souls* …, London 1662. For this work, see J.I. Cope, *Joseph Glanvill*, 11, 87ff.

[46] *Lux Orientalis*, "The preface", f. A [8^{ro,vo}], B 2ro.

[47] Perhaps the fact that More's utterances on this point were scattered through his works, combined with the fame and spiritual authority More enjoyed inside and outside Cambridge, explains why the Vice-Chancellor did not censure More's views on pre-existence.

the businesse, but that there was room for after-undertakers". Glanvill pays scarcely more attention to Jewish opinion than the author of *A Letter of Resolution* had done. He remarks that one of "the great Rabbins ... Mr. *Ben Israel* in his *Problems de Creatione*, assures us, that *Prae-existence* was the *common belief* of all *wise* men among the Jews, without exception". Furthermore, he quotes the "Book of Wisdom", the author of which "certainly was a *Jew*, probably *Philo*". All this, however, only functions as "a *by-consideration*".[48] In this, he differed from More, who attached so much weight to the testimony of Menasseh.

Through Franciscus Mercurius van Helmont, whom he first met in 1670, More came into contact with Van Helmont's Kabbalistic studies and with those of Christian Knorr von Rosenroth.[49] Furthermore, in a letter to Lady Conway of 5 February 1671/72 he speaks about a Jew who told him about Isaac Luria, whom they held "to be the most knowing man of their cabbala of the *Jewes Nation*".[50] More was interested, but also critical, as appears from his *Fundamenta Philosophiae sive Cabbalae Aeto-Paedo-Melissaeae*, in which, says Allison Coudert, he expressed his feelings "eloquently and somewhat heatedly".[51] It found a place in Knorr's *Kabbala Denudata* (1677). In *Fundamenta* the doctrine of the pre-existence of souls is mentioned in a short passage, in which More tries to guard his cherished doctrine against disfigurement and pollution by a Kabbalist hypothesis, according to which the souls originated from the material word.[52] From his "Annotations" to the 1682 edition of Glanvill's *Lux Orientalis* and Rust's *A Discourse of Truth*[53] it becomes clear that More remained loyal to his essentially Platonic doctrine of pre-existence. What strikes us in the author's account of his conversation with Menasseh ben Israel, then already a quarter of a century ago, is the fact that here the only witness for the doctrine of pre-existence who is mentioned by name is "that very ancient and learned Jew *Philo Judaeus*". In the context of the doctrine of pre-existence, Menasseh neither mentions him in his *De Creatione* nor in his *De Resurrectione*, while More only mentions him in passing (in a long list of philosophers) in his *The Immortality of the Soul*.[54] Assuming that the sentence in the "Annotations" in which Philo is mentioned refers to the conversation in question, we may ask whether it was a case of "fausse reconnaissance" on the side of More (*cf.* the "if I remember right") or whether he and the Amsterdam rabbi really discussed Philo when they had their meeting in London.

---

48 *Lux Orientalis*, 52.
49 For this and what follows, see A. Coudert, "A Cambridge Platonist's Kabbalist Nightmare".
50 *Conway Letters*, 352 (Letter 218).
51 "A Cambridge Platonist's Kabbalist Nightmare", 648.
52 C. Knorr von Rosenroth, *Kabbala Denudata*, I 2, Sulzbaci 1677; repr. Hildesheim-New York 1974, 297.
53 Full title in note 1.
54 *Immortality*, 114.

For some people, the idea of the pre-existence of souls was more than an abstract speculation. In a letter of 13 October 1683 Edmund Elys, an Anglican clergyman with mystical sympathies,[55] wrote to More after the decease of Elys' wife: "That *Hypothesis of Praeexistence* would be Probable unto me if I had no other Grounds for it but my Reflexion upon the *Strange Sympathy* that was betwixt us notwithstanding our *Differences in Sex, Education, Bodily Temper* and which sometimes broke out in such words, at which our Enemies took advantage".[56] In fact, Elys went even further than More dared to go: apparently he believed in the paired creation of souls, a doctrine which Menasseh taught but which we do not find with More. That in certain circles the doctrine of pre-existence enjoyed a rather large measure of popularity appears from the publisher's address in *Two choice and useful Treatises*; according to the publisher, "when the book *Lux Orientalis* grew scarce it was so much valued by the more eager and curious searchers into the profoundest points of philosophy, that there was given for it some four or five times the price for which it was first sold".[57]

Not all, however, valued the idea of the pre-existence of the human soul as highly as the Platonists did. Outside the Platonist circle, most Christian theologians considered the doctrine of pre-existence strange and even unorthodox. Glanvill, who revered the moderate Calvinist Richard Baxter—"I affect you no less ardently, than if you were a Metropolitan"—apparently had some misgivings, when he sent his *Lux Orientalis* to Baxter: "... Tis very likely that you will wonder at this exploit; And be yet more surprised when I have told you, that I am the Author ...".[58] Baxter indeed could not appreciate Glanvill's work, as appears from another letter Glanvill sent to him: "Your disapproval of Praeexistence is one of the greatest arguments yett seen against it". Over against Baxter, Glanvill maintained his point of view, though with caution and reserve: "I owe myself an Assertor of the probability of this hypothesis, though I lay not great stress upon it, for I would not build great matters on it ... That the doctrine of Praeexistence is *uncertain*, that is, not strictly demonstrable, I grant. And so I am afraid are most speculations else, except some very few fundamentals".[59]

As an example of a critic from a later generation I quote the English mystic William Law (1686-1761) who—notwithstanding the fact that he recognized

---

[55] See *DNB*, s.v. Elys; *Conway Letters*, 301, n. 2.

[56] Christ's College, Cambridge, MS 21, f. 36A.

[57] See F. Greenslet, *Joseph Glanvill*, New York 1900, 60f.

[58] Glanvill to Baxter, 4 August 1662: Dr. Williams's Library, London, Baxter's Letters, MS 59-1-174; N.H. Keeble and Geoffrey F. Nuttall, *Calendar of Correspondence of Richard Baxter* II, Oxford 1991, Letter 705.

[59] *DWL*, MS 59-1-170; *Calendar* II, Letter 711. This letter has been published (though not quite correctly) in *Bibliotheca Platonica*, 1 (1889), 186-192.

in More "a pious Christian, and of great abilities"—remarked that More "knew nothing deeper than a hypothesis, nor truer of the nature of the soul than that which he has said of its pre-existence, which is little better than that foolish brat descended from it, the transmigration of souls".[60] In more solemn words, but essentially in the same spirit, already in Menasseh's lifetime the doctrine as it was formulated by Menasseh in his *De Creatione* was heavily attacked by the Leiden professor of theology Johannes Hoornbeeck (1617-1666), a redoubtable polemicist and—as a follower of the Utrecht theologian Gisbertus Voetius—a representative of right-wing Calvinist orthodoxy.[61] In 1655 appeared his *Tesjubat Jehudah*[62]—"that book", says Menasseh, "which he later writ against our nation, wherein he hath objected against us, right or wrong, all that he could scrape together".[63] Hoornbeeck's work had an apologetic-controversialist as well as a conversionist character—two aspects, which were closely linked together. In the circle of Dutch seventeenth-century Calvinism we meet with a lively interest in the conversion of the Jews, fostered by the expectation of a general conversion of the Jews in the last days. Furthermore, a number of Calvinist theologians were convinced that this conversion could be advanced by a polemicist approach which aimed at convincing the Jews of their "errors" by means of theological refutation.[64] One of them—in this context perhaps even the most prominent—was Hoornbeeck, whose *Tesjubat Jehudah*, while in many ways an interesting specimen of theological apologetics, pretended to be an appeal to the Jews to turn towards (Reformed) Christianity.

Hoornbeeck first of all differs from the Platonists in his evaluation of the Kabbalah. As we saw, Platonists, while often deficient in knowledge with regard to this point, could have some sympathy with what they considered the Kabbalistic method. No doubt Hoornbeeck knew more about the Kabbalah than most of the Platonists. He had read Jewish authors on the Kabbalah (among them Menasseh ben Israel); also Christian authors such as Reuchlin and Rittangel. But unlike the Platonists he had a deep aversion from all Kabbalistic speculations. Over against Menasseh's statement that through the Kabbalah we come to know "sublimia mysteria", Hoornbeeck remarks that,

---

[60] See J. Hoyles, *The Edges of Augustanism* (International Archives of the History of Ideas, 53), The Hague 1972, 110, quoting from J.H. Overton, *William Law*, London 1881, 407f.

[61] For Hoornbeeck's polemical activities, see J.W Hofmeyr, *Johannes Hoornbeeck als polemikus*, Kampen 1975—a work which only gives a general survey of the subject.

[62] J. Hoornbeeck, *Tesjubat Jehudah sive, pro convincendis et convertendis Judaeis Libri Octo*, Lugd. Bat. 1655.

[63] *Vindicae Judaeorum* (1656), 8, repr. in L. Wolf, *Menasseh ben Israel's Mission to Oliver Cromwell ...*, London 1901; Menasseh, however, appreciated the fact that Hoornbeeck gave short shrift to the "blood accusation".

[64] See J. van den Berg, *Joden en Christenen in Nederland gedurende de zeventiende eeuw*, Kampen 1969.

however ingenious it may seem to be, nothing is more uncertain and fallacious than the Kabbalah: "Ars est, si modo ars dicenda, inventionis ac commenti humani, inanem faciens, atque ridiculam operam...".[65]

His condemnation of the Kabbalah sets the tone for his treatment of the doctrine of the pre-existence of the human soul, to which he pays comparatively much attention. In accordance with the large majority of Reformed theologians,[66] Hoornbeeck was an adherent of the "creationist" doctrine, which held that the human soul was created together with the body: "in hominis generatione creatur anima".[67] As such, he rejected the idea of "traducianism" (held by the Lutherans), and *a fortiori* the idea of the pre-existence of the soul. In connection with all this he opposed the idea of the paired creation of the male and the female soul and the idea of "metempsychosis", which he considered detrimental to the belief in the resurrection: together with which body could or should a soul be presented at the resurrection, which had inhabited various bodies?[68]

The pages Hoornbeeck devotes to the idea of pre-existence are almost a running commentary on Menasseh's expositions of the subject in his *De Creatione* (esp. Probl. XV), which he quotes extensively and literally. In Menasseh's work he distinguishes three kinds of arguments: arguments based on the Old Testament, on the tradition of the wise men among the Jews, and on human reason. With regard to the first category, Hoornbeeck tries to refute Menasseh's appeal to a number of Old Testament texts. He goes from text to text, putting his translation over against that of Menasseh and interspersing his expositions with arguments of a more general or philosophical nature. According to Hoornbeeck, Deut. 29.14 does not say that God enters into a covenant with all souls, but with those who were present and with the "posteri, qui non praesentes erant". In Isaiah 57.16 not all human souls are meant, but "animae hominum qui existunt et vivunt". Of Jer. 1.5 Hoornbeeck gives a quitte different translation from that of Menasseh: "antequam te formarem in utero, novi te", thus making this text a proof-text for the idea of God's prescience and of his election of Jeremiah for the prophetic office. Eccl. 4.2 does not say that the unborn men (here, Hoornbeeck avoids the word "soul") were happy, but only that they were not unhappy. And lastly, Job 38.21 is said "per ironiam ... et non affirmative, sed negative accipiendum".[69]

With regard to Menasseh's appeal to the Jewish fathers or "sages", Hoornbeeck was somewhat sceptical. He noticed that in *De Creatione* Menasseh

---

[65] *Tesjubat*, 94.
[66] H. Bavinck, *Gereformeerde dogmatiek* II, Kampen ^{4}1928, 542.
[67] *Tesjubat*, 329.
[68] *Tesjubat*, 547.
[69] *Tesjubat*, 324-328.
[70] *Tesjubat*, 321.

averred that the idea of pre-existence was common to all Hebrews, while elsewhere, in *Conciliator*, Menasseh said that most of the Hebrews think like this.[70] It is clear that Hoornbeeck saw the doctrine of pre-existence as it was held by the Jews of his own days as mainly a Kabbalistic doctrine, partly derived from Platonic-Pythagorean sources. He did not recognize a rational argument in Menasseh's exposition of the doctrine; on the contrary, exactly this doctrine led to rational impossibilities, and thus Menasseh's appeal to reason he considered spurious. Within the context of scholastic thinking, one argument used by Menasseh seemed to have some validity: if God indeed created everything within the span of six days, then there can be no creation after that time. Hoornbeeck counters this argument, however, by remarking that God also creates "postea", after the "creatio prima". To deny this would mean the denial of the possibility of miracles: in every miracle there is always "aliqua creatio, et productio rei ex nihilo".[71]

It is clear that Hoornbeeck's dislike of Kabbalism, his resistance to Platonism and his rejection of the doctrine of pre-existence should be seen in their interrelationship. Hoornbeeck recognizes that Menasseh's appeal to Plato is not without ground, though sometimes he seems to go even further than Plato. But Hoornbeeck rejects Platonism exactly on those points which are important in connection with the idea of pre-existence. He rather contemptuously dismisses Plato's notion of "reminiscence": " Platonis ista sententia cordatis risum debet, atque a multis saeculis explosa fuit: ut eam nunc reducere velle, in Cabbalistarum gratiam, nihil sit quam nugas nugis addere, et se omni ex parte prostituere".[72] And over against Menasseh's Platonic depreciation of the body—Menasseh describes the body as a most unhappy prison and attributes all human guilt to the body—Hoornbeeck puts his doctrine of the interrelation of soul and body: "A temperamento corporis haud magis anima pendet in suis operationibus, quam a ratione mentis, corpus".[73] Here, the contrast between Platonic and Aristotelian thinking[74] becomes manifest; though in this context Hoornbeeck does not mention the name of Aristotle, as a seventeenth century orthodox theologian he found his philosophical background in Aristotelianism. And as a consistent Calvinist he had, as we saw, no sympathy whatever with Kabbalism.[75] Hoornbeeck's conclusion is, that neither in Scripture, nor in reason or experience is there any indication or vestige of the idea of pre-existence.

---

[71] *Tesjubat*, 329.
[72] *Tesjubat*, 326.
[73] *Tesjubat*, 328, 548.
[74] Cf. Aristotle, *De Anima*, Book I, 1.
[75] For Calvin's and Beza's rejection of Kabbalistic speculations, see D.P. Walker, *The Ancient Philosophy*, 121; for Hoornbeeck also: J.L. Blau, *The Christian Interpretation of the Cabala in the Renaissance*, New York 1944, 111.

As an able Hebraist, who for conversionist reasons was deeply interested in Judaism, and who because of his Calvinist orientation towards the Old Testament had some affinity with certain aspects of Hebrew thinking, Hoornbeeck had a much more profound knowledge of Jewish theology than More had, whose knowledge of Judaism was rather elementary. But because of his Platonic background, More no doubt could better understand Menasseh's intentions. While for Hoornbeeck the word "Kabbalah" had nothing but a negative association, for More (notwithstanding his criticism) the same word had something of a magic sound. And while Hoornbeeck saw Menasseh's doctrine of pre-existence as a compound of nugatory speculations, More shared Menasseh's interest in the radiant world of life and light in which the human souls moved before being confined within the human body. Perhaps this spiritual affinity explains why after many years More still lively remembered his meeting with the Amsterdam rabbi, who like him believed in "pre-existence"—a doctrine, dear to him but repudiated by so many of his fellow-Christians. May we surmise that Menasseh on his side, in those last years of his life, so full of tensions and disappointments, enjoyed his conversation with a Christian theologian who understood and shared his passion for a deeper insight into the mysteries of the soul?

CHAPTER SIX

CONTINUITY WITHIN A CHANGING CONTEXT: THE APOCALYPTIC THOUGHT OF JOSEPH MEDE AND HENRY MORE

The English millenarian William Whiston[1] wrote in his *Essay on the Revelation of St. John*, published in 1706:

> The Learned Dr. Henry Moor, and Monsieur *Jurieu* generally follow Mr. *Mede*, and so are certainly some of our best Commentators on this Book. But where Mr. *Mede* had failed, they generally fail also: and where they advance some new Assertions of their own, they are generally built on some *Interpretations* of their own, contrary to the true Order of the Visions ...[2]

In this passage, Whiston recognizes the great debt seventeenth and early eighteenth century millenarians in and outside England owed to Joseph Mede. Among them was, indeed, the Cambridge Platonist Henry More. Much has been written on Mede's millenarianism, considerably less on that of More.[3] The reason for the greater attention Mede's millenarianism has received is obvious: as Whiston rightly observed, Mede was the leading English millenarian of the seventeenth century, and his influence reached beyond the boundaries of his own country and his own times. It is impossible to get a clear view of later millenarian developments without taking into account the model as laid down by Mede in his *Clavis Apocalyptica* of 1627. But in the passage, quoted above, Whiston somewhat played down the importance of Henry More as a millenarian. Perhaps in seventeenth-century England no one wrote more extensively on the millennium than our Cambridge Platonist, and the philo-

---

[1] For Whiston (1667-1752), see James E. Force, *William Whiston, Honest Newtonian*, Cambridge etc. 1985.

[2] W. Whiston, *An Essay on the Revelation of Saint John. So far as it concerns the Past and Present Times*, Cambridge 1706, 102. For Joseph Mede (1586-1638), see *DNB* s.v.; for Pierre Jurieu (1637-1713), Huguenot theologian, from 1681 onward in Rotterdam, who expounded his millenarian views in his *L'accomplissement des prophéties* (1686), see F.R.J. Knetsch, *Pierre Jurieu. Theoloog en politikus der refuge*, Kampen 1967, esp. ch. XIV.

[3] For Mede's millenarianism, see E.L. Tuveson, *Millennium and Utopia*, New York etc. 1964; R.G. Clouse, "The Rebirth of Millenarianism", in P. Toon (ed.), *Puritans, the Millennium and the Future of Israel*, Cambridge and London 1970; B.W. Ball, *A Great Expectation*, Leiden, 1975; P. Christianson, *Reformers and Babylon*, Toronto etc. 1978; Katherine R. Firth, *The Apocalyptic Tradition in Reformation Britain 1530-1645*, Oxford 1979; R.H. Popkin, "The Third Force in 17th Century Philosophy", *Nouvelles de la République des Lettres* 3 (1983), 35-63; I. Escribano-Alberca, "Eschatologie von der Aufklärung bis zur Gegenwart", in *Handbuch der Dogmengeschichte* IV, Fasc. 7 d, Freiburg-Basel-Wien (Herder) 1987 (also for More).

sophical and theological climate in which he lived gave a special colour to his millenarian views. His form of millenarianism certainly deserves special attention.

Both Mede and More were fellows of Christ's College, Cambridge: Mede from 1613 till his death in 1638, More from 1639 till his decease in 1687. In "The life of ... Joseph Mede, B.D.", to be found in John Worthington's edition of Mede's Works, we read that he was for some time "disquieted with Scepticism" and began to doubt whether the τὸ πᾶν was any more than "a mere Phantasm or Imagination". Soon, however, he shed these existential doubts, though he always was an advocate of a form of methodological doubt: "For he supposed that *To doubt nothing*, and *To understand nothing*, were verifiable alike".[4] Richard Popkin sees a relation between Mede's turning away from Pyrrhonism and his millenarian thinking: "He found his resolution of his sceptical crisis in the truths he discovered in the *Book of Revelation*".[5] Mede developed into a scholar of a broad erudition as well as a mathematical preciseness: a worthy member of the *respublica litterarum*. In theological respect, he steered a middle course between the moderate Calvinism in which he had been brought up and the Arminianism which began to gain ground in England, and though in general he was careful in his utterances, he unambiguously rejected the high Calvinism of the Synod of Dort.[6] At one time, he was suspected of "too much ... tenderness to the Puritan faction; which" (he wrote to his friend William Twisse, the later prolocutor of the Westminster Assembly), "is a crime here, if it be once fastened upon a man, nullo Oceano eluendum",[7] but he remained a loyal son of the Church of England, her sacramental doctrine and her liturgy.

His *Clavis Apocalyptica*, which first appeared in 1627, made him famous. Especially in the circle of established Anglicanism it overshadowed its immediate predecessor, the English Puritan Thomas Brightman's commentary on the Apocalypse, published in Latin in 1609 and in English, under the title *A Revelation of the Revelation*, in 1615.[8] Brightman's work had two aspects; it was a Puritan manifesto as well as a scholarly commentary. Below the surface of Brightman's exposition of the Bible text we sense a deep emotion: that of

---

[4] *The Works of the Pious and Profoundly Learned Joseph Mede, B.D.*, London 1677, II, IV.

[5] Popkin, "The Third Force", 38.

[6] "When that unhappy difference about the point of Predestination and its Appendants ... was blown to so high a flame in the Low-Countreys ... he would often say, he wondered that men would with so great animosity contend about those obscure Speculations", and "when he observ'd some to contend with an unmeasurable confidence and bitter zeal for that black Doctrine of Absolute Reprobation ... he could not forbear to tell some of his Friends, That it was an Opinion he could never digest ...", "Life", *Works*, XVIIIf.

[7] Mede to Twisse, April 1637, *Works*, 850.

[8] For the millenarianism of Brightman (1562-1607), see esp. Firth, *Apocalyptic Tradition*, ch. V.

a man who brings, as he says in the dedication, "matter of exceeding joy and of a most glorious triumph" and who looks forward with ardent expectation to "the coming gladsome dayes".[9] It is in particular this element which made his work popular in the Commonwealth period.[10] His idiosyncratic treatment of the idea of the millennium made him vulnerable, however, to criticism on the scholarly level. In fact, his work was a mixture between the Augustinian conception of a millennium which started with the conversion of Constantine and a futurist millennial expectation. In the process of history he recognized two millennial periods of prosperity for the Church. The first period lasted from the fourth century (the binding of the "dragon" by Constantine) till the fourteenth century (the invasions of the "Barbarous Turke", who raged not only against "the false Church, but against the true one also"). This period had an ambivalent character, because "the Beast" (the Pope, the vicar of the dragon) "was borne together with Constantine". The second period started with the resurrection of the truth (Wiclif and Hus!), "whereby continuance of the truth is promised for a thousand yeares".[11]

Mede rarely mentioned Brightman, and when he did, it was in a critical sense. When at one time Twisse had mentioned the name of Brightman in his correspondence with Mede, the latter wrote: "... if with Mr. *Brightman* and others we begin the Thousand years from *Constantine*, there is no place of Scripture for a Papist to urge for *Saint-worship* like unto this, because the time will fit so just; For it began much about that time ...".[12] On this point, Mede's criticism of Brightman was unfair; indeed, Brightman had anticipated such criticism by stressing the contemporaneity of the birth of the "Beast" with that of Constantine. But the motive of Mede's rejection of Brightman's theory is clear: any concession to the traditional Augustinian view of the millennium could weaken the resistance against Rome.

The year in which Mede's *Clavis* appeared also saw the publication of a work of the German Reformed theologian Johann Heinrich Alsted, *Diatribe de Mille Annis Apocalypticis*, a straightforward defence of the idea of a future millennium.[13] Mede essentially agreed with Alsted's idea that the saints of the first resurrection would reign on earth during the millennium, though he differed from Alsted on some points of interpretation.[14] It was Alsted and Mede,

---

[9] T. Brightman, *A Revelation of the Revelation*, 3d ed., Leiden 1616,f. A 3vo.

[10] See W.M. Lamont, *Godly Rule*, London 1969, 95ff.

[11] Brightman, *A Revelation*, 1036f., 1041, 1044, 1047, 1051.

[12] Twisse to Mede, 2 Nov. 1629; Mede to Twisse, 11 Nov. 1629, *Works*, 758, 760.

[13] For Alsted (1588-1638), see *Theologische Realenzyklopädie* II (1978), 299-303; for Alsted and England R.G. Clouse, "Johann Heinrich Alsted and English Millennialism", *The Harvard Theological Review* 62 (1969), 189-207.

[14] See his "Remains on some Passages in the Apocalypse", *Works*, 600ff., and his letter to Dr. Meddus, 18 August 1629, *Works*, 770ff.

who provided millenarianism with the label of respectability in Protestant circles.

Mede's ideas on the millennium are to be found in his *Clavis* (which became more widely known in the second edition, 1632), in some posthumously published works and in his published correspondence. Their originality lies in the fact that his explanation of the Apocalypse is based on a fairly consistent system of "synchronisms": "paths trodden by few, with much care of sure footing", as an opponent recognized.[15] Mede saw a synchronical relationship between the prophecies in Daniel and those in the Apocalypse, while also within the Book of Revelation itself he saw a very strong synchronical coherence. On the strength of this system, it was possible to make a chart of the events, predicted in the Apocalypse, as indeed was done for the second Latin edition.[16] Mede himself was convinced that his system provided the key for the understanding of the biblical prophecies:

> ... yield me a-while that this which I have exhibited is indeed the true Representation of the *Order* and *Connexion* of the *Apocalyptic Visions*: See then how admirable the use thereof will be for *Interpretation*. For if we can once be assured of the meaning of someone principal Vision, how evident then and ruled will the way be from it to find and discover the rest? Will it not be like a Mariner's Card to guide our way in this mystical Sea?[17]

It was a close-knit, mathematically verifiable system, once its premises were accepted; a system, up to the requirements of modern scholarship, which left or seemed to leave no room for subjective interpretations. Mede even spoke of "the Law of *Synchronistical* necessity".[18] His system enabled him to keep together a historical and a futurist explanation of the Apocalypse, and to base his millenarian views on the—in his opinion solid—ground of a seemingly literal interpretation. Of course, the question could arise why the interpretation of the thousand years as given by Mede was hidden for such a long time. Mede answered this question in a letter to Twisse: "For the Thousand years *Regnum Christi*, it was time for it to be silent under *Regnum Antichristi;* and the *Reign of the Martyrs in the first Resurrection* to be cried down, when Antichrist was blasphemously to advance them before-hand to a Reign derogatory to the glory of Christ their Lord ..."[19] The idea which lies behind this utterance is, that a premature interest in the martyrs" reign as depicted in Revelation 20 could have led and had led indeed to an idolatrous veneration of the martyrs—

---

[15] Thomas Hayn(e) to Mede, 5 June 1629, *Works*, 735.

[16] See Firth, *Apocalyptic Tradition*, 218f., with a reproduction of "The Apocalyptik Type" in the 2nd English edition of 1650.

[17] "Remains", *Works*, 581f.

[18] *Works*, 583.

[19] Mede to Twisse, 11 Nov. 1629, *Works*, 759.

and for Mede, "idolatry" was the great Antichristian sin, the main sign of the apostasy of the Church.[20] The doctrine of the millennium could only safely be proclaimed within the context of a purified Church.

It is clear that Mede's views are marked by what his editor called a "serious and pathetical Expostulation with the Church of Rome".[21] Still, he was not uncritical with regard to the churches of the Reformation. In his letter to Twisse, quoted above, we meet with a very cryptic passage:

> ... there is a Sin whereof the whole body of the Reformation is notoriously guilty; which nevertheless is accounted no Sin, and yet such an one, as I know not whether God ever passed by without some visible and remarkable judgement. This seems to call for a scourge before Antichrist shall go down: And that may be, as far as I know, this feared *Clades Testium* [the fall of the two witnesses]. I will not name it, because it is invidious ...[22]

Twisse did not understand it: "But will you not make us acquainted with that Sin you intimate that cries for vengeance?"[23] Mede, in fact, did not. Perhaps the mysterious passage can be explained from what at a later stage he wrote in a letter to Twisse, in which he expressed his fear that some judgment would befall the Reformed Churches "because out of the immoderation of their zeal they had in a manner taken away all Difference between *Sacred* and *Prophane*".[24] Especially a disregard of the sacrificial character of the Eucharist he considered "sacrilege".

But whatever judgement might befall the Reformed Churches, the main judgement was reserved for the Antichristian Church of Rome. The fall of Antichrist would ring in the millennium, which—contrary to common millenarian opinion—he identified with the "Dies Judicii Magni": the day of judgement would be "a continued space of many Years, wherein Christ shall destroy all his Enemies, and at length Death itself". In his utterances on the future millennium Mede is careful and reserved:

> What the *Quality of this Reign* should be, which is so singularly differenced from the Reign of Christ hitherto, is neither easie nor safe to determine, farther than, That it should be the Reign of our Saviour's Victory over his Enemies, wherein *Satan* being bound up from deceiving the Nations any more, till the time of his Reign be fulfilled, the Church should consequently enjoy a most blissful peace and happy security from the heretical Apostasies and calamitous sufferings of former times.

Mede warned against "gross and carnal conceits of an *Epicurean* happiness

---

[20] "The Apostasy of the Latter Times", *Works*, esp. 643ff.
[21] *Works*, 644.
[22] *Works*, 760.
[23] Twisse to Mede, 16 Nov. 1629, *Works*, 765.
[24] Mede to Twisse, April 1637, *Works*, 850.

misbeseeming the Spiritual purity of Saints". Furthermore, he rejected the idea that the presence of Christ in the millennial kingdom would be "a Visible Converse upon Earth": Christ's kingdom "ever hath been and shall be *Regnum Coelorum* ...". With regard to the conversion of the Jews, he expected that the whole "Nation of the Jews", converted at one moment by "such a *miraculous apparition* of Christ from heaven" as that by which St. Paul was converted, would take a prominent place "together with the *Virgin Christians of the Gentiles* (who are the Surrogate Israel)".[25] Lastly, he believed that the day of judgement would also be the day of the conflagration, predicted in II Peter 3; not a total annihilation, but rather a purification. Heaven and earth "shall be purged and refined for the righteous to dwell therein".[26] In all this, Mede (like Brightman[27] and many others) was convinced that he was in full agreement with "the Opinion of the whole Orthodox Christian Church in the Age immediately following the death of *St. John*".[28] To his thinking, his millenarianism was not a form of heresy, but on the contrary a revival of the tradition of the pure primitive Church. No doubt, it was one of the central elements of his teaching in Christ's College.

Among Mede's students at Christ's College was also Henry More.[29] We may assume that already at that time he fell under the spell of his teacher. In most of More's theological works, his eschatological interest takes an important, often even a dominant place. In this context I mention his "magnum opus theologicum" *An Explanation of the Grand Mystery of Godliness* (1660); furthermore *A Modest Enquiry into the Mystery of Iniquity* (1664), *An Exposition of the Seven Epistles to the Seven Churches (1669), Visionum Apocalypticarum Ratio Synchronistica (1674), Apocalypsis Apocalypseos (1680), A Plain and Continued Exposition of the several Prophecies or Divine Visions of the Prophet Daniel* (1681) and *Paralipomena Prophetica* (1685). The expectation of the coming millennium remained alive with him until the end. In his expositions on this subject there is a certain broadening of the argument, but also much repetition, practically no change and no real development.

More wholeheartedly agreed with the fundamental structure of Mede's eschatology:

> ... he that I am most of all beholden to, is that incomparably Pious and Learned person *Mr. Joseph Mede*, once one of the Fellows of our Colledge, in whose steps

---

[25] "Remains", *Works*, 603f.

[26] "A Paraphrase and Exposition of the Prophecie of St. Peter", *Works*, 613-617.

[27] *A Revelation*, 1052.

[28] Mede to Dr. Meddus, *Works*, 771.

[29] For More (1614-1687), see R. Ward, *The Life of ... Dr. H. More*, London 1710; A. Lichtenstein, *Henry More. The Rational Theology of a Cambridge Platonist*, Cambridge (Mass.) 1962; Sarah Hutton (ed.), *Henry More (1614-1687). Tercentenary Studies*, Dordrecht-Boston-London 1990.

> where he treads right, I thought I was bound to insist, as also in any others as far as they are in a true path.[30]

He was deeply impressed by Mede's "Scheme of Synchronisms", which he saw as a "Synchronical Architecture ... not built upon any Hypothesis but the innate Character of the Apocalyptical Visions themselves". Thus, this scheme of interpretation was not dependent on a fallible theory with regard to the date of the writings of the Apocalypse, as was the case with Grotius' historical exegesis. While Grotius' expositions stand or fall with the way "he fancieth himself able to apply his Historical Materials", and thus "has indeed no Guide at all from the Apocalypse itself", Mede "is directed and limited by the demonstrative Law of those innate *Synchronisms* he had gathered". We shall return to More's criticism of Grotius at a later stage; this may suffice to show how much More felt indebted to the apocalyptic scheme of his teacher. Mede saw the system of synchronisms as a chart on a mystical sea; More, in his turn, considered Mede's hermeneutical approach a safe guide in the "prophetic labyrinth" of the Apocalypse. A verification *a posteriori* was, "that the things that are found to be *Synchronical*, have also a natural Connection and Complication one with another".[31]

Escribano-Alberca remarks that with More the synchronisms of Mede are transformed into axioms,[32] but the difference is only slight. With Mede as much as with More the synchronisms form the solid base of the superstructure, while at the same time More is careful to retain a certain margin of freedom with regard to the interpretation of the synchronisms.[33] In More's synchronical system there are some small deviations from that of Mede—of course, a subject like this offers ample scope for varieties in interpretation. Thus, unlike Mede More differentiates the "seventh Trumpet" into "seven Thunders" (Rev. 10.3,4), which according to More leaves room for a more gradual transition between the "Reign of the Beast" and the "Millennial Reign". Furthermore, Mede "never meddled with the seven Churches", which take such an important place in More's interpretation of the future. And lastly, More differed from Mede in that he identified the "three days and a half the Witnesses laye slain" (Rev. 11) with "the 1260 days of their Prophesying", which as we shall see led him to suppose that in the period of the Middle Ages the "witnesses" were dead and alive at the same time.[34] These small differences, however, do not detract

[30] *Apocalypsis Apocalypseos*, London 1680, 249.

[31] "An Explanation of the Grand Mystery of Godliness", *The Theological Works of ... Henry More*, London 1708, 125 (henceforth abbreviated as *TW*).

[32] "Eschatologie", 54.

[33] Cf. the reserve he makes in parenthesis: "seeing the Truth of Mr. Mede's Synchronisms, as far as respects this present Subject, is so apodictical ...", *loc. cit.*

[34] *Apocalypsis*, 259.

from the fundamental agreement between More's apocalyptic scheme and that of Mede. Accordingly it is self-evident that More strongly protested against the report that shortly before his death Mede was "out of conceit" with his own synchronisms.[35]

Both Mede and More were aware of the danger of a misuse of the biblical prophecies. Uncertainty was better than false certainty. The devil could, according to More (referring to Mede), by making a false computation lead people to believe that Christianity would continue no longer than 365 years, and thus hinder men's conversion to the faith.

> Which, I think, is Argument enough to persuade us how necessary it is that the Holy Prophecies should be wrapt up in Aenigmatical Coverings, and be made of uncertain Interpretation by undeterminable Lubricities, till either Events, or some faithful Interpreter more than ordinarily assisted by God, shall give their clear solution.[36]

No doubt, in speaking of "some faithful Interpreter" he primarily thought of Mede. However this may be, More was assured that ultimately it would be possible to rend the veil of the enigma of biblical prophecy. The sometimes labyrinthine character of the apocalyptic parts of the Bible made him careful, but the time of "uncertain interpretation" had passed. In the "Preface" to his *Theological Works* he wrote:

> I have contributed so much to a clear and certain Way of interpreting them, laying down such assured Grounds and Rudiments, as if a Man carefully observe, and find History applicable within the compass of those Laws, he can no more fail of the right Meaning of a Prophecy, than he will of the rendering the true Sense of a Latin or Greek author, keeping to the Rules of *Grammar*, and the known *Interpretations of Dictionaries*.[37]

This implies, that since the introduction of the synchronistical method of interpretation of the biblical prophecies, which was followed by More, technical skill was a necessary requisite for the understanding of the apocalyptic secrets.

Not only in his millennial expectation, but also in other respects More followed his teacher. He was as loyal to the Church of England as Mede had been: the consideration of her reformed character "must needs make our Mother the Church of *England* look very lovely and amiable to every ingenuous and discerning Eye".[38] As we shall see, his ecclesiological orientation played a not unimportant part in the formulation of his millenarian views. Furthermore, in

---

[35] *Apocalypsis*, 340ff

[36] "A Modest Enquiry into the Mystery of Iniquity, The First Part", *TW*, 525.

[37] "Preface to the Reader", *TW*, VII.

[38] "Mystery of Godliness", *TW*, 715.

line with Mede More professed to seek a middle way between Calvinism and Arminianism,[39] though it should be added that in fact the whole trend of his thinking was quite definitely Arminian,[40] more so than that of Mede. But while this, perhaps, is only a difference in degree, there is a more obvious difference between the two scholars with regard to their philosophical orientation. Mede's philosophical background does not become explicit, but we may assume that it was Aristotelian with Ramist adaptations.[41] More's thinking, however, is coloured by his Platonism; one of our main questions will be, how far Platonist philosophy also affected his millenarian views.

In his *The Great Mystery of Godliness*, which (as we saw) first appeared in 1660, More expressed his belief—such on the ground of the "compute of prophecie"—that the millennium was near at hand.[42] One example of his method of computing may suffice. The "little horn" in Daniel 7 is a part of the Roman empire. Its reign would last three years and a half; this must be converted into 1260 days, which in the prophecies stand for years. This brings us to the Apocalypse, where the woman in the wilderness is said to abide there for a time and times and half a time as well as for 1260 days, which—according to More—"plainly shews the Warrantableness of this Solution". These 1260 days coincide with the time of various other events, mentioned in the Apocalypse, such as "the mournful Prophecies of the Witnesses", "the Whore of Babylon" and the "Succession of the first six Trumpets". It is the period of the Church "lapsed into a degenerate Condition". This period, which in fact covers the period between the time of Constantine and More's own times, is not only the period of the Church, but also of the Empire: the prophecies in the Apocalypse "run parallel in time". Then follows the millennium: the martyrs will be bodily resurrected, and "the true and Apostolical Church" will see a political resurrection.[43]

That More expected the millennium to be "near at hand" becomes still more explicit in his *Visionum Apocalypticarum Ratio Synchronistica*, a small work in the spirit of Mede's *Clavis*. There he states that in the period in which the Roman empire fell apart into many kingdoms because of the invasions of the barbarians (which he dated at about 400), the Church began to favour idolatrous rites such as the invocation of the saints, the cult of images and the adoration of the Eucharist. Thus, old paganism was reintroduced into the empire.[44] Again and again, More emphasized the antichristian character of the Church of Rome. "Antichrist" is not a person who will reveal himself at the

---

[39] "Mystery of Godliness" *TW*, 352.
[40] See J.van den Berg, "The Synod of Dort in the balance", this volume Ch. 1.
[41] Cf. Firth, *Apocalyptic Tradition*, 218.
[42] "Mystery of Godliness", *TW*, 145.
[43] "Mystery of Godliness", *TW*, 123, 143.
[44] "Ratio", *Opera Theologica*, 43.

very end of the world—this he considered a chimerical fiction—but rather the personification of the dominance of "Pagano-Christian Idolatry".[45] The Reformation, on the other hand, implied the resurrection of the two witnesses, whom he saw as types of the Old and New Testament (a revival of pure biblical doctrine) and of the magistracy and ministry (a revival of the right order in State and Church).[46] And nowhere was the restoration of the true church more clearly visible than in the Church of England: "the prophecy of the resurrection of the witnesses fell out most fully and orderly in our English Reformation, where the Ecclesiastical Witness mounted the highest among the Reformed Churches into the Prophetic Heaven".[47] Therefore, its apocalyptic context "should make our Reformation the more Sacred, and awe men off from either violently tearing it in Pieces, or more hiddenly and obliquely corrupting it by foisting in any old out-cast Ware disallowed and rejected by our Pious and Judicious Reformers".[48] No doubt this sentence contains a defence of the middle way of Anglicanism against open or hidden attacks from Puritan or Romanizing quarters.

But although More was deeply committed to the cause of the Reformation, especially in its English form, he did not go as far as to identify the Reformation with the greatest event of all, the beginning of the millennium. In the resurrection of the witnesses, a specimen of the fall of Antichrist was given; but "the Sins of our Churches may prove an Obstacle, to retard the final approaching Ruin of *Antichrist*, and the Hastening of the Philadelphian age".[49] The Church of the Reformation is, like the Church in Sardis, in a very imperfect state—wandering "between Egypt and the Land of Promise, which is the Philadelphian State". In this context, More mentions "the Relaxation of Probity of Life and Manners, and the noisy Debates and Contentions about mere Trifles".[50] In the "Epistle Dedicatory" to John Lord Robarts, Lord Privy Seal, which accompanied the first edition of the *Exposition of the Seven Epistles to the Seven Churches* from which these quotations are taken, More wrote after having mentioned the Philadelphian Church:

> Which therefore cannot but be a Note of main importance for all Reformed States and Kingdomes to steer their Affairs by, namely, to bind their course thitherward

---

[45] "Synopsis Prophetica, or The Second Part of the Enquiry into the Mystery of Iniquity", *TW*, 569.

[46] *Apocalypsis*, 103. In "Mystery of Godliness", however, More states that the "Divisions of Churches" indicate that all is not yet.right, and that the Witnesses are not yet alive ...", *TW*, 142; an idea, which he later rejected: "Preface", *TW*, XIII.

[47] "Preface", *TW*, VIII.

[48] "Mystery of Iniquity" II, *TW*, 716.

[49] "Mystery of Iniquity" II, *TW*, 635; cf. "Ratio", *Op. Theol.*, 44.

[50] "A Prophetical Exposition of the Seven Epistles Sent to the Seven Churches in Asia", *TW*, 762.

whither they are pointed to by the Finger of God himself in his Holy Oracles. For they sail as it were with winde and tide whose carriage of Affairs approaches the nearest to the purpose of Divine Fate.[51]

"Philadelphia" embodied a high ideal: the promise of a blessed future state, a challenge to the Reformed churches and nations to turn away from all that recalled the former state of "idolatry". In this connection, he mentioned a specific form of "idolatry", the erection of a false image of God in the minds of men, which cannot be anything else but the "high Calvinist" image of the God of the absolute decree of reprobation as contrasted with the idea of a God whose essence is universal love.[52]

More did not believe the beginning of the millennium would bear a dramatic character or would be accompanied by miraculous events:

... this only remains for Protestants. That they compute the Approaching of the final Ruin of *Antichrist*, and of the *blessed Millennium*, according to their Advances in the Mystery of *real Regeneration* and the indispensable Duties of Christianity. *The more holy, the more innocent, the more humble, the more vehemently aspiring after heavenly Goods they find one another; the more prudent they be, the more faithful and obedient to the publick Magistrate; the more meek and benevolent towards one another, and the more earnestly they bind all their Endeavours to promote the publick Good and the common Felicity of all Mankind*, (which assuredly will introduce the *Philadelphian* interval) *The more they may conclude the Ruin of Antichrist, and the glorious Reign of Christ with his Saints in the blessed Millennium to be.*[53]

For More, the millennium had first of all a spiritual dimension; Christ's kingdom was a kingdom of peace and love, the empire of the divine virtue of charity, marked by reason, humanity and tender lovingkindness.[54] All this did not detract from the historical and realistic character the expected millennium had for More. In this context, I cannot refrain from quoting a passage from the dedication of the famous sermon More's fellow-Platonist Ralph Cudworth preached in 1647, in the period of the Civil War, befor the House of Commons.[55] Implicitly referring to the millennial expectations of those times Cudworth remarked that justice and righteousness, together with a good peace, well settled in a Commonwealth, are all the outward felicities we can expect, "till that happy Time come, which the *Prophet* foretelleth, and is therefore more than a Platonicall idea ..." More's expositions on the subject,

---

[51] *An Exposition of the Seven Epistles to the Seven Churches*, London 1669, f. A 6[vo].
[52] "Mystery of Godliness", *TW*, 142f.
[53] "Seven Epistles", *TW*, 761.
[54] "Mystery of Iniquity" I, *TW*, 499.
[55] R. Cudworth, *A Sermon Preached before the Honourable House of Commons ... March 31, 1647*, Cambridge 1647 (repr. New York 1930), "To the Honourable House of Commons". Apart from one remark in Part. II, Ch. V, § 91, Cudworth does not deal with the subject of the millennium in his "magnum opus" *The True Intellectual System of The Universe* (1678).

written many years later are quite in line with Cudworth's elementary remarks. More looked forward to "Philadelphian" times, in which the Church would be pure and the life of the whole community would be permeated by the spirit of the Gospel.

Those times would also have a political dimension. We should neither overemphasize nor underestimate the meaning of the word "political" in connection with More's millenarian ideals. The primary motives behind his chiliastic expectations were of a religious nature. "Life" and "Spirit" would be the most essential characteristics of the Philadelphian state.[56] But this did not exclude the political aspect: "That Millennial Happiness that some Men talk so loud of, is not in demolishing of all Ranks and Orders of Superiority in *Church* or *State* ... but in the right Administration of Affairs in both ...".[57] In the period of the binding of Satan, a "Nova Politia" would replace the "Politia Idololatrica". This new "Politia" would be created by a "Concilium"[58]—an idea we also meet with More's contemporary Comenius.[59] In his *Apocalypsis Apocalypseos* More speaks of

> a Polity here upon Earth, and of Divine Institution, and to be settled after the utter destruction of the Whore of *Babylon*, by a Council truly Holy, and *truly Oecumenical*, being persons of pure and upright Spirits, and without all worldly interest, and moreover inspired extraordinarily by the Spirit of God ...[60]

In the way he formulated his views with regard to the political dimension of the millennium his aversion from the radical chiliasm of the Fifth Monarchy Men played a large part.

> It is ... but a Fanatick or Satanick Fury in such that under pretence of ushering in *the fifth Monarchy*, as they call it, would destroy *all Orders and Ranks* in *Church* and *State*, as if *the wrath of man could work the Righteousness* of God: when neither these Orders themselves have an Unholiness in them, nor the Persons haply in possession are less Saints then they that would pull down.

---

[56] Cf. his comparison between the Philadelphian and the Laodicean state: "Laodicea will be left Heir to all the Riches of her Sister Philadelphia ... saving the Life and the Spirit", "Seven Epistles", *TW*, 759.

[57] "Mystery of Godliness", *TW*, 144f

[58] "Ratio", *Op. Theol.*, 39.

[59] Comenius dealt with the idea of an "Oecumenicum Concilium", to be held at the beginning of the "septimum Mundi millenarium", the period of the "universalis reformatio", in his *De rerum humanarum emendatione*, which was not published until this century; II, Prahae 1966, c. 658-681; cf. J.M. van der Linde, *De wereld heeft toekomst*, Kampen 1979, ch. III. There is a parallel between the ideas of More and those of Comenius, and though, as far as we know, there were no direct contacts between the two scholars, Comenius was possibly acquainted with More's poems: M. Blekastad, *Comenius*, Oslo-Praha 1969, 3.

[60] *Apocalypsis Apocalypseos*, 215.

Those who "are gaping after a *fifth Monarchy* in this sense" and thus are "thirsting after Spoil and Blood" will be carried along by the "Tide of Divine Vengeance",

> ... which will ever and anon flow in upon the Church, till a true and sincere Reformation. For there is no *Stability* to the expected ... *till that Church appear that is purely Apostolical in Life and Doctrine.*[61]

More's millennium was a well-ordered society, whose spiritual centre would be a truly reformed Church, which would bear all the marks of the Church of England as More wanted her to be. Like Mede, More was not interested in the idea of a personal reign of Christ on earth, as some chiliasts were.

> But that there may be a *Millennium* ... or a long period of time wherein a more excellent Reign of Christ than has manifested itself yet to the World may take place, truly it seems so reasonable in it self, and there are such shrewd Places of Scripture seem to speak that way, that it is hard for an indifferent Man to gain-say it.

His description of the millennium is based on biblical elements, while at the same time we may discern a slightly Platonic ring. The "Renovation of the State of things" will lead to new heavens and a new earth "wherein righteousness shall dwell; wherein *real Sanctity* and *universal Peacefulness* shall bear Sway". And the power of the Spirit of Christ "shall be more potently felt for the *unpaganizing* of the World, and for the destroying of this spiritual Idolatry, which is the inordinate Affections and fierce Endeavours of the *Animal Life*". More's irenical intention reflected itself in his description of a society in which "all the goodly Inventions of nice Theologers shall ... cease, and all the foolish and perplexing Arguments of the disputacious Schools shall be laid aside ..."[62]

With More, the idea of the conversion of the Jews did not take such an important place as with Mede, but fundamentally there was no difference. He, too, believed that in the millennium "the Jews will be called, and make one part of the Catholic Church ...". Mutations in the Turkish empire "will make for the joyning of the Jews, and it may be some other Eastern People ... with the Church of Christ".[63] Their conversion will take place in a miraculous way, of which Paul is the prophetic type. Some places in Scripture "may incline a rational man to believe that some chief of the Jews, the most able, the most noted and most zealous of them for the Jewish Religion, may be called as Paul was. Whose Testimonies will awake all the Jewish Nation, and cause them more impartially to consider the Truth of Christian Religion". "For fuller

---

[61] "Mystery of Godliness", *TW*, 144f.
[62] "Mystery of Godliness", *TW*, 360f.
[63] *Apocalypsis*, XII, 161.

satisfaction" he referred to Mede. But while Mede spoke with full certainty, More was not so certain: "I do not love to dwell long on an agreement that I cannot so certainly and assuredly master."[64]

Together with Mede, More expected a conflagration of the world after the millennium. The earth and the surrounding air would be purified by fire. In that day, all the faithful "renew their strength, and shall mount up with Wings as Eagles, and be carried far above the reach of this dismal Fate; that is, they shall ascend up in those *Heavenly Chariots* or *Ethereal Vehicles* (the ancient Philosophers speak of) and so enter into Immortality and Eternal rest".[65]

More saw the conflagration as part of the day of judgement, which he did not identify—as Mede had done—with the millennium, but placed after the thousand years. It would be a day of "direful Vengeance", but "the victorious Church of Christ retreats with the rest of the Angelical Hosts, marching up the Ethereal Regions in goodly Order and lovely Equipage ...". The Faithful will now become "free Partakers of all the Rights and Immunities of the celestial Kingdom", where there is "Order and Government without Envy and Oppression, Devotion without Superstition, Beauty without Blemish ... lastly, where there is the Vision of God, the Society of *Christ*, the Familiarity of Angels, and Communion of Saints ..."[66]

As a millenarian, More was no exception in seventeenth century England. He even considered his own interpretation to be the "main Sense of the Protestants".[67] But over against the "prophetic explanation" of the apocalyptic parts of the Bible, of which Mede and More were the most prominent English representatives, stood a different hermeneutical model, represented by no one less than Grotius in his annotations on Daniel and the Apocalypse. It was a scholarly model, based on a primarily historical interpretation, which gave new support to the traditional anti-chiliastic explanation of biblical prophecy. In line with the views of the medieval theologians and of the Reformers, who followed in the steps of Augustine, Grotius placed the beginning of the millennium in the time of Constantine.[68] More, who had a deep respect for Grotius, confessed that he had almost fallen under the spell of the "ingenuities and prettinesses" of Grotius' explanation.[69] But ultimately he remained loyal to Mede, and in more than one of his works he attacked Grotius' exegesis.

---

[64] *Paralipomena Prophetica*, London 1685, 157.
[65] "Mystery of Godliness", *TW*, 156f.
[66] "Mystery of Godliness", *TW*, 314.
[67] "Mystery of Iniquity" II, *TW*, 631.
[68] "... mille istorum annorum initium duci debet ab Edicto Constantini, quod est apud Eusebium, in quo vincti draconis est mentio ...", *Annotationes in Novum Testamentum*, Pars tertia et ultima, Parisiis 1650, 264. For English reactions to Grotius views of the millenium, see also J. van den Berg, "Grotius' Views on Antichrist and Apocalyptic Thought in England", this volume Ch. 7.
[69] "Mystery of Godliness", *TW*, 119.

Of course, essential matters were at stake. If Grotius was right, the interpretation of the struggle between Rome and the Reformation as part of the apocalyptic events would have lost its biblical foundation, and the hope of better times would be a mere speculation. In that case, "this Book of Prophecies [the Revelation of St. John] would be utterly Useless ...".[70] Until the end, More strongly opposed the interpretation, given by "The Favourers *of Rome* and *Grotius*': the latter's exegesis "makes the very pretence of understanding Prophecies ridiculous, and deprives *Christ* of his *Glory* ... and the *Church* of her so *Eminent Priviledge* above all other Religions". The vehemency of More's language can perhaps partly be explained from the fact that in 1680 Grotius' approach enjoyed a fair amount of popularity: Grotius "is now accounted the *Chiefest Interpreter*, and most accommodate to baffle the true and genuine meaning of those Prophecies ...".[71]

A very personal attack on Grotius is to be found in More's commentary on Daniel. After having established that Grotius rejected the opinion of the primitive Church which made the fourth kingdom in Daniel the Roman one (Grotius saw it as that of the Lapides and Seleucides) More remarked: "By which device Grotius forsooth would excuse the Pope from being the little Horn with eyes, and consequently Antichrist". It was a dangerous deviation from orthodox opinion, More thought; to which Grotius had come "as it seems to me partly out of the distaste he had taken against the Reformed Church of Holland for their usage of him, and partly to glaver [to flatter] and curry favour with the Pontifician party".[72]

He was all the more offended when in 1685 the prominent Puritan theologian Richard Baxter rather lightheartedly dealt with the millenarian ideals of Mede, More and others. In his *A Paraphrase on the New Testament* Baxter wrote in connexion with the interpretation of "the Book of Revelations":

> Forty years ago, when I was but young, I studied it (I doubt too soon) and read *Brightman, Napier, Pareus* etc. and after that *Mede, Potter ... Broughton* ... And when since I read Mr. *Durham, Dr. Moor*, etc. and *Grotius*, and Dr. *Hammond*, and many annotators, I confess despair, and more needful business made me do it but superficially.[73]

Ultimately, with regard to the question of the millennium Baxter had more affinity with the opinion of Grotius and of his English follower Henry Hammond, who declared he wrote "in a way which is very remote from the

---

[70] "Mystery of Godliness", *TW*, 138.

[71] *Apocalypsis*, XV, XVIII.

[72] *Exposition of Daniel*, XXXVIIf

[73] R. Baxter, *A Paraphrase on the New Testament ... With an Advertisement of Difficulties in the Revelations*, London 1685, f Q 2[vo]. For the differences between Baxter and More with regard to this point, see also W M. Lamont, *Richard Baxter and the Millennium*, London 1979, esp. 52ff.

conceits of the *Millenaries*",[74] than with those of Mede and More. He refused to follow Mede and More in their straightforward identification of the Papacy with Antichrist; he would neither affirm nor deny that Papacy was Antichrist, but saw no evidence to prove the affirmative. As a matter of fact, he did not think the point very relevant: "I do judge of Popery by the knowledge of its particular Errours and Sins, and not by the Revelations, or any thing which I understand not." In line with Grotius, he saw the beginning of the millennium in the time of Constantine, when "the Kingdoms of the World were made the Kingdoms of Christ: therefore I dread the denying Christ these Kingdoms, and reproaching even the best Ages of his Church on Earth as Antichristian". Of course, he would not deny the usefulness of the Book of Revelation (a point which More so strongly stressed in defence of his millenarian explanation): on the contrary, "it is of exceeding comfortable use: Though I know not whether the New *Jerusalem* will come down from Heaven before, or at the Common Resurrection, it rejoiceth me that it will come ...". Nor did he want to give any support to the "Friends to Papal Usurpation but, it is far more dreadful to the Pope, and all his Flatterers, and Followers, to be plainly condemned by the known Laws of Christ ... than to be under the Dread of a dark and controverted Prophecie".[75]

It were expressions like these, which angered More, who took up the gauntlet in a pamphlet, published under the pseudonym "Philicrines Parrhesiastes". He wrote about "the odd and indeed impious Carriage of R.B." and deeply resented the injury Baxter had done to "the Spirit of Prophecy in the Holy Scriptures" and consequently "to the whole Church of Christ, to the Church of England and to Dr. H.M". More accused Baxter of a sceptical attitude towards "all the Prophecies of the Scripture": "All the advantages of an explanation of prophecy as Mede had given R.B. gives away in an unaccountable Freak of *Scepticism*". Furthermore, he reproached Baxter of having "a Wooden Soul" and "a Stony Heart" with regard to the calling of the Jews.[76] More could not understand how "a Man so operosely and affectedly professing himself for *Peace* and *Love* should be content that God should be so irreconcileably in *Wrath* toward the Nation of the Jews, as to leave them in the lurch for ever ...". Why did Baxter "slur the Learned and Pious Labours of Mr. Mede"?[77]

---

[74] H. Hammond, *A Paraphrase, and Annotations upon all the Books of the New Testament*, London 1659 (first cd. 1653), 941.

[75] Baxter, *Paraphrase*, f.R 2vo, $3^{ro,vo}$, 4ro.

[76] Here, More refers to a rather scathing attack by Baxter on Brightman's views with regard to a miraculous conversion of the Jews: *Paraphrase*, f. Q 3vo, 4ro.

[77] Phililicrines [sic] Parrhesiastes, *Some cursory reflexions impartially made upon Mr. Richard Baxter his way of writing notes on the Apocalypse*, London 1685, f. A $1^{ro,vo}$, 12,3 (published together with *Paralipomena*).

More considered the vindication of Mede's method in interpreting the Apocalypse "the rescuing of the Book it self into the Power and Use it ought to have in the Church: for it is a 'a standing light' to all the ages thereof ...".[78] He was too sanguine in his belief in the value of Mede's interpretation, but Mede was, indeed, still a guide for men of a more enlightened generation like Isaac Newton and William Whiston. In 1680, More discussed his millennial ideas, as expressed in his *Apocalypsis Apocalypseos*,[79] with Newton. At first he thought there was full agreement between him and Newton with regard to "Apocalyptical Notions"; later he perceived there were differences, which, however, did not disturb their friendship.[80] For Newton, not More, but Mede was the great authority in apocalyptic matters.[81] As we saw the same holds true for Whiston, who in his synchronistic system followed the lead of "the incomparable Mr. Mede", though not without some critical remarks in connection with a number of details in Mede's interpretation.[82] There is a remarkable continuity with regard to the basic system, though within a changing context.

In this line of development, More takes a place of his own. The framework of his chiliastic ideas is that of Mede: a system, he believed, which guaranteed a mathematical certainty in the explanation of the apocalyptic parts of the Bible. But his millenarian views are not just a replica of those of Mede—there is a slight change of atmosphere which reveals something of the special character of More's world of thought. It is not easy to detect specifically Platonic traits in his eschatological views, and his millennium is (as much as that of Cudworth) more than, "a Platonicall idea", but still there are some indications of a more or less Platonic approach. I think here of his statement that in the millennium the Spirit of Christ will destroy the endeavours of the "animal life"; also of his description of the "ethereal vehicles" which shall take up the blessed into heaven.[83] In some respects, he was a man of a vanishing world; thus, when he tried to confirm the idea of a "conflagration" through the testimony of the ancient philosophers.[84] But at the same time he was a man of a modern world, when he attempted to prove the reasonableness of the same idea with the help of scientific or semi-scientific arguments.[85] Here as elsewhere

---

[78] "Mystery of Godliness", *TW*, 138.

[79] Newton's copy of the work is in the possession of Christ's College Cambridge(Shelfmark CC. 5. 15); it bears the inscription: Is. Newton Ex dono Rndi Auctoris Feb. 18 1680/1.

[80] More to J. Sharp, 16 August, 1680, in: M.H. Nicolson, *The Conway Letters* (rev. edition, ed. by S. Hutton), Oxford 1993, 478f.

[81] For this, see esp. F.E. Manuel, *Isaac Newton Historian*, Cambridge (Mass.) 1963, 175f.

[82] *Essay*, 86.

[83] For Platonic traits in his description of heavenly life, see Tuveson, *Millennium and Utopia*, 94f.

[84] "Mystery of Godliness", *TW*, 28.

[85] "Mystery of Godliness", *TW*, 159ff.

we meet with a certain dualism between mysticism and rationalism which more than one author on More has noted.[86]

His commitment to the Church of England played a large part in his conception of the millennium. To a certain extent, his description of the millennial state was a projection of the pattern of the Anglican establishment upon the screen of the future: "... there is not any Book in the World that makes more for the Establishment of the *Crown* and *Church of England* than this Holy Book of the Apocalypse".[87] The reverse of this was his fierce rejection of all revolutionary chiliastic conceptions, especially in his "Mystery of Godliness", written under the still vivid impressions of the events of the Commonwealth period. He shared Mede's strong bias against Rome, and in this context his tone could become extremely militant, so when he wrote that Christ himself with his "Apostolical Legions of Reformed Christians" would utterly demolish and destroy "the Papal Empire or Hierarchy".[88] But nevertheless he expected the future conversion of "Rome Pagano-Christian" to "the Ancient, pure and Apostolick Christianity",[89] and though he spoke in high terms of the Reformation he was not blind to the defects of the Reformed Churches. He looked forward to the time when "*Calvinism, Lutheranism, Popery*, and whatever else savours of Sects and Discords of Minds and Opinions shall be melted down into one ... both as to Life and Doctrine, truly Catholick and Apostolical *Philadelphianism*".[90] His description of the "Philadelphian State" reflects his warm and somehow mystically coloured spirituality,[91] which reminds us of congenial traits in continental Pietism. More's millennium is above all a time of charity and justice, in particular towards the poor and the oppressed; a time in which the Church will return to its pristine apostolic purity and in which the world will be at peace: "not a Kingdom of *Belluine Ferocity*, but of *Reason, Humanity*, and *tender Loving Kindness*".[92]

---

[86] Lichtenstein, *Henry More*, 19.

[87] "Mystery of Iniquity" II, *TW*, 713.

[88] *Apocalypsis*, 95. It would be tempting to relate these militant utterances, published in 1680, with the growing anti-Catholic mood in England at that time, but in earlier works, e.g. *Mystery of Iniquity* (1664), we meet with equally strong expressions. In a letter to Archbishop William Sancroft, to whom he sent a copy of his *Apocalypsis Apocalypseos*, More made it clear that he had not written his commentary on Revelation in view of the special circumstances of those times - "But that it is come out so seasonably in this grand tug between Protestantisme and Poperie, I must confess that can not be ascribed to any prudence of mine but merely to Divine Providence", More to Sancroft, 2 January 1679/80, Bodleian Library, MS Tanner 38, f. 115.

[89] "Mystery of Iniquity" II, *TW*, 863.

[90] *TW*, "Preface", XIV.

[91] "An aspirant for mysticism More perhaps was, but a mystic, hardly ...": Lichtenstein, *Henry More*, *loc. cit.*

[92] "Mystery of Iniquity" I, *TW*, 499.

It was a high ideal: inspiring, but at the same time critical: "… this *Apocalyptick* Glass is not only for the *Romanist* but all the Churches of Christendom to look their Faces in".[93]

---

[93] "Mystery of Godliness", *TW*, 142.

CHAPTER SEVEN

GROTIUS' VIEWS ON ANTICHRIST AND APOCALYPTIC THOUGHT IN ENGLAND

In a most interesting essay, Hugh Trevor-Roper depicts Grotius' attitude towards England as a love-affair, "a platonic love for an idealized England".[1] In many respects it was love on both sides, as appears in the field of theology: while Grotius sympathized with the theological climate of the Church of England (or rather with the ideal image he had formed of the *Ecclesia Anglicana*), quite a number of Anglicans highly esteemed him for his moderate and latitudinarian way of thinking. On the English side, however, the esteem was not unmixed: even in the circle of those who to a large extent sympathized with Grotius' theological approach there was criticism with regard to his interpretation of the figure of Antichrist. On this point, the ways sometimes parted.

Sixteenth and early seventeenth century Protestantism, however much divided on many theological and ecclesiastical issues, was marked by a broad consensus regarding the mysterious words in I John 2.18: "Little children, it is the last time: and as ye have heard that antichrist shall come, even now there are many antichrists."[2] In this context, II Thessalonians 2.3-4 also played an important part: "Let no man deceive you by any means; for that day shall not come, except there come a falling away first, and that man of sin is revealed, the son of perdition, who opposeth and exalteth himself above all that is called God, or that is worshipped; so that he as God sitteth in the temple of God, shewing himself that he is God". Furthermore, Antichrist and "the man of sin" were often equated with the "beast" of the Apocalypse with seven heads and ten horns, "and upon his heads the name of blasphemy" (Rev. 13.1). It is clear that the image of the "beast" harks back to pre-Christian Jewish thought, as it is expressed in the prophecies of Daniel, where a "beast" is depicted as speaking great words against the most High, and wearing out the saints of the most High, and thinking to change times and laws (Dan. 13.7). As we shall see, in the period of the Reformation these texts were generally projected upon the Pope or rather upon the papacy as an institution which manifested itself as "antichristian".

The "papal" interpretation was not an invention of the Reformers: it oc-

[1] "Hugo Grotius and England", in Hugh Trevor-Roper, *From Counter-Reformation to Glorious Revolution*, London 1992, 47.

[2] Here, as elsewhere, I quote the *Authorized Version* (1611).

curred already in the later Middle Ages in heretical circles.[3] There is, however, a not inconsiderable difference between the late-medieval and the Protestant identification of the Pope with Antichrist. While certain medieval groups could see one specific Pope as Antichrist because his life and attitude were in radical conflict with the demands of the Gospel, the Reformers tended to identify the institution of the papacy with Antichrist. They saw the papacy as a manifestation of the spirit of Antichrist: it defended and maintained false doctrines which ran counter to the pure message of the Bible as it had been rediscovered by the Reformation, and it persecuted those who wanted to return to the pure and undiluted doctrine of the primitive church. When in Protestant circles "the Pope" was denounced as Antichrist, the identification had not primarily a personal and incidental meaning; it was a pronouncement of an essentially theological nature, directed against an institution which was structurally and fundamentally evil, though of course the boundary-line between the personal and the structural aspects was sometimes blurred. Indignation at the persecution of the "true believers" could lead to an identification of the person of the Pope with Antichrist.

Among the prominent Reformers, Luther was the first who used the term "Antichrist" in connection with the Pope—explicitly in his reaction to his excommunication in 1520: *Adversus execrabilem Antichristi bullam*. In this context, Hans Hillerbrand remarks: "Luther's blunt identification of Pope and Antichrist constituted the watershed in the early Reformation controversy ... The concept of the Antichrist was ... whatever it was theologically, a propaganda tool employed to repudiate the papacy in the strongest way possible".[4] There is with Luther a sideline: he saw the Turk or Saracen as a minor Antichrist, but in the full sense the Pope was Antichrist, because he was active as persecutor of Christ within the church.[5] We meet the same identification between Pope and Antichrist with the other Reformers. Melanchthon wrote about the necessity to counteract the Pope "tamquam Antichristo",[6] and Calvin described the Pope as the leader and head of the impious and execrable kingdom of Antichrist.[7] This view remained a constant element in the Protestant

---

[3] For the interpretation of the figure of Antichrist in the Middle Ages, see Hans Preuss, *Die Vorstellungen vom Antichrist im späteren Mittelalter, bei Luther und in der konfessionellen Polemik*, Leipzig 1906, 4-82; Norman Cohn, *The Pursuit of the Millennium* (1957), London 1970; Marjorie Reeves, *Joachim of Fiore and the Prophetic Future*, London 1976; Richard K. Emmerson, *Antichrist in the Middle Ages*, Manchester 1981; furthermore Gustav Adolf Benrath's contribution to the article "Antichrist" in *Theologische Realenzyklopädie* III (1978), 20-28.

[4] H.J. Hillerbrand, "The Antichrist in the Early German Reformation: Reflections on Theology and Propaganda," in A.C. Fix and Susan C. Karant-Nunn, *Germania Illustrata. Essays ... presented to Gerald Strauss* (Sixteenth Century Essays and Studies XVIII), Ann Arbor 1992, 16f.

[5] Gottfried Seebass, "Antichrist," *TRE* III, 30.

[6] Preuss, *Die Vorstellungen vom Antichrist*, 203.

[7] *Institutio religionis christianae* (1559) IV, VII, 25.

tradition. In the marginal notes to the Dutch "States" translation,[8] which first appeared in 1637, three years before Grotius' *Commentatio ad loca quaedam N. Testamenti quae de Antichristo agunt, aut agere putantur*[9] was published anonymously in Amsterdam, the "Beast" or "Antichrist" was identified as a long succession of persons who tried to suppress the true doctrine of Christ and his church. He would give himself splendid and alluring titles, such as "Holy Father" and "Vicar of Christ." Some Popes could be singled out as pre-eminent representatives of the spirit of Antichrist, such as Gregory VII, no doubt primarily because of his affirmation of the doctrine of transubstantiation.[10] The "Beast" and the "False Prophet" signified the spiritual and worldly dominion of Antichrist "with all its mitred and armed substitutes".[11]

Similar notions prevailed in English Protestant circles.[12] The idea that the papal power was a manifestation of the spirit of Antichrist was a common opinion not only with puritanically-minded authors such as John Foxe (1516-1587), the martyrologist, but also with middle-of-the-road Anglicans such as the famous apologist Bishop John Jewel (1522-1571). The theme returns with seventeenth-century Anglican millenarians, of whom the Cambridge theologian Joseph Mede (1586-1638) is one of the most outstanding representatives; the scheme, which he expounded in his *Clavis Apocalyptica* (1627) and his *In Sancti Joannis Apocalypsis Commentarius* (1632) became the basis for practically all later apocalyptic and millenarian speculations in the English-speaking world. Mede was a consistent futurist: though he did not speculate on the exact date of the millennium, he expected the dawn of the thousand years of peace, predicted in Revelation 20, within a not too distant future. There is a connection between his (traditionally Protestant) conception of Antichrist and his millennial views: the fall of Antichrist (*i.e.* the ultimate defeat of the "Roman" power) would ring in the millennium.[13]

---

[8] In the Commonwealth period they were translated by Theodore Haak (one of the founders of the Royal Society) at the request of the Westminster Assembly: *The Dutch Annotations upon the whole Bible, together with, and according to their verse translation of all the text*, London 1657.

[9] J. ter Meulen and P.J.J. Diermanse, *Bibliographie des écrits imprimés de Hugo Grotius*, 's-Gravenhage 1950 (further *BG*) no. 1100.

[10] *The Heidelberg Catechism* (1563) described the Mass, founded as it was on this doctrine, as a "damnable idolatry" (Answer 80).

[11] See the marginal notes to 2 Thess. 2.3; 1 John 2.18; Rev, 17.4; 20.8 and other places.

[12] For this, see in particular Christopher Hill, *Antichrist in Seventeenth-Century England*, Oxford 1971; Richard Bauckham, *Tudor Apocalypse*, Appleford 1978; Paul Christianson, *Reformers and Babylon: English apocalyptic visions from the reformation to the eve of the civil war*, Toronto etc, 1978; Katherine R. Firth, *The Apocalyptic Tradition in Reformation Britain*, Oxford 1979.

[13] For his millenarianism and that of his pupil Henry More (to be mentioned below), see J. van den Berg, "Continuity within a changing context: the Apocalyptic Thought of Joseph Mede and Henry More", this volume Ch. 6.

As Christopher Hill points out, in the mid-thirties it had suddenly become unfashionable and unpopular to say that the Pope was Antichrist. A number of "Laudians"—followers or supporters of William Laud, the "Arminian" theologian who in 1633 became Archbishop of Canterbury and who, accused of treason and "Popery," was executed in 1645—objected to a too easy identification between Pope and Antichrist. At his trial, Laud declared: "No man can challenge me that I hold the Pope not to be Antichrist; it is a great question even among learned protestants whether he be so or not".[14] His irenic attitude towards the Church of Rome was indeed one of the factors, if not the main factor, which led to his tragic fate. On this point, he fundamentally differed from Mede, who in spite of his tolerant and latitudinarian frame of mind was uncompromising in his anti-Roman demeanour. This is the reason why Mede, though he cannot be considered a Puritan, received posthumous recognition in the Commonwealth period. A first edition of his (largely unpublished) *Works* appeared in 1648. The third edition (1672) contains an anonymous "Life," probably written by John Worthington, the learned theologian who between 1650 and 1660 was Master of Jesus College, Cambridge and who in many ways was a kindred spirit. According to the "Life," Mede constantly asserted,

> That the *Great Apostasie* or *Antichristianism* did (as to one main part thereof) consist in *Spiritual Fornication* or *Idolatry*. Nor need any Protestant be disturb'd at the word *Antichristian* or *Antichrist*, so frequently used by our Author [Mede] when he had to doe with the Roman Polity and the Chief thereof ...

Mede, the "Life" continues, was well aware that the Antichrist or Antichrists mentioned in St. John's Epistles might primarily respect some impostors, who began to appear in the world about the end of the Jewish State, but he thought that what was said of those Antichrists might interpretatively (though not explicitly and directly) be applied to "that *Fatal and Great Apostasie* which was to surprise the Church": to him of whom those other Antichrists were in some sense "Figures or Forerunners".

> For this was his Notion in this particular, He that sets up and substitutes in the room of *Christ* Saints and Angels, as so many Mediatours between us and God, (agreeably to the practice of the Heathens, who of old set up *Daemons* as Agents between the Sovereign Gods and Men,) *eo ipso negat Jesum esse Christum* ...

Mede was not "fondly addicted" to the use of the word Antichrist. He also made use of other forms of speech, suggested to him from the style of that "Mysterious book," the Apocalypse, such as "*Bestia Bicornis, Pseudo-propheta Romanus, Meretrix Babylonica, Regnum Pontificale* etc." Yet "withall

---

[14] Hill, *Antichrist*, 39f.

he was not so weakly nice, as wholly to decline that word [Antichrist] in his Apocalyptick labours."

The author of the "Life" emphasizes that in this he was in line with the Anglican tradition. Archbishop Whitgift had, when he answered for the degree of D.D., defended the thesis: *Papa est ille Antichristus*. And Bishop Andrewes, "his ancient and constant friend," had stated that

> by *Babylon* in *Apocal.* chap. 17 and chap. 18, is meant, *non Roma Ethnica, sed Antichristiana*; and withall evinces the vanity of that poor subterfuge, and yet made use of (as that other also of *Roma Ethnica*) by *H. Grotius* in his Annotations), That by the *Destruction of Babylon* there foretold is to be understood the *Burning of Rome* by the Goths and Vandals about the year 455. As afterwards he makes it clear that *Idolatry* ... is justly charged upon the *Roman* Church ...[15]

The "Life" of Mede was written at a time when the views of Grotius were well known in England. Though some of the Laudians had already called into question the traditional interpretation of Antichrist, Grotius' explicit rejection of the Protestant consensus was a shock to the great majority of English Protestants. Katherine Firth remarks:

> Grotius had done what seemed impossible to most Protestants—he had dispensed not only with the idea that the Revelation comprehended the history of the Church from Christ to the second coming but also with the identification of the Roman papacy with Antichrist. This struck at the heart of the Protestant apocalyptic tradition.[16]

Grotius' *Commentatio ... de Antichristo*, which was published in 1640, two years after the death of Mede, appeared (as we saw) anonymously; at Grotius' own request, "ut quam minimo cum praejudicio legeretur".[17] Apparently, Grotius feared that the *Commentatio* would meet with strong opposition. His fears were not unfounded: in the same year appeared a refutation by Samuel Maresius, at that time professor at the "Illustrious School" of Bois-le-Duc, later professor of theology at the University of Groningen: *Dissertatio de Antichristo*;[18] from the full title it becomes clear that Maresius was aware of Grotius' authorship.[19] In 1641 Grotius answered, now under his own name, in his *Appendix ad interpretationem locorum N. Testamenti quae de Antichristo agunt*. In his exegesis of the relevant texts he gave a historical explanation. He identified "the man of sin," "the son of perdition" of II Thessalonians 2.3 with

---

[15] *The Work of the Pious and Profoundly-learned Joseph Mede, B.D.*, London 1672, XXVIIf. For Whitgift, the "Life" refers to Whitgift's "Life" by Sir George Paule (1609); for Andrewes to his *Tortura Torti* (1609), 183; 188.

[16] Firth, *The Apocalyptic Tradition*, 246.

[17] *BG* 542.

[18] For this and what follows, see D. Nauta, *Samuel Maresius*, Amsterdam 1935, 168-72.

[19] Cf. *BG* 542.

the Emperor Caligula ("Cajus"), "that Wicked" in the same chapter (vs. 8) with Simon Magus (Acts 8.9-25) and "Antichrist" (I John 2,18) with the pseudo-Messiah Barkochba. The blasphemous Beast which rose up out of the sea represented the idolatry of heathen Rome (Rev, 13.I; "ex mari" is "ex populo Romano"), while "the great whore that sitteth upon many waters" (Rev. 17.I) was equally identified with "Roma gentilis."[20] The indefatigable Maresius, with whom Grotius had rather haughtily dealt in his *Appendix*,[21] reacted in a lengthy work: *Concordia discors et Antichristus revelatus. Id est Ill. Viri Hugonis Grotii Apologia pro Papa et Papismo* (two volumes, 1642). The sub-title reveals the core of the controversy. Maresius' accusation that Grotius' publications on "Antichrist" were an apology for the Pope and for the "papal" church was unfair. It is clear, however, that there was a connection between Grotius' irenicism and his view of Antichrist: "... eorum qui schisma esse perpetuum volunt, qui ad ipsum unitatis Ecclesiae ac concordiae nomen confremissent, interest Papam credi Antichristum."[22]

In Reformed circles in the Netherlands the idea that the Pope was Antichrist remained prevalent until far into the eighteenth century. Orthodox Lutherans, too, objected to Grotius' exegesis; thus the well-known polemicist Abraham Calovius tried to refute the "nugae Grotii de Caio" in his *Biblia Illustrata* (1676).[23] Even the Remonstrants did not follow Grotius: in his *Theologia Christiana* the leading Remonstrant theologian Philippus a Limborch defended the general opinion of the Reformers "per Antichristum designari Pontificem Romanum."[24]

In England Grotius was respected as a scholar, though even in the Laudian period, when the prevailing anti-Calvinist climate seemed favourable to the spread of his views, he did not meet with such response as he had hoped for. Laud was cautious and reserved, and Grotius' reputation was somewhat under a cloud, first because of the accusation of Socinianism, then because of his supposed "popish" sympathies.[25] Still, his works were known and read. *De satisfactione Christi* (1617) was published in Oxford in 1636; *De veritate*

---

[20] *Opera Theologica* III, 458, 466, 471ff., 490. See also the "Annotationes" on the New Testament, *Op. Theol.* II/2, 953f., 113f., 1200f., 1214.

[21] He did not mention Maresius's name, but called him "Borborita," a contemptuous word which contained an allusion to the name of his opponent: Des Marets, "of the bog"; see Nauta, *Maresius*, 170 with reference to Bayle's *Dictionnaire* III (ed. 1740), 323.

[22] "Appendix," *Op. Theol.* III, 475.

[23] A. Calovius, *Biblia Novi Testamenti Illustrata* II, Dresdae et Lipsiae 1719, 901-18; cf. 1616ff, 1624, 1841-59, 1880-96. In his criticism of Grotius, Calovius follows Maresius. See also Preuss, *Die Vorstellungen vom Antichrist*, 265 n. 1.

[24] *Theologia Christiana ad praxin pietatis ac promotionem pacis Christianae unice directa*, Amstelaedami 1686, 833; cf. liber VII, cap. XII (pp. 841-45): "Examen sententiae H. Grotii de Antichristo."

[25] Trevor-Roper, "Hugo Grotius and England," 70f.

religionis Christianae (1627) in 1639.[26] In the Commonwealth period his works seem to have been easily available. When in 1653 a friend of Richard Baxter complained that he had not been able to find the works of Grotius (and those of Du Plessis-Mornay and Cameron) in a Westminster library, Baxter wrote back: "Whereas you say that your library has not Grotius, Camero or Mornay, I answer they are common bookes as most in the shops".[27] In 1660 the *Commentatio* was published in England in the seventh volume of the *Critici Sacri*,[28] and thus within easy reach of scholars in the Universities.

Grotius had his critics, but also his supporters. One of the most outspoken among them was the Anglican theologian Henry Hammond (1605-1660), a Laudian, though not extreme.[29] He was on friendly terms with the Calvinist primate of Ireland James Ussher; also with Baxter, who wrote: "I took the Death of Dr. Hammond ... just when the King came in [at his return from the Continent] for a very great loss; for his Piety and Wisdom would sure have hindred much of the Violence which after followed."[30] Hammond was an admirer of Grotius. In a treatise on the Epistles of Ignatius and the doctrine of episcopacy (1655) he inserted "A digression concerning some jealousies spread of Hugo Grotius":

> This very learned, pious, judicious man hath of late among many fallen under a very unhappy fate, being most unjustly calumniated, sometimes as a *Socinian*, sometimes as a *Papist*, and as if he had learned to reconcile *Contradictories*, or the most *distant extreams* ...

Hammond defended him against both charges. He saw him as a friend and admirer of the Church of England, who sought nothing but "a universal reconciliation" of the church:

> ... all that this very learned man was guilty of in this matter, was but this, his passionate desire of the unity of the Church in the bands of peace and truth, and a full dislike of all uncharitable distempers, and impious doctrines ... All which notwithstanding, the temper of that learned man was known to be such, as rendred him in a special manner a lover and admirer of the frame and moderation observed in our Church of *England*, as it stood (shaken, but not cast down) in his life time, desiring earnestly to live himself in the Communion of it, and to see it copied out by the rest of the world.[31]

---

[26] *BG* nos. 925; 948.

[27] Baxter to Abraham Pinchbecke, 26 August 1653: N.H. Keeble and Geoffrey F. Nuttall, *Calendar of the Correspondence of Richard Baxter* I, Oxford 1991, nos. 127; 129.

[28] *BG* nos. 1142; 1143.

[29] See John W. Packer, *The Transformation of Anglicanism 1643-1660 with special reference to Henry Hammond*, Manchester 1969.

[30] *Reliquiae Baxterianae*, London 1696, II, 208, § 66; quoted in *Calendar* I, no. 582 (see also no. 581).

[31] *The Works of ... Henry Hammond* II (sec. ed., London 1684), section II, 45; 47.

Hammond's best known work is *A Paraphrase and Annotations upon all the Books of the New Testament* (1653); it was several times reprinted and it became a classic of seventeenth century Anglican theology. In his introduction to the annotations upon the Apocalypse he claimed his interpretation was original:

> And it has been matter of much satisfaction to me, that what hath upon sincere desire of finding out the truth, and making my addresses to God for his particular directions in this work of difficulty ... appeared to me to be the meaning of this prophesie, hath, for this main of it, in the same manner represented it self to several persons of great piety and learning (as since I have discerned) none taking it from the other, but all from the same light shining in the Prophecie it self. Among which number I now also find the most learned *Hugo Grotius*, in those *posthumous* notes of his on the *Apocalypse*, lately publish'd.[32]

From the Puritan John Owen this elicited the sarcastic remark, transmitted to Hammond by one of Owen's correspondents, "that there are many complaine of your secret vain-glory, in seeking to disclaime the direction from H. Grotius in reference to your comment on the Revelation."[33] However this may be, it is clear that Grotius and Hammond used the same method in their interpretation of the Apocalypse. Hammond's approach to the mysteries of the Book of Revelation was historical and rational, in line with the general trend of his hermeneutics: "... the understanding the Word of God contain'd in the Scripture is no work of extraordinary Illumination, but must be attained by the same means, or the like, by which other writings of men are expounded ..."[34] Of course he did not deny the presence of a prophetic element in the Apocalypse: it would be anachronistic to expect with him or with Grotius a historical-critical approach in the modern sense, but regarded from the vantage-point of the seventeenth century their views of "the thousand years" (Revelation 20.3) were "preterist." Those thousand years, Hammond remarked, noted "the tranquillity and freedom from persecutions that should be allowed the Church of Christ from the time of Constantines coming to the Empire".[35] In his interpretation of II Thessalonians 2.3 and 9 and I John 2.18 Hammond sees "the man of sin," "the son of perdition," "that Wicked" and "Antichrist" as the same person, Simon Magus—here slightly deviating from Grotius, who only identified "that Wicked" with Simon Magus; but the difference is not essential. "The Beast" of Revelation 13,1 denoted "the heathen worship, as it stood at

---

[32] *Works* III, 861. One may wonder who were the other "persons of great piety and learning." Hammond will not have meant Catholic authors such as Luis de Alcazar, a strong opponent of the Protestant interpretation of Antichrist; rather they were English Protestant theologians—perhaps Richard Montagu or Gilbert Sheldon (see Hill, *Antichrist*, esp. 33-40).

[33] Packer, *The Transformation of Anglicanism*, 96.

[34] "A Postscript concerning New light or Divine Illumination," *Works* III, IX.

[35] *Works* III, 937.

Rome"; the "whore" or "harlot" of Revelation 17,1 "the imperial dignity of Rome."[36] Fundamentally, Hammond agreed with Grotius in his interpretation of Antichrist, though it did not detract from his Protestant convictions: in more than one writing he firmly defended the claims of the Church of England over against the "Romanists".

Not all Anglicans of the post-Restoration period were prepared to follow Grotius and Hammond in their approach to the Antichrist problem. The traditional interpretation was strongly defended by the Cambridge Platonist Henry More (1614-1687), a pupil of Mede and, like his teacher, a Fellow of Christ's College, Cambridge. Though on some minor points he deviated from Mede, yet essentially he agreed with him in his interpretation of the Apocalypse.[37] Over against Grotius' method of interpretation he championed that of his revered teacher, and while he respected Grotius as a scholar, he was convinced that (for perhaps excusable reasons) the latter had not penetrated as deeply into the mysteries of the Book of Revelation as Mede had done:

> And because there does nothing so much counterbalance the weight of Mr. *Mede's* Reasons as the Autority [sic] and Luster of that worthily-admired Name of the Learned *Hugo Grotius*, who has interpreted the Revelations to quite another Sense; (the ingenuities and prettinesses of whose expositions had almost imposed upon my self to a belief that there might be some Sense also of the Revelation as he drives at) to make all clear I shall take the pains of exhibiting both to the view of the Reader. Who I hope will not take it ill that so Pious, so Learned and Judicious a Person as Mr. *Mede*, and that in a matter to which he may seem to be peculiarly selected and set apart to by God and nature, to which he mainly applied himself with all possible Care, Seriousness and Devotion, should see further than *Hugo Grotius*, who has an ample Harvest of Praise from other performances, and who by reason of his Political Employments could not be so entirely vacant to the searching into so abstruse a Mystery.[38]

More's fundamental objection to a mainly historical approach of the Book of Revelation such as practiced by Grotius was of a hermeneutical nature: if Grotius were right, and if in consequence the Book of Revelation did not cover the whole development of human history, then it would be "utterly *Useless*." On the contrary, the vindication of Mede's method "is really the rescuing of the Book itself into that Power and Use it ought to have in the Church: For it is a standing light to all the Ages thereof ..."[39] More wanted to rescue the Apocalypse from what he considered a sterile explanation, without any use for

---

[36] *Works* III, 678-83, 825-29, 911-15, 927-31. Though in his interpretation of Antichrist Hammond concentrated on Simon Magus, he emphasized that "man of sin" etc. "should signifie more than one single person, viz. Simon and the Gnosticks" (p. 680).

[37] See Van den Berg, "Continuity,"; this volume Ch. 6.

[38] From *An Explanation of the Grand Mystery of Godliness* (1680), in *The Theological Works of ... Henry More, D.D.*, London 1708, 119.

[39] "Mystery of Godliness," *Theol. Works*, 138.

the church of his own days, and to show that it functioned as a light that clarified the complex spiritual and political situation of the world with which contemporary England had to cope. He did so in particular in his work: *A Modest Inquiry into the Mystery of Iniquity*, which appeared in 1664 as a counterpart to his *Explanation of the Grand Mystery of Godliness*. Now the subject was what he also called "the Mystery of Antichristianism"; a subject, he realized, which at that time was not popular in more educated circles[40] (perhaps in reaction to Puritan times?)—but that made its treatment no less necessary.

To More, Antichrist (in the Apocalypse described as "the Beast" or "the whore of Babylon") was neither a figure from a far-away past nor of a distant future, but "Rome *Pagano-Christian*," or, "the *Roman Hierarchy* (taking *Roman* in the largest Sense) corrupting Christianity with the illicite Doctrines and Practices of Idolatry".[41] In his work on "the Mystery of Iniquity" he devoted two chapters to a refutation of Grotius' interpretation of Apocalypse 13 and 17. He strongly opposed Grotius' identification of "the Beast" with the idolatry of pagan Rome, and declared he was astonished "that a Person of those admirable Parts and Learning, and, as I have always been prone to think, of great Ingenuity, should ever please himself in any such Performance as this". What, More asked, could be "the Cause of this strange Misadventure of his?" More could not believe that Grotius "was in good earnest in this Exposition," but neither did he want to believe that Grotius, a man of ingenuity and integrity, "would willingly and wittingly, in Favour of a Party ... adulterate the true Meaning of the Oracles of God".[42] The apocalyptic themes continued to occupy the mind of More. In 1680 appeared his *Apocalypsis Apocalypseos*, a commentary on the Book of Revelation. It appeared in the after-days of the "Popish Plot" (1678), when in England anti-Catholic feelings ran high, but there was no direct connection, as he made clear in a letter to Archbishop Sancroft, to whom he sent a copy of his book.[43] More's fiercest attack on Grotius occurs in his commentary on Daniel (1681); there he declared that Grotius had excused the Pope from being Antichrist partly because of his distaste for the Reformed Church of Holland "for their usage of him", partly to "curry favour with the Pontifician party."[44] Apparently, to More it was no longer an open question why Grotius had deviated from the traditional interpretation of Antichrist.

In the same year in which More's *Apocalypsis Apocalypseos* appeared, one

---

[40] Hill, *Antichrist*, 148f.
[41] "Mystery of Iniquity," *Theol. Works*, 569.
[42] "Mystery of Iniquity," *Theol. Works*, 630 f.
[43] More to Sancroft, 2 January 1679/80, Bodleian library, MS Tanner 38,f 115; see Van den Berg, "Continuity," 201 n. 88; this volume 100.
[44] *A Plain and Continued Exposition of the several Prophecies or Divine Visions of the Prophet Daniel*, London 1681, XXXVIIf.

of the leading Latitudinarians, Simon Patrick (1625-1707), who in 1688 was appointed Bishop of Chichester, in 1691 Bishop of Ely, published an English translation of Grotius' *De Veritate*.[45] As a Latitudinarian he admired Grotius, whom he defended against the accusations of heresy. To his translation he added a seventh, explicitly anti-Catholic chapter, perhaps in order to make clear that following "the Grotian way" did not necessarily entail a sympathetic attitude towards the Church of Rome.[46] Shortly after the "Glorious Revolution" Patrick encouraged the publication of a millenarian work by the Anglican clergyman Drue Cressener (1642-1718), vicar of Soham near Ely: *The Judgments of God upon the Roman-Catholick Church* (1689). In 1690 Cressener published a second work on the same subject; he realized that his work was "out of fashion," but it could appear thanks to the recommendation of Patrick. At one time, Cressener wrote, he was influenced by "the mollifying pleas of Grotius,"

> But when I came to be acquainted with Mr. Mede's Demonstrations, and had compared them with the monstrous evasions, and absurd strains of wit, that *Grotius* and others were fain to flye to, to turn off the force of them, I gave over all thoughts of the comprehending way.[47]

Richard Baxter (1615-1691) went the other way round. He was a man of an independent mind: a Puritan leader who in 1660 for conscience's sake had the courage to decline the offer of a bishopric; a theologian, who steered a middle course between "High Calvinism" and Arminianism. As Geoffrey Nuttall writes, he "rarely agreed wholly with anyone."[48] Baxter's attitude towards Grotius was ambivalent. He was acquainted with the works of Grotius, and went as far in his appreciations as to write: "I must in Gratitude profess that I have learnt more from Grotius then from almost any Writer ... that ever I read".[49] At the same time, however, in his *The Grotian Religion Discovered* (1658) he strongly objected to Grotius' irenicist attitude towards the Church of Rome. He warned "the Episcopal Party" against "*Grotianism*," and in his

---

45 Symon Patrick, *The truth of Christian Religion; In Six books Written in Latin by Hugo Grotius. And Now Translated into English, With the Addition of a seventh book [Against the present Roman Church*: addition to the title in the 1689 ed.], London 1680 (*BG* nos. 1023, 1024 and 1025-28).

46 For this, see J. van den Berg, "Between Platonism and Enlightenment: Simon Patrick ... and his place in the Latitudinarian movement," this volume Ch. 9.

47 *A Demonstration of the First Principles of the Protestant Applications of the Apocalypse*, London 1960, XIII. For Cressener, see J. van den Berg "Glorious Revolution and Millennium: the "Apocalyptical Thoughts" of Drue Cressener", this volume Ch. 10.

48 G.F. Nuttall, "Richard Baxter and *The Grotian Religion*," in D. Baker (ed.), *Reform and Reformation: England and the Continent c1500 - c1750 (dedicated ... to C.W. Dugmore)*, Oxford 1979, 245.

49 *Calendar* I, no. 234 n. 1.

Grotian Religion he tried to prove that Grotius had turned "Papist" and that "Popery was indeed his Religion."[50] John Maitland, Earl of Lauderdale agreed. In 1658 he wrote to Baxter: "I was in Paris acquainted with Grotius ... and though I was then very yong yet some visits past among us. My discours with him was only in Humanities. But I remember well he was then esteemed such a Papist as you call Cassandrian ...".[51]

Baxter himself deeply mistrusted the way of Cassander, which, he feared, would inevitably lead to Rome. "Cassandrian Papists," he averred, were "levelling all their doctrines to the advancement of the Papall interest."[52] Still, his criticism of the "Grotian religion" did not make him a supporter of More and Cressener in their rejection of Grotius' interpretation of "Antichrist." As a young man he had read millenarians such as Brightman and Mede, since then also More, Grotius and Hammond. The disparate interpretations brought him into confusion: "I confess despair." And though he did not become an outright follower of Grotius and Hammond in their view of Antichrist he refused to identify the Papacy with Antichrist: he thought it would be "far more dreadful to the Pope ... to be plainly condemned by the known Laws of Christ ... than to be under the Dread of a dark and controverted Prophecie."[53] On this point, too, Baxter demonstrated his independence.

More was deeply disappointed that Baxter did not follow Mede, and reacted in a rather bitter pamphlet; he accused Baxter of a sceptical attitude with regard to the "explanation of prophecy."[54] In 1691, Cressener asked Baxter for "a cautious examination" of his second book. He hoped Baxter would come over to his view by owning that the great adversary of the Reformation "is so Pompously set forth to the world in this Prophecy, As the Great Antichrist."[55] No reaction from Baxter is known; he died only a few months afterwards.

One may wonder whether millenarian speculations were indeed as "unfashionable" as Cressener claimed in the dedication of his *Demonstration*. No less a person than Isaac Newton (1642-1727) sympathized with Mede's apocalyptic scheme.[56] He, too, believed that the predictions of things to come relate to the state of the Church in all ages, and though he did not explicitly identify the Pope with Antichrist, in his "observations" on Daniel he explained the elev-

---

[50] *Reliquiae Baxterianae*, London 1696, part I, 280; cf. Nuttall, "Richard Baxter," 249.

[51] The Earl of Lauderdaill to Baxter, 20 September 1658, *Calendar* I, no. 500.

[52] From Baxter's *Christian Concord* (1653), quoted by Nuttall, "Richard Baxter", 246.

[53] Baxter, *A Praphrase on the New Testament ... With an Advertisement of Difficulties in the Revelations*, London 1685, f. Q 2vo; R 2vo; 3ro,vo; 4ro. See also W.M. Lamont, *Richard Baxter and the Millennium*, London 1979, 52ff.; Van den Berg, "Continuity", this volume Ch. 6.

[54] See his *Some cursory reflexions impartially made upon Mr. Richard Baxter his way of writing notes on the Apocalypse*, published in London in 1685 under the pseudoným Phililicrinis [*sic*] Parrhesiastes.

[55] Cressener to Baxter, 2 June 1691, *Calendar* II, no. 1245.

[56] See F.E. Manuel, *Isaac Newton Historian*, Cambridge (Mass.) 1963, 175f

enth horn or king from Daniel 7.24-25, which would speak great words against the most High and would wear out the saints, as "the Church of Rome."[57] A similar approach we find with the famous scientist Joseph Priestley (1733-1804), who as a millenarian also stood in the tradition of Mede.[58] In his *Institutes of Natural and Revealed Religion* (1772-74) he declared he saw in a number of prophecies in the book of Daniel and of the Revelation "the plain characters of the *Church of Rome*," and in his *Notes on Revelation* (1804) he wrote: "The *blasphemy* of the beast, of which the papal power was a part, consists in the Pope's usurping the authority of God ...".[59]

In his *Apologia* (1864) the later Cardinal John Henry Newman (1801-1890) writes that as a boy of fifteen he read Newton on the Prophecies,[60] and became most firmly convinced that the Pope was the Antichrist predicted by Daniel, St. Paul and St. John. "My imagination was stained by the effects of this doctrine up to the year 1843". Gradually, however, he came to other thoughts; but while his reason was convinced, he did not throw off, for some time after, the unreasoning prejudice and suspicion, which he cherished about the (Catholic) Church "at least by fits and starts".[61] Even in Newman's life the after-effects of the traditional Protestant view of Antichrist led a tough existence. In the second half of the nineteenth century however, the identification between Pope and Antichrist just faded away, only to live on in extreme Protestant circles. At last, in his beloved England Grotius prevailed.

---

[57] Sir Isaac Newton, *Observations upon the Prophecies of Daniel and the Apocalypse of St. John*, London 1733, 15; 75.

[58] See J. van den Berg, "Priestly, the Jews and the Millennium", this volume Ch. 13.

[59] J.T. Rutt (ed.), *The Theological and Miscellaneous Works of Joseph Priestley*, New York 1972 (repr. of the edition of 1817-32) II, 190; XIV, 476.

[60] Not Isaac Newton, but Thomas Newton, Bishop of Bristol, who between 1754 and 1758 published his *Dissertations on the Prophecies*.

[61] *Apologia pro Vita Sua*, ed. by M.J. Svaglic, Oxford 1967, 20, 115; cf Ian Ker, *John Henry Newman*, Oxford 1990, 5, 184f.

CHAPTER EIGHT

QUAKER AND CHILIAST: THE "CONTRARY THOUGHTS" OF WILLIAM AMES AND PETRUS SERRARIUS

In the year 1662 a tract was published in the Netherlands under the title *Lucerna super candelabrum.*[1] The Dutch translation, which appeared in the same year, mentioned on the title-page the name of one of the leaders of the early Quaker movement, William Ames; an English edition, also bearing the name of Ames, appeared in the course of the following year.[2] It seems that, partly due to the complex way in which the title-page was formulated, at an early stage the tract was attributed to Ames, an attribution which was perpetuated in the eighteenth and nineteenth centuries. William Sewel, however, the Quaker historian who possessed so much first-hand information on what had happened in the early period of the Dutch Quaker community, found reason to deny the authorship of Ames, though, according to Sewel, Ames had approved of the contents of the work. In her exhaustive biography of the Collegiant and chiliast Petrus Serrarius, one of the Dutch contacts of Ames, Ernestine G.E. van der Wall remarks that the way in which the tract speaks of the "inner light" unmistakably points towards an author of rationalist tendency, *i.c.* Pieter Balling, under whose name it was printed in 1684. She adds, however, that (as appears from the fact that Benjamin Furly translated the tract into English) it found a favourable reception in Quaker circles.[3] There was indeed common ground: it is the message of the Light, "the inward ear, by which alone, and by no other, the voice of God, that is the Truth, can be heard",[4] which is the main theme of the work.

On the first page the author, dealing indirectly with the religious controversies of his times, remarks "that two men, speaking or writing the same words, may nevertheless have different, yea sometimes contrary thoughts". This sen-

[1] The reprint of the Latin version in the Dutch ed. of William Sewel's history of the Quakers (see below, note 6) has as title *Lucerna super candelabro*; W.I. Hull, *The rise of Quakerism in Amsterdam 1655-1665*, Swarthmore 1938, 215 note 444.

[2] I quote from the English edition: *The Light upon the Candlestick. Serving for observation of the principal things in the Book called The Mysteries of the Kingdom of God*, etc., London 1663; *cf. Wing* I (1972), nr. 3007, under the name of William Ames.

[3] E.G.E. van der Wall, *De mystieke chiliast Petrus Serrarius (1600-1669) en zijn wereld*, Leiden 1987, 227. See also A.C. Fix, who in his *Prophecy and Reason. The Dutch Collegiants in the Early Enlightenment*, Princeton 1991, 199-205, gives a broad analysis of *The Light*. While in the first version of this essay I left open the question of the authorship, I am now convinced by the arguments *pro* Balling, which implies that I went too far in speaking of a full conformity between the ideas of Ames and those of *The Light*.

[4] *Op. cit.*, 9.

tence sums up quite well what happened in the Netherlands, when English Quakers first came into contact with Dutch Collegiants; we receive the impression that in the initial stage the two groups felt attracted to each other because they seemed to speak the same language. Soon, however, it became clear that on many points their ideas diverged rather widely. Yet, at the end we may wonder whether under the surface there was not still present a common spirituality, rooted in what R.M. Jones, speaking of "mystical religion", calls "a direct and intimate consciousness of the Divine Presence".[5] We shall meet with all the tensions, but perhaps also with something of the underlying affinity, in the discussions which took place in the years around 1660 between William Ames and Petrus Serrarius.

William Ames set foot on Dutch soil for the first time in the spring of 1656, driven by an indomitable urge to spread the message of the Light also in the Low Countries, where only six years later, at the end of 1662, he was to find his grave.[6] It seems that he already possessed some knowledge of the Dutch language, with which he came to be well acquainted within a short time. We do not know the date of his birth, but probably on his arrival in Holland he was middle-aged; he had served in the army of the King, with the navy and in the Parliamentary army, and after that he had worked as a Baptist minister in Ireland. From Sewel's work as well as from his own writings we get the impression that he was an intelligent, courageous and energetic man, eager to convert others to the doctrine which had "pierced through" him, when "one who was sent by the Lord ... declared that that which convinced man of Sin, was the Light of Christ".[7]

Ames was not the first English Quaker who worked in the Netherlands, but soon he became the recognized leader of the Dutch Quaker community. His task was not an easy one. There were difficulties within the Quaker community, caused by unbalanced people: W.C. Braithwaite remarks, that the soil in Holland was not stony as it had been in Ireland and Scotland, but shallow, bringing forth rank and short-lived growths.[8] And the magistrates, though in general rather tolerant, could be hostile towards strangers who seemed to upset the stabilized order in church and society. More than once Ames was led before the magistrates and even imprisoned, but he bore his adversities with that mixture of quiet patience and almost defiant boldness, which is one of the secrets of the early Quaker movement. To those, and particularly to the Amsterdam magistrates,

---

[5] R.M. Jones, *Studies in Mystical Religion*, London 1909, XV.

[6] For the following passage see Hull, *op. cit.*, and J.Z. Kannegieter, *Geschiedenis van de vroegere Quakergemeenschap te Amsterdam,* Amsterdam and Haarlem 1971. Hull often refers to the classic works of G. Croese, *Historia Quakeriana,* Amstelodami 1695, and of W. Sewel, *Histori van de opkomste, aanwas en voortgang der ... Quakers,* Amsterdam 1717; Kannegieter gives additional information regarding the grounds of his researches in the Amsterdam archives.

[7] W. Ames, *A Declaration of the Witness of God, manifested in the Inward Parts,* ²1681, 12.

[8] W.C. Braithwaite, *The Beginnings of Quakerism,* London 1970, reprint of 2nd ed., 408.

who in 1657 wronged him, and in him the Light, he announced the judgement of the Lord in words which have an apocalyptic ring:

> Cry and complain about the misery which shall come over you, for the Lord is coming with a retaliation, vengeance and heat, to avenge the innocents' blood, and he wants to root out totally the evil-doers and the hypocrites from the earth, and the beast and the false Prophet will perish together, who have arranged themselves against the light ...[9]

But there were also softer tones:

> ... and we do not wish evil to those who have wronged us, but we rather wish that the Lord may open their eyes, and that they may follow the light in their consciences, which will show them the evil they have brought about, and their injustice.[10]

In view of all the troubles they met, it is amazing to see with how many people and groups Ames and his friends came into contact. Only in passing do we mention Ames's visit to "a Jew at Amsterdam that by the Jews is cast out",[11] possibly Spinoza,[12] to whom Ames may have been introduced by one or more of Spinoza's friends in the circle of the Amsterdam Collegiants, perhaps by Serrarius, who only a few years later acted as an intermediary between Spinoza and the secretary of the Royal Society at London, Henry Oldenburg.[13] With the dominant Reformed Church, relations were strained to the utmost. The ministers looked with deep disapproval upon people who not only bitterly attacked the existing churches, but who even "disturbed" the church services by interrupting the preacher; it was the Amsterdam consistory which in 1657 directed the attention of the magistrates to the actions of the Quakers.[14] In their turn, the Quakers were shocked by what they considered the persecuting spirit in the "official" church. Ames wrote to Jacobus Koelman, one of the protagonists of the "Further Reformation", who had attacked the Quakers:

> I believe that such a pretended congregation which persecutes, banishes, imprisons, strikes, stones, reviles, etc., those of which they must confess that they are of a better conversation than they themselves are ... are not the congregation of Christ but the

[9] *Een verklaringe van den onrechtvaerdighen handel van de Magistraten van Amsterdam, tegens Willem Ames, ende Humble Thatcher, voorghevallen in den jare 1657*, 7.
[10] *Op. cit.*, I.
[11] Ames in a letter to Margaret Fell, 17 April (O.S.) 1657, found and printed by Hull, *op. cit.*, 205.
[12] Thus, more positive still than Hull, Kannegieter, *op. cit.*, 328f.
[13] See: K.O. Meinsma, *Spinoza en zijn kring*, 's-Gravenhage 1896, 227, 244f, 251; A.R. Hall and M.B. Hall (eds.), *The Correspondence of Henry Oldenburg* II, Amsterdam 1966, 97, 381, 391, 567.
[14] Kannegieter, *op. cit.*, 17; R.B. Evenhuis, *Ook dat was Amsterdam* III, Amsterdam 1971, 331ff.

> synagogue of Satan. Oh, how appears the devouring wolf under the sheep's clothing.[15]

The Remonstrants, too, were severely criticized: over against the Rotterdam minister Albertus Holthenus, who, according to Ames, held the religion of the Remonstrants to be a perfect religion, Ames remarked that "this people", while singing with David that they were enfeebled and brokenhearted, is "neither enfeebled nor broken or bowed down, but many of them are adorned with gold, pearls, knots of ribbons and costly apparel, thereby showing that they follow the lust of their eyes and the greatness of life ...".[16] Besides, the Remonstrants whom Ames met denied the continuation of special revelations and emphasized that in these present times Scripture is the only way and means to come to the knowledge of God and of his will.[17]

Only with the Mennonites were relations somewhat different. Ames chided the Leiden Mennonites because in a dispute they had called in the help of an Arminian—it was like Saul going to the witch of Endor—but he felt obliged to add:

> Now let no one apply this to himself who is not guilty! for I do not accuse all for the faults of some; for I know that there are many amongst you in several places, in whom there is a hunger and thirst after righteousness ...[18]

In Amsterdam, Ames had come into contact with Mennonites who were also members of the Collegiant society. Now the Collegiants—most of whom were at the same time members of a Remonstrant or a Mennonite congregation—had a number of things in common with the Quakers.[19] They came together in meetings for mutual edification and there was full freedom of speech though not for the women; they were critical of the institutional aspects of church life; in particular, some of the early Collegiants believed in the possibility of a direct inspiration by the Holy Spirit, and, while at a later stage most of the Collegiants moved in a more rationalist direction, in the period around 1660 at least a number of Collegiants, such as Adam Boreel, a patrician from Zeeland,[20] and Petrus Serrarius, were of a mystical and chiliastic bent. One of the leading Collegiants was the Amsterdam Mennonite preacher

---

[15] "Aen Jacobus Coelman, Prediker, door William Ames", in William Ames and John Higgins, *De valsche propheten bekent aen haere vrughten,* 1659, 26f.

[16] "Eenige dwaelingen der Remonstranten ...", in *De valsche propheten*, 17-20.

[17] *De valsche propheten*, 19; Ames, *Een ghetuyghenis des Wets van de Geest des Levens in de binnenste deelen* ..., 1659, 3.

[18] *Een ghetuyghenis des Wets* ..., 6f.

[19] For the Collegiants see J.C. van Slee, *De Rijnsburger Collegianten*, Haarlem 1895; for the contacts between Collegiants and Quakers esp. 386-92. Now also Fix, *Collegiants*.

[20] For him as a representative of the Collegiant movement see J. Lindeboom, *Stiefkinderen van het Christendom,* "s-Gravenhage 1929, 342ff.

Galenus Abrahamsz, who at first had some sympathy with the Quakers, even so that his opponents (belonging to the more conservative Mennonite group) accused him of having both his feet in the Quakers' barge.[21] But this was not true. Sewel writes in his *History*:

> *W. Ames* found also some reception among the Baptists there, who at first were pleased with him, but J. Stubs did not use them so well, as Dr. *Galenus Abrahams* once told me, who compared *Ames* to a Musician that play'd a very melodious tune, and Stubs to a Disturber of the harmonious Musick, tho" *Ames* afterwards for his great Zeal, was found Fault with also.[22]

The "XIX Articles" of 1657, written by Galenus and D. Spruyt, contained an implicit criticism of Quakerism; Ames in his turn attacked Galenus; others also took part in the discussion (on the side of Galenus, among others, Serrarius); the number of pamphlets and the vehemence of the attacks and counter-attacks make W.I. Hull use the term, "the war of pamphlets".[23] According to Sewel, during Ames's lifetime the conflict between him and the Collegiants remained unsolved.

> In his Sickness, which was a lingring Disease, he was told, that among the Baptists and Collegians, it was said of him, That he had changed his judgment, and was grieved for having judged them wrongfully. But to this he said, It was not so, but that he still judged their Way of Worship, especially their Disputations and Will-Worship, to be out of the Way of the Lord. And in this belief he died in peace.[24]

The message of Ames, as we meet it in the pamphlets he wrote, was concentrated upon the one great theme of the Light, which convinces of sin and thus enables man to overcome the world[25] and to enter into the Kingdom of Christ. Was it this central theme of his message, was it something which radiated from his personality, or perhaps a combination of these and other factors, which attracted some of the Collegiants when they came into contact with Ames? No doubt it was in their circle that the first meeting between Ames and Serrarius took place. From a few remarks, made by Serrarius in a pamphlet against Ames, we may conclude that initially not only was he himself impressed by

---

[21] H.W. Meihuizen, *Galenus Abrahamsz 1622-1706*, Haarlem 1954, 6o.
[22] W. Sewel, *The History of the Rise, Increase and Progress of the Christian People called Quakers*, London 1725, 133.
[23] Hull, *op. cit.*, 232ff. The large number of Quaker tracts, published in the Netherlands in this period, corresponds with the peak in the publication of English Quaker tracts in the same years. See Mrs. M.J.F. Bitterman, "The Early Quaker Literature of Defense", *Church History* 42 (1973), esp. 204.
[24] *Op. cit.*, 366.
[25] For the various aspects of this expression, used by Ames in his *A Declaration of the Witness of God*, 15 see G.F. Nuttall, "Overcoming the world: the early Quaker programme" in D. Baker (ed.), *Sanctity and Secularity: The Church and the World*, Oxford 1973, 145-64.

the Quaker message, but also through him others came under Quaker influence: "a number of plain pious souls, who are deceived and ensnared by these false *Lights* (to which, inadvertently, I may have given some occasion) ...".[26] Already the way in which Ames and Serrarius addressed each other in their pamphlets makes it clear that the two men knew each other rather intimately; at any rate we know that the meeting between Collegiants and Quakers, in which Adam Boreel bitterly attacked the Quakers because of the Nayler affair[27] and the young Quaker John Higgins no less vehemently inveighed against Boreel, was held in the house of Serrarius;[28] at this meeting, which took place on 24 August 1660, Ames, too, was present.[29] The clash marked the break between Quakers and Collegiants; "the war of pamphlets", in which Ames and Serrarius came to take opposite sides, had already begun some years earlier.

Petrus Serrarius or Serarius, whom Ames—in a rather rash judgement—considered the most bitter opponent of the Quakers in the Netherlands,[30] was born in London, where he was baptized as Pierre Serrurier in the French Church of Threadneedle Street on the 11th May 1600.[31] In 1620, he was admitted to the Walloon College at Leiden,[32] where he stayed till 1623.[33] No doubt, already there he met John Dury, whom some years afterwards he was to succeed as a minister in Cologne and with whom he was to have such friendly contacts at a later stage of their lives.[34] In 1623 Serrarius was accepted as a probationer in the Walloon churches. From 1624 to 1626 we find him in the province of Zeeland working as an assistant in Middelburg, Flushing and

---

[26] P. Serarius, *Van den Waere Wegh tot God, Tot Bewijs Dat niet alle LICHT dat in de Duysternisse schijnt, den Wegh zy tot God. Gestelt Tegens "t Voorgeven van William Ames ...*, Alckmaer 1661, AI2ro. Possibly Serrarius was even the translator of the first Quaker pamphlet which was translated into Dutch, that of William Dewsbury, *The Discovery of Man's Returne to his first Estate* (1654); the Dutch ed. of 1656 was translated by "P.S.": H.J. Cadbury, "Joshua Sprigge on the Continent", *Journal of Friends Historical Society* (hereafter *J.F.H.S.*) 45 (1953), 60-3.

[27] The conduct of James Nayler soon became known in Holland and led to a strong anti-Quaker agitation. See: Hull, *op. cit.*, 237-54.

[28] *Adam Boreel ontdeckt door sijn Vruchten,* Amsterdam 1662.

[29] Serrarius gives his account of the meeting (with its date) in his: *Van den Wegh tot God,* A2ro,vo; Ames in his: *De Misslagen en Valscheden Wederleydt, die gevonden zijn in de Extracten uyt de Schriften van Jacob Adriaensz Waere,* Amsterdam 1661, 12ff.

[30] Ames, *Het waere Licht beschermt, Ende de Onnooselheydt van de Eenvoudige bevrijt van de onwaerheden ende valsche Beschuldigingen door Petrus Serrarius op haer geleyt ...*, 1661, A1vo.

[31] Moens, W.J.C., *The Registers of the French Church of Threadneedle Street, London,* Lymington 1896, *Publications Huguenot Society London* IX, 35. For these and the following biographical data, see now the work (mentioned in note 3) by Ernestine G.E. van der Wall, who in 1977 participated in the preparation of this article.

[32] *Livre Synodal* I, La Haye 1897, 285, 287.

[33] G.H.M. Posthumus Meyjes, *Geschiedenis van het Waalse College te Leiden 1606-1699,* Leiden 1975, 191.

[34] G.H. Turnbull, *Hartlib, Dury and Comenius,* London 1947, 273, 293, 296f., 382. Dury stayed in the Walloon College till about March 1621: Posthumus Meyjes, *loc. cit.*

Groede.[35] In the spring of 1626, he was inducted as a minister in the Walloon church of "Du Verger" (secret name for Cologne); the acts of the consistory contain the interesting detail, that he had in his house a number of books, left by Dury.[36] We may just wonder whether perhaps it was the reading of these books which made him leave the ministry of the church at Cologne and ultimately brought him to proclaim himself "*Ministrum Euangelii in Ecclesia universali*".[37] We know that when he left Cologne in 1628 he was suspected of doctrinal errors,[38] though the nature of these errors does not become quite clear. It is sometimes assumed that he was dismissed in Cologne on account of chiliastic ideas, but we have grounds to suppose that at that time he was not yet a chiliast; it seems, however, that he had come under the influence of mystical tendencies which somehow alienated him from the strict Calvinism of his church.[39] In a work which he wrote shortly before his death, he confessed his sympathy for the great mystics: the author of the *Theologia Germanica*, Tauler, Ruysbroeck, Suso, Thomas à Kempis, John of the Cross and Dionysius the Carthusian;[40] at any rate, this is the line which runs through almost all his works and made him feel sympathetic, though sometimes only for a time, to those who shared his mystical interest. Gottfried Arnold, himself so deeply influenced by the mystical tradition, recognized in Serrarius a kindred spirit: he called him "an impartial teacher and witness of the truth".[41]

After some wanderings—in 1629 he wrote a letter to Dury from Groningen[42]—Serrarius settled in Amsterdam, where in 1630 he married Sara Paul van Offenbach.[43] In 1640 the Walloon synod, probably on behalf of or at the instigation of the Middelburg consistory, thought of making use again of the services of Serrarius, but—apparently on the grounds of information obtained from the Walloon consistory at Amsterdam—the Walloon synod, held

---

[35] *Livre Synodal* I, 315, 317, 319.

[36] R. Löhr (ed.), *Protokolle der Wallonischen Gemeinde in Köln von 1600-1776*, Köln 1975, 128f.

[37] Th. Crenius, *Animadversiones Philologicae et Historicae* II, Lugd. Bat. 1696, 47 (quoting Maresius).

[38] *Livres des Actes* I (Bibl. Wallone, Amsterdam), f. 145ro: "Notre frere Pierre Serrurier venu du Verger pour voir ses parents ayant donné quelque soubcon d'erreur en la doctrine, a esté trouvé bon que l'Eglise d'Amsterdam en prenne exacte cognoissance ...."

[39] W. Rood in his *Comenius and the Low Countries,* Amsterdam 1970, 149, states that he was dismissed as a result of his chiliastic views; D. Nauta, however, quoting Bayle's *Dict. hist. et crit.* III, fol. 325, mentions *"les erreurs fanatiques de Swenckveldius"* as the cause of the conflict: *Samuel Maresius,* Amsterdam 1935, 332 note 199.

[40] *Responsio ad Exercitationem Paradoxam Anonymi cujusdam, Cartesianae Sectae Discipuli*, Amsterodami 1667, 52.

[41] G. Arnold, *Fortsetzung und Erläuterung oder Dritter und Vierdter Teil der unpartheyischen Kirchen- und Ketzer-Historie*, Frankfurt a/Mayn 1729, 1092.

[42] Turnbull, *op. cit.*, 127.

[43] *Doop- en trouwboeken* [hereafter: *D.T.B.*] Frans-Ger. Kerk [Walloon Church], gemeente Archief [Municipal Archives; hereafter: G.A.] Amsterdam, nr 437, 11.

at Zierikzee, decided not to go further in this matter, but to recommend him to the care and the prudence of the Amsterdam church.[44] Still, from the fact that in 1640 the Walloon brethren in Zeeland initially were inclined to renew the contact with Serrarius, we may gather that at least at that time they did not consider him a real heretic.

The information we possess about his Amsterdam period—he lived there until his death in 1669[45]—is of a very fragmentary character. We receive the impression that he lived in an *otium* of a probably rather comfortable character; the Groningen professor of theology Samuel Maresius, speaking of the chiliastic speculations of Serrarius, ironically remarks: "qui eo quod abundes otio istis speculationibus libentius indulges".[46] He found time to translate from German, English and Latin, to write a number of theological works, and to have personal contacts with a variety of people.[47] An impartial judgement of his character is that of his opponent Maresius: "Est certe vir ille, bonus, pius ac bene doctus".[48] Serrarius moved in the circle of the Amsterdam Collegiants and was a great friend and admirer of Galenus Abrahmsz,[49] though we have no reason to suppose that he joined the Mennonite community. For a time, he was under the spell of the world of ideas of Antoinette Bourignon, from whom at last he was alienated by a deep conflict, in which their common friend Comenius took the side of Antoinette.[50] The friendship with Dury—based on a spiritual affinity, though perhaps they did not agree in all things[51]—lasted till the end. A special mention must be made of his interest in the alchemical activities of Franciscus Mercurius van Helmont,[52] to all intents a mystic, who because of this was even held to be a Quaker in the latter part of his life.[53] Serrarius was also known for his friendly contacts with a number of Amsterdam Jews; we shall return to this in the context of an exposition of his eschatology.

---

[44] *Livre Synodal* I, 421, 423. Here I differ from Goeters, who gives the impression that it was Serrarius himself who refused to come to Middelburg; see W. Goeters, *Die Vorbereitung des Pietismus in der reformierten Kirche der Niederlande*, Leipzig 1911, 48.

[45] He was buried on 1 October 1669: *D.T.B.* Frans-Ger. Kerk, G.A. Amsterdam, nr 1130, 295.

[46] S. Maresius, *Chiliasmus Enervatus ad D.P. Serarium*, Groningae 1664, 2[vo]; for the controversy between Maresius and Serrarius see: D. Nauta, *op. cit.*, esp. 332-5.

[47] In describing Serrarius' personal contacts, Goeters (*loc. cit.*) wrongly states that he frequently travelled in England and that because of this his chiliastic views possibly originated from English sources.

[48] Maresius, *op. cit.*, 6.

[49] C.B. Hylkema, *Reformateurs* I-II, Haarlem 1900, 1902, *sparsim*; Meihuizen, *op. cit.*, 63.

[50] Marthe van der Does, *Antoinette Bourignon, Sa vie (1616-80), son oeuvre*, Groningen 1974, 109, 120, 134.

[51] On Dury's reaction to the criticism of the Amsterdam minister John Rulice with regard to his contacts with Serrarius and his circle, see Turnbull, *op. cit.*, 296

[52] J. Crossley (ed.), *The Diary and Correspondence of Dr John Worthington* ... III, Part I (Chatham Society), 1985, 105ff.

[53] *Op. cit.*, 100.

The "primitiae" of his studies are the theses on the question whether the church can totally decline, which he defended on 6 July 1622 in the Walloon College at Leiden; his conclusion is, that in a period of general persecution and apostasy the church can totally lose its external splendour, while yet the internal (and essential) state of the church remains intact.[54] It would be tempting to see at least something of his later ideas on the church prefigured in these theses, and indeed, the anti-triumphalist emphasis returns in more than one of his later publications, but we should not forget that often theses like these were no more than an echo of the teacher's views; and no doubt what Serrarius defended was quite in accordance with orthodox doctrine and theology (*cf.* art. XXVII of the *Confessio Belgica).* In 1647 there appeared a new Dutch translation of Tauler's works from the German "to the service of the general impartial Christendom", partly or even wholly made by Serrarius.[55] In 1654, Serrarius wrote a foreword to a translation of seventeen sermons of Joshua Sprigge on the future glory of the church.[56] Now Sprigge's eschatology had a mystical character; he emphasized the fact that the second coming of Christ is a spiritual matter, a coming of Christ in the heart of man; in this, as we shall see, his views resemble those of the Quakers. It is exactly this element by which Serrarius was deeply moved: he thoroughly sympathized with Sprigge's view that the "future glory" does not refer to the external form of the church, but to the internal work of God in the conscience of man. "There are some to whom Christ has already come and who are day by day enjoying him, while others look forward in painful suspense, calculating the times and the years of his coming according to the Scriptures, without knowing it is so close at hand".[57]

Here, like Sprigge, Serrarius speaks more the language of a mystic than that of a millenarian. But only a few years later we find him defending, though not without hesitation, the chiliast position over against Moyse Amyraut, who in 1654 had attacked chiliasm in his *Du Regne de Mille Ans*; according to Wallmann his work against Amyraut is the best introduction in the chiliastic world of thought of those times.[58] It is not easy to combine the more mystical eschatology of 1654 with the later chiliastic utterances, but however this may be,

---

[54] *Explicatio Quaestionis an Ecclesia possit deficere* ... quam favente Deo Opt. Max. praeside ... D. Danielo Colonio ... tueri annitat in collegio Petrus Serrarius Londino-Anglus ..., Lugd. Bat. 1622, *passim.*

[55] *Johannis Tauleri Opera* ..., Hoorn 1647.

[56] For Sprigge see *DNB* LIII, 426f.; Braithwaite, *op. cit.*, 264, 566f.; Th. Sippell, "The Testimony of Joshua Sprigge", *J.F.H.S.* 38 (1946), 24, 28; and the article by H.J. Cadbury, mentioned in note 26.

[57] J. Sprigge, *De Getuygenisse Eener Aenstaende Heerlijkheyt* ... in "t Nederlands getrouwelijk overgezet door P.S., Amsterdam 1716, 4vo.

[58] J. Wallmann, *Philipp Jakob Spener und die Anfänge des Pietismus*, Tübingen 1970, 330f. For the causes of Serrarius' hesitation see the preface of his *Assertion du Regne de Mille Ans ou de la Prospérité de l'Eglise de Christ en la Terre* ..., Amsterdam 1657; by the various devout and pious persons who were seeking the kingdom of God within themselves and who might be hurt

from 1657 onward we meet in Serrarius a staunch and consistent defender of the millenarian position. In 1659 he wrote a work, *The treading underfoot of the Holy City*, which appeared together with a translation of a work of the sixteenth-century mystic Christian Entfelder, *On the many Separations which have this year arisen in Belief* (1530).[59] Serrarius wrote this work—and added his translation of Entfelder's work—in order to defend his friend Galenus Abrahamsz against the attacks of an anti-Collegiant Mennonite.[60] The dominant motif with Serrarius is that of the decline of the present-day churches as compared with the apostolic church: all churches have deviated so far that we should not expect a restoration of the congregation of Christ unless God intervenes in a miraculous way. On this point his view of the church coincides with his chiliastic opinions: there will be no renewal of the church until the Jewish nation will be converted to Christ, who then will reign on earth together with his saints.[61]

We mention some other works in which his chiliasm becomes manifest. In 1661 Serrarius published his *Answer to the Book, published in the year 1659 ... on the Apostasy of the Christians*,[62] in fact an enlargement of the argument of his former work, now used as a refutation of an anonymous work of a very unorthodox character, *Of the Apostasy of the Christians.*[63] This work of Serrarius is interesting not only because it contains a clear and succinct explanation of Revelation 20,[64] but because of its expositions on the doctrine of predestination and the authority of the creeds. With regard to the first point, Serrarius tries to steer a middle course between Arminianism and the doctrine of absolute predestination, and his view has some affinity with the ideas of the school of Saumur;[65] with regard to the second point he expresses his fear of all credal formulations which do not simply repeat the words of Scripture.[66] Still,

---

by his exposition of an external kingdom on earth, "*comme si on vouloit les amuser à des choses de dehors pour les empescher en la poursuite des choses internes et purement spirituelles*" could be meant the English Seekers, but also the Quakers with whom Serrarius had come into contact in 1656 or 1657 (*3ro,^{vo}).

[59] P. Serarius, *De vertredinge des heyligen stadts,* ofte Een klaer bewijs van "t VERVAL der Eerste Apostolische Gemeente ... Mitsgaders Christiaen Entfelders Bedenckinge over de veelderley Scheuringen ende Dwalingen ..., Amsterdam 1659. For Entfelder, see *The Mennonite Encyclopedia* II, 226f.; R.M. Jones, *Spiritual Reformers in the 16th and 17th centuries*, London 1914, 39ff.

[60] For the background of this controversy see Meihuizen, *op. cit.*, 61ff.

[61] See esp. 10-16 and the questions, put in the addendum to the work which follows the translation of Entfelder.

[62] *Antwoort op "t Boeck in "t Jaer 1659 uytgegeven Van de Apostasie ofte, Afval der Christenen* ... Amsterdam 1661.

[63] The author afterwards appeared to be the former *assessor* of the Court of Holland, Lancelot van Brederode. See S.B.J. Zilverberg, "Lancelot van Brederode en zijn geschrift 'Van de Apostasie dat is van den Afval der Christenen'", *Nederlands Archief voor Kerkgeschiedenis* 50 (1970), 230-43.

[64] *Op. cit.*, 14.

[65] *Op. cit.*, 153f., 160ff.

in a letter which he sent to Maresius in 1662, he stated that he believed no doctrine among Christians was more in accordance with the Scriptures than reformed doctrine.[67] This letter was written in order to accompany the gift of a little book, *A Further Message on the occasion of the great Conjunction of all Planets, in the Sign of Heaven, called Sagittarius, to happen the 1/11 December Anno 1662*.[68] In this work—to which Maresius replied in his *Chiliasmus Enervatus*—Serrarius combined his chiliastic interpretation of the relevant Old and New Testament passages with a number of very elaborate astrological speculations. He expected the speedy arrival of the fifth monarchy, the time in which the stone cut without hands (Dan. 2.34, 35) would humiliate all earthly kingdoms and fill the earth with its presence. The work is also remarkable because of its very sympathetic attitude towards the Jews—a sympathy which manifested itself in various ways; it earned for Petrus Serrarius and his brothers Louis and Joseph the praise of their fellow chiliast Jean de Labadie.[69]

In his last published work,[70] *Responsio ad Exercitationem Paradoxam Anonymi cujusdam, Cartesianae Sectae Discipuli*[71] Serrarius attacked the rationalist propositions of the anonymous author[72] of the work *Philosophia S. Scripturae Interpres* ("Eleutheropoli", 1666). Over against the rationalist approach, Serrarius defends the mystical and pietist tradition with regard to the interpretation of Scripture, which maintains "*interpretationem S. Scripturae non esse humanarum virium, sed gratiae divinae opus*"; the right interpretation of Scripture is a matter of "*interna revelatio*", "*internus afflatus*". He fully realized that because of this he would be accused of "enthusiasm", but to this he replied: "*Quid enim est Enthusiasta proprie, nisi qui profitetur dari* ἐνθουσιασμούς, i.e. *Spiritus Divini afflationes*". In this context, the Quakers are mentioned:

Non enim sani theologi eas ideo rejicient, quia de Lumine et Spiritu, internisque

---

[66] *Op. cit.*, 150.

[67] Maresius, *op. cit.*, 6; according to Maresius, whose favourable judgement of the person of Serrarius we mentioned above, he was "ἰδιογνώμων ac creditus in Schwenckfeldianismum pronior".

[68] *Naerder Bericht wegens die groote Conjunctie ofte "t samenkomste van allen Planeten in het Teecken des Hemels, ghenaemt de Schutter, te geschieden den 1/11 December Anno 1662*, Amsterdam 1662. An English translation appeared in the same year under the title: *An Awakening Warning to the Wofull World;* also a Latin edition, entitled: *Brevis Dissertatio De fatali* et *admiranda ... Planetarum Conjunctione ...*

[69] J. de Labadie, *Oordeel der liefde en gerechtigheyt over den jegenwoordighen toestandt der Joden*, Amsterdam 1667, f. A2[vo], 3[ro]. No doubt De Labadie was influenced by Serrarius in his chiliasm: see Wallmann, *loc. cit.*

[70] A commentary on the Apocalypse, at one time as a manuscript in the possession of Gottfried Arnold, was never published: Arnold, *loc. cit.*

[71] See note 40; a Dutch edition appeared in the same year.

[72] The Amsterdam medical doctor Ludovicus Meyer; *Nieuw Nederlandsch Biografisch Woordenboek* V, 342ff.

> Illuminationibus loquuntur; sed tantum, quia de Spiritu quodam jactitant qui supra S. Scripturas, imo contra S. Scripturas sese effert, et plus arrogantiae et ostentationis quam humilitatis prae se fert.[73]

The differences between Serrarius and the Quakers revealed themselves as early as 1657. In a pamphlet, which appeared in that year, Ames rejected the objections, brought up by Serrarius and by an unknown author "F.D." against twenty-three questions, put by Ames.[74] The main subject of this early discussion was the central question of the relation between Scripture and Spirit. Serrarius emphasized the indispensability of the work of the Spirit for the right understanding of "the sense of God and of Jesus Christ", and in this, of course, Ames agreed with him, though with a proviso which, in the form of an *argumentum ad hominem,* is typical of what might be called Ames's "existential" approach: "If you own in your life, what you express in words, the spirit will not condemn you". But the Quakers objected to the juxtaposition of Scripture and Spirit, external and internal knowledge: we know Christ first of all internally, through the Spirit, through the Light.[75] Here we touch upon the point which, ten years later, Serrarius was to formulate as a "boasting on the Spirit which raises itself above, yea even against the Scriptures".

In his *The treading underfoot of the Holy City*, Serrarius had implicitly criticized the views of the Quakers with regard to the restoration of primitive Christianity in its purity. He shared with the Quakers the view of church history as a history of apostasy from the apostolic ideal. At the same time, he agreed with Galenus, who in the "XIX Articles" (which contained a succinct exposition of his views) had remarked that nowadays no church or congregation was in conformity with the situation of the first and unique church, "to which alone is given in the New Testament the names of a congregation of God, Bride, Spouse, body of Christ".[76] Furthermore, he held—on this point he was more explicit than Galenus—that this restoration could only come about through a dramatic, an apocalyptic intervention of God, which the Quakers arbitrarily anticipated in their activities. To this, Ames replied in his *The Light which shines in the darkness proved to be the Way to God*:

> Well Peter, what an outcry has there been amongst you against me because of the judging of others? And do you now judge all men as being outside the congregation of Christ? What, has Christ in these times no body which is separate from the world?

---

[73] *Op. cit.* f. C3^{ro}; 49; 51f.

[74] *Een Wederlegginge van een Boeck, ghenaemt Antwoort op 23 Vragen, door F.D. als mede een Wederlegginge van een andere Antwoort, die door P.S. daer opgedaen was, waer in syne dwaesheyt ontdeckt is* ..., 1657; though I have not been able to trace the work of Serrarius to which Ames refers, it is easy to reconstruct the argument from what Ames writes.

[75] *Op. cit.*, 1ro, 2ro,^{vo}.

[76] G. Abrahamsz and D. Spruyt, *Nader verklaringe van de XIX Artikelen,* Amsterdam 1659, f. a 3ro (art. XII).

> ... has there nothing been left in the whole wide world, on the ground of which some people could be called the Apostolic Congregation of Christ?

On this point, Ames brings in the subject of eschatology, which was so closely bound up with the ecclesiological question. According to Serrarius, the coming restoration of the church could only be expected in the time of the millennium; but over against this Ames argued that the day had arrived in which God would appear in his glorious light and would be appearing in many thousands of his saints. "If you do not believe in the Light, the day of God will pass by you ... God has a people, in which Christ lives, and which can truly say: here is Christ."[77]

Here we meet with one of the most characteristic elements of early Quaker eschatology.[78] It was not undramatic; it even had millennial traits. George Fox wrote in 1654:

> The mighty day of the Lord is coming, that all things must be brought to light, and all your secrets brought to light ... the candle is lighted, the day does appear that God will rule in his Saints above the heathen, above the wicked and the ungodly men ... the eternall God will rule and reign in his Saints, and be admired, magnified and glorified in them above you all.[79]

It sounds like a Fifth Monarchy pamphlet, but the eschatological scheme is different: Fox believed that the prophecy of Daniel with regard to the fifth monarchy had been fulfilled with the coming of Christ on earth in order to establish his spiritual kingdom in the hearts of men:

> ... and this fifth kingdom the Kingdom of the Messiah is spiritual, and doth subdue the power of darkness, and gather people up into unity, and is not to be understood literally, for it is everlasting ...[80]

This is the background of Ames's eschatology. As we saw above, with him, too, the "dramatic" element was not lacking, but his ultimate interest lay elsewhere: in the struggle between light and darkness, between the Light and the anti-Christian powers, as it takes place in the heart of men. Serrarius was deeply interested in the *externa* of eschatology, in the unfolding of eschatolo-

---

[77] Ames, *Het Ligt dat in de duisternisse schijnt beweesen den Weg tot God te sijn ...*, Amsterdam 1660, 6ff.

[78] For early Quaker eschatology see Hugh Barbour *The Quakers in Puritan England,* New Haven and London 1964, esp. 181-90; T.L. Underwood, "Early Quaker Eschatology", in P. Toon (ed.), *Puritans, the Millennium and the Future of Israel,* Cambridge and London 1970, 91-103; B.W. Ball, *A Great Expectation. Eschatological Thought in English Protestantism to 1660,* Leiden 1975, esp. 192-211.

[79] G. Fox, *Newes Coming up out of the North Sounding towards the South,* London 1654, 6.

[80] G. Fox, *An Answer to the Arguments of the Jewes ...* [1661], esp. II.

gical events in the course of history, in what would happen to the people of Israel in the time of the millennium, in the future glory of the earthly kingdom of Christ. In 1661 he published his *Of the true Way to God,* in which he put the following questions to Ames and Higgins:

> Whether at one time all the blessings, Deut. 28, intended for the people of Israel, will receive their turn on earth, as all the curses will have had their time?
> Whether before the last Judgment the God of Heaven will establish a Kingdom on earth, in which justice will prevail and in which there will be a fullness of peace?[81]

Ames, however, was scarcely interested. In his *The true Light protected*—a reply to *Of the true Way to God*—he put over against the chiliastic expectations of Serrarius his Quaker views, which have recently been characterized as a form of "realized eschatology".[82] When Serrarius argued that the great time had not yet come because the nations did not yet walk in the light of Jerusalem (Rev. 21.24)—and he took this expression quite literally—Ames shortly replied that those who are saved already walk in the light.[83] And he would not deny that something would happen in the future—the Quakers did not abandon the traditional eschatological scheme as such[84]—, but what in the eyes of Serrarius took a central place, to Ames was only of marginal importance: to the questions of a more eschatological nature, put by Serrarius, he devoted no more time and space than that of a monosyllabic "yes". Serrarius had maintained he knew "all this and much more" (the eschatological scheme) through "the flesh of Christ", *i.e.* on the grounds of his external word; to this, Ames retorted: "Well, Peter, this is highly boasted, as if you know everything, and we nothing; I think you have it not through his spirit, but I am content with what I know."[85]

Ames thought of Serrarius as a man who was proud of his carnal wisdom; conversely, Serrarius saw in the Quakers people who thought they already possessed that for which they ought to wait in patience and humility. On 17 March 1660 (O.S.) Serrarius wrote to an English friend, the Seeker John Jackson:

> Your sober word I have runn through with great delight my spiritt symbolizing with yours and glorifying God both for the clearness of the truth and of the expressions of it. Would to God this people might increase both in multitude and earnestness ... Are these your seekers in England? Then I'le rather joyne with them, than with such

---

[81] *Van den Waere Wegh tot God,* 120.
[82] For the application of the term to Quaker eschatology, see the studies of T.L. Underwood and B.W. Ball, mentioned in note 78.
[83] Ames, *Het waere Licht beschermt,* 20.
[84] See also Underwood, *op. cit.*, 103.
[85] *Het waere Licht beschermt*, 20; 33.

> as presume they have found and possessed. Better is a poor man in his uprightness acknowledging his want than a rich man that perverteth his words (saith Solomon) and makes show to bee what hee is not. This controversy beginneth to bee much ventilated in these parts.[86]

In this letter, Serrarius refers to John Jackson's *A Sober Word to a Serious People* (London 1651), an interesting exposition of the Seekers' point of view,[87] with which Serrarius clearly was more in sympathy than with that of the Quakers, who, of course, are meant by those who "have found and possessed". Here he was perhaps less than fair to the Quaker point of view, which was not that of the *beati possidentes;* George Fox himself had used the word "possessors", but with him it stood in the context of a *theologia crucis*: "Be not professors but possessors and take heed of getting above the cross ..."[88] Still, Serrarius did not condemn the Quakers in everything; he recognized the legitimacy of their speaking about the Light, the Spirit and internal illumination. In spite of all differences, of all their "contrary thoughts", Quaker and chiliast had a common background in their deep reverence for the work of the Spirit in the heart of man. In view of this background, I close this tribute to a scholar, who has written such an inspiring work on the Holy Spirit in the life and thought of Puritans and Quakers,[89] by quoting from a hymn, possibly written by the English archbishop Stephen Langton, but attributed by Serrarius to the Early Church:[90]

> Veni sancte Spiritus
> et emitte caelitus
> lucis tuae radium.
> Da tuis fidelibus
> in te confidentibus
> sacrum septenarium.
> Da virtutis meritum
> da salutis exitum
> da perenne gaudium.[91]

---

[86] A manuscript copy of this letter—which Dr Nuttall brought to my notice—is found between two tracts of Jackson in the Friends' Library, London, *Tracts* Vol. 309.

[87] For the author and his book see R.M. Jones, *Studies in Mystical Religion,* 458ff.

[88] G.F. Nuttall, *Studies in Christian Enthusiasm, Illustrated from Early Quakerism*, Pendle Hill (Pa., U.S.A.) 1948, 44.

[89] This study originally appeared in a volume of essays published in honour of Geoffrey Nuttall. The work in question is *The Holy Spirit in Puritan Faith and Experience*, Oxford 1946.

[90] *Responsio*, *op. cit.*, 58: "Toto corde cum Primitivae Ecclesiae ad Deum sitientibus Animabus saepe repetamus Canticum illud ..." Serrarius reads l. 3, "verbi tui radium".

[91] See: F.G.E. Raby (ed.), *The Oxford Book of Medieval Latin Verse,* Oxford 1959, 375f.; J.W. Schulte Nordholt, *Hymnen en Liederen*, Hilversum, etc., 1964, 134f., 219.

CHAPTER NINE

BETWEEN PLATONISM AND ENLIGHTENMENT: SIMON PATRICK (1625-1707) AND HIS PLACE IN THE LATITUDINARIAN MOVEMENT

On the 21st of December 1673, John Evelyn noted down in his Diary: "Dr. *Patrick* preached the first serm: to the Household at W[hite] hall on 4. Phil: 4 most patheticaly seting forth the Love of God; and the obligation we had to rejoice in it".[1] At the time, Simon Patrick was a well-known and respected London preacher. He also was a prolific author; not a deep scholar, but a man with a practical mind, a ready pen and a broad range of interests, whose works would meet with a good deal of success and recognition. I shall attempt to assess his place in the Latitudinarian movement by marking out some characteristic traits of his world of thought; in this context, special attention will be given to the reception of some of his works in the Netherlands.[2] For Patrick's biography I made use of his autobiography (published in 1839), and a manuscript biography by a younger contemporary, Samuel Knight, prebendary of Ely, which is based on the manuscript autobiography,[3] while I also consulted A. Taylor's "Preface" to his edition of Patrick's *Works*.[4]

Like a number of other Latitudinarians, Patrick, who was born in 1625 and thus grew up in the period just before the Civil War, had a more or less Puritan background. According to Knight's biography

> His fathers diligence in his calling did by no means interfere with his constant and regular performance of religious duties in his family, and the public worship of God, which gave occasion to those who had too little religion themselves to stigmatize him with the name of a puritan, ...

while his mother had been educated with "the rules of the practice of piety".

In 1644, Patrick went up to Cambridge. His father had provided him with recommendations to Benjamin Whichcote, recently appointed Provost of

---

[1] E.S. de Beer (ed.), *The Diary of John Evelyn* IV, Oxford 1955, 29.

[2] For the reception of Latitudinarian works in the Netherlands (with a short passage on Patrick), see J. van den Berg, "Eighteenth Century Dutch translations of the works of some British latitudinarian and enlightened theologians", *Nederlands Archief voor Kerkgeschiedenis* 59 (1979), 194-212.

[3] *The Auto-biography of Simon Patrick, Bishop of Ely*. Now first printed from the original manuscript, Oxford 1839 (as far as I know, the MS biography is no longer extant); "Life of Symon Patrick, by Dr. Knight, Prebend of Ely", MS University Library Cambridge, Add. 20 (the following quotations are from pages 5 and 7).

[4] A. Taylor (ed.), *The Works of Symon Patrick D.D.* I, Oxford 1858.

King's, and to Ralph Cudworth, then a Fellow of Emmanuel, but ultimately his way led to Queens' College, where he fell under the spell of John Smith. In his autobiography, Patrick records a conversation with Smith on the doctrine of "absolute predestination",

> which I told him had always seemed to me very hard, and I could never answer the objections against it, but was advised by divines to silence carnal reason. At which he fell a laughing, and told me they were good and sound reasons which I had objected against that doctrine, and made such a representation of the nature of God to me, and of his goodwill to men in Christ Jesus, as quite altered my opinion, and made me take the liberty to read such authors (which were before forbidden me) as settled me in the belief that God would really have all men to be saved, of which I never after made a question, nor looked upon it as a matter of controversy, but presumed it in all my sermons.[5]

Patrick had the rare experience of being twice ordained: first as a Presbyterian minister; some years later, when he had become convinced of the necessity of episcopal ordination, by Bishop Hall of Norwich, a moderate Anglican, who as an ejected Bishop had to ordain him in private. At that time, in and after 1654, a transition from a certain form of Presbyterianism to an explicit Episcopalianism was not exceptional; in 1657, there were even great disputes about episcopal ordination in Emmanuel College.[6] Patrick became Vicar of Battersea and, after the restoration in 1662, Rector of St. Paul's, Covent Garden; in the preceding year, a royal mandate had annulled his election as Master of Queens' College. He won fame as a preacher, and in 1671 he was appointed chaplain to the King. He was also a good and devoted pastor: in 1665—the year of the plague—he remained in London to excercise his ministry. His letters to Lady Gauden,[7] written in that same year, which have been preserved and published, are in general not of a scholarly nature, such as Henry More's letters to Anne Conway, but their value lies in the fact that they make us understand better the mind and personality of the author. He saw the plague as a judgement of God on the wickedness of the population of London. In a letter of 30 September 1665 he quoted 2 Esdras 16.19, 20: "Behold, famine and plague, tribulation and anguish are sent as scourges for amendment. But for all these things they shall not turne from

[5] *Auto-biography*, 18f.

[6] R.S. Bosher, *The Making of the Restoration Settlement. The Influence of the Laudians 1649-1662*, London 1957, 38.

[7] Elizabeth Gauden was the wife of Dennis Gauden, head commissioner of the victualling department of the Navy, brother of John Gauden (Bishop of Winchester). The Gaudens lived in Clapham, but at the time of the plague Elizabeth stayed with a sister-in-law at Hutton Hall near Burnwood, Essex: *The Works of Symon Patrick* IX, 571, note a. The original correspondence is now in Cambridge University Library, MS.Add. 19. Taylor, who had no access to the original letters, based his edition of the correspondence (in *Works* IX, 571-617) on an abridged transcription: 445, notes i and j. I quote from the Cambridge MSS.

wickednesse ...".[8] Still, he kept open the possibility of an "amendment" after death, as appears from a letter of 10 October 1665, when the plague was already decreasing:

> Some people I see are past mending; att least in this world. What course God may take with them in the next, wee cannot tell. And if wee should intimate to them any such hopes, it would but make them worse and more incapable of favour. Yet the philosophers I see spoke it out: For Simplicius commenting upon Epictetus, saith that they who will not be made better by that book of his, cannot possibly be amended by any thing but the paines of hell. I know not how I fall into this argument; it is I suppose from my pitty towards many wretched creatures whom I wish happy; and that desire sure is not disagreeing to the laws of christianity.[9]

In the difficult situation of 1665, he read Epictetus,[10] and he endeavoured "to practice the philosophers lesson and to rejoice both liveing and dying".[11] His attitude at that time, indeed, had something of a Stoic quality. But at the same time, his letters to Lady Gauden have a Platonic flavour: "This Body doth not seeme to be made for a constant quiet habitation. It is a handsome prison, and if wee be not alwayes chained up, but sometimes gaine our liberty, it is a very great favour".[12] And together with all this, a more modern, Cartesian-rationalist trend manifests itself in a passage in which he chides Lady Gauden, who suffered from melancholy, because she imputes the indisposition of her body and mind and the troubles of her child to the influence of evil spirits.

> You want a little more philosophy to make your religion more satisfactory to you ... Now all passions we feele work upon the blood and make a new contexture there of parts, as appeares by the very outward lineaments of the face. To this different configuration of the animal spirits there, are most of the alterations you feele to be ascribed.[13]

And, last but not least: central to his thinking as it manifests itself in this correspondence is the idea of the love of God—it is significant that again and again he uses for God the term "the Almighty Love".[14]

In the summer of 1681 a number of London ministers agreed to write a short commentary on the Bible. Patrick promised to make notes on Ecclesiastes and the Song of Songs, but

---

[8] ULC, Add. 19, f. 29.

[9] ULC, Add. 19, f. 35. For the Cambridge Platonists and the idea of universal redemption, see D.P. Walker, *The Decline of Hell. Seventeenth-Century Discussions of Eternal Torment*, London 1964, esp. Ch. VIII.

[10] See also his letter of 7 Oct. 1665, ULC, Add. 19, f. 33.

[11] 19 Oct. 1665, ULC Add. 19, f. 40.

[12] Undated; ULC, Add. 19, f. 15.

[13] See note 12. Patrick wrote to Henry More about Lady Gauden's depression: see More's letter to Patrick, 5 Oct. 1673, Bodleian Library, MS Tanner 42, f. 38.

[14] Thus in the letter quoted above, and in a letter of 10 June 1676, f. 59.

> that design came to nothing, by the fears of Popery, which shortly ensued; when all our labours were engaged to keep our people firm in their religion, and discover the errors of the Romish Church.[15]

From that time onward, as one of the leading London ministers Patrick was deeply engaged in the struggle against Rome, which became the more vehement after James II's accession to the throne.[16] Patrick's opposition to Rome displeased the King, who according to Patrick had complained to the Archbishop about the ministers of London, "who preached too much against Popery, and named me in particular, who he said was a good man, but leaned too much on the two Deans" (Edward Stillingfleet and John Tillotson).[17] In that period, he was unpopular in Catholic as well as in right-wing Protestant circles; the Bishop of Lincoln pointed out as Patrick's adversaries "both Papists in the Church of Rome and some zealous dissenters in our Church".[18]

After the Glorious Revolution Patrick was one of those who were singled out for advancement. Gilbert Burnet recommended a number of members of the London clergy to William III: Tillotson, Patrick, Tenison, Stillingfleet, Sharp, Sherlock, Wake and Fowler, with one exception (John Sharp) well-known Latitudinarians. According to Burnet, Patrick was "a great preacher, and a man of eminently shining life, who will be a great ornament to the Episcopal order".[19] His sermons were appreciated at court, as appears from a letter of Burnet, who was so pleased by Patrick's "Excellent Sermon" that he intended to ask the Queen to order it to be printed; "but indeed her Majestie prevented me"—she declared she already wanted to take steps to have the sermon printed.[20] Patrick became Bishop of Chichester and, in 1691, Bishop of Ely,[21]

---

[15] *Auto-biography*, 98.

[16] For the opposition of the Latitudinarian Churchmen and Patrick's part in it, see M.C. Jacob, *The Newtonians and the English Revolution 1689-1720*, Ithaca and New York 1976, esp. Ch. 2; G.M. Straka, *Anglican Reaction to the Revolution of 1688*, Madison (Wisconsin) 1962, 17f.

[17] *Auto-biography*, 98.

[18] Thomas [Barlow, Bishop of] Lincoln to the Dean of Peterborough, 22 Febr. 1685, Queens' College, Cambridge, MS 73, f. 20 (quoted with the permission of the President and Fellows of Queens' College, Cambridge). In 1679 Patrick became Dean of Peterborough; he remained Rector of St. Paul's: *DNB* XLIV, 46.

[19] Burnet to the Prince of Orange, undated, probably written from Exeter: S.W. Singer (ed.), *The Correspondence of Henry Hyde, Earl of Clarendon and of his brother Laurence Hyde, Earl of Rochester*, London 1828, II 281. For a later, slightly more critical judgment, see Burnet's *History of his own Time* I, Oxford 1823, 326 (= folio ed. I 189f.): "Patrick was a great preacher ... a laborious man in his function, of great strictness of life, but a little too severe against those who differed from him ... He became afterwards more moderate".

[20] Burnet to the Dean of Peterborough, undated, Queens' College, Cambridge, MS 73, f. 48. Perhaps it was Patrick's sermon on Col. 3.15, preached before the Queen at Whitehall and printed in the course of 1689 (*British Museum Gen. Cat. of Printed Books*, 180, 677).

[21] For the political aspect of the episcopal appointments of 1690-1691, see Burnet, *History of his own Time* IV, 132 (= folio ed. II 77): "this great promotion was such a discovery of the king and queen's designs, with relation to the church, that it served much to remove the jealousies, that some other steps the king had made, were beginning to raise in the whigs ..."; according to

where he served till his death in 1707: a man who assiduously performed his episcopal duties and whose pen did not rest. And from time to time he came up to London to attend the meetings of the House of Lords; so in December 1705, when as a good Latitudinarian he expressed his concern about the way young students had protested against the candidacy for Parliament of two "worthy gentlemen", one of whom was Isaac Newton.[22]

As far as we know, Patrick's first public performance was the preaching of a funeral sermon for his beloved teacher John Smith, who died in 1652. The text (2 Kings 2.12: And Elisha saw it, and he cried, My father, my father, the chariot of Israel, and the horsemen thereof) is indicative of the great admiration he fostered for Smith. The sermon appeared in 1660, together with Smith's *Select Discourses*. Patrick characterized Smith with an adapted quotation from Gregory of Nazianzus which has a Platonic ring: "His country was heaven, his town or city was the Jerusalem which is above, his fellow-citizens were the saints, his nobility was 'the retaining of the divine impressions and stamps upon his soul, and being like to God the archetype and first pattern of all goodness'. And indeed the preserving of the heavenly symbols that are in our souls ... he often spake of ...".[23] As we shall see, in fact Patrick never moved far from the teaching of Smith.

I mention a few other publications of the many which in the course of time Patrick sent to the press. His earliest publications are two tracts on the Sacraments: *Aqua Genitalis*, on Baptism (1659) and *Mensa Mystica, on* the Lord's Supper (1660). Patrick has not—as perhaps the titles of the works might make us surmise—a high sacramental doctrine: Baptism is a seal of the covenant between God and man,[24] the Lord's Supper a seal of the love of God in the gift of his Son. Thus in line with the Anglican tradition he strongly attacks the doctrine of transubstantiation: "They that would have more than such things as these in this Sacrament [that of the Lord's Supper] are in danger to have nothing at all".[25] This does not detract, however, from his deep reverence for the Sacraments, which at a later stage would lead to his plea for frequent communion.[26] In fact, his sacramental doctrine was not unlike that of Calvin, as the Catholics perceived who according to Patrick "in scorn and pride" called the Lord's Supper as celebrated by the Anglicans: "Calvin's Supper and Communion".[27] Patrick, however, does not appeal to Calvin, but rather to Erasmus,

---

Burnet, all those who had been appointed or promoted were men "of moderate principles".

[22] R.S. Westfall, *Never at Rest, A Biography of Isaac Newton*, London 1980, 626.

[23] John Smith, *Select Discourses* (4th edition), Cambridge 1859, 505f. (quoting from Gregory of Nazianzus, Orat. 8, § 6).

[24] *Aqua Genitalis. A Discourse concerning Baptism*, London ^{4}1684, 407, 441 (continuing pagination with the 5th ed. of *Mensa Mystica).*

[25] *Mensa Mystica*, London ^{3}1676, f. [B 7 ro, 8 ro].

[26] *Diary of John Evelyn* I, 30.

[27] *Mensa Mystica*, f. 4 (= 3)v^{o}.

for whose views he felt a deep sympathy, especially because Erasmus, as Patrick quotes him, wanted to have Jesus painted before the eyes of men "not sowre and harsh; but just as he is, Friendly, Sweet, and Amiable".[28] This quotation set the tone for many of Patrick's later works.

In 1662 appeared a short pamphlet under the title *A Brief Account of the New Sect of Latitude-Men*.[29] It was written by "S.P. at Cambridge"; I think that although there is no absolute proof, there is no reason to doubt the usual attribution of the pamphlet to Simon Patrick. *A Brief Account* is a most interesting little work; Gordon Rupp rightly remarks that Patrick "never achieved anything as sparklingly impressive in any of his later writing".[30] The style—witty and lively—is that of Patrick at his very best, while the contents are typical for a man who was deeply committed to the cause of the new way of thinking as it had manifested itself in the works and public utterances of the Cambridge Platonists. The author is at pains to show that the so-called Latitudemen or Latitudinarians are loyal Anglicans, who "highly approve that vertuous mediocrity which our Church observes between the meretricious gaudiness of the Church of *Rome*, and the squalid sluttery of Fanatick conventicles". Their ideal is the Church of "the first and purest ages". He does not think it credible that they should hold any other Doctrine than the Church holds,

> since they derive it from the same fountains, not from the *Spinose school-men, or Dutch systematicks*,[31] neither from *Rome* nor *Geneva*, but from the Sacred writings of the Apostles and Evangelists ...

They want to discern between the "modern corruptions" and the "ancient simplicity" of the Church. Patrick rejects the accusation that the Latitudinarians listen too much to their own reason. There is no point in divinity, "where that which is most ancient does not prove the most rational, and the most rational the ancientest; for there is an eternal consanguinity between all verity; and nothing is true in Divinity, which is false in Philosophy, or on the contrary ...".

The theology propounded in this pamphlet, is that of a moderate Anglicanism with a strong Arminian bias: the author rejoices in the fact that "the

[28] *Aqua Genitalis*, 500.

[29] I used the facsimile edition with an introduction by T.A. Birrell, Los Angeles 1963.

[30] *Religion in England 1688-1791*, Oxford 1986, 29 n. 1. Taylor doubted the authenticity of the pamphlet and did not dare to give it a place in his edition of the *Works* (see *Works* 1, Editor's Preface). According to T.A. Birrell, however, Taylor's arguments are far from conclusive: "Introduction", I. I concur with Birrell's arguments in favour of the attribution to Patrick but I would rule out the possibility (left open by Birrell) that it was written by a supporter: why should a supporter create a wrong impression by using the initials S.P.?

[31] Apparently, Patrick refers to the predestinarian theology of the Synod of Dort (1618-19).

freedom of our wills, the universal intent of Christ's death, and sufficiency of God's Grace, the conditions of justification [*i.e.*: no justification without manifest signs of a holy life in obedience to the will of God][32] ... do again begin to obtain". Life is more important than doctrine or ritual: "I shall always think him most consciencious who leads the most unblameable life, though he be not greatly scrupulous about the externals of Religion".[33] In the field of philosophy he is no great admirer of Aristotle, and quite definitely not of "the generality of his Interpreters". The Latitudinarians embrace "a method of philosophy which they think was a much antienter than *Aristotle*, as you conceive *Oxford* was before *Cambridge* ... Christian Religion was never bred up in the *Peripatetick school*, but spent her best and healthfullest years in the more *Religious Academy* ... ; let her old loving Nurse the *Platonick Philosophy* be admitted again into her family ...".[34] But he combines the Platonic philosophy with a new way of philosophizing which, though he does not mention the name, cannot be anything else than that of Descartes; after all, this was the year in which More wrote that the true ancient philosophy "did consist of what we now call Platonism and Cartesianism".[35]

Furthermore, the author implicitly pleads for a measure of toleration within the Church when he depicts her as an indulgent Mother "that will not unnecessarily impose upon the judgement or practice of her Children". As regards those who are outside the Church, by their moderation the Latitudinarians "are most likely to win upon the minds of dissenters, who are too many to be contemned". But moderation does not entail sympathy: he sees the Presbyterians, together with the "Papists", as "potent Enemies ... who watch all opportunities of subversing the best Church in the world".[36] Patrick's criticism of Dissent would become still more explicit some years later, when he published his *A Friendly Debate*.[37]

In 1664 appeared Patrick's best known work, *The Parable of the Pilgrim.* It never attained such a measure of popularity as, shortly afterwards, Bunyan's *Pilgrim's Progress* would receive, and it certainly lacks the dramatic quality of the latter work, but its charm lies in the mildly Platonic atmosphere which pervades the "parable". "We are ... of kin to two Worlds, and placed in the

---

[32] For the relation between justification and "holy life" in seventeenth century Anglican theology, see in particular C.F. Allison, *The Rise of Moralism*, London 1966.

[33] *Brief Account*, 9-11.

[34] *Brief Account*, 14, 24.

[35] A. Lichtenstein, *Henry More. The Rational Theology of a Cambridge Platonist*, Cambridge (Mass.) 1962, 10 (quotation from the "Preface General" to More's *Collection of Several Philosophical Writings* 1662). Margaret Jacob thinks it possible that in Simon Patrick's more modern philosophical orientation the influence of his brother John Patrick played a part: *The Newtonians*, 43.

[36] *Brief Account*, 11ff.

[37] For a discussion of this work, see below.

middle between Heaven and Earth. With our Heads we touch the one, and with our Feet we stand upon the other".[38] The theology behind the book is the same as that which we found in the *Brief Account*: the pilgrim is free to choose; he knows God is a God of love, not a cruel tyrant whose image is like that of a Devil,[39] and his religion is marked by an indissoluble unity between faith and practice, justification and obedience. The *Parable* particularly opposes the antinomian brand of Calvinism which exalts "Free Grace" at the cost of active obedience; the theology of "those that would turn me into a Stone, and render me at once as humble, and as lumpish and melancholy too, as the earth itself".[40] But the polemic elements are counterbalanced by an irenic tendency: it quite astonished the pilgrim "to see that so many men did dream that the way to *The Vision of Peace* lay through the field of strife and war; and that we must come to live together in endless love hereafter, by living in perpetual frays and brawls in the world where we now are".[41]

Such "frays and brawls" were engendered, however, by Patrick himself when in 1669 he published his *A Friendly Debate between a Conformist and a Non-Conformist*;[42] a work which was followed by three *Continuations*, in which the polemical tone became stronger and stronger. A central point in the *Friendly Debate* is that of the place and function of reason in religious life. One of the objections of the Non-Conformist to a fictitious Anglican minister, a "Mr. Dulman" is, that when he endeavours to open the Scripture "he doth not do it in a Spiritual way, but only Rationally". The "Conformist" replies: "Do you think that these two words, *Spiritual* and *Rational*, are opposed the one to the other? If they be, then *Spiritually* is as much as *Irrationally* and absurdly ... I find nothing so powerful as the Christian Doctrine rationally handled".[43] Another prominent aspect of the *Friendly Debate* is its anti-Calvinist bias, strengthened by Patrick's strong resistance against antinomian tendencies he perceived in the circle of the Dissenters. When the Non-Conformist remarks that according to the Conformists "good works are necessary to our justification", Patrick makes "Conformist" reply that such is indeed true, when we see Salvation as "the final and absolute justification at the day of judgment".

---

[38] *The Parable of the Pilgrim*, London 1665, 152.

[39] *Parable*, 28. This very strong anti-Calvinist expression is in line with Henry More's protest against an absolute decree of reprobation; according to More, those who favour this idea make themselves "Puppets ... of that great Idol of theirs (for it is no God) that wills, as they say, merely because he wills": *An Explanation of the Grand Mystery of Godliness* X, V, 6, *Theological Works*, London 1708, 353.

[40] *Parable*, 17f.

[41] *Parable*, 11.

[42] The work appeared anonymously, but the authorship soon became known. It won him the favour of the Archbishop of Canterbury, Gilbert Sheldon, who before had been critical of Patrick: *Auto-biography*, 59f.

[43] *A Friendly Debate*, London 1669, 2, 5, 11.

Furthermore "Conformist" remarks that his minister "doth not tickle us meerly with a soft Story of the great love of *Jesus Christ* towards Sinners; but labours to beget in us an ardent love to him. And lest we should run away with a pleasant Fancy, he makes us understand wherein this love consists, viz. in Obedience to him to the very death ...".[44]

Of course, Patrick was aware of the fact that not all Dissenters were antinomians. To a certain extent he sympathized with Richard Baxter, whom in a later stage of the discussion he even defended against the charge of unorthodoxy,[45] as, in 1680, he would also do in a personal discussion with the ultra-Calvinist layman Lewis (Louis) du Moulin, who had attacked Patrick as well as Baxter because of their supposed deviation from the doctrine of justification.[46]

Baxter, in his turn, had some sympathy for Patrick. In his autobiography we read: "He [Patrick] had before written a Book called the *Pilgrim*, which with many laudable things, had sharply pleaded that *Obedience must enter the definition of Justifying Faith* ... He was one of those then called a Latitudinarian, a sober, learned, able Man, that had written many things well, and was well enough esteemed". Baxter was all the more shocked at the tone and the tendency of *A Friendly Debate:* "this Book was so dis-ingenuous and virulent as caused most Religious People to abhor it for the strain and tendency, and probable Effects". Patrick generalized: "he speaketh to the Nonconformists in general (though acknowledging some sober Persons to be among them) that which is nothing to the cause of Non-conformity; and laboureth to prove that the Religion of the Non-conformists is *foolish*, ridiculous, *etc.* As if he should have thought to prove the Religion of *Christians*, or *Protestants* foolish, because there are ignorant persons among them". Baxter did not speak "out of partiality" against Patrick: "for he was pleased to single me out for his Commendations, and to exempt me from the Accusations. But it made my Heart grieve to perceive how the Devil was only the gainer, whilst Truth and Godliness was not only pretended by both parties, but really intended".[47] It seems that Patrick's friends, too, were not always quite happy with his polemical style; in his autobiography he mentions that many of his friends thought the

---

[44] *A Friendly Debate*, 10, 109.

[45] *A Further Continuation and Defence, or, A Third Part of the Friendly Debate*, London 1670, 260f.

[46] In his last illness, Du Moulin (who lived in Patrick's parish) asked Patrick's forgiveness for his attacks; on this occasion Patrick mentioned the name of Baxter: *Auto-biography*, 85. For Du Moulin's attack on Patrick, see his *A Short and True Account of the Several Advances the Church of England hath made towards Rome*, London 1680, esp. 31ff.; for Du Moulin's retractation: *The Last Words of Lewis du Moulin*, London 1680, esp. 6-10; for Baxter and Du Moulin: R. Baxter, *Reliquiae Baxterianae* ... published by Matthew Sylvester, London 1696, Lib. I (Part 1), 110, and G.F. Nuttall, "Dr. Du Moulin and *Papa Ultrajectinus*", *Nederlands Archief voor Kerkgeschiedenis* 61 (1981), 205-213.

[47] *Reliquiae Baxterianae*, Part III, 39f.

beginning of the *Second Continuation* was written "in a way a little too jocular".[48]

It was Patrick's sincere intention in writing against the Dissenters "to persuade them in a kind manner to join with us; at least not to have us in contempt ...".[49] Thus, his *Friendly Debate* was an apology for the Church of England as well as a plea for "comprehension". There is a natural affinity between Latitudinarianism and the ideal of "comprehension": a certain degree of latitude was needed to accept at least the more moderate Dissenters within the fold of the Church of England. Only an "indulgent mother" would be able to come to terms with her dissenting offspring. In the idea of comprehension, idealistic and pragmatic motives went hand in hand: the unity of the Church was a divine command, it was also thought to be a prerequisite for the continuation of the Protestant establishment, and it would strengthen the Protestant cause in the ungoing struggle with Rome.

When, after the "Glorious Revolution", comprehension no longer was a workable option, the idea of toleration as embodied in the *Toleration Act* of 1689 fitted quite well into the prevailing Latitudinarian framework of those days. Fellow-Protestants, who together with the leading Latitudinarian Anglicans had withstood the Roman threat and who were prepared to take the oaths of allegiance and supremacy, were no longer considered "potent enemies" of the Church. This does not imply, however, that Latitudinarians were always as tolerant in practice as their ideals might make us surmise. When Bishop of Ely, Patrick praised the Rector of Doddington for having stemmed the progress of "the Anabaptist faction"; a schoolmaster, who belonged to that group, would certainly not receive a licence.[50] Did he consider the work of the schoolmaster as part of "the squalid sluttery of Fanatick conventicles", about which he had written in 1662?

In 1673 appeared a work of a less polemical nature, a devotional work in the full sense of the word: *Advice to a Friend*, written for his future spouse. It is perhaps his deepest work; certainly a work in which the Platonic influence is dominant and pervasive, more than in any other of his writings.

> If a Soul inclosed in this Body can see and apprehend so much of God; o what a sight of him shall it have, when it is freed from these Chaines? If whilst we look out of these Windowes of Sense, such a glorious Majesty present itself before us; in what an amazing splendor will the Divinity appear, when there is nothing to interpose between us, and its incomparable beauty?

True religion should at least reflect something of this light and beauty: "look

---

[48] *Auto-biography*, 60.

[49] *Loc. cit.*

[50] S. Patrick to the Rev. Mr. Williams, 22 August 1697, British Library Add. 5831, f. 148.

upon Religion as a most pleasant thing, and represent it to yourself with a face as fair and beautiful as you can".[51] No wonder—just to give one example of the impression the *Advice* made even a long time after its first publication—that in 1710 Henry Newman, secretary of the Society for Promoting Christian Knowledge, offered to lend a copy of the work to a correspondent who suffered from "melancholy".[52] The accentuation of the "pleasant" character of the Christian religion is one of the distinguishing marks of the Latitudinarian pastoral approach. Patrick's devotional works, his biblical expositions,[53] his exertions to defend the Church of England against her real or potential enemies and his pastoral activities as a bishop made him, in the words of J.H. Overton, "one of the chief instruments in that revival of church life which marked the last years of the seventeenth century".[54]

As we saw, in the years which preceded the "Glorious Revolution" Patrick was one of the leaders of the Anglican opposition to the growing influence of Rome. The fact that now the Catholics were considered the most imminent threat to the Anglican establishment made him shift the front of his polemical activities from the Dissenters to the Church of Rome. In 1680—two years after "the Popish plot"—he published a revised translation of Grotius' *De Veritate Religionis Christianae*, to which he added a seventh book, "Against the Present Roman Church".[55] As a Latitudinarian, he sympathized with Grotius' theological views. In the preface to the translation he highly praised the Dutch scholar who "fell into disgrace in his own Country", and he defended him against those who had accused him of heresy. Certainly he wrote in the spirit of Grotius when he remarked in Book VII: "... following the Scriptures, we shall embrace a Religion of admirable simplicity".[56] It is not impossible, however, that on one point at least he differed from Grotius: there are indications (though the evidence is circumstantial), that he shared the millenarian ideals of some of his Anglican contemporaries.[57] But while people such as Henry More or Drue Cressener strongly denounced Grotius' anti-chiliastic explanation of Revelation and his refusal to identify the papacy with Antichrist for fear

---

[51] *Advice to a Friend*, London 1673, 51, 79.

[52] L.W. Cowie, *Henry Newman, An American in London 1708-43*, London 1956, 10.

[53] Between 1679 and 1685 he published a series of paraphrases, from the Book of Job to the Song of Solomon, and between 1695 and 1706 a series of commentaries on the historical books of the Old Testament.

[54] *DNB* XLIV, 46; cf. G.V. Bennett: "... the Williamite bishops made great efforts to turn their clergy's attention to pastoral concerns"; in this context he mentions Patrick as one of those bishops who "travelled out into remote corners of their diocese", *The Tory Crisis in Church and State 1688-1730*, Oxford 1975, 21.

[55] *The Truth of Christian Religion* ... Now translated into English, with the addition of a seventh book, by Simon Patrick, London 1680.

[56] *The Truth*, London 1694, 24.

[57] For this, see Margaret C. Jacob, *The Newtonians*, 108.

that the acceptance of Grotius' views would weaken the Protestant cause,[58] Patrick took a wiser course. In stead of criticizing Grotius, he compensated for the lack of anti-Catholic bias in Grotius by writing his "seventh book", thus creating the impression (or giving the illusion) that his sharp anti-Catholic stand was in line with "the Grotian way".

In the course of time, some of Patrick's works found their way to the Netherlands in Dutch translation.[59] His edition of the English translation of *De Veritate* with the seventh book already appeared in Dutch translation in 1686;[60] it went through five editions, of which the last one (1728) also contained the two treatises added by Jean le Clerc to his edition of *De Veritate*.[61] In the middle years of the eighteenth century, other works of Patrick were translated into Dutch. Between 1740 and 1757 appeared a biblical commentary in seventeen folio volumes: "Explanation of the entire Holy Scripture, taken from the English explanations by Patrick, Polus and Wells", which for the Old Testament contained much material from Patrick.[62] It gained a large popularity in the Netherlands. The first volume was published with a recommendation by the Leiden professor Joan van den Honert, dated 1 Oct. 1739. Van den Honert was a theologian in the tradition of Coccejus; orthodox, but not extreme.[63] As a Calvinist he opposed the Remonstrants, but at the same time as a child of the eighteenth century he somehow sympathized with the toleration ideal, in this context quoting with approval John Locke and Benjamin Hoadly.[64] In his recommendation to the commentary, he praised the English authors, but (though at that time he probably was not yet aware of Patrick's theological position)[65] as a cautious man he made a general proviso: "no one should think

---

[58] See J. van den Berg, "Continuity within a changing context", this vol. Ch. 6, and "Glorious Revolution and Millennium: the "Apocalyptical Thoughts" of Drue Cressener", this vol. Ch.10.

[59] See this article note 2.

[60] H. de Groot, *Van de waarheid des christelyken godsdiensts* ... uit het Latijn vertaalt door Joachim Oudaan ... Althans met een Zevende Boek vermeerdert, in het Engels geschreven door Dr. Simon Patrik, Rotterdam 1686.

[61] See J. ter Meulen et P.J. Diermanse, *Bibliographie des écrits imprimés de Hugo Grotius*, La Haye 1950, 523-525.

[62] *Verklaring van de geheele H. Schrift, uit de Engelsche verklaringe van Patrik, Polus, Wels*, Amsterdam 1740 (1741)-1757. Polus is Matthew Poole (1624-1679), Wels is Edward Wells (1667-1727). Of Volume I, a first ed. appeared in 1740, a second ed. in 1741.

[63] For Van den Honert, see *Biographisch Woordenboek van Protestantsche Godgeleerden in Nederland* V (1931) s.v. and now also: J. van Eijnatten, *Mutua Christianorum Tolerantia*, Firenze 1998.

[64] In the Dutch translation of his academic oration "De mutua christianorum tolerantia" of 1745: *Academische redenvoering over de onderlinge verdraagzaamheid der Christenen*, Leiden 1745, also published in Van den Honert's *Derde versameling van heilige mengelstoffen*, Leiden 1747. He quoted Locke and Hoadly from a Dutch translation: *Verzameling van eenige verhandelingen over de verdraagzaamheid en vrijheid van godsdienst*, Amsterdam 1734.

[65] Apparently he did not read English (the auction catalogue of his books, *Bibliotheca Honertiana*, Lugd. Bat. 1758, contains no English books), and Patrick's theologically controversional *Parable* had not yet appeared in Dutch translation.

that I, speaking thus of this work, agree with everything which is to be found in it, and that I nowhere differ from the authors ...".[66]

In 1744 appeared a translation of *The Devout Christian instructed how to pray* of 1672;[67] perhaps for Remonstrants it provided an alternative for the existing "Reformed treasury of prayer", which had its origin in the seventeenth century Puritan tradition.[68] Two years later, a translation of the *Parable of the Pilgrim* was published,[69] which seems to have had a fair amount of popularity: there was an identical reprint in 1752, and a shortened edition in 1773, with a preface by the translator, according to whom the work had found so many readers that there were almost no more copies available.[70] It is interesting that in the shortened edition none of the expressions which implied an anti-Calvinist bias were expunged or even softened.

Conservative Calvinists considered the *Parable of the Pilgrim* a threat to Reformed orthodoxy. For Antonie van der Os, a young minister of the Reformed Church with enlightened ideas, the fact that he (as his opponents asserted) had recommended the *Parable* to the members of his first congregation had unhappy results: it was used as an additional charge in a heresy suit which in 1755 led to his deposition. The Reformed Church of that time was not in all respects "an indulgent mother". In a recent study on Van der Os it has been argued (I think on good grounds) that presumably Van der Os was the translator of the *Parable*.[71] However this may be, there clearly are parallels between his world of thought and that of Patrick.

Van der Os was a pupil of Van den Honert. Perhaps partly for personal reasons, possibly also because in the course of time his sympathy for the toleration ideal had deepened, Van den Honert came forward as a staunch defender of the accused minister, much to the astonishment and disappointment of many orthodox. Theologically, Van den Honert's position was somewhat ambivalent. He shared Patrick's dislike of ultra-Calvinist "antinomian"

---

[66] *Verklaring* I ²1741, X. See also his preface to Volume IV (1742), VI, where he defends the English authors against the insinuation that they were not interested in inner and spiritual knowledge; to Volume V (1742), I, where he mentions Albert Schultens' esteem of Patrick as an exegete, and to Volume VII (1744), I, where he gives unstinted praise to "the great Simon Patrick".

[67] *De aandachtige Christen onderricht hoe hy Godt zal bidden en danken, of een Gebede-boek voor huisgezinnen*, Amsterdam 1744.

[68] See J. van den Berg and G.F. Nuttall, *Philip Doddridge (1702-1751) and the Netherlands*, Leiden 1987, 44.

[69] *Geschiedenis van den reiziger naar het hemelsche Jerusalem* ... naer den zesden druk in het Nederduitsch vertaelt, en met kopere Plaeten versierd, Amsterdam 1746.

[70] *Geschiedenis* etc., Amsterdam 1773, * 2ro. In *From Abbadie to Young*, Veenendaal 1980, 95, J. van der Haar mentions an edition (of which only Volume I has been preserved) which appeared in 1776 (apparently unabridged).

[71] R.A. Bosch, *Het conflict rond Antonius van der Os, predikant te Zwolle 1748-1755*, Kampen 1988, 20 vv. For Patrick, Van der Os and Van den Honert, see also 48, 105f.

tendencies, but on the other hand he could not agree with the theological context of Patrick's reaction to antinomianism. In the period in which he was deeply engaged in the defence of Van der Os he attacked Patrick's *Parable*, no doubt with the purpose of safeguarding himself against the accusation of Arminian sympathies. Patrick (Van den Honert asserted) had rightly opposed the misuse of the doctrine of free grace, but in doing so had fallen himself into the semi-Pelagian error.[72]

In the meantime, the Dutch translation of Patrick's *Advice to a Friend* had also appeared.[73] The preface, written by the translator, breathed an enlightened spirit. According to the translator, Patrick's *Parable* had made such progress in the Netherlands, "that it had survived all stirrings of stupid ignorance and overstrict party spirit and had won the esteem of almost all judicious people among those who love true piety".[74]

Of course it was Patrick's theology, his rejection of the doctrine of absolute predestination, his emphasis on the universal love of God, his insistence on the connection between faith and obedience, his plea for a return to the simplicity of the primitive church, which evoked the sympathy of enlightened Protestants, the criticism of conservative Calvinists. But he was no more a radical than his Cambridge teachers were. He shared their moderate orthodoxy, their broad-minded adherence to the fundamental tenets of the Anglican Church, of which he was such a loyal son. When we compare his teachings with those of the leading Cambridge Platonists, whom he so much admired, it becomes clear that most of what he taught had already been said by them. Just like them, he valued reason too highly ever to become an enthusiast; just as with them, a mild and tempered mysticism prevented him from becoming a rationalist.[75] But he was no deep philosopher, nor had he a speculative mind. He was, in a broad sense, a Platonist, but hardly a Neoplatonist. That he did not sing the praise of Hermes Tresmegistus, as the younger More did, is evident: that was already *passé* when Patrick went up to Cambridge. But he rarely mentions Plotinus, and he does not recur to the *theologia prisca*, which meant so much

---

[72] J. van den Honert, *Het geloov der vaderen, ten spore der kinderen*, Leyden 1753, 54. Van den Honert did not convince all his opponents; even after his death, two ultra-orthodox authors stated that in his struggle against "inner Christianity" Van den Honert himself had made use of Pelagian or semi-Pelagian arguments: A. Comrie and N. Holtius, *Examen van het Ontwerp van Tolerantie* X, Amsterdam 1759, XXX.

[73] *Bestieringen tot een heilig leven*, bij wijze van een raad aan een vrind in "t Engelsch beschreven door den beroemden Heer Simon Patrick ... naar den derden druk uit het Engelsch vertaald en met Kopere Platen versierd, Amsterdam 1752.

[74] *Bestieringen*, f. 5vo.

[75] Especially A. Taylor strongly emphasizes the continuity between the Cambridge Platonists and Patrick; he sees Patrick as the most faithful and diligent exponent of the principles of the Cambridge School in their application to the theory and practice of religion and morality: S. Patrick, *Works* I, XXXI note g.

[76] Auto-biography, 26.

to his Cambridge teachers. His theology is a mixture between the Platonist and the Erasmian-Grotian tradition. It was his main purpose to preach a religion that was clear without becoming cold, simple without losing its essential depth-dimension. To him, the centre of religion was the awareness of the love of God, which, as he remarked in his autobiography, he preached to mankind as the most evident truth.[76] In this, he stood in the tradition of John Smith, who in his *The Excellency and Nobleness of True Religion* had remarked:

> A good man, that finds himself made partaker of the Divine nature, and transformed into the image of God infinitely takes pleasure in God, as being "altogether lovely", according to that in Canticles, Totus ipse est desideria; and his "meditation of God is sweet unto him". St. John, that lay in the bosom of Christ, who came from the bosom of the Father, and perfectly understood His eternal essence, hath given us the fullest description that he could make of Him, when he tells us that "God is love; and he that dwelleth in God, dwelleth in love"; and, reposing himself in the bosom of an Almighty goodness, where he finds nothing but love and loveliness, he now displays all the strength and beauty of those his choicest and most precious affections of love, and joy, and confidence.[77]

This quotation from his beloved teacher may serve as an epitome of the heart and core of Patrick's theology. On that Sunday in December 1673, the year in which Patrick wrote his moving *Advice to a Friend*, John Evelyn, indeed, understood what was the essence of his message.

---

[77] J. Smith, "The Excellency and Nobleness of True Religion", in *Select Discourses*, 434. "Desideria" is a literal translation of the Hebrew plural מַחֲמַדִּים (Cant. 5.16).

CHAPTER TEN

GLORIOUS REVOLUTION AND MILLENNIUM: THE "APOCALYPTICAL THOUGHTS" OF DRUE CRESSENER

On 22 November 1687, Drue Cressener, vicar of Soham in the diocese of Ely, wrote to his friend Henry Plumptre:

> I have been almost buried in my Apocalyptical Thoughts for these several months ... I do now acquaint you, that I am in a condition to write Prognostications of the Affairs of almost all Kingdoms for these Hundred Years next following.

How much the subject fascinated him and how deeply he was convinced of the issue of his prognostications also appears from another letter to Plumptre, written on 21 February 1688 (O.S. 1687):

> I am more and more confident, as Apocalyptical Men use to be, of the strength of my Conclusions; And from thence send you the News of a continual increase of the flourishing State of the Church very shortly to begin, and to continue to the end of the World; And therefore desire you to take special Care of your Health, and to desire all good People to do so, that they may be so happy as to live to see a full confirmation of this Prediction ...

Cressener supposed the next year (1689) would be "a year of Wonders for the Recovery of the Church". He was thrilled at the prospect: "My Pen runs before I am aware of it; For my Head is full, and I think I have got one to ease my self upon, and so I desire you to bear it patiently ...".[1]

While he followed the great events of his own time with deep intensity, Cressener himself had a very uneventful life.[2] Born in 1642 in Bury St. Edmunds, in his sixteenth year he went up to Cambridge, where he studied first at Christ's College, later at Pembroke Hall, of which he became a fellow in 1669. In Christ's he no doubt was taught by Henry More, who in the period after the Restoration would become the most prominent Anglican

---

[1] Cf. his letter to Plumptre of 28 February 1688 (O.S. 1687), in which he wrote that he agreed with Jurieu that a resurrection of the "Reformed Religion" in France in 1689 was highly probable. The letters to Plumptre are printed in D. Cressener, *The Judgments of God upon the Roman-Catholick Church*, London 1689, sig. Ttl-3.

[2] Dru[e] Cressener, son of Thomas, was baptized on 13 January 1641/2; see Bury St. Edmunds, St. James Church Parish Registers, Baptisms 1558-1800 (with thanks to Suffolk Record Office, Bury St. Edmunds). The list of incumbents in Soham Parish Church mentions him as Drugo Cressner. For his life, see *DNB* s.v. (gives a wrong birthdate); J.Venn and J.A. Venn, *Alumni Cartabrigienses* I, Cambridge 1922, s.v.

millenarian.[3] Cressener was ordained in London in 1677; in the same year he became vicar of Waresley, in 1678 also proctor of the University of Cambridge. In 1679 he moved to Soham, where he stayed as vicar till his death in 1718. From 1700 he was also prebendary of Ely; perhaps he owed his appointment to the influence of the Bishop of Ely, Simon Patrick, with whom he was acquainted since the turbulent years which preceded the Glorious Revolution.

It was in those years that he started writing his first book, *The Judgments of God upon the Roman-Catholick Church. From its First Rigid Laws for Universal Conformity to it, unto its Last End.* What follows on the title-page is in fact a summary of its contents; we are informed that the book gives

> A Prospect of these near approaching Revolutions, Viz. the Revival of the *Protestant* Confession in an Eminent Kingdom, where it was totally suppressed. The last end of all *Turkish* Hostilities. The general Mortification of the Power of the *Roman Church* in all Parts of its Dominions. In Explication of the *Trumpets* and *Vials* of the *Apocalypse*, upon Principles generally acknowledged by *Protestant* Interpreters.

The book contained testimonies from a number of people, among them Simon Patrick, Thomas Burnet and Henry Plumptre, which should make it clear that the main part was written before the events of the Glorious Revolution.[4]

Patrick was a leading figure in the circle of London ministers who strongly opposed the growing influence of Rome in the reign of James II and who welcomed the Glorious Revolution; as a theologian, he was a typical representative of the Latitudinarian tendency in the Church of England.[5] It is not clear whether he himself was a millenarian. Cressener wrote that Patrick's encouragement "was the great Motive to me to enter into the more obscure and uncertain parts of the Prophecy",[6] which at least seems to indicate that Patrick was in sympathy with millenarian studies, though his support for Cressener may have been caused as much by Cressener's uncompromising anti-Catholic stand. Thomas Burnet, master of the Charterhouse, was also a prominent Latitudinarian. He was deeply interested in scientific subjects, especially in the theories about the origin and development of the earth. In 1681 he published the first part of his *Telluris Theoria Sacra*; it appeared in 1684 in an English version: *Theory*—from the fourth edition (1719) onward *The Sacred Theory*—*of the Earth*. When Cressener had almost finished his book, probably

[3] For More's millenarianism, see J. van den Berg, "Continuity within a Changing Context—the Apocalyptic Thoughts of Joseph Mede and Henry More"; this volume Ch. 6.

[4] Patrick, Burnet and Plumptre declared in March 1689 (N.S.) that they had read the chapters 1-19 "near a year ago". Thomas Paget and Samuel Freeman wrote that these chapters were in their hands "when the Bishops were sent to the *Tower* [June, 1688], and then offered [apparently for approbation] to Lambeth": *Judgments*, sig. A4rV.

[5] For his theological position, see J. van den Berg, "Between Platonism and Enlightenment: Simon Patrick (1625-1707) and his Place in the Latitudinarian Movement"; this volume Ch. 9.

[6] Cressener to Plumptre, 22 November 1687, *Judgments*, sig. Tt2v.

in May 1688 (he had come as far as the nineteenth chapter) he received a manuscript copy of the second part of Burnet's *Theoria*, which apparently circulated among his London friends.[7] Cressener was highly pleased with the "Learned and Ingenuous Discoveries" of his "Honoured Friend", whom no doubt he knew since their common time at Christ's College:[8]

> I do wholly subscribe to his opinion about the necessity of the literal Acceptation of the first part of the 21st Chapter of the *Apocalypse*, concerning the Resurrection of the Saints: And from thence to acknowledge the unquestionable grounds we have for a Blessed *Millennium* here upon Earth.[9]

Their thoughts on the Millennium ran parallel, though as we shall see the centre of gravity of Cressener's work differed from that of Burnet.

Henry Plumptre possibly was the Plumptre of Nottingham who was involved in a conflict, caused by James II's proceedings against the charter of Nottingham corporation.[10] If so, he certainly shared the political views of the London circle of Latitudinarian clergy; no doubt he was a close friend, as Cressener entrusted him with his private "Apocalyptical Thoughts".

Furthermore, William Lloyd, Bishop of St. Asaph's, was interested in Cressener's work.[11] He asked for the manuscript, which he received before June 1688, when together with six other bishops he was sent to the Tower.[12] He was a convinced millenarian; John Evelyn, who on more than one occasion discussed with Lloyd the subject of biblical prophecy, called him "this prophetick bishop'[13]—perhaps not without a tinge of irony.[14] He propagated

---

[7] See M.C. Jacob and W.A. Lockwood, "Political Millenarianism and Burnet's *Sacred Theory*", *Science Studies* 2 (1972), 270.

[8] Referring to this early relationship Margaret C. Jacob even suggests that Cressener may have been one of the Anglican sources of Burnet's millenarianism: *The Newtonians and the English Revolution 1689-1720*, Ithaca (N.Y.) 1976, 108. Anyhow, both Burnet and Cressener were pupils of Henry More. As appears from his testimony, Burnet had read Cressener's manuscript in the early spring of 1688; by then his *Theoria sacra* had already appeared. Neither there, nor in the millenarian expositions in his *De statu mortuorum et resurgentium tractatus* (London 1727), does Burnet directly refer to contemporary authors; besides, his expositions have not, as those of Cressener have, a very explicit historical scope. In the aftermath of the Glorious Revolution, however, his eschatological views were influenced by the great events of those days: while in 1727 he wrote that the resurrection of the witnesses had not yet taken place, in 1691 he wrote in a letter to John Patrick: "... the resurrection of ye Witnesses goes on very well in Savoy and Dauphiné"; Burnet to J. Patrick, prebendary of Peterborough, Bodleian Library, Oxford, MS Tanner 26, f. 44. The letter can be dated from a P.S. in which the surrender of Dublin to the Duke of Ormonde is mentioned.

[9] *Judgments*, 288.

[10] *DNB*, s.v. Henry Plumptre (the son), president of the Royal College of Physicians.

[11] For Lloyd, see A. Tindal Hart, *William Lloyd 1627-1717*, London 1952.

[12] *Judgments*, sig. [b4v].

[13] E.S. de Beer (ed.), *The Diary of John Evelyn* V, Oxford, 1955, 25.

[14] Cf. Evelyn, *Diary* V, 20, on Lloyd's "long since opinions concerning great Revolutions to be at hand for the good of the Christian orthodox Church", or 322, on Lloyd's "old discourse"

his millenarian views till the end of his life; there is an amusing story about a meeting between Queen Anne and Lloyd in 1712, at which the old bishop tried to convince the Queen that within four years the Church of Rome would be utterly destroyed and the Millennium would begin.[15]

The millenarianism of men such as Thomas Burnet, Lloyd and Cressener was indeed marked by a strong, sometimes even vehement anti-Catholic bias, which especially in the period between the "Popish Plot" and the Glorious Revolution fell in with the mood of many Anglicans who saw the Anglican establishment threatened. The combination between apocalyptical expectations and anti-Catholic fervour was combustible material, which could become dangerous when used by the opponents of James II. Though, as Margaret Jacob points out, Burnet's work as such did not justify active resistance, there were difficulties with regard to the obtaining of a publishing licence.[16] The second part of the *Theoria* was published after the Revolution, in 1689.[17] We may assume that because of similar difficulties the licensing of Cressener's *Judgments* was held up. It was not published until after the Revolution, in 1689, the same year in which the second part of Burnet's book appeared, and it contained a long dedication to the new King, in which Cressener remarked that to those who would believe his interpretation of prophecy it would be like "a Voice from Heaven, not only for present comfort to themselves, but to call for their best assistance to Your Conduct". William received a special place in the series of apocalyptical events: "We have seen you at the Head of almost all the several kinds of *Peoples*, and *Nations*, and *Tongues*, that would not suffer the *dead Bodies* of *the Witnesses* to be buried. We our selves were thereupon in a manner made the First-fruits from the Dead upon their approaching *Resurrection*."[18]

One year later, in 1690, appeared his second and last book, *A Demonstration of the First Principles of the Protestant Applications of the Apocalypse*; like his first work published in London, though this time not printed for Richard Chiswell, as his *Judgments* had been, but (for reasons which we shall discuss below) for another London bookseller, Thomas Cockerill. The second work is an attempt to corroborate the main points of the first book by means of reasonable argumentation; almost inevitably it does not contain much new material. The contents of the book are summarized in a number of "rules" or "proposi-

---

concerning the destruction of Antichrist etc.

[15] Note of Lord Dartmouth (who was present at the meeting) to Gilbert Burnet's *History of my Own Time*, 2nd ed., I, Oxford, 1723, 327f.; cf. Tindal Hart, *William Lloyd*, 177f.; Jacob, *Newtonians*, 127.

[16] Jacob, *Newtonians*, 118f., 112.

[17] Or perhaps already in December 1688: Jacob and Lockwood, "Political Millenarianism", 270, note 11.

[18] *Judgments*, sig. A[2r-v].

tions", not only printed in the text but also on folding pages. In June 1691, a few months before the decease of the venerable Puritan theologian Richard Baxter, Cressener sent him a letter on the subject and the system of the book:

> Sir, this I did offer to the censure of some learned criticks before I printed it; And their encouragement as well as mine owne greater scepticalnesse in the whole processe of my endeavour under it, does make me very desirous to have your cautious examination of it.

But in fact Cressener wanted to convert Baxter, whom he knew to be more fundamentally "scepticall" with regard to millenarian speculations, to his own views regarding the identification of Rome with Antichrist:

> I should think it is a very happy advantage to the Reformation if after your former opposition of it you should now impartially owne, that its Great Adversary is so pompously set forth to the world in this Prophecy, as the Great Antichrist.

Cressener also gave practical advice: "To save ye trouble of turning to the quoted Rules ... bee pleased to let the Tables of ye Propositions lye open before you, As is usuall in Mathematicall proof.'[19]

The use of the latter term is indicative of Cressener's method. Joseph Mede had tried to interpret prophecy according to "the law of synchronistical necessity", and Henry More had claimed that his method of interpretation gave as much certainty as the translation of a Latin or Greek author in accordance with "the rules of grammar and the known interpretations of Dictionaries".[20] For Cressener, however, this was not sufficient: "there is still wanting a clearer Evidence." Especially in regard of "the Friends of the Grotian way" it was necessary to show that Cressener's interpretation (which fundamentally was in line with that of Mede and More) was "much more certain" than that of Grotius, whom Baxter seconded.[21] Still, Cressener realized that even his method, built like that of Mede and More on the idea of a "synchronistical" relationship between the prophecies in Daniel and the Apocalypse which made it possible to chart with more or less precision the course of history, did not guarantee "a Mathematical Evidence about such matters". But he tried to come as near to such evidence as was possible: the only way to make the Apocalypse appear as "the Word of God to *us*" (i.e. as a prophecy, delivered for the instruc-

---

[19] Cressener to Baxter, 2 June 1691, Dr. Williams's Library, London, Baxter Correspondence III, f. 15. The letter was written in reply to a (not extant) letter from Baxter: N.H. Keeble and G.F. Nuttall, *Calendar of Correspondence of Richard Baxter* II, Oxford 1991, 321. For Baxter and Cressener, see also W.M. Lamont, *Richard Baxter and the Millennium*, London, 1979, 59-62, and for Baxter's "former opposition", Van den Berg, "Continuity", this volume, Ch. 6., 97f.

[20] Van den Berg, "Continuity", this volume Ch. 6, 90.

[21] *Demonstration*, XIIIf.

tion and comfort of the Church of his own days) was "to prove and not to guess at the meaning of it".[22]

This time, too, Cressener had some difficulty in having his book published, though now for different reasons. In the dedication—now to Queen Mary—he attributed the unwillingness of the publishers to a general lack of interest in millenarian studies: "The Enquiry into these matters is so out of fashion, and lies under so general a prejudice, that I found the Press every-where affrighted from undertaking the Charge of this Publication." Ultimately, thanks to Simon Patrick's warm recommendations he had been able to find a publisher.[23] Perhaps the publishers were also deterred by Cressener's way of writing; he himself feared "that the dry strictness of the Reasonings in it, will turn away more from perusing it, than the strength and cautiousness of it will please".[24]

Cressener attributed a high value to his predictions. In the Dedication he wrote: "If they prove to be satisfactorily clear, Religion and Empire being the Subject-matter of them, they seem to be the most proper Object of the Meditation of Christian Princes." He hoped that Her Majesty's favourable regard of his performance would procure "the Royal Stamp" upon it and thus make it "the Currant Study of the Age again".[25] But this hope was not fulfilled: in the coming years, interest in millenarian speculations would be at a low ebb, and apparently Cressener did not feel stimulated to write more on the subject. With regard to millenarian publications, his pen, which had once run so quickly, was at rest for the remaining part of his life. Still, in later years, too, the study of the subject occupied him, as appears from a letter to Simon Patrick on the prophecies of Daniel, which ends on a charming note of self-knowledge: "But when I am upon this subject, I am apt to bee too tedious for wch I beg your pardon for."[26]

Cressener had not always been an opponent of "the Grotian way". In his younger years he was much impressed by Grotius' irenicism, which in the view of English millenarians was closely bound up with his non-millenarian interpretation of the Apocalypse:

> I was once very much taken with the mollifying pleas of *Grotius*, and others of the Reconciling way; and apprehended it possible for the chief Heads of the Roman Communion to condescend to an expedient for a general Reconciliation. But when I came to be acquainted with Mr. *Mede*'s Demonstrations, and had compared them with the monstrous evasions, and absurd strains of wit, that *Grotius* and others were fain to flye to, to turn for the force of them, I gave over all thoughts of the comprehending way.[27]

---

[22] *Judgments*, sig. b2r-v.
[23] *Demonstration*, sig. alr.
[24] *Demonstration*, I.
[25] *Demonstration*, sig. alv.
[26] Cressener to Bishop Patrick, 15 September 1694, Bodleian Library, MS Tanner 25, f. 216.
[27] *Demonstration*, XIII.

One may wonder whether the political and religious developments in England made him turn from the irenical Grotius to the militantly anti-Catholic Mede. The personal influence of his teacher More, who was a pupil and admirer of Mede, may also have played a part. However this may be, it is clear that Mede, who had succinctly formulated his millenarian views in his *Clavis apocalyptica* (1627), became his great authority. But just as other followers of Mede did, he tried to vindicate his independent judgment by criticizing the great master on details. "Apocalyptical thoughts" leave ample scope for a range of minor variations.

While the framework of Cressener's millenarian concept is essentially that of Mede, he was indebted to the Huguenot theologian Pierre Jurieu for the application of his scheme within the context of contemporary political developments. Jurieu, too, was a millenarian in the spirit of Mede.[28] One year after the revocation of the Edict of Nantes, in 1686 (he was then in exile in the Netherlands) he published his main exposition of the subject, *L'Accomplissement des prophéties*; it appeared in English translation in 1687.[29] When Cressener read this work, either in the French edition or in the English translation of 1687, but at any rate before he wrote his *Judgments*, he was deeply struck by Jurieu's interpretation of the two witnesses of Rev. 11. Understandably, in millenarian circles there was much speculation about the identity of the witnesses and the place and time of their death and resurrection. Mede, who identified the witnesses with the churches of the Reformation, saw their death and resurrection as a future event, "adhuc implendum".[30] In 1629 he wrote: "I conceive not this *Clades* [*Testium*] to be such as should extinguish the persons or whole materials (as I may so speak) of the Reformed Churches, but the publick Fabrick of the Reformation". He was uncertain, however, with regard to the exact nature of the event: "It would make somewhat perhaps for understanding the degree of this *Clades*, if we could certainly tell what were that πλατεία τῆς πόλεως, wherein the *Witnesses* should lie for dead; and whether those of the *nations, tongues* and *people*, which should hinder the putting of them into graves, were *friends* or *foes*. They may seem to be *friends* ..."[31]

For Jurieu, the death of the witnesses was not an object of speculation, but grim reality.[32] In France, the antichristian powers had silenced the voice of the

[28] For Mede's influence on Jurieu, see F.R.J. Knetsch, *Pierre Jurieu, theoloog en politicus der refuge*, Kampen 1967, 206.
[29] *The Accomplishment of the Scripture Prophecies ... Faithfully Englished from the New French Edition ... Enlarged with the Applications of Daniel, and the Revelation*, London 1687.
[30] "De occisione testium", *The Works of ... Joseph Mede*, London 1677, [924].
[31] Mede to William Twisse, 11 November 1629, *Works*, 761.
[32] For this and what follows, see Knetsch, *Jurieu*, chap. 14, and "Pierre Jurieu (1637-1713) and his Comment on the Glorious Revolution" in J. van den Berg and P.G. Hoftijzer (eds.), *Church, Change and Revolution*, Leiden 1991, 145-166.

faithful witnesses. But there was hope for the future: according to the prophecy of Rev. 11 the witnesses would rise again and stand upon their feet. Jurieu expected that the resurrection of the true church in France would take place by means of a conflict between the French king and the Pope which would shatter the power of Antichrist as embodied in Rome. In a publication of 1687, *Apologie pour l'accomplissement des prophéties*, which was not translated into English and which perhaps escaped Cressener's attention, Jurieu declared that his predictions with regard to the dates of the great events were his private opinion. This does not detract, however, from the fact that he expected a speedy revival of the true church. After some time, this would be followed by the fall of the papal power. Patience was needed: "Il faut assigner un temps de quelque longueur pour la dernière chute du Papisme",[33] but it would certainly not be an interminable time; in this context, Professer Knetsch speaks of the "short-windedness" of Jurieu's apocalyptical concept.[34] According to Jurieu, the destruction of Antichrist would take place in the beginning of the next century and be followed by the reign of Jesus Christ on earth.[35]

In the dedication of his *Judgments* to William III Cressener described Jurieu's interpretation of the prophecy of the two witnesses as a "discovery", and in the preface he wrote: "Monsieur Jurieu must indeed be allowed to have given the World the first Alarme of the death of the Witnesses at this present time." At the same time, however, he noticed that in England the grounds which Jurieu gave "had the ill fortune ... to be received but as his Conjectures". The apparently lukewarm reception of Jurieu's work made Cressener decide "to clear up the foundation, that he depended upon, and to add a new proof of mine". When his *Judgments* was published (as we saw, after the Glorious Revolution) Cressener was afraid that his work would be seen as a *vaticinium ex eventu*, "a politick conjecture from the present State of Affairs"; therefore he was at pains to procure testimonies which made it clear that his work was written at a time when there was "the thickest cloud" over the Reformed Churches in almost all parts of Europe.[36]

This "thickest cloud" was, of course, the actual or threatening persecution by Rome. Jurieu, a Huguenot exile in the Netherlands, wrote from the background of the dispersed Reformed Church of France, whose witness in the mother country had almost totally been silenced. He was also deeply im-

[33] *L'Accomplissement des prophéties ou la délivrance prochaine de l'église*, Rotterdam, 1686, 149 *(in margine)*.

[34] Knetsch, *Jurieu*, 209.

[35] Cf. the sub-title of *L'Accomplissement:* "Ouvrage dans lequel ii est prouvé, que le Papisme est l'Empire Antichrétien; que cet Empire n'est pas éloigné de sa ruïne; que la persecution presente peut finir dans trois ans et demi. Après quoi commencera la destruction de l'Antichrist, laquelle s'achevera dans le commencement du Siecle prochain: Et enfin le regne de Jesus-Christ viendra sur la terre.'

[36] *Judgments*, Dedication and Preface, sigs. A[I]v, b4r-4.

pressed by the fate of the Waldensians, driven from their valleys in Savoy; in 1686, he was asked to become their intercessor with the Dutch States General.[37] Cressener wrote from the vantage-point of the English church, still by law established, but (as many thought) threatened in its existence by the Romanizing politics of James II. It is difficult to assess to what extent these fears were realistic. On the one hand, the events of 1679 and the year after, when all England was in the grip of the threat of a "Popish Plot", had shown how easily unfounded rumours and accusations could lead to an anti-Catholic hysteria which was out of touch with reality. On the other hand, the letters, written by James's Catholic secretary Edward Coleman in the years before 1679 were, indeed, incriminatory.[38] After his accession to the throne in 1685, it was clear to all observers that James looked forward to the triumph of Catholicism in England, which, he hoped, would come about by means of infiltration and conversions, and after 1686 his attitude towards the Anglican church became definitely hostile; as one historian writes: "He blundered on with the blind optimism of a man whose mind was determinedly closed to any thought of failure.'[39] The fate of the Huguenots strengthened the anti-Catholic mood in England, and the support James officially gave them was not quite unambiguous.[40] To us, it seems incredible that in the 1680's a religious landslide could have taken place in England, but we should not forget that less than half a century before, in the period of the Commonwealth, the Church of England had almost been wiped away by a landslide to the other side. Also in later seventeenth-century England the religious and political equilibrium was precarious, though perhaps less than some feared and others hoped.

The events of 1685 gave new fuel to the anti-Catholic mood, and led to a renewed emphasis on the traditional identification of the Catholic church (or the papacy) with Antichrist. On this point, Cressener was not less explicit than Jurieu, but he wanted to strengthen the equation of Rome with Antichrist by means of a coherent and consistent exegetical argumentation. In this context, the identification of the Beast, mentioned in the Book of Revelation, with the fourth Beast of Daniel 7 is pivotal. Therefore, Cressener strongly criticized Grotius's historical interpretation of the term "the Beast",[41] which made its application to the present-day Roman church impossible. According to

[37] J.F. Martinet, *Kerkelyke geschiedenis der Waldenzen*, Amsterdam ²1775, 108.

[38] J. Kenyon, *The Popish Plot*, London 1972, *index*; R.W. Jones, *The Revolution of 1688 in England*, London 1984, 78; J. Miller, *Popery and Politics in England 1660-1688*, Cambridge 1973, 137ff.

[39] Miller, *Popery*, 202.

[40] Jones, *Revolution*, 112f.

[41] Grotius saw "Bestia quarta terribilis atque mirabilis" of Dan. 7.7 as the Macedonian dynasties which ruled over Syria and Egypt; *Annotata ad Vetus Testamentum* II, Lutetiae Parisiorum 1644, 436; cf. 414 (on Dan. 2.40).

Cressener, "the Beast, and the false Prophet are the chief Ruling Power of the present Church of Rome", and "*Babylon* signifies the City of *Rome* in a state of Ecclesiastical Domination".[42] In the Dedication of his *Demonstration* to Queen Mary, he complained about the "General Unconcern" with regard to this point, which he saw as "the effect of the Popish Marriages in the Three Last Reigns".

> Nothing was more the Doctrine of our Church to the end of the Reign of King James the First, than the Charge of *Babylon*, and Antichrist, upon the Roman Church; but it seemed something too rude a Charge, both to Church and Court, when the Queen came to be concerned in it.[43]

In his defence of the antiquity of his doctrine over against the modern interpretation, given by Grotius and his followers, he appealed to Archbishop James Ussher, who had given a long list of authorities in support of his thesis that Babylon signified Rome under the Pope and that the Papacy may be said to be "the *Beast that was, and is not*, and yet *is*".[44] And by means of rather tortuous reasoning he even tried to show that the fifteen arguments, used by Bellarmine to prove that the Church of Rome was the true church in fact proved that is was Babylon.[45]

When Cressener wrote his *Judgments*, the "Witnesses" were still in sackcloth, the "Beast" still triumphant. According to Cressener, one of the main sins of the Roman church was "the forcing Men against their Consciences to reverence the Roman Authority in Points of Faith and Worship for the only Rule and Standard of Christian Truth". The sin of the heathen emperors was their tyranny against the church; the Christian emperors became spiritual dictators to the consciences of men; now the degenerate church wants to enforce all to "an Uniformity in the Roman Worship". This is the great provocation, which calls for God's judgments.[46] These judgments will begin within a short time. The witnesses are dead, but thanks to their friends they are not buried; no doubt, Cressener thinks here of the reception the exiled Huguenots had found in other Protestant countries. The time of their resurrection is near: "the Recovery of the True Church" will take place in 1689, or ultimately in 1690.[47]

---

[42] *Judgments*, "Suppositions for the Second Part", nos. 1 and 5 (on folding page, unpaginated).
[43] *Demonstration*, sig. alv.
[44] *Demonstration*, iv; "The Consent of the Ancients Concerning the Fourth Beast in the Revelations", London, 1690 (printed as an appendix to *Dem.)*, 35. See N. Bernard (ed.), *The Judgments of the Late Arch-Bishop of Armagh, and Primate of Ireland, of Babylon (Rev. 18.4) Being the Present See of Rome*, London 1659, esp. 126f.
[45] *Demonstration*, 8; see R. Bellarminus, *Disputationes de controversiis Christianae fidei adversus huius temporis haereticos*, ed. 3a, I, Ingolstadii 1590, Lib. IV "De notis ecclesiae", cap. 3-18 (c. 1299-1363).
[46] *Judgments*, 55-65.
[47] *Judgments*, 96-98.

Cressener acknowledged that he derived his interpretation of the prophecy of the two witnesses from Jurieu:

> however different I am from *Monsieur Jurieu* in almost every thing else, yet I was extreamly surprised with the light that he has given to the Prophecy about the Death of the Two Witnesses from the present face of the Protestant Churches all over *Europe*.[48]

Even the probable dates he gives for their resurrection are the same as those we find in Jurieu's works.[49] Just as it is the case with Jurieu, his expectations, seemingly based on nothing but his interpretation of biblical prophecy, are in fact to a large degree determined by the political situation. In 1687, change was already in the air. When, only one year later, the Glorious Revolution took place, Cressener saw the events in England as a sign that the Protestant cause would also prevail in those countries where the witness of the Reformed Church had recently been silenced. The passage in the Dedication on the death and the resurrection of the witnesses[50] of course refers primarily to France, where only recently the witnesses had been killed.

Initially, he identified the killing of the witnesses with the Revocation. Contrary to Jurieu, whose interpretation of ἐπὶ τῆς πλατείας he rejected, Cressener asserted that the resurrection of the witnesses could take place outside France. But that was only a theoretical difference: "... it is very difficult to imagine, where this can happen, but in the Kingdom of *France*." For various reasons, other countries did not qualify for the great event, but "the Gallican Church, in the present state of it, seems to be already on the fair way to a thorough Reformation".[51] Possibly Cressener had in mind the *Four Gallican Articles* of 1682, which had denied the dominion of the Pope over things temporal.[52] In Huguenot circles, there was some sympathy for the Gallican theory—Jurieu saw the Huguenots as consistent Gallicans—, but it was mixed with deep disappointment at the fact that it was the Gallican church itself which persecuted the Huguenots.[53] For Anglicans it was still more easy to see a parallel between their own church and the Gallican church; only some decades later the broadminded Archbishop Wake suggested that a new reformation might ensue from a union between the Anglican and the Gallican church.[54] Cressener was very sanguine. Now was the time when the fourth vial (Rev. 16.8, 9) was to be

---

[48] *Judgments*, 82.
[49] Knetsch, *Jurieu*, esp. 207f.
[50] See above, 156, n. 36.
[51] *Judgments*, 140.
[52] For "la Déclaration" or "les Quatres Articles de 1682", see *Dictionnaire de théologie catholique*, IV, Paris 1924, 185-205.
[53] Knetsch, *Jurieu*, 104.
[54] N. Sykes, *William Wake, Archbishop of Canterbury 1657-1737*, I, Cambridge 1957, 260.

poured out over the sun, which in its turn would scorch men with heat. In Cressener's scheme, the sun stood for the Sun-King, Louis XIV, whose quarrels and wars would vex and humiliate "the Papal and Imperial Interest".[55] Here, knowledge of contemporary political events and ignorance with regard to their background are mixed in a curious way: at that time, Protestantism had more to fear from a fanatical King than from a moderate Pope. But even if he had known this, it probably would not have changed his views. In the apocalyptic times in which he lived anything was possible; to Plumptre he wrote: "Upon this occasion I cannot but mention to you, that the King of *France* either has not long to live, or must be really made *The Most Christian King* within these few Years.'[56]

The pouring out of the last vials would mean the utter destruction of the Beast and thus usher in a new era, the time of the Millennium. Just when he started the nineteenth chapter of his work, which would deal with the Millennium, he received, as we saw, a manuscript copy of the second part of Thomas Burnet's *Theoria*. The works of Cressener and Burnet had a different scope: while Cressener was mainly interested in the relation between prophecy and history, Burnet was primarily interested in the relation between prophecy and geology. His interest in the future fate of the earth coloured Burnet's millenarian views, which, in their turn, influenced those of Cressener, in particular with regard to the theory of a conflagration which would change the face of the earth. We find the connection between conflagration and Millennium already with Mede, who based it on 2 Peter 3: "Christ our Lord shall come, when the *Beatum Millennium* is to begin ... in flaming fire; by the Divine and miraculous efficacy whereof the *World* that now is shall be refined, and delivered from the bondage of corruption ...".[57] More saw the idea of a conflagration confirmed by "the Opinion ... of ancient Heathens and Jews".[58] Burnet's point of departure in his description of the conflagration was "the doctrine of the Stoicks"; Scripture (especially, of course, 2 Peter 3) was for him "a second witness".[59] Cressener wrestled with the subject. With Burnet, he believed that the great judgments of God upon the world are ordinarily executed by the concurrence of the natural disposition of things.[60] Now, the consummation of God's judgments on the Church of Rome would be brought

---

[55] The attitude of Innocent XI with regard to the Glorious Revolution was initially passive, though it seems that at a later stage he regretted not having come to the assistance of James II; J. Orcibal, *Louis XIV contre Innocent XI*, Paris, 1949, 75, n. 350; for James II and the Pope, see Miller, *Popery*, 229-38.

[56] Cressener to Henry Plumptre, 28 February 1687/8, *Judgments*, sig. [Tt4r].

[57] Mede, *Works*, 618.

[58] H. More, *Theological Works*, London 1708, 28.

[59] Thomas Burnet, *The Theory of the Earth*, Book II (1691), new. ed. under the title *The Sacred Theory of the Earth*, London/Fontwell 1965, 251.

[60] *Judgments*, 292.

about by the pouring out of the last three vials and the sounding of the last trumpet, which would inaugurate "the Last Ruine of *Babylon* and the Beast",[61] or—in terms of the doctrine of a conflagration—"the burning of the Seat of Antichrist". The progress of the conflagration would be gradual and slow; so much so that there would be room for a pure state of the Christian Church "betwixt the ruine of the Beast and the last end of the Conflagration". The Christian Church would not only continue but increase after the conflagration of the Roman territories. The partial conflagration of the world (which might lead to a change for the better of the climate in other parts of the world) would be the means for the conversion of Jews and heathen in all parts of the world, "the Conversions [sic] of the Kingdoms of this present World, into the Universal Kingdom of the Lord and of his Christ. And from that time may Christ be said to begin to Reign with his Father for ever, tho the *Millennium* will be his more peculiar share of that Reign". The last sentence is unclear: it reflects an uncertainty in Cressener's thinking with regard to the place of the Millennium in the context of the apocalyptical scheme—either within the time of the conflagration, "in those parts of the world which were yet untouched and entire", or after the conflagration, when the New Jerusalem would descend from heaven.[62]

Cressener's expectations seemed to find a partial fulfilment through and after the Glorious Revolution. A greater revolution in the state of affairs of the world was still to come, but—as Cressener wrote in his dedication to William—"that which makes the fairest promise of the near approach of this time, is Your Majesty's unexpected success in these Nations, which has given a perfect new turn to all the affairs of Europe ... It is manifest, That in all appearance the next causes are now in Action." For the adversaries—Cressener thought here first of all of the persecutors of the Huguenots in France—no other way would be open but to grant freedom of religion; this would lead to a conversion of the whole Kingdom of France without any violent methods, and to a general mortification of the Roman church in all parts of its dominion, "as would make it sink by degrees into nothing".[63] But for the Reformed churches a new future would dawn; they are "but scattered Altars, and particular Synagogues, till they come all to be united into one Universal Temple at the end of the Consecration of the Christian Church, that is, at the end of the Vials and of all the Enemies of Christ".[64]

Cressener wrote all this before or in March 1689. In the summer of the same year, not the conversion of France, but the "glorieuse rentrée" of the Waldensians into the valleys of Piedmont took place; an event which created a deep impression in England. John Evelyn mentions a conversation between

[61] *Judgments*, 215.
[62] *Judgments*, 290-95.
[63] *Judgments*, sigs. [A1v, A3r].
[64] *Judgments*, 187.

a number of leading clergymen in the London residence of Bishop Lloyd. All of them were "not a little surpriz'd' at what had happened in *Savoy*"; even, it seems, Lloyd himself, though he had already for a long time affirmed that the Waldensians were "the 2 Witnesses spoken of in the Revelation who should be Kild, and brought to life againe".[65] Cressener tried to fit the "glorieuse rentrée" into his chronology of the death and resurrection of the witnesses. If their death did not take place at the time of the Revocation itself, but just a bit later, at the time of "the last Considerable Abjurations of the new Converts", then the resurrection of the witnesses three days [= years] after their death "must fall just about the time that the *Vaudois* did Revive". He added—we find it in the dedication of his second book, *Demonstration*, to Queen Anne—:

> The Proper Kingdom of *France* did indeed seem from the present Posture of Affairs, to be the most likely to be the first Scene of this Revival. But it has been shewn, that there is nothing in the Prophecy that does fix the first beginning of it there; And that the Persecution in *France*, and *Savoy*, being executed by the same Instruments, may very well pass for one and the same thing.

The fact that the Turkish power—the second woe of the Apocalypse—seemed to come to an end strengthened his conviction. All evidence pointed the same way.[66] Of course, like so many millenarian schemes, his scheme, too, was adaptable to circumstances. But his belief in the essential value of his "apocalyptical thoughts" remained unshaken: "The Foundation of a Building may be setled upon a Rock, though some parts of the Superstructure should fall for want of immediate and close coherence of it".[67]

Does Cressener's further silence on the subject mean that he was a disappointed man? In his lifetime, William and Mary both died. The tide did not turn in France, and though in England the future of Protestantism was now safe, in large parts of Europe the power of Rome was as strong as ever. And while he was not in all respects a man of the past—I think here in particular of his sympathy for the theories of Thomas Burnet, which with regard to the dramatic aspects of the apocalyptical events contained a demythologizing element—in general his approach was, as he knew himself, indeed out of fashion. But in his aversion from Rome and his hope for a revival of Protestantism he reflects something of the fears and hopes of at least a number of contemporary Anglicans in the time of the Glorious Revolution. Perhaps this event, through which he believed his predictions would be confirmed and his expectations would be fulfilled, was also his glorious moment, his finest hour.

---

[65] Evelyn, V, 25 (18 June 1690).
[66] *Judgments*, 110ff.
[67] *Demonstration*, sigs. A3v, 4r.

CHAPTER ELEVEN

DUTCH CALVINISM AND THE CHURCH OF ENGLAND IN THE PERIOD OF THE GLORIOUS REVOLUTION[1]

In the summer of 1680 Henry Compton, Bishop of London, approached the High Anglican Thomas Ken, at that time chaplain to Princess Mary at the Court of the Stadtholder in The Hague, for information on the opinions of the Dutch theologians regarding the differences between the Church of England and the Dissenters. In the period of the aftermath of the "Popish Plot", a number of leading Anglicans thought it important to renew the attempts at comprehension of the more moderate Dissenters into the Church of England in order to strengthen the cause of Protestantism.[2] In this context, it could be advantageous if a number of Reformed theologians who themselves were loyal members of a church with a presbyterian form of church government, would declare that they had no fundamental objections to a reunion of the Presbyterians with an episcopally governed church. Shortly before, Mary's former chaplain William Lloyd, who in the autumn of 1680 became Bishop of St Asaph, had already made a similar request to Ken, and when his request was unsuccessful he had asked Compton to approach Ken. Neither Lloyd nor Compton, however, succeeded in moving Ken to supply them with the information they needed. On 19 August Ken wrote to Compton:

> ... I cannot apprehend the judgments of the generality of those Dutch divines, with whom I have conversed, to be worth the asking, or very creditable to urge, should they give it for us, they for the most part rather despising than studying classical antiquity; and the classical authors which many of them read with most deference are our English Non-Conformists; so that if the factious party should countermine us in this particular, I am persuaded that more of our Divines here [*i.e.* the Dutch theologians] would be for them whom they call their Brethren and esteem as the great Doctors of the Reformed Church [the Presbyterians], than for us whom they censure for at least half papists.

Ken even thought an approbation of the Church of England by Dutch divines would be dangerous, because this could lead them to expect from the Anglicans a recognition of the validity of the "orders" of the Dutch church. Next they might demand that the Princess would come to their sacrament, and then, "farewell all Common Prayer here for the future". A particularly difficult point

---

[1] I thank the librarian and staff of Lambeth Palace Library for their kind assistance.

[2] See R. Thomas, "Comprehension and Indulgence", in G.F. Nuttall and O. Chadwick (eds.), *From Uniformity to Unity*, London 1962, 189-254.

was that of the reordination of non-Anglican ministers on their joining the communion of the Church of England: "... the resentment they have at our reordaining them sticks in their stomach".[3]

It is clear that Ken was not the ideal intermediary between the Church of England and the Dutch theologians. He did not know, or perhaps did not want to know, that not all Dutch theologians were as strongly opposed to the Church of England and as much averse to the study of Christian antiquity as he had painted them in his letter to Compton. There was at least one Dutch Calvinist whose attitude towards the Church of England was very positive: the Leiden professor of theology Fridericus Spanheim (the younger).[4] He was not the only one who held the Church of England in high esteem, but he certainly was one of the most outspoken defenders of the English church in the Netherlands. Fridericus Spanheim was a son of a theologian of the same name, who had taught in Geneva and in Leiden. He studied in Leiden, where the renowned Johannes Coccejus was one of his teachers. After a professorship of fifteen years at the University of Heidelberg he returned to Leiden in 1670, where he succeeded Coccejus, who had died in 1669. He spoke with much respect of his teacher and predecessor, but he did not follow him in his theology. At the time when Spanheim assumed his position in Leiden, tensions were running high between the "Coccejans" on the one hand and the Utrecht theologian Gisbertus Voetius and his friends and followers on the other. The Coccejans were more progressive in theology, more free in practical matters such as the observance of the "Sabbath" and more inclined towards accepting new intellectual developments such as the philosophy of Descartes than the "Voetians" were. Voetius was the "grand old man" of the right wing of the Reformed Church: strict in doctrine, a "precisian" in practice, sympathizing with the writings of the orthodox English Puritans. Gilbert Burnet, who met him in 1664, disliked what he called his peevishness and that of his party; he thought him "a dour and rigid man". In general, Burnet was very critical of Dutch theology: "I did not admire the learning of Holland; I found little spirit among the professors at Leyden".[5] It is clear that Burnet's Latitudinarianism and Dutch Calvinism did not mix at all well. In 1669, the year of Coccejus's death, Voetius was reconciled with his former opponent Samuel Maresius (Des Marets), a Groningen professor of French descent, who was a conservative Calvinist but did not share Voetius' "precisian" attitude and Puritan sympathies. The reconciliation was brought about by Johannes van der Waeyen, at

---

[3] Bodleian Library Oxford (hereafter: BLO), Rawl. MSS c. 983, fol. 53, quoted from A. Tindal Hart, *William Lloyd*, London 1952, 26f.

[4] For Fridericus Spanheim (1632-1701), see D. Nauta, "Fri(e)dericus Spanheim", in *Biografisch lexicon voor de geschiedenis van het Nederlandse Protestantisme* (hereafter: *BLGNP*) II, Kampen 1983, 411-13.

[5] H.C. Foxcroft, *A Supplement to Burnet's History of my Own Time*, Oxford 1902, 91.

that time minister in Leeuwarden, who later would become an outspoken Coccejan with Cartesian sympathies, and who as such would come into sharp collision with Spanheim. In view of Van der Waeyen's later development it is ironic that he was instrumental in bringing together Voetius and Maresius, who now joined hands in their struggle against the innovators, the "novatores".

Spanheim was not a Voetian—he was too independent for this—but he was a conservative such as his father had been and Maresius was, and in the theological struggles of his time his sympathies were more with the Voetians than with the Coccejans, especially when they were inclined towards Cartesianism. The "novatores" found in him a fierce, sometimes bitter opponent. He also wrote against the Remonstrants, but in his *Controversiarum de Religione ... Elenchus* (1694) he distinguished between those who held to the original teaching of Arminius and who (apart from the doctrine of predestination) agreed with the orthodox on the essential points of doctrine, and those whom because of their Socinian inclinations he considered more heretical.[6] In the same work he also devoted a chapter to the English Latitudinarians. He declared he did not intend to detract from their piety and their erudition, but according to Spanheim they valued human reason too highly and thus rejected the Pauline doctrine of election and reprobation as incompatible with natural notions. Primarily they were called "Latitudinarians" because of a certain latitude in church order and discipline. Spanheim realized that they also took a certain liberty in the interpretation of the Articles of Faith; it was on this account that he expressed the wish that they might not extend their doctrinal latitude outside the limits of the Anglican and Scottish confessions. While he was a strict Calvinist, for the sake of the propagation of the Gospel and the opposition against "Antichrist" he stressed the necessity of "concordia" or at least "tolerantia" between all orthodox Protestants.[7] In October 1688, on the eve of the Glorious Revolution, he wrote to a Swiss colleague that the only hope for the Protestant churches, threatened by the antichristian powers (the Catholic states), lay in a mutual confederation that also comprised the powers that governed them and the theologians who assisted them in the work of the Lord.[8] Churches, princes, magistrates, theologians—they should combine their forces in the struggle against Rome. Here we meet with what certainly was an important factor in his Anglican sympathies. He shared those sympathies with his father who, in the dedication of one of his works to Archbishop Ussher and some other leading Englishmen, had testified to his broad affections towards all the British churches, whose very distinguished "praesules"

---

[6] *Controversiarum de Religione cum Dissidentibus Hodie Christianis ... Elenchus ...* (1649), in *Opera Omnia*, 3 volumes, Lugd. Bat. 1700-3, III, c. 848.

[7] *Opera* III, c. 997-9, 889.

[8] F. Spanheim to A. Klingler (Basel) 28 Oct. 1688, University Library Basel, Bibl. Fr. Gr. MS G2 I, 28, f. 195 (apographon).

(bishops), whose faithful pastors, whose flourishing flocks, he wrote, we esteem and love in the Lord. In this context, he spoke of the lovable face of the English churches and the reverence and zeal which could be observed in church life in England. No doubt this reflects his own experience, and as such it is an almost nostalgic memory of the time he spent in Oxford, before taking up his chair in Geneva in 1626.[9]

The younger Spanheim visited England in 1679. In Oxford he enjoyed the hospitality of Edward Bernard, Professor of Astronomy;[10] through correspondence they would remain in friendly contact. He also met a number of Anglican ecclesiastical leaders. In a manuscript in the library of Lambeth Palace which is from Spanheim's hand and which should be dated 1689 we read, "... j'ai l'honneur de connoître ... Monsieur l'Archevêque de Canterbury ... Messeigneurs les Evêques de Londres, d'Asaph, d'Eli etc".[11] William Sancroft was suspended as Archbishop on 1 August 1689, to be succeeded by John Tillotson in 1691; so either the manuscript was written before Sancroft's suspension, or, if later, at a time when Spanheim was not yet aware of what had happened to Sancroft. The Bishop of St Asaph was Lloyd, who later became Bishop of Lichfield and after that Bishop of Worcester. Probably Spanheim knew Lloyd already from the time of his chaplaincy at The Hague.[12] Of special interest were his contacts with Compton; it is possible that Compton all the more readily complied with Lloyd's request to approach Ken because of the information he had received from Spanheim a year before. In 1681 Spanheim wrote a letter to Compton, to which we shall return. In this letter, which was published by Spanheim in the same year, the Leiden theologian reminded the bishop of their conversation on the various forms of church government—a prelude to what he would later write and publish on this subject.[13] Given the fact that Spanheim, though sympathetic towards the Church of England, never renounced his Presbyterian brethren, it would be remarkable if there had been no personal contact with at least some of the leading Presbyterians, but apart

---

[9] F. Spanheim [pater], *Dubiorum evangelicorum pars tertia*, Geneva 1655, f. e 2 rv. For the elder Spanheim see D. Nauta in *BLGNP* III, 410-11.

[10] From 1668 till 1669 Bernard had stayed in Leiden in order to consult the oriental manuscripts in the University Library (*DNB* s.v.); perhaps one of Bernard's Leiden contacts had provided Spanheim with an introduction. After his return home, Spanheim thanked him warmly for his "humanitas": Spanheim to E. Bernard, 31 March 1679, BLO Smith MS 5. fol. 329.

[11] "Pensée d'un Theologien désintéressé de deça la mer ...", Lambeth Palace Library (hereafter: LPL), Gibson Papers, MS 935, 76.

[12] For Lloyd's broadminded attitude towards Mary attending the services in the English Church at The Hague, served by a "nonconformist minister", see Rosemary van Wengen-Shute, "The English Church in The Hague during William and Mary's Time", in P.G. Hoftijzer and C.C. Barfoot (eds.) *Fabrics and Fabrications*, Amsterdam 1990, 52.

[13] The letter was printed in Spanheim's refutation of Bossuet's *Exposition de la doctrine catholique* (1671): *Specimen Stricturarum ad Libellum Nuperum Episcopi Condomiensis* (1681), in *Opera* III, c 1015-16.

from one letter to the Rotterdam Presbyterian minister Joseph Hill[14] no correspondence has come to light.

After the first abortive attempts to elicit information on the opinions of Dutch theologians through Ken, Compton directly approached some continental theologians: the French ministers Samuel de l'Angle and Jean Claude, the Leiden Professor Etienne (Stephanus) le Moyne, originally a Frenchman, who had received a doctor's degree in Oxford in 1676,[15] and his colleague Spanheim. Letters from De l'Angle, Claude and Le Moyne were published (with an English translation) in 1681 by Edward Stillingfleet (then Dean of St Paul's, later Bishop of Winchester)in his *The Unreasonableness of Separation*, in which, albeit with certain reservations, he had advocated a union between Episcopalians and Dissenters.[16] Spanheim's letter was not included. According to the extreme High Anglican scholar Henry Dodwell (who had been with Lloyd in the Netherlands[17] and during a visit to Leiden at that time had become personally acquainted with Spanheim), this was because the latter had written too coldly on the Church of England.[18] Spanheim, however, averred that Stillingfleet had not included his letter because it had already been published, so that there was no need to publish it again; an explanation which is not quite satisfactory.[19]

Spanheim's letter, though sympathetic towards the Church of England, was indeed more restrained than those of the others, in particular that of his colleague Le Moyne, who gives the impression that he considered "le gouvernement Episcopal" to be the normal form of church government. Le Moyne strongly attacked the Dissenters, who had broken away from the Church of England: "Je regarde ces gens là, comme des perturbateurs de l'Eglise, et qui sont infalliblement animés d'un esprit de sédition". In view of the present state of affairs (of course the impending danger from Rome), they should be well aware of the fact "qu'il n'y a qu'une bonne réunion qui puisse prevenir les

---

[14] See below, note 58.

[15] De l'Angle and Claude ministered to the famous Temple de Charenton. For De l'Angle (who was born in England and had received an Oxford doctorate), see E. and E. Haag and H. Bourdier. *La France Protestante* (second edition) I, c. 1040f. (s.v. Baux); for Claude, IV, c. 449-76. Claude afterwards complained about the fact that his letter had been published, and wrote a very critical letter to Compton in April 1681: D. Neal, *The History of the Puritans* (new edition), London 1837, III 224, (new) note. For Le Moyne, see *Nieuw Nederlandsch Biografisch Woordenboek* X, c. 634-36; for his Oxford degree: J. Foster, *Alumni Oxonienses* (Oxford, 1892), III/IV, 1028.

[16] He warned against forming a faction of former Dissenters within the Church of England: "... if the design be to bring them in as a Faction to bridle and controll the *Episcopal Power*, by setting up forty Bishops in a Diocess against one ... let them not call this a Design of Union". *The Unreasonableness of Separation*, London [3]1682, "The Preface", xc.

[17] Francis Brokesby, *The Life of Mr Henry Dodwell*, London 1715, 39f.

[18] Dodwell to Spanheim, 11 March 1685, BLO MS Cherry 22, f. 10-17. It is in this letter that Dodwell refers to their meeting in Leiden.

[19] See Spanheim's *Epistola* against Van der Waeyen (cf. note 26), in *Opera* II, c. 1111.

maux dont l'Angleterre est menacée".[20] Apparently, Le Moyne had sent his letter through Jean (or John) Durel, minister of the Episcopal French chapel of the Savoy, a fierce defender of the order and liturgy of the Anglican Church and an equally fierce opponent of Dissent.[21] Later, he complained that Durel had left out a number of more moderate passages.[22] Whatever the case, Spanheim had been more cautious than his Leiden colleague, though he shared his Anglican sympathies and his anti-Catholic bias. It is significant that (as we have seen) his letter was printed as a kind of preface to a work which contained a strong refutation of the views of Bossuet. Fear of Rome and love of the Anglican Church were complementary.

After having praised Compton for his humanity, prudence and moderation, Spanheim remarked in his letter that the Dutch were not envious of the British churches on account of their constitution, and that conversely he knew the British did not condemn the overseas churches because of their system of government. Spanheim's fundamental thesis is that from the beginning there had been room in the Christian church for a variety of systems of church polity. As early as the times of the Apostles, the order of the church was varied and changeable ("varia ac mutabilis"). The Apostles and their successors thought it sufficient if everything took place with order and decency, under the government of bishops, pastors, ministers ("Episcopi, Pastores, Ministri"). Furthermore he remarked that it would be difficult if there was a contrast between the forms of government in state and country on the one hand, and in church and religion on the other. In doing so, he implicitly indicated that an episcopal form of church government went better with a kingdom such as England than with a republic such as the Netherlands. There should be common ground between the orders in church and state. Thus for England the best form of church government was that of the "communio episcopalis", provided the idea was dismissed that the episcopal form of church polity was of divine right or that salvation depended on external ceremonies. A union between Episcopalians and Presbyterians would be important in view of the threat from Rome, an argument we also noted in Le Moyne and which at that time was indeed one of the strongest incentives to union or comprehension. Of course he referred to the "Popish Plot" when in this context he spoke of the force of a nefarious

---

[20] I quote from Spanheim's edition of Le Moyne's letter in "Epistola", *Opera* II, c. 1251.

[21] For this, see his *Sanctae Ecclesiae Anglicanae adversus Iniquas atque Inverecundas Schismaticorum Criminationes Vindiciae*, London 1669, in which he defended episcopacy as "de jure divino" (pp. 364-98); furthermore his *A View of the Government and Publick Worship of God in the Reformed Churches beyond the Sea*, London 1672, with many letters from French Reformed theologians in favour of the episcopal system. In the latter work, he condemned those Dissenters who in the period of the restoration did not join the Church of England as "Canaanites" who had still remained in the land: f. A 3^{rv}.

[22] E. Calamy, *An Historical Account of my Own Life*, ed. by J.T. Rutt, London ^{2}1830, 175; cf. [An.] *Bonasus Vapulans, or, some Castigations given to Mr John Durell*, London 1672, 80f.

conspiracy, worse than that of Catalina! Spanheim's letter to Compton implied a full recognition of the legitimacy of episcopacy, and its main tendency was acceptable to Latitudinarian Anglicans as well as to moderate Presbyterians. His views may not have been acceptable to more extreme High Church theologians such as Dodwell, but they were certainly in tune with those of mediating seventeenth-century Episcopalians such as James Ussher or the Scottish Archbishop Robert Leighton.[23]

One may wonder whether Spanheim's moderate letter had any impact on the English situation; it probably had none at all. It had, however, an unexpected repercussion in the Netherlands. As we saw, Spanheim was a convinced opponent of Cartesianism, and he took an active part in the anti-Cartesian reaction which in 1676 led to the condemnation of Cartesianism by the curators of the University of Leiden and to the deposition of the leading Coccejan theologian of those days, his aged colleague Abraham Heydanus.[24] Some years later, in 1682, Johannes van der Waeyen, who was one of the leading Cartesian-Coccejan theologians, retaliated in a lengthy preface to a commentary on Galatians. Van der Waeyen had been a minister of the church at Middelburg, but in 1676, at the height of the troubles between the Voetians and the Coccejans, the intervention of William III in the local conflicts led to his deposition and his banishment from the province of Zeeland.[25] One year later, the favour of the Frisian Stadtholder Hendrik Casimir II, who lived in open conflict with his cousin William III, procured him a professorship at the University of Franeker. The Franeker Professor strongly attacked Spanheim for his role in the agitation against the Leiden Cartesians: he averred that Spanheim, though pretending to be moderate, had been one of the instigators of the troubles.[26] Spanheim answered in 1682 in an *Epistola Responsoria*, in which he also dealt with the matter of church government; he wanted to defend himself against rumours regarding his loyalty to the presbyterian system, which were current in the circles around Van der Waeyen (who had taken exception to Spanheim's letter to Compton).[27]

---

[23] For their views, see N. Sykes, *Old Priest and New Presbyter*, Cambridge 1956, 134-37.

[24] In his *De Novissimis circa Res Sacras in Belgio Dissidiis*, Lugd. Bat. 1677, written in October 1676, some months after the deposition of Heydanus, he presents himself, however, as a moderate and irenical theologian; he repeatedly quotes Heydanus, and though he does not criticize the edict of the curators he disclaims any responsibility for it: see especially 158ff. Perhaps he was somewhat embarrassed by its far-reaching effects.

[25] For Van der Waeyen as a theologian, see C. Sepp, *Het godgeleerde onderwijs in Nederland* II, Leiden 1874, 297f., 307f.; for the conflict in Middelburg *inter alia* M. van Empel and H. Pieters, *Zeeland door de eeuwen heen*, Middelburg 1959, 558f.

[26] J. van der Waayen [sic], *De brief tot den Galaten*, Leeuwarden 1682, 36.

[27] F. Spanheim, *Epistola Responsoria ad Amicum de Nupera Praefatione Johannis van der Waayen Literis Referentum, in qua etiam de Variis Ecclesiarum Politiis, atque Finiendis Belgarum Litibus, agitur*, Lugd. Bat. 1682; see *Opera* II, c. 1032. *Cf.* Van der Waeyen, *Galaten*, 120-9.

The discussion, which in part perhaps had a political background, continued. In 1683, Van der Waeyen published an *Epistola Apologetica* against Spanheim; the tone of his "letter" (in fact a rather lengthy book) was personal and satirical. He ridiculed his Leiden colleague for the latter's Anglican sympathies and contacts: "you will see Spanheim jumping, running, attempting I do not know which, in order neither to lose favour with the Bishops or the Episcopalians, nor to give the impression of rejecting openly the doctrine of the Confession to which he had subscribed".[28] Van der Waeyen accused Spanheim of deviation from the *Confessio Belgica*, which clearly taught a divinely prescribed and sanctioned form of church polity, in which all "verbi divini ministri" have the same power and authority. The interpretation of Articles XXX and XXXI of the Confession as given by Van der Waeyen is an interesting counterpart to the High Anglican view of a "jure divino" existing form of episcopal church government. According to Van der Waeyen it is the presbyterian form of church polity, with as its central doctrine the idea of the equality of ministers, which is taught in the New Testament, is founded on divine right, and is confirmed by the Confession of the Dutch Church. He emphatically denied that in the time of the beginning of the Christian church there was such a form of episcopacy as is to be found in the Anglicana. When in the course of the second century the Bishops were exalted above the Presbyters, the way was prepared for antichristian developments within the church. It was a great fault of the British Church that it had partly retained the hierarchical system, together with so many rites and ceremonies, and even had restored it (Van der Waeyen was thinking of he events of 1660) after it had been abrogated. Furthermore, the "hierarchicals" accepted the doctrines of the Remonstrants, and even of the Socinians. Van der Waeyen gives a long list of heresies which were to be found in Anglican authors and which had been condoned by "ille Henricus" (Henry Compton) upon whom "noster Fridericus" sponges: "Sic vides quae monstra alat Ecclesia Hierarchica".[29]

Spanheim was deeply shocked by this vehement attack. First he reacted in the annotations added to a second edition of his *Epistola* against the "fictions and abuses" of his antagonist,[30] and shortly afterwards in a more systematic work, *Animadversiones*, which dealt with "the varied and free polity of the churches".[31] Spanheim was backed by the curators of Leiden University, who sent an angry letter (printed in the second edition of the *Epistola*) to the cura-

---

[28] *Ad Philalethium Eliezerem adversus Nuperas Friderici Spanhemii Literas Epistola Apologetica*, Franequerae 1683, p.116.

[29] *Ibid.*, 417.

[30] *Epistola ad Amicum de Praefatione Frisiae Accusationibus, cum Animadversionibus Necessariis ad Censuras, Fictiones et Contumeliis Famosae Scriptionis Johannis ván der Waijen*, Trajecti ad Rhenum 1684. It is this edition which was published in *Opera* II, c. 997-1104.

[31] *Animadversiones de Ecclesiarum Politia Varia et Libera*, Lugd. Bat. 1684; also in *Opera* II, c, 1105-1260. I quote the *Epistola* (second edititon) and the *Animadversiones* from the *Opera*.

tors of the University of Franeker. They were irritated at the way Van der Waeyen had dealt with the English bishops in general and the Bishop of London in particular, whom they praised highly for his piety, his erudition and his temperance.[32] How angry Spanheim himself was, appears not only from his published works, but also from a number of private letters. In his letter to Archbishop Sancroft,[33] to whom he sent a copy of his *Animadversiones*, he spoke contemptuously of Van der Waeyen ("quidem Wayenus") as a weakminded babbler, who had infamously attacked the system of the Anglican Church. To Edward Bernard he wrote that he considered Van der Waeyen's work (or satire, "si satyra est") a sordid and inerudite writing, rather demoniacal than human.[34] And in a letter to his Dutch friend Gisbertus Cuperus he remarked that, apart from anonymous writings, since Christian times no more virulent work had ever appeared.[35]

In his *Epistola* and his *Animadversiones*, Spanheim strongly denied that he deviated from the *Confessio Belgica*. With regard to this point, he was confronted with a not inconsiderable problem. In Article XXXI, the Confession states, "And regarding the ministers of the Word (divini Verbi ministri), in whichever place they may be, they have one and the same power and authority, being together servants of Jesus Christ, the only universal Bishop and only Head of the church". This passage runs parallel to Art. XXX of the *Confessio Gallicana*: "Nous croyons tous vrais pasteurs ... avoir mesme authorité et égale puissance". Van der Waeyen, who was convinced that he had a strong case against Spanheim and who no doubt was happy to be able to convict the Leiden heresy-hunter of heresy, had gone so far as to suggest that Spanheim secretly wanted to introduce episcopacy and caesaropapism into the Dutch Church, an accusation Spanheim indignantly rejected.[36] Spanheim did not see the passages from the Dutch and French confessions as confessional statements of universal and timeless validity, but as regulations of the churches in the Netherlands and France in their specific situation. The idea of equality was not a matter of "jus divinum". With regard to the "disciplina ecclesiastica", Christ and the Apostles had only prescribed what was substantial and necessary. Not everything which was in use in the apostolic church was binding on all Christians. Spanheim rejected the idea that the church in the times of the Apostles was marked by an equality of ministers. The "episcopi" and the

---

[32] Spanheim emphasized in a preface to the *Epistola* that the Leiden curators had acted on their own accord: he had not requested their intervention.

[33] Spanheim to W. Sancroft, BLO, Tanner MS 32, f. 51. The tone of the letter is indicative of Spanheim's personal acquaintance with the Archbishop.

[34] Spanheim to E. Bernard, 1 June 1684, BLO, Smith MS 5, fol. 335.

[35] Spanheim to G. Cuper(us), 1 July 1683, Koninklijke Bibliotheek, The Hague, MS 72 C26, 6. Spanheim's preoccupation with the criticism of his orthodoxy also appears from a short letter to his Basel colleague Johann Zwinger, 30 May 1684, UB Basel, Bibl. Fr. Gr., MS III 16, fol. 93.

[36] "Epistola", *Opera* II, c. 1033f.

"presbyteri" were not in all aspects equal; right from the beginning there had existed a distinction in degree, a "discrimen graduum". The "episcopi" were superintendents, inspectors, curators. The "presbyteri" had various tasks: some of them functioned as preachers, others took part with the bishops in the government of the church. None was called priest ("sacerdos"), for there were no more sacrifices after the final sacrifice of Christ; nonetheless, Spanheim condoned the use of the term "priest", for example by the "Bohemians". Also in the purified churches of the Reformation there was a certain "discrimen graduum"; as well as in the French and the Dutch churches it existed in fact in all Reformed churches.[37] Furthermore, the churches which were not episcopally governed had always respected the way of government of the Church of England. In this context, he referred to the Synod of Dort, just as Le Moyne had done in his letter to Compton: "Ceux de Hollande ... montrèrent bien qu'ils avoyent pour l'Eglise Anglicane une profonde veneration". Van der Waeyen had countered this argument by stating that the respect the Dutch showed to the English delegates was due to the fact that they represented the Crown of England, but Spanheim did not agree. He has the story that when the Bishop of Llandaff (George Carleton) recommended the episcopal system as an expedient against schism and heresies, the President of the Synod, Johannes Bogerman, remarked he regretted that the Dutch Church had no bishop: "Domine, non sumus adeo felices".[38]

Naturally, there remained some problems. One of these was the function of lay elders. Spanheim doubted whether it was necessary to have such elders, "presbyteri secundi ordinis", in all churches. A more complex problem with regard to the question of comprehension (as Ken had already noticed) was that of reordination. Spanheim could imagine a new imposition of hands as a sign of reconciliation, as was used in the ancient church for those who, having lapsed in the period of persecution, returned to the church. He expressed, however, the wish that, were Presbyterian ministers to join again the Church of England, the "hierarchic brethren" would not impose the laying on of hands as a necessity nor make the efficacy of their ministry dependent on an external rite.[39]

Spanheim sent a copy of the *Animadversiones* not only to Sancroft (whose reaction we do not know), but also to Dodwell, who was the very opposite of

---

[37] "Animadversiones", *Opera* II, c. 1139-46. Spanheim rarely mentions the Scottish Church, perhaps because of its special position: though originally Presbyterian, it was now under episcopal government.

[38] "Epistola", *Opera* II, c. 1060. For this, Spanheim's source was a work by one of the English delegates at the synod, Joseph Hall: *Episcopacie by Divine Right*, London 1640, 15 f.; cf. Durel, *A View*, 118. As far as I can see, the Dutch sources are silent on this point. For the Synod of Dort and Episcopalianism, see W. Nijenhuis, *Ecclesia Reformata*, Leiden 1972, chapter IX: "The Controversy between Presbyterianism and Episcopalianism surrounding and during the Synod of Dordrecht 1618-1619".

[39] "Animadversiones", *Opera* II, c. 1141, 1175f.

a Latitudinarian; the biographer of the late Archbishop John Tillotson called him art "altitudinarian" whose ideas Tillotson quite emphatically disliked.[40] Dodwell—for whom indeed the efficacy of the ministry was dependent on what Spanheim saw as "external rites"—reacted to the book in a highly critical way.[41] He was prepared to concede that Spanheim had defended some individual persons against the attacks of Van der Waeyen, but he had not defended the Church of England as such: "on the contrary, you do not defend, but you undermine our church" ("... Ecclesiam nostram non defendis, sed subruis"). Ironically, Dodwell remarked that when Spanheim excluded from his defence all those who disagreed with Calvin or Dort, or who thought the episcopate necessary for the church, he was indeed an excellent patron of "our church" and the ecclesiastics! He reproached Spanheim for not criticizing men such as Prynne and Baxter and for sympathizing in fact with the more moderate ("mollioribus") non-conformists.

In his answer Spanheim showed himself disappointed at Dodwell's misjudgement of his intentions. Explicitly he distanced himself from the "rigidiores Presbyteriani", and he emphasized that he had never promoted nor even read works of non-conformist authors.[42] To Bernard he complained that having defended the episcopal dignity from the most terrible slander, and "your Oxford" from the stain of Socinianism or semi-Pelagianism, he had not deserved such bad grace from the side of Dodwell.[43] The correspondence between Spanheim and Dodwell broke off, to be resumed about ten years later, apparently by Dodwell. In 1695, Spanheim wrote in answer to a letter from Dodwell that he had never intended to accuse people whom he revered of Papism or Pelagianism, as Van der Waeyen had done; further, that it should be possible to retain the friendship while dissenting on obscure and dubious matters. This letter shows Spanheim's more moderate side; at the same time it confirms us in the impression we receive from his correspondence of 1684, that he underestimated or somewhat played down the differences in theological climate between the churches in England and in the Netherlands. Perhaps Dodwell would have been strengthened in his negative opinion of Spanheim's views, if he had known that one of the prominent younger Dissenters, Edmund Calamy (the historian of Dissent), spoke not without sympathy about Spanheim's views on comprehension. Calamy knew Spanheim from a short visit to Leiden, where he attended one of Spanheim's lectures.[44]

This visit took place in the winter of 1688-89, at the time of the Glorious Revolution, which, though not fundamentally, yet quite drastically changed

---

[40] Thomas Birch, *The Life of the Most Reverend Dr John Tillotson*, London 1752, 400.
[41] For Dodwell's letter, see note 18.
[42] Spanheim to H. Dodwell, 12 Sept. 1684, BLO Cherry MS 99.
[43] Spanheim to E. Bernard, 31 Oct. 1684, BLO Smith MSS 5, 339.
[44] Calamy, *Historical Account*, 174.

the English political and ecclesiastical situation. In this context, the idea of comprehension received a new momentum: for a short period, moderate Anglicans and Presbyterians believed that a comprehension of at least part of the Dissenters would be a viable option. No one expected that all Dissenters would join the mother church: even if the attempts at comprehension had succeeded, an "Act of Toleration" would have been necessary on behalf of those who had drifted too far away from the Church of England to consider a reunion. Comprehension and toleration were not opposite alternatives, but rather complementary possibilities.[45] Whether William III was strongly committed to the cause of comprehension is not quite certain. Jonathan Israel thinks a weakening of the privileged position of the Church of England would not have been too unwelcome to William;[46] a very strong Church of England would perhaps have been less easily manageable than an Anglican Church which had an important Dissenting community as its counterpart. On the other hand, however, a partial comprehension could have been a political asset, because it would have strengthened the influence of the Latitudinarians, and more in particular that of the "Williamite Bishops" within the Church of England. We may also wonder whether Spanheim and other Dutch theologians, who apparently had good relations with the court at The Hague, would (as we shall see) have gone to such great pains in the matter of comprehension if there had not been some political backing. However this may be, it is beyond doubt that Mary was personally in favour of comprehension. She was a deeply religious woman, devoted to the Church of England and to the Protestant cause,[47] while at the same time she was certainly not ill-disposed to the Presbyterians; during her stay in the Netherlands she had often attended the services led by Presbyterian ministers in the English church at The Hague.[48]

After her return to England, Mary—now Queen—requested Spanheim to write a "judicium" about the "Anglican affairs".[49] Perhaps she hoped that a moderate, mediating study by a comparative outsider, an orthodox and respected member of a presbyterially governed continental church, who had visited England and could be supposed to have some goodwill in Anglican as well as in Presbyterian circles, would contribute to bridging the gap and so from outside would assist in bringing about the desired union. There exist a

---

[45] See J. van den Berg, *The Idea of Tolerance and the Act of Toleration*, London 1989, 14f.

[46] J.I. Israel, "William III and toleration", in O.P. Grell and others (eds.), *From Persecution to Toleration*, Oxford 1991, 151f.

[47] See J. van den Berg, "Religion and Politics in the life of William and Mary", in *Fabrics and Fabrications*, especially 36f.

[48] G F. Nuttall, "English Dissenters in the Netherlands", in *Nederlands Archief voor Kerkgeschiedenis* 49 (1978), 51f.

[49] In a letter to William Lloyd he mentioned it as: "Meum de rebus Anglicanis judicium, quale mihi sapientissima Reginarum expresserat": Spanheim to the Bishop of Coventry and Lichfield, 13 Nov. 1695, British Library (herafter BL) Stowe MS 755, f. 36.

number of manuscript versions of Spanheim's "judicium" which, apart from minor variations, essentially comprise a shorter and a larger version. The longer version was printed posthumously in the second volume of Spanheim's *Opera Omnia* (1703), edited by the Leiden Professor Johannes a Marck.[50] By that time, however, it was no longer up-to-date. In retrospect, Calamy wrote, "... which Tract well deserves to be read and considered, though it had no effect".[51] The Bodleian Library has a copy of the Latin text of the shorter version.[52] Lambeth Palace has two shorter versions (not identical) in French, together with a copy of the larger (definitive) Latin version.[53] Another copy of this text, virtually identical, is in the British Library.[54] A copy of the first version was forwarded to the Queen, who sent to Spanheim a most favourable reaction.[55] In her turn, she forwarded the manuscript to Tillotson, then Dean of St. Paul's, and asked his advice on the matter. Tillotson wrote to Spanheim that he had read his tract with much pleasure ("avide ... et summa cum delectatione"); at that time, however (the beginning of 1691) the climate was not favourable to comprehension, and thus for tactical reasons he advised that its publication should be postponed until the time should be more auspicious.[56]

Apparently, Spanheim was not quite happy with the first version. He wrote an extended version, which (according to a note in both extant copies) should be preferred above the version which was read by the late Archbishop Tillotson.[57] Furthermore, he added a note in which he explicitly stated that the work should only he published if the Archbishop of Canterbury (Thomas Tenison) gave his permission and if the moderate brethren (the Presbyterians who were not hostile towards the idea of comprehension) did not judge it unsuitable for furthering a union with the Anglican Church. In November 1695

---

[50] "Expetitum judicium super dissidio Anglicano et capitibus, quae ad unionem seu comprehensionem faciunt", II, c. 1262-1312.

[51] Calamy, *Historical Account*, 175

[52] "Comprehensionis Anglicanae momentum, obices, ad eam motiva", BLO, Add. Ms A 214, f. 82-100

[53] LPL. Gibson Papers, MSS 932.75, 773. Ms 932.75 is not signed , but presumably partly written in Spanheim's hand; Ms 935.35 (unsigned), presumably wholly in his hand.

[54] BL, Harl. MS 5253 (dated 1690).

[55] Spanheim to the Bishop of Coventry and Lichfield , 3 Nov. 1695 (see note 48): "... judicium , de quo faventissimum responsum tuli ..." The Ms the Queen and Tillotson read was possibly one of the two versions in Lambeth Palace: they are among the Gibson Papers, of which the larger part came from Archbishop Tenison (Catalogue, LBL, III). After Tillotson's death they may have passed into the possession of Tenison. For the Queen asking Tillotson's opinion, see Tillotson's letter to Lady Russel, 25 Oct. 1690, printed in Birch, *Life of Tillotson*, 228.

[56] Tillotson to Spanheim, 6 Feb. 1691 (NS), *ibid.*, 234-6.

[57] The date on the copy in BL (1690) poses a problem: the note in question dates from after the death of Tillotson (22 Nov. 1694), and as appears from what follows Spanheim sent copies of the larger version to his English contacts in 1695. If the date is not a mistake, Spanheim perhaps started revising the first version in 1690, but for one reason or another did not divulge it until five years later.

he wrote to William Lloyd that, urged by learned men from the Presbyterian discipline, he had submitted his "judicium" to Tenison.[58] From this it appears that while on good terms with a number of Anglicans Spanheim also had good relations with Presbyterians, whom he considered his brethren. In 1695, Spanheim rightly was not optimistic about the prospects of a union: he doubted whether these were times in which the more prudential Nonconformists could be induced to a union, he wrote. And almost as if with a deep sigh he added, this was once the desire of our very pious Queen.[59]

In the extended version, which was posthumously printed, Spanheim started by remarking that the abolition of the penal laws was not sufficient to bring about a union; on the contrary, there was a danger of drifting farther apart. He warned against extremism on both sides. On the one side, a number of Anglicans considered their form of church government immutable, because it was sanctioned by divine law;[60] on the other side, the more rigid Dissenters saw their form of church discipline, with their equality of ministers, their government of the church by ministers and lay elders, and sometimes also the independence of the (local) churches, as a divine and apostolic institution. Amongst many on both sides, however, there existed a considerable consensus with regard to the fundamental points of doctrine and the form of worship. Many Anglicans, Spanheim observed, were prepared to have "communio sacra" in Presbyterian services, while members of overseas Reformed churches gladly went to communion in Anglican churches; he thought the opportunities for comprehension were favourable. It should, however, be a comprehension without equivocation and without the use of force.

With regard to ecclesiastical offices his main thesis is that, apart from the French, Dutch and Scottish churches (in the interim, the Church of Scotland had returned to its Presbyterian tradition), there existed everywhere inequality in authority. On this point there also existed differences within the non-episcopal churches. Examples of the points at issue are as follows: was their office of President of the Synod allocated by rota or (more like the episcopal officer) perpetual? Were their lay elders chosen for life or only for a certain period? What was the particular function of magistrates in a consistory? One receives the impression that for Spanheim the office of lay elders was of marginal importance; on this point, he clearly deviated from the system of his own

[58] It is not clear who those Presbyterians were, but we know that he had sent one of his writings on the affair of comprehension to Joseph Hill (probably the elder), minister of the English Presbyterian Church at Rotterdam: Spanheim to J. Hill, 22 Dec. 1693, BL Add. MS 4277, fol. 162.

[59] For Mary's desire for union, see also F. Spanheim, *Laudatio Funebris ... Mariae II*, Lugd. Bat. 1695, 57.

[60] In one of the shorter French versions (LPL, Gibson Papers 912.75) he explicitly mentioned Dodwell.

church. In a certainly more confidential document, an opinion on the "Articles of Comprehension" (1689), Spanheim even wrote that in his view the exercise of ecclesiastical discipline by lay-elders is not self-evident: "I mean those elders who are in nothing equal with ye Ministers of ye Word, whose Office is so often only for a Time, who have taken no Holy Orders, who have not been ordained by Imposition of Hands; who for ye most part are Illiterate and Working Men ...".[61]

As regards the liturgy, in his *Judicium* he again warned against extremes. He could, just to give one example, understand the Dissenters' objections to endless repetition in set forms of prayer, but at the same time he conceded that the long extemporaneous prayers of the Presbyterians were not always edifying. And though in the Anglican liturgy there were still relics of papal superstitions, it would be wrong to see all Anglican rites as "superstitious". So Spanheim does not object to, for example, the wearing of vestments as such; on this point, Hooper had acted too strongly.[62] Kneeling at communion can be a posture of reverence, though the oldest practice was that of sitting at the table;[63] it can be dangerous, however, when it is connected with the idea of a "praesentia realis".

Of course, for Dissenting ministers the greatest barrier was that of reordination. Spanheim strongly warned against such a form of reordination of non-episcopal ministers as would invalidate their former ordination. He could, however, accept a new imposition of hands as a sign of their "aggregation" into the Anglican church. The idea of a conditional reordination contained the danger of equivocation. Spanheim thought rather of a renewal of the ordination, such as had been given to Paul and Barnabas when they went out to the heathen. He ended his exposition with the very serious cautionary appeal, not to give room to any form of equivocation and tacit reservations, and not to lend an ear to rumours such as that after comprehension the Episcopalians would try to oppress the Presbyterians, or the Presbyterians would try to form a faction within the Church; such rumours were incompatible with the apostolic law of love.[64]

---

[61] I quote from the English translation of the "Avis demandé à un Theologien par delà la Mer Sur les Articles de la Comprehension", BLO Add. MS A 213, ff. 29-52 (French), ff 57-79 (English); the quoted passage on f. 70. The author is not explicitly mentioned, but the "Avis" refers to "mon Traitté de la diversité des Disciplines ... imprimé 1684".

[62] In this, he was in line with Calvin's moderate advice in the "Vestments controversy"; see W. Nijenhuis. *Calvinus oecumenicus*, 's-Gravenhage 1959, 205ff.

[63] Anglicans objected to receiving communion sitting: see Stillingfleet, *The Unreasonableness of Separation*, LXXXIII; cf. Durel, *A View*, 54f., who remarked that the Bohemians even considered it an "Arian" custom: the Arians, taking Christ "for a meer man, did think themselves ... good enough *to sit with him* at his own Table".

[64] For this summary of the contents of the *Judicium*, see in particular *Opera* II, c. 1263ff., 1289, 1296ff., 1308f., 1312.

For a theologian who in his own country was known as a conservative Calvinist, and even seen by some as a heresy-hunter, the *Judicium* is a remarkably mild exposition. Still more remarkable perhaps is a short note without date or signature which is among the papers on comprehension in Lambeth Palace and which is possibly also from Spanheim's hand: "Memoire pour leurs Altesses Royales sur les Affaires de Religion".[65] It has a strongly anti-Socinian tendency. The author remarks that their Royal Highnesses can banish from the church "ce malheureux esprit de tolerance pour le Socinianisme". He is more cautious, however, with regard to Arminianism. He recognizes the extent to which Arminianism ("ces opinions contre la pure doctrine de la grace et de la predestination") has pervaded the Anglican Church; there, "elles sont communes et presque universelles". They are however, not as dangerous as the Socinian errors, though in political respect Arminianism, too, is dangerous: Arminians are secret enemies of the Prince of Orange. The advice is to deal leniently with Arminianism and to suffer the liberty of opinion, but to oblige the theologians of the Anglican Church in a gentle way ("Par des voyes douces") by no means to deviate from the seventeenth Article of the Anglican Confession (which deals with the doctrine of predestination). The document ends with a short exposition on "la grande Affaire", the reunion of the Presbyterians with the Anglican Church, In order to bring this about, it would be at the discretion of their Royal Highnesses to expunge some ceremonies which in themselves contained nothing that was wrong, but which were "indifferent" and thus could be sacrificed for the sake of peace.

When, in the spring of 1689, the proposed Act of Comprehension was dropped and the matter was referred to Convocation,[66] Burnet saw this as "the utter ruin of the comprehension scheme",[67] though later he realized that too many concessions to the Dissenters could have caused a schism in the Church of England.[68] Perhaps Tillotson still had some hope. He took a very active part in the work of the Royal Commission for the review of the liturgy, which met in the autumn of 1689. It had a double purpose: many members thought that a revision (what we might call a "modernization") would make the liturgy more palatable to the spirit of the age or "the humour of the people", while at the same time making it more acceptable to the Presbyterians.[69] How much

[65] LPL, Gibson Papers, MS 937.77.

[66] See, *inter alia*, D.R. Lacey, *Dissent and Parliamentary Politics in England, 1661-1689*, New Brunswick 1969, 232ff., and J. Spurr, "The Church of England, Comprehension and the Toleration Act of 1689", *English Historical Review* 104 (1989), 927-46.

[67] Birch, *Life of Tillotson*, 165.

[68] G. Burnet, *History of my Own Times* (new edition) V, Oxford 1823, IV, 58f.; (in the first edition, II 32f.).

[69] T.J. Fawcett, *The Liturgy of Comprehension 1689*, Southend 1973, 25-45, 207 ("The humour of the people").

Tillotson was involved in "la grande affaire" appears from his "list of concessions which will probably be made by the Church of England for the union of Protestants".[70] The concessions were far-reaching. Many of them ran parallel to what Spanheim had written. Tillotson's Low Anglican position appears clearly from the fact that in his view, "those who have been ordained only by presbyters shall not be compelled to renounce their ordination", but for the sake of those who would doubt the validity of such an ordination he proposed a form of conditional reordination: "If thou art not ordained, I ordain thee." As we saw, this was a point on which Spanheim had great reservations.

Through Stillingfleet the seven points were sent to Hans Willem Bentinck, Earl of Portland, who more than any other at that time had the ear and the trust of the King.[71] Portland in his turn asked the advice of a number of Dutch theologians: Spanheim, of course, and also Henricus Pontanus (minister at The Hague), Daniel des Marets (Walloon minister at The Hague),[72] Jacobus Trigland (Professor at Leiden University, whose uncle had been the teacher of William III), and Hermannus Witsius (at that time Professor at Utrecht University; in 1685 he had been a member of a delegation, sent to England in order to congratulate James II, and on that occasion had met a number of leading Anglicans and Dissenters).[73] Pontanus collected the answers and sent them on 11 October 1689 to Bentinck, together with letters from Trigland and Witsius and a short exposition from the hands of Des Marets and an unknown French colleague.[74] Furthermore, the Bodleian Library has the French and English text of an extensive commentary from Spanheim's hand on the Articles of Comprehension.[75] It is interesting to see how far these Dutch theologians, all of them conservative Calvinists, were prepared to go. They consented with only some minor criticisms to practically all the points which Tillotson had proposed. One point, however, remained difficult: that of the ordination by bishops. Again Spanheim warned against any form which might be interpreted as reordination. Trigland, who saw the matter of comprehension as a great and godly design,[76] also had his difficulties with regard to what he saw as one of

[70] LPL MS 954, r.31, printed *inter alia* by Fawcett, 25f.

[71] They were sent on 13 Sept. 1689; see the copy in Tillotson's "Memoranda" in BL, Add. MS 4236, fol. 318b.

[72] Des Marets had contacts with William III through his botanical interests and occupations; in 1692 he even became "Controller General of His Majesty's Household in the Netherlands". See D.O. Wijnands, "Hortus Auriaci", *Journal of Garden History* 8 (1989), 77ff.

[73] See J. van Genderen, *Herman Witsius*, 's-Gravenhage 1953, 70-4. He had a profound interest in Puritan theology.

[74] The answers, collected by Pontanus, in LPL, Gibson Papers, MS 932.71; Witsius's letter: 932.72; Trigland's letter: 932.74; the letter of Des Marets and his colleague (signature illegible): 932.73.

[75] See note 61.

[76] "[Een] groot en godvruchtigh dessijn ... een Werck gelijk elck verstandig en vroom Patriot moet wensen": Trigland to Portland, 6 Oct. 1689.

the most delicate problems. For the future he did not object to a form of episcopal ordination of all ministers, but conditional ordination could suggest that before his ordination the ordinand would have illegally fulfilled his function. Witsius, an irenical orthodox theologian with pietist tendencies, thought the fourth point, of the reformation of manners (a point which as we know was very near to the Queen's heart),[77] should have precedence over the other points. With regard to the matter of (re)ordination he was more lenient than Trigland or Spanheim: if a conditional reordination without renunciation of the earlier ordination could be made palatable to those whom it concerns, very much might be gained. He added that he was not sufficiently at home in the English situation to be able to determine whether or not such a form of reordination would imply an indirect confession of the invalidity of the former acts of office.[78] In all these matters, he expressed a deep trust in the King: "My Lord the King is wise after the wisdom of an angel of God, which gives me confidence". To these papers was added an unsigned copy of a letter from a minister who served, or more probably had served, a Dutch church in England. He wrote that he looked upon the Church of England as "our very dear sister" ("onse allerliefste suster")[79]—a late answer to what, earlier in the century, Bishop Joseph Hall wrote about the continental Reformed Churches: "We love and honour those sister churches as the dear spouse of Christ".[80]

Was Ken right in his negative judgement on the attitude of the continental (in this case, Dutch) Reformed theologians towards the Church of England? Perhaps in part: no doubt on this point Van der Waeyen was more representative of popular feelings and of the views of the average minister than Spanheim was. According to Calamy, who (as we have seen) himself sympathized with Spanheim, even some of the latter's friends and neighbours charged him with being too favourable towards the Church of England.[81] But even if Spanheim did not represent the opinions of the majority of Dutch Calvinists on this point, as far as we can see this did not detract from his fame as an orthodox Reformed theologian. And he did not stand alone: such solidly orthodox theologians as Trigland and Witsius shared his appreciation of the Church of England and

---

[77] D.W.R. Bahlman, *The Moral Revolution of 1688*, New Haven 1957, 16ff.

[78] Witsius to Portland, 10 Oct. 1689.

[79] According to the *Catalogue* the letter was enclosed in that of Witsius, and thus sent from Holland. The author mentions Jacobus Alting (who, as he writes, had heen ordained a "priest" in the Church of England) as his teacher at the University of Groningen. If indeed the author was no longer in England, the only candidate for the authorship of the letter I can find is Gerardus van der Port, who matriculated in Groningen in 1670 and who served the Church of Austin Friars from 1680 till 1685, when he exchanged London for Amsterdam, where he died in 1691. See *Album Studiosorum Academiae Groninganae*, Groningen 1915, c. 106; J.H. Hessels, *Ecclesiae Londino-Batavae Archivum* III, Part 2, Cambridge 1897, Index *s.v.*

[80] Sykes, *Old Priest and New Presbyter*, 75.

[81] Calamy, *Historical Account*, 174.

were as much in favour of "comprehension" as he was. They would not have liked to see the system of the Anglican Church introduced in the Netherlands, but it was good for England provided that, as Witsius wrote to Portland, a reunion between Anglicans and Presbyterians would not be prejudicial to some foreign churches, which should remain in their old system of church government and their old laudable customs.

What were the motives which led Spanheim and other Dutch theologians to be so favourably inclined towards comprehension and to go so far in their appreciation of the Anglican Church? We have remarked that the fear of a Catholic usurpation of power, fanned by the events in France and the politics of James II, played an important part. The Church of England was not only the largest Reformed sister church, but also the church of the English nation, which if it remained firmly Protestant was one of the strongest bulwarks against the threats from Rome. Unity between English Protestants would strengthen the influence of the anti-Roman forces; conversely, disunity could cause cracks in the bulwark. Des Marets and his colleague even wrote in their letter on comprehension that a reunion of Anglicans and Presbyterians could be "le coup le plus mortel que le papisme puisse recevoir". In addition, Spanheim's friendship with some of the leading Latitudinarian Bishops as well as his loyalty to William III certainly played a part. In his funeral oration for Spanheim his colleague Trigland remarked that no one was more intimate with, more agreeable and precious to the Anglican Bishops and to the King than Spanheim was—a rhetorical exaggeration, as such proper to the genre, but in this case containing a significant kernel of truth.[82] Politically, the Latitudinarian church leaders were supporters of William's politics; culturally, Spanheim respected them as learned and erudite scholars, fellow-members of the republic of letters.

More explicitly theological factors may also have contributed to his attitude in this matter. Spanheim was a traditionalist, not in the Voetian-Puritan line, but in that of Maresius and of the leading French Reformed theologians and churchmen. As such, he looked back to the early period of the Reformation, a time in which, he believed, the division between Episcopalian and Presbyterian forms of church government was not as clear and disruptive as at a later stage. Something of this early situation he saw continued, if not in his own church, then in a number of other continental Protestant churches. Further-

[82] J. Trigland, *Laudatio Funebris Frid. Spanhemii F.F.*, Lugd. Bat. 1701, 36. On 17 February, Henry Compton was present in Leiden, where he attended Gronovius' oration on the return of William III; on that occasion he will certainly have met again his friend Spanheim: G.D.J. Schotel, *De Academie te Leiden in de 16e, 17e en 18e eeuw*, Haarlem 1875, 382. At the beginning of his oration, Gronovius addressed Compton with special homage as "reverendissime et illustrissime praesul": Jacobus Gronovius, *Felix Adventus in Bataviam ... Wilhelmi Britanniarum Regis*, Lugd. Bat. 1691, opposite 1.

more, his patristic studies had strengthened his conviction that the forms of church government had always been varied and changeable. This made it all the more easy for him to support the attempts at comprehension.[83] They were, however, doomed to failure. Ironically, it was Spanheim's admired friend Compton who on 21 November 1689 in Convocation contributed to wrecking the comprehension scheme by backing the High Anglicant Dean of Gloucester William Jane as "prolocutor".[84] The "very dear sister" and the "brethren" remained apart, and Spanheim's wish, uttered at the end of his *Judicium*, that in the history of the English churches a union might inaugurate the era of the "concordia fratrum", was not fulfilled.

---

[83] For Spanheim's views with regard to the differences in worship between Anglicans and Presbyterians, see also a disputation, defended by one of his students and no doubt, as was usual, written by the professor: J. Waser, *Disputatio Theologico-Historica* ..., Lugd. Bat. 1696. It pleads for "diversitas" in liturgical matters with preservation of the "consensus fidei" (f. D 1ro,^{vo}).

[84] See E.F. Carpenter, *The Protestant Bishop, being the Life of Henry Compton, 1632-1713, Bishop of London*, London 1956, 164ff.; according to Carpenter, "personal considerations swayed his judgment, and gave his actions a bewildering inconsistency".

CHAPTER TWELVE

THE IDEA OF THE PRE-EXISTENCE OF THE SOUL OF CHRIST: AN ARGUMENT IN THE CONTROVERSY BETWEEN ARIAN AND ORTHODOX IN THE EIGHTEENTH CENTURY

In his *Briefe betreffende den allerneuesten Zustand der Religion und der Wissenschaften in Gross-Brittanien* (1752) the German theologian Georg Wilhelm Alberti wrote (in a postscript to a letter on the Trinitarian controversies):

> Ich habe vergessen, von einer andern Meynung, betreffende die Lere von der h. Dreyeinigkeit, etwas zu sagen, welche doch manchen angesehenen Gönner gehabt hat, auch noch hat: ich meyne die Praeexistenz der Seele Christi ... Der neueste Verteidiger der Lere von der Praeexistenz der Seele Christi, welcher zu den Gründen seiner Vorgänger vor diese Meynung noch mehrere hinzu gethan, ist D. Isaac Watts, von welchem man dergleichen nicht vermuten sollte. Er hat schon lange diese Meynung geheget, wie er meldet, und sie zu der Zeit, da seine Gemüts- und Leibeskräfte am stärkesten gewesen, untersuchet, und höchst wahrscheinlich gefunden; doch seinen Aufsatz davon bey dreissig Jahre liegen lassen, ob sich vielleicht das Wahrscheinliche dieser Meynung verlieren mögte; weil dis aber nicht geschehen, so hat er ihn endlich A. 1746 drucken lassen.[1]

In 1746 a work by Watts on Christology did indeed appear, under the title *The Glory of Christ as God-Man display'd*; first anonymously, then (in a reissue of the same year) with the author's name on the title-page.[2] If Alberti is right as regards the time which elapsed between the writing and the publishing of the work, *The Glory of Christ* was written before 1720.[3] As we shall see, in the years after 1720 Watts published a number of works on christological subjects. In spite of what Alberti mentions, the reasons for the delay in publishing *The Glory of Christ* remain somewhat mysterious; the more so, as before 1746 he had already touched on the doctrine of the pre-existence of the human soul of Christ in more than one work. However this may be, *The Glory of Christ* distinguished itself from earlier works by the fact that here this doctrine was fully and explicitly discussed, as appears from the title of the third discourse: "The Glories of Christ as God-Man displayed, by tracing out the early exist-

---

[1] G.W. Alberti, *Briefe*... (III), Hannover 1752, 742, 745.

[2] "The title is a cancel": *British Museum Gen. Cat. of Printed Books 253*, c. 993. I used the edition of this work in *The Works of ... Isaac Watts*, ed. by D. Jennings and the late P. Doddridge VI, London 1753, 762-861.

[3] Alberti's information is confirmed by, or perhaps borrowed from, a passage in *The Glory of Christ*, where Watts remarks that Henry More's *The Great Mystery of Godliness*, which appeared in 1660, was published "near threescore years ago": *Works* VI, 853.

ence of his human nature as the first-born of GOD, or as the first of all creatures, before the formation of this world".

The Independent minister Isaac Watts (1674-1748) was one of the most prominent English Dissenters.[4] He was a voluminous author; in his own times his works enjoyed a large degree of popularity abroad as well as in England.[5] The hymns he wrote (some of which have become classics) are a mirror of his evangelical spirituality. While essentially orthodox[6] and a defender of the Trinitarian tradition, he was a man of a mild and irenic attitude. In 1720, at a time when "the Arian controversy"[7] began to divide the Dissenting community, he still thought "a happy medium might be found out to secure liberty and the gospel together".[8] His theological approach and his stand amidst the conflicts of his day may be characterized as a Dissenting *via media.*

The Arian controversy started right at the beginning of the eighteenth century, in 1702, with the publication of a work by a Presbyterian minister in Dublin, Thomas Emlyn (1663-1741): *An Humble Inquiry into the Scripture Account of Jesus Christ.*[9] For his arianizing ideas, Emlyn was imprisoned, but this could not stop the spread of his views; one of the historians of Dissent, Michael R. Watts, remarks that it was Emlyn's Arianism which became the prevailing heresy of the early eighteenth century.[10] Arianizing tendencies not only spread within the Dissenting circle, but also within the Church of England. When in 1712 Samuel Clarke, rector of St. James's, Westminster, well known for his support of Newton and his controversy with Leibniz, published his *The Scripture-Doctrine of the Trinity*, in which he taught the subordination of the Son to the Father, he was accused of Arianism, though (like, to a certain extent, Emlyn) he did not consider himself an Arian.[11] He could only escape

---

[4] His main biographies are: T. Milner, *The Life, Times and Correspondence of the Rev. Isaac Watts, D.D.*, London 1834; A.P. Davies, *Isaac Watts. His Life and Work*, London 1948.

[5] For his popularity in the Netherlands, see: J. van den Berg and G.F. Nuttall, *Philip Doddridge (1702-1751) and the Netherlands*, Leiden 1987, esp. ch. II.

[6] For this, see T. Milner, *Life*, 724-729; A.P. Davies, *Watts*, 109-126.

[7] For "the Arian controversy", see J.H. Colligan, *The Arian Movement in England*, Manchester, 1913; E.M. Wilbur, *A History of Unitarianism* II, Cambridge (Mass.), 1952, 236-270; R. Thomas, "Presbyterians in transition", in C.G. Bolam and others, *The English Presbyterians*, London 1968, 113-218; M.R. Watts, *The Dissenters* I, Oxford, 1978, 371-382.

[8] Quoted from R. Thomas in *The English Presbyterians*, 170.

[9] For Emlyn, see esp. E.M. Wilbur, *Unitarianism*, 244ff. Emlyn gave an account of the proceedings against him in "A true Narrative of the Proceedings ... against Mr. Thomas Emlyn". *The Works of Mr. Thomas Emlyn* I, London 1746, 1-79.

[10] *The Dissenters* I, 373.

[11] For Clarke"s attitude towards traditional Arian doctrine, see J.H. Colligan, *The Arian Movement in England*, 37. Clarke explicitly declined to be called an Arian, while Emlyn, who sympathized with Clarke, declared he did not agree wholly with Arius (nor with Socinus): "A true Narrative", *Works* I, 16. Still, from some passages in Emlyn's "A Vindication of the Worship of the Lord Jesus Christ, On Unitarian Principles" (1706; *Works* I, esp. 276f.) and in his "A Vindication of the Bishop of Gloucester's Discourse" (1707; *Works* I, esp. 377f.), we may deduce that ultimately, in spite of his reservations, he sympathized with Arius.

ecclesiastical prosecution by promising to keep silent on the subject, but of course his ideas as laid down in his work could not be silenced; they exercised a not inconsiderable influence, especially in the Dissenting community. All this resulted in a mounting tension within the circle of the Dissenters which came to a head in 1719, when at a conference of the London Dissenting ministers, held at Salters' Hall, a narrow majority opted for liberty with regard to the interpretation of the doctrine of the Trinity.[12]

It should be added, that among this majority only a few were indeed Arians; furthermore, that most of those who objected against the orthodox Trinitarian creed were not Socinians: they saw Christ as a pre-existent being, which even might be called God, subordinate to the Father but far exalted above all human beings, and thus able to act as Mediator in the work of atonement. This form of Arianism left much of the traditional theological concepts intact. The theology of the eighteenth-century Arians was a mixture of biblicism and rationalism. Influenced as the arianizing theologians were by the rationalist method of John Locke, they were protagonists of a free and open inquiry into the Scriptures, and they refused to submit to the authority of credal formulas for which they found no warrant in the Bible. This does not imply that they were radicals who wanted to turn upside down the whole structure of traditional theology; their Arianism could, however, easily drift into an explicitly antitrinitarian form of Unitarianism, as indeed happened in many cases in the second half of the eighteenth century.[13]

Isaac Watts had not taken part in the Salters' Hall conference, nor did he want to be identified with one of the two conflicting parties as to the question of subscription or non-subscription to certain credal formulas.[14] But he was deeply concerned about the Trinitarian controversy as such, as appears from a dissertation he published in 1724 under the title "The *Arian* invited to the orthodox faith: or, A plain and easy method to lead such as deny the proper deity of *Christ*, into the belief of that great article".[15] Watts' irenical spirit is revealed in the preface to the three *Dissertations* of which "The *Arian* ..." formed part:

> I would not willingly call every man an enemy to *Christ*, who lives under some doubts of his supreme godhead. My charity inclines me to believe that some of them,

---

[12] For "Salters' Hall", see R. Thomas, "The Non-Subscription Controversy amongst Dissenters in 1719: the Salters' Hall Debate", *Journal of Ecclesiastical History* 4 (1953), 162-186.

[13] For the transition from Arianism to Unitarianism, see E.M. Wilbur, *Unitarianism*, ch. XV, XVI, and H.L. Short,"From Presbyterian to Unitarian", in *The English Presbyterians*, 219-235; furthermore J. van den Berg, "Priestly, the Jews and the Millenium", this volume Ch. 13. Emlyn already used the term "Unitarian", but his Arian "Unitarianism" should not be identified with the more radical Unitarianism of a later generation.

[14] For Watts and "Salters' Hall", see T. Milner, *Life*, 322ff.

[15] The first of three *Dissertations relating to the Christian doctrine of the Trinity, Works* VI, 493-544.

> both read their bibles carefully, and pray daily for divine instruction to lead them into all truth: That they honour and adore that glorious person whom they believe to be the brightness of his Father's glory, and by whom he created the worlds, who condescended to take a human body, and to die for sinners ...[16]

Furthermore, in "The *Arian* ..." Watts distinguished between "the ancient Arians" who believed the Son and the Holy Spirit to be "mere creatures", and "the modern refiners of the *Arian* scheme", who have granted that there is "a peculiar, strict and perfect union and communion, between the Father and the Son"; for this, he referred to Clarke's *Scripture-Doctrine of the Trinity*.[17] "Where is", Watts asked, "the inconvenience, or difficulty, of allowing this to be called a personal union, whereby what is proper to God may be attributed to *Christ*, and what is proper to the man *Christ* may be attributed to God ...?"[18] It is interesting that it was precisely in the context of an "invitation to Arians" that Watts mentioned for the first time in his works the doctrine of the pre-existence of Christ's human soul

> which seems to be the most obvious and natural sense of many scriptures, if we can believe that it was formed the first of creatures before the foundation of the world, and was present with God in the beginning of all things, which is no hard matter for an *arian* to grant. Then we also justly believe this union between God and man to have begun before the world was, in some unknown moment of God's eternity: For when the human soul of *Christ* was first brought into existence, it might be united in that moment to the divine nature.[19]

Here, the idea of the pre-existence of the soul of Christ is used by Watts as a bridge to span the gap between the Arian and the orthodox. Watts realized that in doing this he was in danger of being himself accused of Arianism. In the preface to four *Dissertations relating to the Christian doctrine of the Trinity* of 1725 he wrote that if a man "explain the trinity according to the ancient *Athanasians* ... he is censured perhaps as a downright tritheist. If he follow the scholastic scheme ... which has been called modern orthodoxy, he incurs the charge of *sabellianism*. If he dare propose the doctrine of the pre-existent soul of *Christ*, and follow bishop *Fowler*, Mr. *Fleming* and others, he is accused of favouring the *arian* and *nestorian* errors, even though all this time he strongly maintains the proper deity of *Christ* ...".[20] He knew quite well, that even "the nicest care" could not exempt a man from "these inconveniences". It was perhaps his awareness of the possibility of such inconveniences which made him hesitate to publish his broader and more fundamental exposition of the

---

16 *Works* VI, 499.
17 The reference is to Part 1, 594 and 600 of Clarke's work.
18 *Works* VI, 505.
19 *Works* VI, 507.
20 *Works* VI, 547.

doctrine of the pre-existence of Christ, which (as we saw) did not appear before 1746.

Just like the other works on the Trinity and on Christology, this work, too, was defined by the context of the Arian controversy. Watts thought the Socinian doctrines had been effectively refuted by many learned authors; now, the point at issue was whether or not Christ in his "complex person" included the godhead: "This is the great and important question of the age".[21] In the attempts to solve this question, the doctrine of the pre-existence of Christ's soul could play an important part:

> ... if, by a more careful inspection of the word of God, we shall find it revealed there with unexpected evidence, that the "human soul of our Lord *Jesus Christ* had an existence, and was personally united to the divine nature, long before it came to dwell in flesh and blood" ... will not such thoughts as these spread a new lustre over all our former ideas of the glory of *Christ* ... ?[22]

Watts was indeed convinced that Scripture offered plentiful evidence for the doctrine he advocated. Many texts, especially in the New Testament, affirm the pre-existence of Christ. Some of them directly refer to his divine nature. Other texts "carry not with them such a full and convincing evidence of his godhead as utterly to exclude all other interpretations". Lastly, there are also texts which "in their most natural, obvious and evident sense seem to refer to some intelligent being belonging to our Lord *Jesus Christ*, which is inferior to godhead"; these texts "most naturally lead us to the belief of the pre-existence of his human soul". In a note, Watts explains that if in this connection he speaks of the soul of Christ as being an angel or an angelic spirit, he means that the soul of Christ was without a body, or was a messenger of God the Father; and if he speaks of him as a super-angelic spirit, he intends to express that Christ's soul had "both natural and deputed powers far superior to angels".[23] Of course he wanted to prevent possible misunderstandings with regard to expressions which, taken out of their context, somehow smacked of Arianism.

One of his main proof-texts was Phil. 2.5, 6, 7. According to Watts, the Arians raise a plausible objection against the "vulgar explanation of the trinity and the divinity of Christ", because "that scheme allows no real self emptying, no literal and proper abasement and suffering of the Son of God", but only a "nominal suffering". The Son of God himself "really suffered nothing ... but was all the while possessed of the highest glory, and of the same unchangeable blessedness": the godhead himself is "impassible", and thus cannot really suffer pain or loss, nor undergo "proper sensible humiliation, shame or sor-

[21] *Works* VI, 731.
[22] *Works* VI, 803.
[23] *Works* VI, 805f.

row". All objections of the Arians are solved, however, if we apply the notion of self-emptying to the pre-existent soul of Christ. This doctrine of the pre-existence of Christ's soul

> sets the whole scheme of the self-denial and sufferings of *Christ*, in as glorious and advantageous a light as their doctrine can pretend to do; and yet at the same time secures the divinity of *Christ*, together with all the honours of it's condescending grace, by supposing this pre-existent soul always personally united to his divine nature. Thus all this sort of pretences for the support of the *arian* error is destroyed at once, by admitting this doctrine.

The same doctrine also helps us in defending the doctrine of Christ's deity against other "cavils" of the Arians. They consider a number of things mentioned in the Old Testament, such as the eating and drinking with Abraham, the wrestling with Jacob etc. "too mean and low condescensions for the great God of heaven and earth to practice". But again, all difficulties are solved if we see these events as appearances of "this glorious spirit"[24]—a human soul, which was "like a glass through which the godhead shone with inimitable splendor ...".[25]

Watts found corroborative evidence for the doctrine he defended in the testimony of the ancient Jews, among whom "there was a tradition of the pre-existence of the soul of the *Messiah*". In this connexion he referred to Philo's exegesis of Ex. 23.20 and to the Septuagint translation of Is. 9.6. Furthermore, he quoted the *Pesikta*:[26] "After God had created the world, he put his hand under the throne of his glory, and brought out the soul of the *Messiah*, with all his attendants, and said unto him, Wilt thou heal and redeem my sons after six thousand years? He answered, I am willing to do so ...". Also in cabbalistic literature the pre-existence of the Messiah's soul is mentioned, and though, according to Watts, "we allow no more credit to these traditions than to other *jewish* tales, yet it discovers their ancient notion of the pre-existence of the soul of the *Messiah* ...".[27] And in ancient christian tradition the doctrine was also to be found: "*Origen* seems to be a believer of the pre-existent soul of *Christ*".[28]

---

[24] *Works* VI, 841f.

[25] *Works* VI, 825.

[26] The quotation is borrowed from Bishop Fowler's *A Discourse of the Descent of the Man-Christ Jesus from Heaven* (see below). In Oxford, where Bishop Fowler had studied, three mss. of the *Pesikta de Rav-Kahana* (one of the oldest homiletical midrashim) have been preserved: *Encyclopaedia Judaica* XIII, c. 333ff.

[27] *Works* VI, 821f.

[28] *Works* VI, 853. For Origen and the doctrine of the pre-existence of the soul of Christ, see M.E. Wiles, "The Nature of the Early Debate about Christ's Human Soul", *Journal of Ecclesiastical History* 16 (1965), 142f.; R. Lorenz, "Die Christusseele im Arianischen Streit", *Zeitschrift für Kirchengeschichte* 94 (1983), 37.

Furthermore, Watts could refer to a number of modern authorities, who shared his opinions on this point. Just as the doctrine of the millennium was long obscured,

> and yet now it has arisen into further evidence, and has obtained almost universal assent, so this doctrine of *Christ's* pre-existent soul, though it might have lain dormant several ages, yet since that excellent man doctor *Henry More* has published it near threescore years ago in his "great mystery of godliness", it has been embraced, as bishop *Fowler* asserts, "by many of our greatest divines, as valuable men as our church can boast of; though most of them have been too sparing in owning it, for fear, I suppose, of having their orthodoxy called in question".[29]

On one important point, however, Watts differed from More: he rejected the idea (held, as we shall see, by More and Origen) that not only the soul of Christ, but all souls were pre-existent, "for which opinion I think there is neither in scripture nor in reason any just foundation ...".[30]

Next to More, Watts mentioned a number of other authors who also held the doctrine of the pre-existence of Christ's soul. Among them was Robert Fleming (1660-1716), a Presbyterian minister of Scots descent, educated in the Netherlands, to whose *Christology* (3 vls., 1705-1708) Watts more than once refers,[31] and Edward Fowler (1632-1714), Bishop of Gloucester, who formed a link between the Cambridge Platonists and the eighteenth-century authors on the subject and to whom because of this we shall return below.[32] Alberti remarks: "Es ist diese Meynung auch ausser England von einigen angenommen worden, wobey ich mich aber nicht aufhalte".[33] Of this, I have only been able to find one instance:[34] a French work, anonymously published in London in 1739 under the title *Dissertation Théologique et Critique, Dans laquelle on tâche de prouver, par divers passages des Saintes Ecritures, que l'Ame de Jésus-Christ étoit dans le Ciel une Intelligence pure et glorieuse, avant que d'être unie à un corps humain dans le sein de la Bienheureuse Vierge Marie*. In his preface, the author gives the impression that his views are new, and that his work is purely the result of his own studies.

---

[29] *Works* VI, 853.

[30] *Works* VI, 823.

[31] "His 'Christology' ... shows that while himself orthodox on the person of Christ, he was resolutely opposed to any form of subscription": *Dictionary of National Biography*, s.v. Fleming.

[32] For adherents of the doctrine of the pre-existence of the soul of Christ, see also J.A.B. Jongeneel, *Het redelijke geloof in Jezus Christus* (diss. Leiden), Wageningen 1971, 75.

[33] G.W. Alberti, *Briefe*, 746.

[34] Apart, perhaps, from the rather eccentric Dutch Cartesian layman Willem Deurhoff (1650-1717), who according to some of his opponents taught the pre-existence of Christ's soul: B. de Moor, *Commentarius perpetuus in Johannis Marckii Compendium* III, Lugd. Bat. 1765, 695.

> Il ne nous paroît pas qu'aucun motif humain nous ait induit le moins du monde a prendre le sentiment que nous avons adopté. Nous avons suspendu notre jugement pendant bien des années, nous avons lu et relu, surtout le Nouveau Testament ...[35]

One of his critics, Armand de la Chapelle, minister of the Walloon church at The Hague,[36] wrote in a review of the *Dissertation* in the *Bibliothèque Raisonnée*: "Il n'est *nouveau* par rapport à l'Angleterre"; yet he remarked that one should not doubt the author's solemn declarations as regards this point.[37]

According to the *Dictionnaire* of J.B. Ladvocat,[38] the author was Pierre Roques (1685-1745), minister of the French church at Basle, whose theology in general was of the same type as that of Watts.[39] It is peculiar, though of course not impossible, that a French author should have developed spontaneously a doctrine which for quite a number of years had already been defended by English authors, one of whom (Henry More) he could even have read in Latin.[40] However this may be, the author of the *Dissertation* brought forward the doctrine of the pre-existence of Christ's soul with no less vigour than Watts did. Like Watts, he rejected the idea that all souls were pre-existent:

> Il y a peu de gens qui croient que les ames soient éternelles, et il est facile de réfuter cette hypothèse. Nous disons la même chose de l'opinion de ces Docteurs Juifs qui croient la pré-existence des ames, et qui ont enseigné qu'elles avoient été toutes créées au commencement du monde.

This he knew from John Lightfoot's *Horae Hebraicae et Talmudicae*, from which he quoted: "Repositorium est, ait R. Salom., et nomen ejus est Goph: atque a Creatione formatae sunt omnes animae quae erant nascendae, atque ibi repositae".[41]

---

[35] *Dissertation*, f.[*3ro].

[36] According to *Nieuw Nederlandsch Biografisch Woordenboek* VII, s.v., he wrote the theological reviews in the *Bibl. Raisonnée*; cf. [J.B.] Ladvocat, *Dictionnaire Historique Portatif* II, La Haye, 1754, s.v. Roques.

[37] *Bibliothèque Raisonnée des ouvrages des savans de l'Europe* XXIV (1740), 135. La Chapelle referred to the Cambridge Platonists Henry More, Joseph Glanville and George Rust, whose opinions he knew from a work, entitled *Two choice and useful Treatises*, London 1682. His astonishment would have been still greater, had he known that a number of other authors had defended the idea of the pre-existence of Christ's soul more emphatically than the authors he mentioned had done.

[38] *Dictionnaire II, loc. cit.*

[39] For Roques and his theology, see J. van den Berg, "Le Vray Piétisme: Die aufgeklärte Frömmigkeit des Basler Pfarrers Pierre Roques", *Zwingliana* 16 (1983), 35-53.

[40] A Latin edition of More's *Opera Omnia* appeared in London in 3 vols. between 1675 and 1679; a reprint of the theological volume in 1700. See the bibliography in F.I. Mackinnon (ed.), *Philosophical Writings of Henry More*, New York, 1925, 240f.

[41] *Dissertation*, 4. Lightfoot refers to "R. Solomon" (Rashi) and other Jewish authors in his notes on John 9.2; he has, however, his reservations with regard to the general acceptance of the idea of the pre-existence of souls among the Jews: "Horae Hebraicae et Talmudicae impensae in Evangelium Sancti Joannis" (1671) in J. Lightfoot, *Opera Omnia* II, Roterodami 1686, 638.

Another parallel with Watts is that the author of the *Dissertation* also hoped the doctrine of the pre-existence of Christ's soul would be a means to bring the Arians and the orthodox together. His tone is even more conciliatory than that of Watts:

> ... on pourroit peut-être par ce moïen rapprocher les sentimens des Ariens et des Orthodoxes au sujet de la divinité du Sauveur. Les Ariens ont cru qu'il y avoit en J.C. quelque nature excellente qui avoit existé dans le ciel, et qui étoit inférieure au Dieu souverain ... En cela ils avoient raison ... Les Orthodoxes au contraire suivent l'Ecriture, lorsqu'ils enseignent que la Parole, qui est le Dieu Créateur des cieux et de la terre, a habité réellement et purement en J.C. ... Toute la vérité ne paroît pas se trouver toute entière, ni dans l'un, ni dans l'autre de ces deux systèmes; mais en réunissant ces deux opinions ... on a un système complet et lié de tout ce que l'Ecriture nous enseigne de la personne de notre grand Médiateur ...[42]

Yet, however irenic he was, at the same time the author strongly maintained he was essentially orthodox: "Nous le déclarons donc hautement encore, nous sommes fort éloignés du sentiment des Ariens et des Sociniens".[43] While La Chapelle had no difficulty in admitting this, he strongly criticized the idea of the pre-existence of the soul of Christ and the arguments used by the author in support of his thesis. The doctrine of a pre-existent soul of Christ, destined to animate a human body for the work of redemption implied that this work preceded the work of creation—an idea, acceptable only to supralapsarians! Furthermore, the created pure Intelligence which was identified with the soul of Christ differed only in terminological respect from the Second Person of the Arian Trinity. In the context of this doctrine, the divine nature of Christ would be completely useless ("inutile"). Besides, would not this doctrine lead to a recognition of three natures in one person? And lastly, why should only one soul be pre-existent; would it not be easier to believe in the pre-existence of all souls?[44] Another critic, the Genevan pastor François de Roches, was prepared to concede that the doctrine proposed in the *Dissertation* could help to explain some obscure passages in Scripture, but would it not be better to leave these in obscurity than to risk "d'ébranler des Véritez très consolantes pour l'Homme pécheur"?[45]

As we saw, Edward Fowler, Bishop of Gloucester (1632-1714) formed a bridge between the Cambridge Platonists and later authors on the pre-existence of Christ's soul. He was a friend and protégé of Henry More, whom he admired and from whom he borrowed some of his ideas,[46] but Principal

---

[42] *Dissertation*, 113.
[43] *Dissertation*, f.[*3ro].
[44] *Bibliothèque Raisonnée* XXIV, 135-138.
[45] F. de Roches, *Défense du Christianisme* II, Lausanne et Genève, 1740, 246.
[46] *DNB*, s.v.; cf. F.J. Powicke, *The Cambridge Platonists. A study* (1926), Hamden (Conn.) 1971, 151, 197.

Tulloch cautions us not to consider him a Cambridge Platonist: "He had but slight hold of the principles of the Cambridge theology, and has sketched them ... from a superficial and somewhat confused point of view".[47] In 1706 Fowler published *A Discourse of the Descent of the Man-Christ Jesus from Heaven; together with His Ascension to Heaven again* ... Fowler thought the doctrine of the pre-existence of the soul of Christ could be used as an argument in the struggle with the Socinians "for its depriving them of the Advantages they have for the Retorting of the Charge against them of wresting Scripture".[48] "For further Satisfaction" Fowler referred the reader to Henry More's *An Explanation of the Grand Mystery of Godliness* (1660). It sounds improbable, when he adds: "Which I never happen'd to look into, till after I had penned what I thought sufficient upon that Part ...",[49] but perhaps Fowler only wanted to say that, though acquainted with More's ideas, he had compared his own work *a posteriori* with that of More. Still, there is a difference between More and Fowler. Like More, Fowler appeals to the fact that this doctrine was "a Doctrine of the ancient *Jewish* Church".[50] More was primarily interested in the doctrine of the pre-existence of all souls, which he also met with in Jewish tradition;[51] a subject about which Fowler wrote in an almost sceptical tone, when he remarked that "the Fanciful Rabbins" grafted upon the pre-existence of "their *Messias*" the pre-existence of all souls. At any rate, in Fowler's view the doctrine of the pre-existence of the soul of Jesus was not dependent on that of the existence of all human souls before the creation of the body.[52] With the followers and successors of the Cambridge Platonists, the accent indeed had shifted from a full-fledged Platonist position to a more rationalist attitude.

Fowler was attacked by the Dean of St. Paul's, William Sherlock (1641-1707), who elaborately excused himself for attacking "a Venerable Prelate, for whom I have had an old Friendship, and a very particular Respect and Honour". He thought it, however, unavoidable to devote a chapter of his *The Scripture Proofs of our Saviour's Divinity Explained and Vindicated* (1706) to a refutation of Fowler's *Discourse*, because "it nearly affects the Cause of Christianity, in its most vital and fundamental Parts: which I hope his Lordship was not aware of ...".[53] According to Sherlock, the Bishop, by assuming a union between the soul of Christ and the Second Person in the Trinity, jumbled

---

[47] J. Tulloch, *Rational Theology and Christian Philosophy in England in the Seventeenth Century* II, Edinburgh 1874, 439.

[48] *Discourse*, 44.

[49] *Discourse*, 66.

[50] *Discourse*, 25.

[51] See J. van den Berg, "Menasseh ben Israel, Henry More and Johannes Hoornbeeck on the preexistence of the soul", this volume Ch. 5.

[52] *Discourse*, 41, 33.

[53] *Scripture Proofs*, 219.

Arianism and Nestorianism together, "an *Arian* Soul, and a *Nestorian* Union".[54]

To this accusation, Fowler indignantly replied in a new work, which appeared in the same year.[55] In his turn, Fowler indirectly accused Sherlock of heresy by referring to the fact that the latter had been indicted of Socinianism or tritheism because of his *A Discourse concerning the Knowledge of Jesus Christ (1674)*.[56] In the context of our subject it is interesting to note that Sherlock's supposed "tritheism" had made Emlyn turn away from trinitarian doctrine.[57] Again, Fowler appealed to More; furthermore, as Watts (probably following Fowler) would do some decades later, he mentioned the fact that just as the doctrine of the millennium, which he connected with the name of Joseph Mede, had lain in obscurity for some time, his doctrine had lain in obscurity since Origen.[58]

More than once we have mentioned the name of Henry More (1614-1687), one of the leading Cambridge Platonists, with whom the doctrine of the pre-existence of the soul of Christ in its new form originated. As we have already seen, More, as a Platonist, was most of all concerned with the idea of the pre-existence of all souls. In the context of an exposition of this doctrine he teaches the pre-existence of the soul of Christ, which according to him is implied in many places of the Old and the New Testament. With regard to the Old Testament, he refers to the fact that in the "*Apparitions* of *Angels* to the ancient *Patriarchs*, it was *Christ* himself that appeared";[59] in this context he quotes Calvin's commentary on Daniel: "In eo nihil est absurdi, quod Christus aliquam speciem humanae naturae exhiberet antequam manifestatus esset in carne".[60] From the New Testament, More mentions a number of texts from the gospel of St. John (3.13, 31; 6.26, 38; 17.4, 5); furthermore, Phil. 2.6, 7, 8 and 1 John 4.2. In connection with the last text, he remarks: "Here St. *John* seems to cabbalize ... that is, to speak in the Language of the Learned of the Jews: For the genuine Sense is: *He that confesses that Jesus is the Messiah come into the Flesh, or into a Terrestrial Body, is of God*: Which implies that he was, before he came into it".[61]

---

[54] *Scripture Proofs*, 248.
[55] *Reflections upon the Late Examination of the Discourse of the Descent of the Man-Christ Jesus from Heaven* ..., London 1706.
[56] *Reflections*, 10.
[57] With regard to Sherlock and his sympathizers, Emlyn even used the term "polytheism": "A Narrative ...", *Works* I, 15.
[58] *Reflections*, 115.
[59] *An Explanation of the Grand Mystery of Godliness* (1660) in *The Theological Works of ... Henry More*, London, 1708, 16.
[60] More refers to an *obiter dictum* in Calvin's commentary on Dan. 10.16-18: J. Calvinus, "Praelectiones in Danielem Prophetam", *Corpus Reformatorum* LXIX (*Opera Calvini* XLI), c. 210 (here, "exhibuerit").
[61] *Loc. cit.*

There is a line running from More to Watts, though in the eighteenth century the idea of the pre-existence of Christ's soul received a different function as a mediating doctrine in the struggle between the Arians and the orthodox. As such, however, it had no results whatever. The Arians could not accept it because of its Trinitarian background. *A fortiori* it was unacceptable to the successors of the Arians, the Unitarians, to whom such metaphysical speculations as the doctrine of a pre-existent angelic being which at the same time was the Second Person in the Trinity were utterly alien. And the orthodox thought it a dangerous doctrine, which weakened rather than strengthened the orthodox position because of its supposed concessions to Arianism. After Watts, the doctrine simply fades away; even Watts' friend and admirer Philip Doddridge (1702-1751) only mentions it in passing, without any sign of agreement.[62] If Goethe had been aware of all this, it would have confirmed him in his opinion, expressed in the well-known lines:

> Zwei Gegner sind es, die sich boxen,
> Die Arianer und Orthodoxen,
> Durch viele Säcla dasselbe geschicht,
> Es dauert bis an das jüngste Gericht.[63]

---

[62] P. Doddridge, *A Course of Lectures on the Principal Subjects in Pneumatology, Ethics and Divinity*, London 1763, Lecture CXXIII, Solution 6.
[63] From the "Zahme Xenien", *Werke* V (1. Abt.), Weimar, 1893, 130.

CHAPTER THIRTEEN

JOSEPH PRIESTLEY, THE JEWS AND THE MILLENNIUM

In one of his publications on apocalyptic thought, Richard H. Popkin mentions Joseph Priestley as an eighteenth-century believer in the idea of a "triumphant apocalypse", a transformation of the world which would result in a wonderful and glorious future for humanity.[1] Priestley's millenarianism (or millennialism) has been dealt with in two studies, both of which concentrate on its political aspects.[2] In this essay, written in honour of Professor Popkin, a scholar whose studies in this field have so much stimulated the interest in millenarianism and its concomitant phenomena, I intend to give special attention to the connection between Priestley's theological position, his attempts to bridge the cleavage between Jews and Christians and his expectations with regard to the future restoration and conversion of the Jews.

Joseph Priestley (1733-1804) was a prolific writer in the field of theology. While not a deep or epoch-making theologian, his works reveal that he was a scholar of a broad theological erudition. His critical mind could lead him to take a radical stand on disputed theological matters—according to family tradition he was a man of "violent convictions"[3]—but his religious commitment and his firm loyalty to what he considered the authentic Christian tradition are beyond all doubt. In his theological development he went through various stages, each of which represented a specific strand in the complex of opinions within eighteenth-century English Dissent.[4]

Born into a dissenting family,[5] he was reared, first by his parents, then by an aunt, in the spirit of a traditional but not bigoted Calvinism. His mother was

---

[1] R.H. Popkin, "The Triumphant Apocalypse and the Catastrophic Apocalypse", in A. Cohen and Steven Lee (eds.), *Nuclear Weapons and the Future of Humanity*, New York 1986, 131-138.

[2] C. Garrett, *Respectable Folly: Millenarians and the French Revolution in France and England*, Baltimore and London 1975, ch. 6; J. Fruchtman Jr., *The Apocalyptic Politics of Richard Price and Joseph Priestley: A Study in Late Eighteenth-Century English Republican Millenarianism*, Philadelphia 1983.

[3] Thus wrote a descendant, Hilaire Belloc's daughter Eleanor Jebb, in the "Foreword" to a historical novel on Priestley: J.G. Gillam, *The Crucible*, London 1954, XI.

[4] For his religious and theological development, see first of all his *Memoirs* of 1806, of which the most recent edition is that by J. Lindsay, *Autobiography of Joseph Priestley*, Bath 1970; furthermore, A. Holt, *A Life of Joseph Priestley*, 1931, repr. Westport, Conn. 1970; E.M. Wilbur, *A History of Unitarianism in Transylvania, England, and America*, Cambridge, USA 1952, ch. 16; and M.R. Watts, *The Dissenters from the Reformation to the French revolution*, Oxford 1978, 471-490.

[5] "His Parents were members of the Congregational Church at Upper Chapel, Heckmondwike": *DNB*, *s.v.*

"a woman of exemplary piety"; his father, who carefully taught him the Westminster Catechism, "also had a strong sense of religion, praying with his family morning and evening", and in later life became fond of the writings of George Whitefield, while his aunt "was truly Calvinistic in principle, but ... far from confining salvation to those who thought as she did on religious subjects".[6] While at a later stage he drifted far away from his Calvinistic background, he remained a convinced Dissenter, who in public life championed the political rights of Dissenters[7] and in his personal life retained some of the most characteristic elements of the Dissenting tradition: the emphasis on family prayers[8] and on Sunday observance.[9]

The deviations from traditional doctrine appeared already when he was a young man. The elders of the congregation in which he had always attended refused to admit him as a communicant member: they did not think him "quite orthodox" because he did not believe that all the human race was liable to the wrath of God only on account of the sin of Adam.[10] After being for a short period influenced by a "Baxterian" minister[11] he became an Arminian, but "had by no means rejected the doctrine of the trinity or that of the atonement". For three years he studied at the Dissenting Academy in Daventry, then became the minister of a Dissenting church in Needham Market,[12] where in his theological views he went one step further. Though he had made it a rule "to introduce nothing that could lead to controversy into the pulpit", it was soon found out that he had become an "Arian" and thus had crossed the critical boundary between Trinitarian and anti-Trinitarian thinking. Still, he had not yet gone over to the more extreme Socinian position with its denial, not only of the full divinity, but also of the pre-existence of Christ. When, between 1761 and 1767, he was a tutor at Warrington Academy, he and his friends, who were all Arians, even wondered at the only Socinian minister in the neighbourhood. The more radical step was taken in Leeds, where since 1767 he was minister of a Presbyterian congregation. It was not an unusual step: for quite a number of "rational Dissenters" (and for a handful of Anglicans) Arianism was a

---

[6] *Autobiography*, 71.

[7] Fruchtman, *Apocalyptic Politics*, 53.

[8] *A Serious Address to Masters of Families with Forms of Family-Prayer* (1794; 1st ed. 1769), in *The Theological and Miscellaneous Works of Joseph Priestley*, ed. J.T. Rutt, (1817-1832) repr. New York 1972, [henceforth, *Works*] XXI. 429-473.

[9] "The Observance of the Lord's Day vindicated": *Works* XX, 330-351. He did not plead, however, for a rigid form of Sunday observance: *cf. Autobiography*, 74

[10] For this and for what follows, see *Autobiography*, 73, 79.

[11] For the so-called "Baxterian Middle Way", see R. Thomas, "Presbyterians in Transition", in C.G. Bolam and others (eds.), *The English Presbyterians*, London 1968, 134ff.; J. van den Berg and G.F. Nuttall, *Philip Doddridge (1702-1751) and The Netherlands*, Leiden 1987, 8.

[12] In the period of Priestley's ministry it became a distinctly Presbyterian congregation because of his refusal to accept support from the orthodox "Independent fund": see J. Goring, "The Break-Up of the Old Dissent", in *The English Presbyterians*, 214.

transitional stage on the road to a clear-cut Unitarian theology, which was marked by an exclusive concentration on the idea of the unity of God, but in the process of transition Priestley played a prominent part.[13] Priestley's decision to become "what is called a Socinian" was prompted by the reading of Nathaniel Lardner's "Letter concerning the Logos".[14] From that time onward he was a convinced and consistent Unitarian: "... after giving the closest attention to the subject, I have seen more and more reason to be satisfied with that opinion to this day, and likewise to be more impressed with the idea of its importance".[15]

Within a comparatively short period Priestley had moved from a moderately conservative to a very progressive theological position. He considered himself more a reformer than an innovator, as appears from his well-known remark made in the "General Conclusion" of his *An History of the Corruptions of Christianity* (1782), in which he defended himself against an attack by Bishop Richard Hurd: "it is not a *progressive religion*, but a *progressive reformation* of a corrupted religion, that is pleaded for". Though of course as a Unitarian he rejected the theology of the Reformers, he could appeal to the progressive character of the sixteenth-century Reformation: "If the Reformation was not progressive, why does not this bishop prefer the state of it under John Huss and Jerome of Prague to that of Luther and Cranmer?".[16] The overarching theme of his theological works is the ideal of the restoration of Christianity to its primitive purity. In this ideal the past and the future, and thus the historical and the eschatological element, are intertwined. Of course, the great problem was how and where to find the criteria for a reconstruction of the past which could serve as a pattern for Priestley's "progressive reformation". In an illuminative essay on Priestley's "rational theology" Margaret Canovan has shown that there was an inherent paradox in Priestley's approach. Priestley was a convinced Christian who believed in the necessity of revelation, but who at the same time was guided by a simplistic rationalist concept of truth: because truth was true for all times, true religion could not have a particular historical reference. All theological "accretions" had to be removed in order to reach the firm ground of pure undefiled truth. This process however, created a vacuum which was filled by an "eighteenth-century interpretation, smuggled in as part of the fact itself. His purpose, then, was to understand history in order to reject it".[17]

---

[13] For this, see Wilbur, *History of Unitarianism*, 293-315 and H. L. Short, "Presbyterians Under a New Name", in *The English Presbyterians*, esp. 219-235,

[14] Published in 1759 under the pseudonym Philalethes: *A Letter writ in ... 1730 concerning the question whether the Logos supplied the Place of a Human Soul in the person of Jesus Christ.*

[15] *Autobiography*, 93.

[16] *Works* V, 503.

[17] Margaret Canovan, "The Irony of History: Priestley's Rational Theology", *The Price-Priestley Letter* 4, (1980), 16-25.

While Priestley adhered to the idea of revelation, as a critical historian he rejected the idea of a literal inspiration of the Bible.

> This high notion of inspiration is as *unnecessary*, with respect to the proper use of the Gospel history, as it is indefensible in itself. All the great ends of the Gospel will be sufficiently answered, if provision be made for the credibility of the *principal facts*, such as the reality of the *moral discourses*, and especially of the *miracles, death, and resurrection* of Christ, as a proof of his divine mission, and a confirmation of our faith in the assurances he has given us with respect to a general *resurrection*, and his second coming to judge *the world, and to reward all men according to their works.*[18]

This moderate critical attitude gave him freedom to dispense with those elements which ran counter to his Unitarian conviction (*e.g.*, the idea of a miraculous conception of Christ),[19] while it left room for a belief in the fulfilment of the most important biblical prophecies. For Priestley there was a verifiable connection between prophecy and event: the Old Testament prophecies with regard to the Messiah were already partly fulfilled; the same was the case with Christ's prophecies regarding the Jewish people,[20] and the "corruptions of Christianity" had already been foretold in the Book of Revelation.[21]

Priestley launched a full-blown attack on what he considered the principal corruption of Christianity, the doctrine of the Trinity, in the tracts he published in 1770 under the title *An Appeal to the Serious and Candid Professors of Christianity*. The fifth of these tracts (which seem to have had a very wide circulation)[22] contains an exposition on the doctrine of the Divinity of Christ, which Priestley strongly and unequivocally denied. "If you ask who, then, is Jesus Christ, if he be not God; I answer ... that 'Jesus of Nazareth' was 'a man approved of God—by miracles and wonders and signs, which God did by him'. Acts.11.22"; and in order to leave no one in doubt with regard to his intention, he added that "man" must mean "the same kind of being with your-

---

[18] "Preface" to *A Harmony of the Evangelists, in Greek* (1777), *Works* XX, 10.

[19] See in particular his expositions on this subject in *An History of Early Opinions concerning Jesus Christ (1786)*, *Works* VII, 57-129. In his discussion with David Levi (to be mentioned below), he shielded himself against the consequences which might be drawn (and which Levi indeed drew) from his rejection of the miraculous conception: "As to the disbelief of the miraculous conception drawing after it the disbelief of the whole Gospel history, judge from fact, and not from imagination ... To say nothing of myself, can it be shewn to have been the case with any other person who has thought as I do with respect to this subject?", *Works* XX, 255.

[20] *Institutes of Natural and Revealed Religion* II, (1763); *Works* II. 177ff.

[21] Notes on the Books of Scripture (1804), *Works* XIV, 443, where Priestley in his introduction to the notes on Revelation writes: "... the correspondence of the prophecy with the events, is so striking, as of itself to prove its divine origin".

[22] Wilbur even mentions the almost incredibly high circulation of 60,000 copies; according to Wilbur, from the date of the appearance of the *Appeal* as a turning-point, "one can trace a revival of devotion and active zeal for their cause among the rational Dissenters": *History of Unitarianism*, 297f.

selves". The belief in "the doctrine of the Divine Unity" justified a separation from those churches which held to Trinitarian doctrine. Besides,

> the great offence to Jews, Mahometans, and the world at large, being the doctrine of the Trinity, it is highly necessary that societies of Christians should be formed expressly on this principle of the Divine Unity, that it may be evident to all the world, that there are Christians, and societies of Christians, who hold the doctrine of the Trinity in as much abhorrence as they themselves can do. For the conversion of Jews and Mahometans to Christianity, while it is supposed to contain the doctrine of the Trinity, no person who knows, or has heard of Jews or Mahometans, can ever expect.[23]

The intention of his theological and philosophical works was apologetic, as appears from what he wrote in his autobiography:

> I can truly say, that the greatest satisfaction I receive from the success of my philosophical pursuits, arises from the weight it may give to my attempts to defend Christianity, and to free it from those corruptions which prevent its reception with philosophical and thinking persons, whose influence with the vulgar, and the unthinking, is very great.[24]

In the context of his apologetic theology Jewish religion played a not inconsiderable part. In his first major theological work, *Institutes of Natural and Revealed Religion*, which appeared in three volumes between 1772 and 1774, he declared that "the Jewish and Christian revelations ... have so close a connection that they must stand and fall together". While for Priestley the Christian religion was "the completion of the whole scheme", he used the term "this truly catholic religion" in the context of a number of observations which related to "the Jewish and Christian religions, jointly".[25] Priestley saw the idea of the unity of God—the only object of worship and praise—as the great doctrine which holds together the Old and New Testament, Jewish and (true) Christian religion:

> Considering how strongly this great article, the worship of one God only, is guarded in all the books of Scripture, it would seem impossible that it should ever be infringed by any who profess to hold the books of the Old and New Testament for the rule of their faith and practice; and yet we shall see that this very article was the subject of one of the first and the most radical of all the corruptions of Christianity. For upon the very same principles, and in the very same manner, by which dead men came to be worshipped by the ancient idolaters, there was introduced into the Christian church, in the first place, the idolatrous worship of Jesus Christ.[26]

---

[23] *Works* II, 394f.
[24] *Autobiography*, 111.
[25] *Works* II, 120, 154.
[26] *Works* II, 280.

The same theme is fundamental to what is no doubt his best-known, perhaps also his most notorious theological work,[27] *An History of the Corruptions of Christianity*, which appeared in two volumes in 1782.[28] The opening passage is unambiguous: "*The unity of God* is a doctrine on which the greatest stress is laid in the whole system of revelation. To guard this most important article was the principal object of the Jewish religion". The Jews expected a Messiah "in whom themselves and all the nations of the earth should be blessed; but none of their prophets gave them an idea of any other than a man like themselves in that illustrious character, and no other did they ever expect, or do they expect to this day". Jesus "made no other pretensions". The teaching of the apostles was consonant with that of the prophets and of Jesus, and also the ancient Jewish Christian church held the opinion "that Christ was simply a man, and not either God Almighty, or a *super-angelic being*". The "primitive Jewish church" was "properly Unitarian".[29]

Because of his theological position, Priestley had a special interest in the Jews, who indeed through the ages were believers in the fundamental doctrine of the Divine unity.[30] He had a sharp eye for the evils perpetrated by Christians against the Jews in the course of history; perhaps no other work on church history paid so much attention to "the sufferings of the Jews" as his *A General History of the Christian Church* (1790).[31] England was not less guilty than other countries: "We may say that we of this generation, have not persecuted the Jews, and that they have no particular reason to complain of *us*. But they were grievously persecuted by the English nation in former times, and have much to complain of *them*".[32] Of course his mentioning the many acts of cruelty against Jews and heretics also, or even primarily, served to expose the persecuting spirit of "corrupted" Christianity, but this does not detract from the sympathy with the Jews and their fate to which his works testify.

In 1786 appeared his *Letters to the Jews, inviting them to an amicable discussion of the evidences of Christianity*;[33] in an advertisement he declared

---

[27] For legal steps, taken in the Netherlands in connection with the Dutch translation of the first volume, see J.P. Heering, "Ten strijde tegen het verlichte Christendom!", in *Op de bres, 200 jaar Haagsch Genootschap tot verdediging van de christelijke godsdienst (1785-1985)*, 's-Gravenhage 1985, 8ff. The sources do not authenticate the story, mentioned by Thomas Peirson in his *Bibliotheca Peirsoniana* and repeated by the editor of Priestley's *Works* (V, 13n.) that the book "was burnt by the hands of the common hangman in the city of Dort".

[28] Priestley originally intended to make it the fourth part of the *Institutes: Works* I, 158n.

[29] *Works* V, 16-19.

[30] *History of Early Opinions*, Book III, ch. I: *Works* VI, esp. 377ff.

[31] *Works* IX, 59f., 117f., 257f., 292, 364ff., 462ff., 580ff.

[32] *Discourses on the Evidence of Revealed Religion* (1794), Disc. VIII (On the Prophecies concerning the Dispersion and Restoration of the Jews): *Works* XV, 298.

[33] The title is reminiscent of that of Philippus van Limborch's *De veritate religionis christianae amica collatio cum erudito Judaeo*, Goudae 1687, which Priestley had read (*Works* XX, 243), and there is a certain parallel between Van Limborch and Priestley in their juxtapo-

that the *Letters* were printed chiefly to be distributed among the Jews and that he had the intention to have them translated into Hebrew "if there should appear to be any prospect of their answering the end for which they were composed".[34] Priestley evidently hoped, and possibly even expected, that a Unitarian presentation of Christianity would bridge the gap between Jews and Christians by taking away the theological stumbling-blocks which prevented the Jews from accepting Christ as the promised Messiah:

> Your dislike of *Christians*, and your abhorrence of their faith, is not to be wondered at, when it is considered how much you have suffered by their cruel oppressions, and how contrary their doctrines have been to the fundamental principles of your religion. You are the worshippers of the one living and true God. But, besides him, the generality of Christians have paid divine honours to Jesus Christ, and in a great measure also to those dead men whom they have called *saints*, who were no more the proper objects of worship than images of wood and stone, the work of men's hands. But at this day the cruel usage you have met with from Christian nations is happily much abated. Christians in general, and especially more civilized among them, are disposed to treat you with equity and humanity; and if you *now* make inquiry into their faith, you will find that many of them have rejected, as abuses and corruptions of it, those doctrines which you so justly abhor.

With regard to the rejection of "corruptions" Priestley saw a parallel between Jews and Christians: while God in the course of his providence had entirely cured the Jews of the least propensity to idolatry, in like manner he was now opening the eyes of the Christians to bring them back to the worship of himself alone. For Priestley, Unitarianism implied a shedding of the influence of Platonic philosophy which had led to the doctrine of the Trinity and its "idolatrous" consequences; to a large extent, it was a return of Christianity, for so long contaminated and corrupted by Greek thinking, to its Jewish background.

At the same time, however, he stated (though with reluctance) that in these present times the Jews lived under the cloud of God's displeasure: they had accepted the divine mission of Moses, but they rejected the divine mission of Jesus, the suffering Messiah. He emphasized that an acceptance of the divine mission of Jesus did not stand in the way of the messianic expectations of the Jews. In this context, he distinguished between the suffering Messiah, announced by the prophets, and the prince of the house of David, under whom the Jews would enjoy the great prosperity, promised to them in the latter days: "All the temporal glory that you expect, will certainly be your lot; and the

---

sition of the miracles of Moses and those of Christ as proof of their "missio divina" (*De Veritate*, 152). For the latter point, see P.T. van Rooden and J.W. Wesselius, "The Early Enlightenment and Judaism ..." *Studia Rosenthaliana* 21 (1987), 146 (with thanks to Dr. Van Rooden).

[34] *Works* XX, 227. A learned Jew in Birmingham had promised to do the translation: Priestley to T. Lindsey, 14 July 1786: *Works* I, 395. In the editor's footnote there is confusion between the *Letters* and the "Address" of 1791.

Messiah that you look for will come".[35] He had already elaborated this point in an article in the *Theological Repository:* "Observations on the Prophecies relating to the Messiah, and the future Glory of the House of David".[36] There, he had distinguished between two personages: the Messiah, foretold by the Prophets, and the prince under whom in the future the Israelites would enjoy their great prosperity. None of the Prophets had ever called this prince the Messiah, but only David, or a branch from the stock of David. The two personages had been confounded by "Christian critics, from the age of the apostles to the present day", but the Jews, too, had confounded the character of the Messiah with that of "the future restorer of their nation".[37]

Priestley expected that the glorious future of the Jews in their own country would be accompanied by their conversion to Christianity. This did not imply, however, that the Jews had to join one of the Christian churches. "On the contrary, since you are still to be distinguished as *Jews*, no less than as *Christians*, it will be more convenient for you to form a separate church, and to keep your sabbath as you now do".[38] With regard to the latter point, the continuation of Mosaic law after the restoration of the Jews to their own country, Priestley had been more explicit in the *Theological Repository* of 1786.[39] Not only the keeping of the sabbath, but also holy feasts (Priestley mentions Passover and the Feast of Tabernacles), sacrifices, circumcision—it should all be continued (though perhaps with "favourable alterations", made in Mosaic ritual by divine authority) after the restoration of the Jews to their own country and after their concomitant conversion to Christianity. Priestley was aware of the fact that this seemed to be contradictory to Paul's teaching with regard to the Jewish law, but it was merely a seeming contradiction: Paul only wanted to safeguard the freedom of the gentiles with regard to Jewish ritual. As a critical theologian, Priestley felt free to remark that not all the expressions of the apostle were sufficiently guarded, and that his reasoning was sometimes hasty and inconclusive. Nowhere, however, had Paul explicitly stated that Mosaic ritual was no longer binding for Jewish Christians. In this context, Priestley even went so far as to state that after the return and the conversion of the Jews "the service of the Temple will be resumed, and be perpetual; and that the Gentiles will join in some parts of it, though they will not be circumcised, or conform to the whole law, as Jews".[40]

---

[35] *Works* XX, 228, 243.

[36] Pamphilus (= Priestley) in: *Theol. Repos.* 5, (1786); *Works* XII, 411-442.

[37] *Works* XII, 440f.

[38] *Works* XX, 245.

[39] Hermas (= Priestley), "Of the Perpetuity of the Jewish Ritual", *Theol. Repos.* 5 (1786); *Works* XII, 442-482.

[40] *Works* XII, 481. For the occurrence of the idea of the restoration of Jewish ritual, including the worship in the Temple, with seventeenth-century millenarians, see E. G. E. van der Wall, *De mystieke chiliast Petrus Serrarius (1600-1669) en zijn wereld*, Leiden 1987, 375-384.

As appears from a postscript to his *Letters*, Priestley did not foster the illusion that his tract would "of itself" make any of the Jews convert to Christianity: "Your conversion must be the result of your own diligent study and impartial inquiry".[41] The main purpose of his *Letters* was to emphasize that if the Jews accepted the historical evidence for the miracles of Moses, they should *a fortiori* accept the historical evidence for the miracles of Christ, "because the history of his miracles is more within the limits of certain history". This, in its turn, could lead to a recognition of the divine mission of Christ as well as of that of Moses.

> Diligently, then, compare the historical evidence of the two religions. Both, you will find, are, in reality, but one. They are perfectly consistent with, nay, they imply each other, and must stand or fall together.[42]

Soon, however, it appeared that Priestley's *Letters* did not answer the end for which they were composed. In 1787, the learned Jewish scholar and controversialist David Levi published a spirited reply to Priestley's *Letters*.[43] Apparently, on the side of the Jewish community in England there had been some hesitation to enter the lists against Priestley. With the Jewish leaders there was some fear that engaging in religious disputes "might be construed as reflecting on, or tending towards disturbing the national religion, as by law established", while moreover "the generality of our learned men being foreigners, are deficient in the proper idiom and phraseology of the English language". Levi, however, considered the first argument groundless, "thanks to God, the Reformation, and glorious Revolution". Besides, "we live in an enlightened age, in which the investigation of theological points is accounted laudable". The second argument was of greater weight; Levi saw himself as David fighting against a Goliath who came with the sword of elegance of diction, the spear of criticism and the shield of sophistry. But like his great namesake, David Levi hit his opponent in his most sensitive spot, *i.e.*, his Unitarian conviction.

---

41 *Cf.* what he wrote to Joshua Toulmin, 6 October 1786: "I am glad that my 'History' [*An History of Early Opinions concerning Jesus Christ*] and 'Letters to the Jews' have given you any satisfaction. I find they are much noticed by that people in this country, but I do not expect to make any converts soon; their prejudices against Christianity are deep rooted": *Works* I, 1, 396.

42 *Works* XX, 250.

43 *Letters to Dr. Priestly* [sic] *in answer to those he addressed to the Jews*, London 1787: a second edition, with different page-numbering but for the rest identical, appeared in the same year. For Levi, see *DNB; Encyclopaedia Judaica* (with different dates of birth and death); T.M. Endelman, *The Jews of Georgian England 1714-1830*, Philadelphia 1979, esp. 263. Levi, who moved in English literary circles, had a good command of the English language (though not an elegant style) and was also (perhaps partly thanks to his friend Henry Lemoine) well versed in English theology. Apparently, Priestley did not expect a reply from this side; on 23 October 1786 he wrote to C. Rotherham "I do not find that any Jews in England will reply to my letters to them; but they say I shall probably have an answer from a Jew at Vienna": *Works* I, 1, 397.

While Priestley supposed that his rejection of the doctrine of the Trinity would make him an acceptable partner in a Jewish-Christian discussion, Levi attacked him exactly on this point: "permit me, Sir, to ask you, whether you sincerely intend, in this discussion, to defend Christianity?". To Levi it was incomprehensible how a man who rejected the miraculous conception of Jesus could be entitled to the appellation of a Christian in the strict sense of the word:[44]

> Whether the generality of Christians have just reason to pay divine honours to Jesus, or not, as you observe ... is not my business at present to inquire, but ought to be settled among Christians themselves; and that, (if I may presume to give my opinion in so weighty a cause) before you attempted to convert the Jews to Christianity. For do but figure to yourself, dear Sir, how ridiculous it must appear, for you to invite the Jews to embrace, what you yourselves do not rightly understand. This, is such an absurdity, that I am surprised and astonished, when I reflect, how it was possible that a Divine and a Philosopher, of your distinguished rank, in the republic of letters, should overlook.[45]

Furthermore, Levi also attacked the main argument of Priestley's *Letters*: the miracles of Jesus as a proof of his divine mission. For Levi it was manifest "that miracles *only* were not sufficient to establish a firm belief in the divine mission of Moses; much less can those of Jesus, and which you freely acknowledge, cannot vie with those recorded of Moses, in point of *magnitude and splendour*, be thought so".[46] And reflecting upon a sentence in Priestley's *Letters* which began with the words: "Had Jesus been that impostor ...", Levi remarked that according to Priestley's hypothesis Jesus indeed must be that impostor. In this context he quoted Josiah Tucker, the moderately orthodox Dean of Gloucester, known among other things for his plea for the naturalization of the Jews, who in his *Brief and Dispassionate View of the Difficulties attending the Trinitarian, Arian and Socinian Theories* (1774) had written that Jesus was either "that great I AM which had an existence, not only before Abraham, but before the world began, or else he must have been one of the falsest and the vilest of the human race".[47]

Offended at the tone of Levi's attack, Priestley reacted in a second set of *Letters to the Jews* (1787), not directed to Levi personally but to the Jews in general.[48] It was, of course, Levi's assertion that Priestley was not entitled to

---

[44] Levi, *Letters*, 4-9.

[45] Levi, *Letters*, 29.

[46] Levi, *Letters*, 71f. Rather incautiously, Priestley had written that, though none of the miracles of Christ can be said to vie with some of those recorded by Moses in point of splendour and magnitude, yet with respect to notoriety and frequency they were abundantly to show that there could be no trick or collusion in the case: *Works* XX, 237.

[47] Levi, *Letters*, 89. For Tucker, see Endelman, *The Jews of Georgian England*, 37f.

[48] On 11 June 1787 he wrote to Theophilus Lindsey: "I have received David Levi's Letters.

the appellation of a Christian which had hurt him most of all: "You must be ashamed that one of your body should have begun this important discussion in a manner so unworthy of you. To make any reply to such a calumny would answer no purpose".[49] Again he emphasized "the proper, that is the historical evidence of Christianity", which attested to the great and leading facts in the Gospel history, the account of the doctrines, the miracles, the death and resurrection of Christ. In this context, he strongly denied that the disbelief in the miraculous conception would draw after it the disbelief of the whole Gospel history, and he repeated what he had said before: the story of the miraculous conception had not the testimony of the age in which it was promulgated; it was an interpolation, and as such had no historical credibility.[50] It is clear that Priestley did not reject the miraculous conception because he thought such a miracle impossible. He argues against it as a critical historian, but the implicit presupposition is of a theological nature: belief in the supernatural conception of Jesus is inextricably connected with Trinitarian doctrine, and the main stumbling-block for the Jews to accept the messianic claims of Jesus.

After a lapse of time, David Levi replied in a second set of *Letters to ... Priestley*.[51] His principal defence against Priestley's emphasis on the historical character of the miracles of Jesus was, that he did not think miracles as such a proof of a divine mission. With regard to this point, he appealed to Conyers Middleton, who in his *A Free Inquiry into the Miraculous Powers which are supposed to have subsisted in the Christian Church* (1749) had shown that miracles such as Jesus performed also occurred elsewhere.[52]

The discussion between Priestley and Levi was not continued. Given the

---

They are below my expectation; so much so, that I hardly think it will be worth while to reply to them; but give notice that I hope to receive something more to the purpose. I shall draw up something ...". Lindsey thought Levi's letters "a very indifferent performance", but (as he wrote on 7 July to a correspondent) "One is glad ... that real Jews answer, as that may bring them in by degrees to the discussion of the question": *Works* I, 1, 410.

[49] *Works* XX, 252.

[50] *History of Early Opinions*, Book III, ch. XX: *Works* VII, esp. 100f.; cf. Canogan, "Irony of History", 22.

[51] D. Levi, *Letters to Dr. Priestley, in Answer to his Letters to the Jews* II, London 1789. Levi explained the delay in answering partly from lack of time, partly from "the consternation into which the greatest part of our nation were thrown on the appearance of my reply to your first letters", 3. But Levi's brave opposition to Priestley also excited admiration: Endelman mentions a curious inscription on an etching, published in 1789, of a fight between a Jewish and a Christian pugilist: "The Christian pugilist", went the inscription, proved himself "as inferior to the Jewish hero as Dr. Priestley when opposed to the Rabbi [sic], David Levi": *The Jews of Georgian England*, 220.

[52] Levi, *Letters*, II. 43. For Conyers Middleton, see *DNB s.v.*; G. Rupp, *Religion in England 1688-1791*, Oxford 1986, 375f. Middleton, however, had excepted (for tactical reasons?) the first century from his criticism of the credibility of miracles: "... there is no sufficient reason to believe, from the testimony of antiquity, that any miraculous powers did ever actually subsist in any age of the Church, after the times of the Apostles": *Free Inquiry*, 3rd ed. London 1749, XCI.

rather acrimonious nature of their discussion it is not very probable that Levi was among the group of Jews who in 1790 or 1791 heard Priestley giving a "discourse" on the resurrection of Jesus in Essex Chapel, London (Theophilus Lindsey's Unitarian chapel)[53] and who afterwards had "an amicable conference" with Priestley, which made him remark: "A freer intercourse with Jews and Christians would have a good effect on both".[54] In his discourse Priestley had called Christ "our Lord", which apparently had offended some of his Jewish hearers. Because of this, Priestley prefixed an "Address to the Jews" to the first edition of the discourse.[55] In this "Address" he again made clear his Unitarian position. Jesus was "as one of your nation, a humble worshipper of the God of your fathers, and he instructed his followers to worship no other than him. These Christians are called *Unitarians* ...". Perhaps reflecting upon a rather minimalizing remark by Levi on the Unitarians—"your sect, (which are but a handful)"[56]—Priestley stated that things were ripening apace for a general declaration in favour of Unitarianism. This would mean that the "great abomination" of "the idolatrous worship of Jesus Christ" would be removed. Then Christianity would resume its "pristine vigour" and enlighten and bless the whole world, and "the unspeakable obligations we are under to you will be repaid by our services, in your conversion to Christianity".

Priestley's last address to the Jews was written in America in 1799 and published as an appendix to his *Comparison of the Institutions of Moses with those of the Hindoos and other ancient nations* (1799).[57] As the full title: "An Address to the Jews on the present state of the World and the Prophecies relating to it" indicates, the main emphasis of this address was eschatological. In Priestley's thinking, apocalyptic speculation took a prominent place. Like so many English theologians, he was a millenarian in the tradition of Joseph Mede, whose *Clavis Apocalyptica* (1627) made millenarianism in England respectable,[58] though (as we shall see) he did not follow Mede in all respects. His millenarianism had a traditional aspect, embedded as it was in a theological thinking which, however innovating and unorthodox, had retained a number of elements from the background in which he had been reared. Neither his Unitarian theology nor his philosophical materialism or his scientific interests implied a positivist outlook. In many ways a rationalist, he was at the

[53] In 1799, however, he mentioned Levi as "a person whom I well know and respect": "Address to the Jews", *Works* XX, 299.

[54] First published in 1791; later in *Discourses on the Evidence of Divine Revelation* (1794): *Works* XV, 325-348.

[55] *Works* XX, 275-280. For Priestley's account of the "amicable conference", see 275n.

[56] Levi, *Letters*, 77.

[57] The "Address" is printed separately in *Works* XX, 281-300.

[58] For Mede's millenarian views, see R.H. Popkin, "The Third Force in 17th Century Philosophy", *Nouvelles de la République des Lettres*, 3 (1983), 35-63 and J. van den Berg, "Continuity within a changing context", this volume Ch. 6.

same time a man of deeply rooted religious convictions. He believed in the reality of miracles, in the resurrection of Jesus, in the fulfilment of prophecy, and his critical method did not prevent him from accepting many of the biblical records as to a large degree historically trustworthy. During his visit to Paris in 1774 he astonished his agnostic hosts because he "chose on all occasions to appear as a Christian".[59] But they will also have noticed that his Christianity was of a special brand, marked as it was by the optimism of his age with regard to the future development of mankind. With Priestley (as with most millenarians) we should not make a sharp distinction between a "pessimistic" millenarianism which emphasizes the dramatic effects of God's judgements and a more "optimistic" millenarian expectation in which the joyful character of the glorious time to come is dominant; in Priestley's millenarianism, both elements are present, though with him the mixture is different from that which coloured the eschatology of former millenarians. Nor should we see a contrast between the religious and the political elements in his millenarianism. Garrett rightly points out that Priestley's millenarian ideas were far more respectable and conventional than some of his other opinions and that his acceptance of the ideology of the French Revolution had the effect of intensifying his millenarianism: "It is thus impossible to separate his political opinions from his religious convictions".[60] Rather than seeing a contrast between the two elements we might (with Fruchtman) express the relations between them in the categories of "interaction" and "interdependence".[61] Priestley's progressive views coloured and sometimes transformed, but never effaced the traditional pattern of his eschatology.

In the third part of his *Institutes*, which appeared in 1774, Priestley gave a clear exposition of his millenarian expectations. Some of his sources are explicitly mentioned. Of course he had read Joseph Mede; furthermore, Daniel Whitby and Bishop Thomas Newton;[62] and last but not least the philosopher David Hartley.[63] For Hartley he had a deep admiration: "Next to the Bible, Hartley's ""Observation [sic] on Man"" is the book that I have recourse to,

---

[59] *Autobiography,* 111.

[60] Garrett, *Respectable Folly*, 133.

[61] Fruchtman, *Apocalyptic Politics*, 2ff; for a supposed contrast between "optimistic" and "pessimistic" elements, see 38ff.

[62] *Works* II, 365ff. Whitby, an Anglican theologian with Unitarian tendencies, published in 1703 a *Paraphrase and Commentary on the New Testament;* between 1754 and 1758, Bishop Newton published his (at that time apparently rather popular) *Dissertations on the Prophecies which have remarkably been fulfilled, and at this time are fulfilling in the world* (3 volumes).

[63] *Works* II, 370. At the time when Priestley wrote his *Institutes*, his friend Richard Price had already given evidence of an inclination towards millennial thinking in his discourse on Providence (in *Four Dissertations*, [London, 1767]). His utterances on this point, however, were at that time still vague and uncertain. I consulted the Dutch translation: *Vier Verhandelingen*, Harlingen 1768, 95f.

when I would read to do my heart good".[64] Hartley saw "the present Circumstances of the World" as "extraordinary and critical, beyond what has ever yet happened". He thought it probable that all the "present Civil Governments" would be dissolved and overturned because of their inherent corruptions. The same fate would befall the ecclesiastical powers of the Christian world; the Church of Rome, but also "all the rest", all those churches which have followed her example. When, however, by great tribulations the Christian Church would have recovered from her corruptions, true and pure religion (called "the Kingdom of Righteousness, of the Saints, the New Jerusalem, etc. ") would finally be established. In these events, the Jewish people would play a special part:

> As the Downfal of the *Jewish* State under *Titus* was the Occasion of the Publication of the Gospel to us Gentiles, so our Downfal may contribute to the Restoration of the *Jews*, and both together bring on the final Publication of true Religion.[65]

All this found an echo in Priestley's *Institutes*.[66] Calamitous events, represented in the Book of Revelation by the outpouring of the seven vials, would lead to a fundamental change in the ecclesiastical and political situation of the world. Antichrist (by Priestley virtually identified with the Church of Rome) would be destroyed,[67] together with the Turkish power, "which has so long been in possession of the Holy Land",[68] and "the forms of government ecclesiastical and civil, which now subsist in Europe" would be dissolved. Something, "more favourable to the virtue and happiness of mankind" would take their place.

> The present kingdoms of Europe are unquestionably represented by the feet and toes of the great image which Nebuchadnezzar saw in his political dream: and upon the

---

[64] "Letter to the Rev. Mr. Venn" (1769), *Works* XXI, 339. In 1775, Priestley edited a new, shortened edition of Hartley's *Observations*.

[65] D. Hartley, *Observations on Man, his Frame, his Duty, and his Expectations*, London 1749, facs. ed, Gainsville, Florida 1966, II, 455, 361, 370, 156, 375,

[66] In his introduction to Priestley's autobiography, Jack Lindsay poses a close connection between Hartley's principle of "the association of ideas", which resulted in an optimistic belief in the progressive development of mankind, and Priestley's millenarianism: "The notion of the Second Coming and the Millenary Rule of the Saints is secularised into that of human perfectibility brought about by the providential workings of the Association Principle" (*Autobiography*, 37). No doubt there was influence: we may assume that Hartley's philosophy strengthened the optimistic trend in Priestley's eschatology, but this does not imply a total "secularization" of Priestley's millenarianism. The religious impetus remained a vital element in his apocalyptic expectations.

[67] Priestley does not mention explicitly "all the rest" of the Christian churches, as Hartley had done, though from the sequel of his exposition it is clear that on this point also there is no real difference between his views and those of Hartley.

[68] In this context, Priestley refers to the outpouring of the seventh vial (Rev. 16.17) and to Daniel 11.40-45, 12.1.

> feet of this image will fall the stone, cut out of the mountain without hands, which represents the kingdom to be set up by Christ.

Thus far, Priestley's views more or less fit into the conventional millenarian scheme. Contrary to traditional millenarians such as Mede and Bishop Newton, however, he rejected with Whitby a literal interpretation of the millennium. Christ himself will not reign in person upon earth, nor will the martyrs actually rise from the dead and live with him: "considering the figurative language of prophecy, it is more probable, that the revival of the *cause* for which they suffered is, in reality, the thing denoted by it". No more should the term of a thousand years be taken literally: that would be much too short for mankind to reach its "mature state". Lastly, after the millennium there will be "another prevalence of infidelity and wickedness, which will bring on the last crisis and final dissolution of the world", followed (in prophetical description) by "a new heaven and a new earth".[69]

In Priestley's expositions on the millennium, as given in his *Institutes*, the political ferment is already present. He wrote this work on the eve of the American Revolution. From a letter to Lindsey (23 August 1771) it appears that he thought the "dismal catastrophe", predicted by Hartley, to be near at hand: "I shall be looking for the downfal of Church and State together. I am really expecting some very calamitous, but finally glorious events".[70] The French Revolution, with which he sympathized—his radical views triggered off the well-known "Birmingham riots" and ultimately led to his emigration to the United States in 1794[71]—gave a new impetus to his millenarian ideals. After his arrival in America he told John Adams (who became President in 1796), that the French Revolution was opening a new era in the world and presented a near view of the millennium.[72] In 1797 he believed that the temporal power was at an end, and that this would be followed by other great changes in the state of Europe and the world at large. "All Christians, however, will look forward with joy to the bright close of the calamities that will accompany these events".[73] As Anne Holt remarks, he read the news-sheets of the day with the Book of Daniel open before him.[74] He derived "a noble consolation

---

[69] *Works* II, 364-371. For his "figurative" interpretations of the words "new heaven and new earth", and his rejection of the idea of a "conflagration", see his Notes on II Peter 3: *Works* XIV, 419.

[70] Garrett, *Respectable Folly*, 130, with references to *Works* I, 1, 146.

[71] For this, see Holt, *Life*, 145-178.

[72] Quoted by Garrett, 133. Later, different views with regard to the events in France were one of the causes of an estrangement between Priestley and Adams: "I suppose, too, he was not pleased that I did not adopt his dislike of the French", Priestley to Rev. T. Belsham, I I January 1798: *Works* I, 2, 391.

[73] Priestley to Mr. Russell, 19 April 1797: *Works* I, 2. 377.

[74] Holt, *Life*, 207.

... from the prophecies of scripture",[75] though the interpretation of prophecy sometimes confronted him with difficulties. "I am persuaded, however, that our principal difficulty arises from the uncertainty of the reading, and the difficulty of translating. If we knew what Daniel really wrote, I am persuaded we should now understand him better than he did himself".[76]

In those last years of his life, so full of personal tensions and political upheavals, he looked forward the more fervently to the daybreak of the millennium. On one point, he had changed his opinion. Under the influence of two articles, written by R.E. Garnham in the *Theological Repository* of 1786 and 1788,[77] Priestley revoked his former opinion that there would be no "personal appearance of Christ upon earth" during the millennium. Now he believed that at the beginning of the millennium Christ would come "in the clouds, so as to be seen by all", then to return to the same state in which he is at present (no doubt, on the earth), and so continue till the general resurrection, and govern the people of Israel, and the world, as the Hebrew nation were directed by the *Shekinah*".[78] But was the time of Christ's coming really near? He believed it, but at the same time he was hesitant. The fulfilment of the most important prophecies is, no doubt, at hand:

> and yet a good many years may intervene before the scene of calamity is passed. I fully expect the personal appearance of Jesus ...; but this will hardly be before the restoration of the Jews, of which there are no symptoms at present. The Turkish empire must fall, before that event, and the neighbouring powers do not seem to be disposed to meddle with it. But, great changes in the disposition of men may take place in a short time, and things least expected come to pass.[79]

In all Priestley's expositions on the millennium, the idea of the restoration of the Jews takes a central place. In the *Institutes* he states that according to many Old Testament prophecies the Jews shall return to their own country, and shall possess it many years in peace. It will be a return of the Ten Tribes as well as of Judah: "this nation is still to be distinguished by God, and to be the medium of his communications to the rest of the world".[80] The theme returns time and again. It gave a special colour to the *Letters to the Jews*. It was elaborated in the discourse "Of the Prophecies concerning the Dispersion and Restoration of the Jews", in which he assigned to the Jews a dominant role in the renewal of the world: "by means of this one chosen nation, all mankind are to be brought to the knowledge, worship and obedience of the true one God".[81] But

---

[75] Priestley to T. Lindsey, 27 August 1797, *Works* I, 2, 383
[76] Priestley to T. Lindsey, 16 November 1797, *Works* I, 2, 388
[77] For this, see Garrett, *Respectable Folly*, 131ff.
[78] Notes on all the Books of Scripture, IV (1804); *Works* XIV, esp. 505.
[79] Priestley to T. Belsham, 5 June 1798: *Works* I, 2, 401.
[80] *Works* II, 368.
[81] *Discourses on the Evidence of Revealed Religion* (1794): *Works* XV, 297

nowhere did he express it more forcefully than in his "Address to the Jews" of 1799, written (as he remarks in the opening sentence) by "a Christian who from his early years has entertained the greatest respect and veneration for your nation".

Writing for Jews, Priestley did not refer to the Book of Revelation, but to the Old Testament prophets, and in particular to the prophecies of Daniel, in which (as we have seen) at that time he was deeply immersed. Many prophets had enlarged, said Priestley, on the restoration and future glory of the Jews, but "Daniel, who barely mentions your restoration, gives several notes of the time". Three nearly coincident events had to take place before the glorious time: the breaking up of the present European monarchies, the extinction of the Papal power and the overthrow of the Turkish empire. For Priestley, history was demonstrating the truth of prophecy. No one could have confidence in the permanence of the monarchies of Europe, who considered what had happened in France. A still more ominous event (though it passed with little notice) was the fall of the Papal power. The Turkish empire was already on the verge of destruction; Palestine, now part of the Turkish empire, almost uninhabited, wholly uncultivated, empty, was ready to receive the Jews. But at the same time he cautioned the Jews not to be too sanguine. "When I say at hand, I do not mean this year or the next, or the next twenty or thirty years: for what are twenty or thirty years to the duration of your sufferings, and especially to that of your future prosperity?".

Priestley expected that the return of the Jews would be followed by a complete restoration, which would entail the acknowledgment that Jesus was a true prophet and that it was a great sin to put him to death. This conviction would be produced by his personal appearance at the beginning of the millennium. Conversion to Christianity (by which he meant, of course, to true, uncorrupted Unitarian Christianity) would not imply, however, a denial of the truth of Jewish religion. On the contrary: "Your restoration cannot fail to convince the world of the truth of your religion; and in those circumstances your conversion to Christianity cannot fail to draw after it that of the whole world".[82]

In his utterances on the Jews, various strands of his theology come together. A philo-Semitic trend is clearly recognizable. If his remark with regard for the veneration he had for the Jews "from his early years" is not a retroprojection, his philo-Semitic sympathies preceded his transition to Unitarianism, though once he was a convinced Unitarian his rejection of Trinitarian thinking no doubt reinforced his respect for his "brethren in the belief in the unity of God". And, of course, his radical rejection of all Greek accretions in Christian theology considerably contributed to his Judeo-Christian orientation. His image of Jewish religion was to a large degree modelled upon the Old Testament,

[82] *Works* XX, 281-300.

interpreted in eighteenth-century categories. He was, however, not quite unacquainted with later Jewish theology.[83] There were also some personal contacts with—probably more or less enlightened—Jews, but there are no grounds to suppose that these contacts had a deep or intensive character.

His millenarianism had various aspects. Fundamentally it was traditional, and as such already contained a philo-Semitic tendency: all millenarians who stood in the tradition of Mede saw the restoration and conversion of the Jews as a constituent part of the apocalyptic scenario. Furthermore, in the context of his apologetic theology, in which the fulfilment of prophecy belonged to the "evidences of revealed religion",[84] contemporary events functioned as a verification of the prophecies with regard to the approach of the millennium; in fact a vicious circle, which is the weak spot of most millenarian conceptions. The news-sheets were read in the light of Daniel, the prophecies were interpreted by means of the news-sheet. But of this Priestley was not aware: in this clear and rational thinker there was an element of almost enthusiastic optimism, which made him look forward with eager expectancy to the great events of the future. An underlying assumption in all this is that these events not only entailed a revolutionary renovation of society, but also a return of Christian religion to its pristine Unitarian purity. In this renewal of religion the converted Jews—believers in the unity of God and in the messianic character of Jesus—would have a central function. This expectation could make him approach the Jews as "a Christian, who reverences your nation, is a believer in the future glory of it, and is a worshipper of the God of your fathers, without admitting any other to share in the rights of divinity with him".[85]

---

[83] See, e.g., his quotations from Jewish scholars in *History of Early Opinions, Works* VI, 384ff.; VII, 282ff.

[84] *Institutes*, part 1, ch. III: *Works* II 170-190.

[85] In the opening sentence of the first *Letters to the Jews: Works* XX, 227.

CHAPTER FOURTEEN

ORTHODOXY, RATIONALISM AND THE WORLD IN THE NETHERLANDS OF THE EIGHTEENTH CENTURY

As far as the Protestant countries are concerned the eighteenth century, "the age of reason", might as well be called "the age of revival". On the one hand, we meet with a strong desire to escape the snares of this world by concentrating upon the mysteries of salvation: the road to sanctity is a narrow road, to be trodden in fear and trembling. On the other hand there are those for whom this world is a world full of new and unexpected possibilities, a world to be explored and to be made instrumental to the fulfilment of the divine plan with regard to the development of humanity in its secular context. Naturally, also in the eighteenth century "sanctity" and "secularity" were not seen as in themselves mutually exclusive concepts. While many revivalists looked forward to the enlightenment of this world by the knowledge of God, many men of the Enlightenment saw before them the prospect of the sanctification of the world by the combined influences of reason and revelation. Some of the fathers of the Enlightenment—notably John Locke and Gottfried Wilhelm Leibniz—were essentially committed to the cause of Christianity, while on the other hand protagonists of the Pietist and revival movements such as August Hermann Francke and Jonathan Edwards cannot in fairness be accused of an anti-rational attitude and of a lack of interest in the well-being of this world. Nevertheless, within the circle of eighteenth-century Protestant Christianity there were conspicuous differences with regard to the evaluation of and the attitude towards the world in which the Christian community, while living in the expectation of the coming Kingdom, still had to find its way and its place.

These differences are connected with a perennial problem in the history of Christianity: the question how to interpret and how to deal with the ambivalence of the concept "world" as it occurs in the sources of the Christian tradition. In the Johannine as well as in the Pauline writings, the world is God's good creation, loved and redeemed by Him—the knowledge of this aspect of the world can lead to a form of Christian "thisworldliness"—, but at the same time we meet with the idea that this world is the totality of unredeemed creation, hostile to God, a threat to Christian life—to love this world is incompatible with a true love of God.[1] The tension, inherent in the ambivalent character of the concept "world" in the New Testament, was activated rather than re-

[1] H. Sasse in *Theologisches Wörterbuch zum N.T.* III, Stuttgart 1938, 867-98.

solved by the concurrence of classical and Christian traditions in the period of the Renaissance. Especially the seventeenth century was marked on the one hand by a worldliness which had not developed into the secularism of the Enlightenment,[2] but did prepare the way for it, on the other hand by a concentration upon the essential qualities of Christian life which in Catholic as well as in Protestant circles could lead to a special emphasis on the distance between the Christian and the world. Eighteenth-century Christianity inherited an unsolved problem. Bunyan's Christian had to find his way in a world which according to at least some of his fellow-Christians was not a vale of tears and darkness, but if not a heaven on earth, then still a field full of new light and new promise.

To what extent do we find this tension in the Dutch eighteenth century situation? In order to get a clear view of the context of our problem, it is necessary first of all to have a look at the development of Dutch church life in the eighteenth century. The Netherlands were a country with a pluralistic religious situation, although almost until the end of the century the Reformed Church was the "public" or "privileged" church: it made use of the old church buildings or of newly built, sometimes monumental churches, its ministers were paid out of public funds, only its members could hold public offices of some importance in the state. All this gave to the Reformed Church an influential position in the midst of Dutch society, which it tried to mould by its preaching and its discipline. But it did not lead to the founding of a Calvinistic theocracy in the Netherlands: for this the influence of the Reformed Church, as a national church structurally weak because of the absence of a national synod during the larger part of the seventeenth century and the whole of the eighteenth century, was not strong enough, the counter-balance of the influence of more or less "Erasmian" magistrates often too strong. Moreover, precisely the public position of the Church could make the exercise of a strict Calvinistic discipline rather difficult. In this context, the Nijmegen case of 1752-3 is illustrative.[3] When the consistory of the Reformed Church of Nijmegen refused to admit to membership two young people of comparatively high rank because of their masonic sympathies—the consistory considered membership of the lodge incompatible with full church membership—the States of the Province of Gelderland successfully intervened; no doubt the most important factor in the attitude of the States was, that if these young people were not accepted as full members of the church this would wreck their political career. Such an example, which could of course be multiplied, shows the reverse of the Reformed Church's privileged position: too often the church had to compromise, too often it was forced to take a course which by precisians could be interpreted as a dangerous adaptation to the pattern of this present

[2] P. Gay, *The Enlightenment* I, London 1967, 314.
[3] S.D. van Veen, *Uit de vorige eeuw*, Utrecht 1887, 45-100.

world. With an implicit awareness of the dangers of this privileged position of the dominant church the Dutch seventeenth-century Catholic church leader Neercassel,[4] a precisian with Jansenist inclinations, wrote about his co-religionists who were "without offices in the republic, without a voice in the council, without power in government": "Let the Catholics rejoice, because it has been granted to them to make sure of their salvation in lowliness, in order not to fall into peril in high places."[5]

In spite of a formal unity in doctrine (ministers had to subscribe to the Belgic Confession, the Catechism of Heidelberg and the Canons of Dort), within the eighteenth-century Reformed Church a variety of tendencies was to be found, each of which represented a particular way of thinking as well as a particular type of spirituality. From the seventeenth century, the church of the eighteenth century had inherited the differences between the followers of two leading theologians, Voetius[6] and Coccejus.[7] The Voetians were the more conservative party. They combined a scholastic-aristotelian theology with a Puritan way of life.[8] In the practice of piety they were deeply influenced by English and Scottish Puritan authors, many of whom saw their works translated into Dutch[9]—the Voetians were sometimes even nicknamed "Scottish clerks".[10] Like the Puritans, they were precisians; their Sunday observance was very strict, and as far as possible they held aloof from worldly pomp and pleasures. In politics, the Voetians were strong supporters of the Orangist party; socially, they found their stronghold in the lower middle class. The followers of Coccejus were different in more than one respect. Many of them tried to combine the biblical thinking of Coccejus[11] with the philosophy of Descartes. It is difficult to see a direct connection between the unphilosophical theology of Coccejus and the philosophy of Descartes; probably many Coccejans followed the French philosopher because his modern outlook was more in accord with their somehow rather open and dynamic thinking than was static Aristotelianism.[12] With at least some Coccejans, their sympathy for Cartesian think-

---

[4] Johannes Baptista van Neercassel (1623-86), apostolic vicar from 1663.

[5] Joan Baptist (Neercassel), *Bevestigingh in "t Geloof en Troost in Vervolgingh*, Brussel 1670, 385ff, 402ff.

[6] Gisbertus Voetius (1589-1676). See A.C. Duker, *Gisbertus Voetius*, 3 vols. and reg., Leiden 1897-1915.

[7] Johannes Coccejus (1603-1669). See G. Schrenk, *Gottesreich und Bund im älteren Protestantismus vornehmlich bei Johannes Coccejus*, Darmstadt 1967 (1st ed. 1923).

[8] For an analysis of the ideas of the Voetian party see W. Goeters, *Die Vorbereitung des Pietismus in der reformierten Kirche der Niederlande*, Leipzig 1911, 53-120.

[9] One of the most important translators was the Voetian minister Koelman; a list of the works he translated in A.F. Krull, *Jacobus Koelman*, Sneek 1901, 352-7.

[10] J.C. Trimp, *Joost van Lodensteyn als piëtistisch dichter*, Djakarta and Groningen 1952, 41.

[11] G. Schrenk remarks that the theology of Coccejus preeminently aims at being a biblical theology (*Gottesreich und Bund*, 14).

[12] For Dutch Cartesianism see J.A. Cramer, *Abraham Heidanus en zijn Cartesianisme*, Utrecht

ing led to a greater appreciation of the possibilities of human reason than was to be found in the Voetian circle. In practical affairs such as Sunday observance and matters of dress and fashion the Coccejans were less strict than the Voetians; their attitude was more in keeping with the climate of opinion among the higher classes of Dutch society, from which the "burgher oligarchy" was recruited, although we get the impression that sometimes even Coccejan ministers were still too strict for patricians and scholars of the "Erasmian" tradition.

In the course of the eighteenth century, the old cleavage between Voetians and Coccejans was gradually superseded by other differences. To the average church member, preaching meant more than theological niceties or philosophical speculations. In certain quarters of the church, especially, but not exclusively among the common people of town and country-side those preachers were popular who preached in an "experiential" way. Of course they were to be found among the Voetians, with their traditional sympathy for the "practice of piety", but also among the Coccejans there were preachers who appealed to the emotions rather than to the intellect; the people distinguished them from the Cartesian Coccejans as the "serious" Coccejans, who had strong affinities with the more pietist or "living" Voetians. Among the leading eighteenth-century Dutch Pietists we find Coccejans (such as the Utrecht professor Lampe)[13] as well as Voetians (like W. Schortinghuis, the minister of the village of Midwolda in the Province of Groningen):[14] their differences were blurred by their common pietist interest. A remnant, more extremely Voetian, whose representatives preferred the name of "Calvinist" to the name of "Reformed",[15] remained vocal until halfway through the eighteenth century; it sympathised with the Pietists and took their side in the heated controversies

1889; J. Bohatec, *Die cartesianische Scholastik in der Philosophie und reformierten Dogmatik des 17. Jahrhunderts* I, Leipzig 1912; M.J.A. de Vrijer, *Henricus Regius*, 's-Gravenhage 1954; E.J. Dijksterhuis and others, *Descartes et le Cartésianisme hollandais*, Paris and Amsterdam 1950; C. Louise Thijssen-Schoute, *Nederlands Cartesianisme*, Utrecht 1989 (1st ed. 1954); E. Bizer, "Die reformierte Orthodoxie und der Cartesianismus" in *Zeitschrift für Theologie und Kirche* 55 (1958) 306-72; T. Verbeek, *Descartes and the Dutch*, Carbondale and Edwardsville (USA) 1992. Cramer only assumes an external connection between Coccejanism and Cartesianism, but others are more inclined to assume an internal relationship between both systems.

[13] Friedrich Adolph Lampe (1683-1729); see G. Snijders, *Friedrich Adolph Lampe*, Harderwijk 1954. Contrary to contemporary Dutch usage (pietistically minded Dutch authors usually avoided the word "Pietist" and its derivatives because of their pejorative associations) in this essay I use the words "Pietist" etc. to denote the advocates of a form of piety which strongly emphasized the crucial importance of personal religious experience ("experiential" piety).

[14] Wilhelmus Schortinghuis (1700-50); see J.C. Kromsigt, *Wilhelmus Schortinghuis*, Groningen 1904; M.J.A. De Vrijer, *Schortinghuis en zijn analogieën*, Amsterdam 1942.

[15] N. Holtius and A. Comrie, *Examen van het Ontwerp van Tolerantie* X, Amsterdam 1759, XII.

of the day. On the other hand the leading non-pietist Coccejans tried to vindicate their own orthodoxy in their discussions with Pietists and rationalists. Their most influential spokesman was the Leiden professor Van den Honert,[16] who was not inclined to accentuate the differences between Voetians and Coccejans. He was a typical theologian of the middle way; while some Pietists accused him of rationalist traits in his theology, the more liberal theologians saw in him an intolerant defender of the Calvinist system. However this may be, the Reformed Pietists as well as their theological opponents considered themselves orthodox: in their sometimes sharp discussions, both sides time and again appealed to the Reformed confessions. Their struggles took place within the context of an unmistakable loyalty to the Calvinist tradition, which, however, in the heat of the controversy was not always mutually recognised.

A more liberal and rationalist tendency mainly revealed itself within the circle of the Protestant Dissenters, especially the Mennonites and the Remonstrants or Arminians. In this context, it is necessary to make some preliminary remarks. In the first place: in spite of the leniency of the Dutch spiritual climate, the Netherlands did not prove a fertile soil for the development of radical Enlightenment ideas; Holland did not produce a Toland, a Tindal, a Voltaire, a Rousseau. Furthermore, in the Netherlands of the eighteenth-century there existed an eclectic attitude with regard to various philosophical systems; in its turn, this attitude strengthened the tendency towards a moderate rationalism which had affinities with and was influenced by the thinking of the German philosopher Christian Wolff.[17] The precarious balance between reason and revelation in the Wolffian system coincided with what has been called the moderately rationalist doctrine of religion of John Locke.[18] From this it follows, that a rationalist influence on theology often led to what Peter Gay, speaking of Wolff, called a "gently modernized Protestant orthodoxy".[19] But some went further; their mixture of Christian thinking and rationalist influences led to a form of Christian rationalism which placed them somewhere outside the circle of traditional orthodoxy. As we shall see, even

---

[16] Johannes van den Honert (1593-1758); see *Biographisch Woordenboek van Protestantsche Godgeleerden* IV, "s-Gravenhage 1931, 232-46.

[17] For the influence of the philosophy of Wolff in the Netherlands see A.W. Bronsveld, *Oorzaken der verbreiding van het rationalisme in ons land*, Rotterdam 1862, 115-29; H.H. Zwager, *Nederland en de verlichting*, Bussum 1972, 76.

[18] See the title of the chapter on Locke in E. Hirsch, *Geschichte der neuern evangelischen Theologie* I, Güttersloh [3]1964, 271-92. *Cf.* Hazard's remark on the eighteenth-century alliance between rationalism and empiricism: "... l'esprit du XVIIIe siècle, tel qu'il prend ses racines dans le XVIIe, est rationaliste par essence, et empiriste par transaction", P. Hazard, *La crise de la conscience européenne* II, Paris 1961, 10.

[19] Gay, *The Enlightenment* I, 331; *cf.* the Dutch philosopher F. Sassen on the orthodox Protestant Enlightenment in his *Johan Lulofs (1711-1768) en de reformatorische verlichting in de Nederlanden*, Amsterdam 1965.

with regard to them the word "rationalists" must be used with all proper reserves: although their world-view as well as their spirituality were not inconsiderably influenced by the spirit of the Enlightenment with its more optimistic appraisal of the possibilities, hidden in man's reasonable nature, their rationalist inclinations did not imply a rejection of the value of divine revelation and of the necessity of man's striving for sanctity with the help of God's grace. Moreover, the boundary-lines between a more orthodox and a more rationalist way of thinking often were not so clearly drawn as to allow of a facile classification within the well-defined framework of any particular group: deep cross-currents and unexpected affinities sometimes blurred the image.

That a more liberal attitude towards traditional values and a greater openness towards new tendencies first of all appeared in the circle of the Dissenters is connected with their specific historical development. The Mennonites, divided as they were among a number of sometimes conflicting groups, had not been able to achieve a united stand with regard to matters of doctrine and practice. While some eighteenth-century Mennonites still clung to the strictest traditions of their sixteenth-century ancestors, others had moved into a different direction. Their more liberal doctrinal outlook was attended with the loss of much of the traditional strictness of life, in line with the development in the latter part of the seventeenth century which made an unknown critic remark in a satirical poem: "Formerly the Mennonites were in the world, but now the world is in their midst."[20] As a matter of fact, those more modern followers of Menno Simons usually did not call themselves "Mennonites", but preferred the more formal name of "Doopsgezinden" ("Baptists"). Their shift towards a new outlook and a new way of life had some connection with the social changes which had taken place in the Mennonite circle: while the early Mennonites mostly belonged to the lower strata of society,[21] many of their descendants had attained positions of wealth and social influence. One of the leading spokesmen of the more rationalist wing of the Mennonite community was the Frisian preacher Stinstra,[22] well known in the English-speaking world because of his heavy attack on the revival movement of c. 1750. When John Wesley had read his *Pastoral Letter against Fanaticism*, the English translation of a tract in the form of a warning letter to the Frisian Mennonites,[23] he

---

[20] N. van der Zijpp, *Geschiedenis der Doopsgezinden in Nederland*, Arnhem 1952, 152.

[21] For this (with a correction of the traditional Mennonite view with regard to this point) see A.F. Mellink, *De Wederdopers in de Noordelijke Nederlanden*, Groningen 1953.

[22] Johannes Stinstra (1708-1790); see C. Sepp, *Johannes Stinstra en zijn tijd*, 2 vols. Amsterdam 1865-66.

[23] J. Stinstra, *Waarschuwinge tegen de geestdrijverij vervat in een brief aan de Doopsgezinden in Friesland*, Harlingen 1750. I quote from the first English translation: John Stinstra, *A Pastoral Letter against Fanaticism, Address'd to the Mennonists of Friesland translated from the original Dutch by Henry Rimius*, London 1753. For the English translations, see *The Richardson-Stinstra Correspondence and Stinstra's Prefaces to Clarissa*, ed W.C. Slattery, Carbondale etc 1969, 214ff.

wrote in his *Journal*: "He is doubtless a well-meaning man, but deeply ignorant of the subject he treats of; and his arguments are of no force at all ... They utterly overthrow many of the grand arguments for Christianity". Many years afterwards, Wesley wrote: "In truth, I cannot but fear Mr. Stinstra is in the same class with Dr. Conyers Middleton ... The very thing which Mr. Stinstra calls fanaticism is no other than heart-religion."[24]

The Remonstrants had been even more accessible to liberal opinions. The eighteenth-century descendants of those who had been ejected from the Reformed Church by the Synod of Dort of 1618-19 formed a small group in which, due to its Erasmian traditions and the high intellectual level of its leaders, there was a lively interest in new currents in European thinking. In particular, John Locke's ideas found a ready response among the leading Arminians: together with his colleague Jean le Clerc (Clericus), the editor of the *Opera* of Erasmus, the Amsterdam professor Philippus van Limborch, who in the winter of 1683 had first met Locke when both men had been invited by a medical doctor in Amsterdam to be present at the dissection of a dead lioness, became the protagonist of Locke's philosophy in the Netherlands.[25] Eighteenth-century Remonstrant theology as a whole was deeply influenced by the spirit of the Enlightenment.

The leading Remonstrant theologian of the second half of the century, the Amsterdam professor Van der Meersch may serve for an example. He was on the cross-roads of German and English influences. In a cultural and theological review, the *Algemeene Bibliotheek*, he introduced German Christian rationalist authors like the Lutheran abbot Jerusalem[26] to the Dutch. Bishop Warburton, whose *The Divine Legation of Moses* was translated into Dutch by Van der Meersch, thought very highly of the Arminian Dutch professor and of the Remonstrant fraternity in general. In a letter of 21 March 1762 he wrote to his Dutch friend: "For ever since I could distinguish right from wrong, I have had a predelection for the Arminian Church, founded on the true principles of Christian liberty, by a succession of heroes; I would call them saints, tho' not of the roman fabric, yet made of better stuff, of Erasmus's own texture; but stronger ...", and nine years later (4 April 1771) he wrote, referring to the "persecuting spirit of Calvinism": "... though the ministers of the Calvinistical church of Holland do not, nor are ever likely to abate their *intolerant* principles, yet in this inlightened age (for which it is principally indebted to your heroes), it is to be hoped, your magistrates will no longer add terror to their *brutum fulmen*".[27]

---

[24] J. Wesley, *Journal*, London ³1960, IV, 72 (8 June 1753) V, 426 (12 Aug. 1771).

[25] P.J. Barnouw, *Philippus van Limborch*, 's-Gravenhage 1963, 33.

[26] Abraham Arend van der Meersch (1720-92); Johann Friedrich Wilhelm Jerusalem (1709-89); for the latter's theological radicalism, see Hirsch, *Geschichte* IV, 31ff.

[27] J. Tideman, "Briefwisseling tusschen den Hoogleeraar A.A. van der Meersch en den Bis-

The spirit of the Dutch Protestant Enlightenment is vividly epitomised in the works of two women authors: Elizabeth Wolff, a minister's wife, and her friend Aagje Deken, who together wrote some novels in which the whole spectrum of Dutch life in the second half of the eighteenth century is reflected. We are confronted with various types: the hypocrite pietist brother Benjamin but also the genuinely pious Stijntje Doorzicht ("Christine Discernment")—she attended the services of Wilhelmus Peiffers, an Amsterdam minister who recommended the works of Doddridge and other English theologians to the Dutch public—; the tolerant minister Redelijk ("Reasonable") and the mildly orthodox professor Maatig ("Moderate"), probably the Leiden professor Hollebeek, Elizabeth Wolff's much-admired brother-in-law, who tried to introduce the "English way of preaching'into Holland,[28] and with them quite a number of other characters, taken from life, who together form a cross-section of the Dutch Protestant population of those days. How did they all, orthodox people and rationalists, followers of Calvin and people of Erasmian texture, conservative theologians and daring innovators, pietist and anti-pietist Christians, deal with the problem of the Christian's relation to the world?

This question has a twofold aspect, a theoretical as well as a practical one. We may ask, whether their view of this world with its light and its shadows was—contrary to the spirit of the age—of a more pessimistic, or—in accordance with contemporary feeling—of a more optimistic nature. But we may also ask what was their answer to the many practical questions with regard to the Christian's participation in the social and cultural life of his own enlightened eighteenth-century surroundings. These two aspects are so closely interwoven that it would be inadvisable to treat them separately.

Let us first of all turn to those of a strong pietistic bent. We have already mentioned the Utrecht professor Lampe, who showed a combination of the spirituality of the seventeenth-century Voetian circle in Utrecht and the Reformed Pietism of north-west Germany—two forms of spirituality which in spite of their different background yet had many elements in common. Lampe was known and respected as a man of a deep and genuine piety. A remarkable instance of the esteem in which Lampe was held by congenial spirits can be found in a work which appeared anonymously in Denmark in 1742-3 under the title: *Menoza, en Asiatisk Printz.*[29] It was written by the Danish Pietist Erik

---

schop van Gloucester, William Warburton (1761-1771)", *Kerkhistorisch Archief* 3, Amsterdam 1862, 417-25. See also C.W. Roldanus, "Nederlandsch-Engelsche betrekkingen op den bodem van 'Arminianisme'", *Tijdschrift voor Geschiedenis* 58 (1943) esp. 21.

[28] Ewald Hollebeek (1719-96); for him, see L. Knappert, *Geschiedenis der Nederlandsche Hervormde Kerk gedurende de 18ᵉ en 19ᵉ eeuw*, Amsterdam 1912, 131ff, 153ff.

[29] I used the German translation: *Menoza, Ein Asiatischer Prinz ... Aus dem Dänischen übersetzt*, 3 vols., Hollstein n.d., probably 1746.

Pontoppidan,[30] and it contained the story of the travels of an imaginary Asian prince who, converted to Christianity, went out in search of real Christians of whom he only found a very few. Lampe was one of them; here the story has an authentic ring, because Pontoppidan himself had visited Lampe on his travels to England and Holland in 1720-21; partly at least, the story of Menoza's travels is founded upon Pontoppidan's own experiences. After visiting England, where he had come into contact with some pious Presbyterians and had made the acquaintance of Archbishop Wake, Menoza came to the Netherlands, a country which could be called a *compendium universi*. A Dutch minister told him, that the kingdom of Christ still had many true adherents in Holland, although they formed a small number, compared with those who served the God of this world. In Amsterdam and again in Utrecht he met Le Clerc, who was rather critical of his Utrecht colleague Lampe: he thought him too stern a moralist, and besides somewhat sectarian, and too much of a zealot. This, however, did not deter our Indian prince; he thought it might be with Lampe as with other "spiritual" people in Europe, whom Satan made objects of slander in order to promote his own kingdom; he would be a stupid devil if he did not act like this! Menoza noted that Lampe's adherents were called "fijnen" (the precise people)—a common nickname for Dutch precisians; according to Menoza it was invented by Satan, who incites his instruments to point out those who are not prepared to walk on the broad highway of this world. In this context, Menoza mentions a conversation with Lampe with reference to a story he had heard from his landlord, whose brother-in-law had joined the precisians and consequently had neglected his affairs to the extent that he now had to eat the dry bread of poverty. Was there indeed, as popular opinion would have it, a connection between his religious attitude and his economic failure? No doubt many seventeenth-century Dutch Puritans would have denied such a connection; Lampe however answered the question in the affirmative: now that the merchant let himself increasingly be guided by his conscience, he also suffered in a material sense, but the cross he had to bear was a noble cross. Formerly, our merchant had been guilty of various nasty tricks, which in Holland are called "the soul of commerce", but since the love of Christ had taken possession of his soul, all this had changed. To be among the wolves without being able to howl with them, to live in the midst of a wicked generation without being able to go along with them, all this makes the Christian's path a thorny one. He, who follows Christ must be prepared to suffer worldly loss—yet a blessed loss, when we turn our eyes to the future economy in the world to come.[31]

---

[30] Erik Pontoppidan (1698-1764). See *Dansk Biografisk Leksikon* XVIII, Copenhagen 1940, 458-66 and J.W. Vink, "Erik Pontoppidan en zijn stichtelijke roman 'Menoza'", *Tijdschrift voor Geschiedenis* 68 (1955), 33-58.

[31] *Menoza* III, 3-23.

It is all in line with what Lampe remarks in his best-known work, an exposition on the mystery of the covenant of grace, written in 1712, which, translated into Dutch, became a popular work of edification in the Netherlands. Satan often makes use of this world as a means to stir up persecutions against the children of God or to arrange such objects as may stimulate the evil which is in them. Therefore, the world is the second main enemy of God's children. It is like a tempestuous sea, where flood follows flood in order to devour the little ship of the faithful.[32] Naturally, this view of the world has its consequences for daily practice: "Let all worldly entertainments be as nothing in your eyes. Make it manifest by utterly despising these things that now you have found something which is better. They who have tasted the heavenly Manna no longer take delight in the fleshpots of Egypt ..."[33] In his sermons, too, Lampe was uncompromising with regard to the world and its vanities: as man is but ash and dust, and his body is but a maggot's bag, why would people bother about appearances and pleasures. Fashion is but a "livery of Satan", beauty is but a passing thing: let the bones in the grave be your mirror.—One may wonder whether according to Lampe it still would be possible for a Christian to live in high places in the midst of the world. Lampe does not go so far as to deny the possibility altogether, but in a sermon preached before the Dowager Princess of Orange at Soestdijk he remarked that because of the dangers of court life it had become well-nigh impossible to combine life at court with true Christianity.[34]

The same spirit of ascetic, world-denying Christianity is met with Schortinghuis, one of the most outspoken and controversial eighteenth century Dutch Pietists. His work on "Inner Christianity",[35] which appeared in 1740, aroused a storm of protest—not only from the side of more rationalist opponents, but also from theologians who were akin to him in their emphasis on the spiritual experience of the inner man, like the redoubtable Groningen professor Antonius Driessen, who shortly before had written: "... grace is experiential ... It is experience which awakens the hope of a better life ..."[36] The main point of attack was Schortinghuis' supposed sympathy with what used to be called: "corrupt mysticism"; however, some of the most conservative Voetians like Alexander Comrie, a minister of Scottish descent defended his orthodoxy.[37] Schortinghuis had strong affinities with German Reformed Pietism and accordingly with Lampe, while in his main work he also mentions a

[32] F.A. Lampe, *De Verborgentheit van het Genaade-verbondt*, Amsterdam 1735, 490.
[33] Lampe, *Verborgentheit*, 627.
[34] Snijders, *F.A. Lampe*, 24ff.
[35] W. Schortinghuis, *Het Innige Christendom*, Groningen 1740. I used the 4th ed., Groningen 1752.
[36] A. Driessen, *Oude en Nieuwe Mensch*, Groningen 1738, 459.
[37] A.G. Honig, *Alexander Comrie*, Utrecht 1892, 281.

number of English and Scottish authors, amongst whom were Francis Rous, John Bunyan and William Guthrie.[38]

For Schortinghuis, the true church is the inner church, true knowledge inner knowledge, true sanctity inner sanctity. Everything is concentrated on the heart of man and on man's inner contemplation of Jesus' heavenly glory. With great approval he quotes Van Lodensteyn's poem—dear to Dutch Pietists:— "High, on high, my soul, fly upwards, for it is not here below ... All that you see on earth, all that you hear on earth ... all that you wish on earth, is not worth your costly heart."[39] One of the persons in his dialogues is "man without grace", who in fact stands for the more moderate orthodox; this person remarks that he has not much sympathy with the narrow precisians, who want to appear in angelic purity; man lives in this world and must converse with the world, rather than wanting to be holier than others. But of course his remarks evoke a heavy protest: those who reject the precisians' attitude condemn themselves and are hostile to inner sanctity and its outward fruits.[40] The great sin of conformity to this world is not only a matter of external conduct, but of a wrong orientation of inner man. People may be outwardly religious, while yet their roots and their whole natural state are vicious.[41] If they knew, what a profound comfort the beloved of the Lord often experience, it would make them truly zealous "to change all the foolish and idle joys for those blissful, joyful tears ..."[42]

Between the predominantly pietistic and the more moderate orthodox there was a difference of emphasis rather than a fundamental difference with regard to the general pattern of life. In 1746 Van den Honert published his *The Church in the Netherlands considered and admonished to conversion*[43]—a lengthy complaint about and protest against the decline of religion and the defection of the country; in this it was in keeping with earlier works like Hondius' *Black Register of a thousand Sins*,[44] Witsius' *The Lord's Dispute with his Vineyard*[45] and Fruytier's *The Struggles of Zion*.[46] As we have seen, Van den Honert was

[38] An analysis of Schortinghuis's language in an unpublished paper of Ms. G. Recter (Vrije Universiteit, Amsterdam) "Een onderzoek naar het pietistische taalgebruik van ds. Willem Schortinghuis in zijn boek 'Het Innige Christendom' uit 1740". For Rous's influence, see J. van den Berg, "The English Puritan Francis Rous and the Influence of his Works in the Netherlands", this vol. Ch. 3.
[39] Schortinghuis, *Innige Christendom*, 549.
[40] *Ibid.*, 256.
[41] *Ibid.*, 136.
[42] *Ibid.*, 233.
[43] J. van den Honert, *De Kerk in Nederland Beschouwd, en tot Bekeering vermaand*, Leiden 1746. For this work, see now J. van den Berg, "Een achttiende eeuwse Coccejaan ..." (Full title, this volume, 270 (Bibliography. *sub* 1991)).
[44] J. Hondius, *Swart Register van duysent Sonden*, Amsterdam 1679.
[45] H. Witsius, *Twist des Heeren met syn Wijngaert*, Leeuwarden 1669.
[46] J. Fruytier, *Sions Worstelingen*, Rotterdam 1713.

a staunch opponent of the Dutch Pietists; however, with regard to the practice of daily life his strictness, although different in some respects, was not essentially less than that of those he opposed. In this the non-pietist orthodox could hardly afford to be outdone by their more pietistic brethren, whose views of sanctity and sanctification they thought to be one-sided and even dangerous; in this context, Van den Honert himself remarked that an emphasis on practical theology and evangelical morality would be a good remedy against an influx of enthusiasm into the church.[47]

The tone of Van den Honert's work is different from that of Schortinghuis. Though he, too, used the word "inner experience" in a positive sense, he was critical of the way this element was emphasised by the Pietists.[48] He paid due attention to the many questions with regard to man's personal relation to Christ,[49] but he was also deeply interested in the Christian's responsibility for public life. On this point, the contrast between Van den Honert and Schortinghuis was of a relative character. In Schortinghuis' work we indeed find something like a "regent's mirror", but it is only marginal and is mainly concerned with the inner life of pious and impious magistrates.[50] Van den Honert is less inner-directed than Schortinghuis, whose Pietism he disliked and who even became one of the main targets of his theological attacks. He does not address himself first of all to the small circle of the godly remnant, but rather to the much larger group of confessing Reformed Christians in general, many of whom bore the burden of responsibility in high places. In his *The Church in the Netherlands* he draws a very vivid picture of eighteenth-century Dutch social life, particularly in the upper middle classes, of which he had a rather poor opinion: "Truly, when we observe the country, we find it filled with impieties." Van den Honert tries to show, that those who have not been able to conquer the country by the force of their weapons have now conquered it by their morals. The Dutch "have become ridiculous copies of ridiculous neighbours ... To be a Dutchman is an original sin according to the men of this world."[51] The cultural influence of Catholic France manifests itself in many ways—it is a threat, not only to the stability of Dutch life in general, but most of all to a life in the true spirit of Reformed Christianity. People rightly complain about the decay of life with the common people, the so-called "small congregation", but the attitude of the rich and the prominent is no better: they take no measures against the desecration of the Sabbath, against the taverns and brothels where even on the Lord's day the rich spend their time.[52] Nor do they

---

47 Van den Honert, *De Kerk*, 215.
48 *Ibid.*, 220ff, 273.
49 His work "Man in Christ", *De Mensch in Christus*, Leiden 1749, gave testimony of a genuine interest in the matter of man's personal salvation.
50 Schortinghuis, *Innige Christendom*, 47-59.
51 Van den Honert, *De Kerk*, 24.
52 *Ibid.*, 332ff.

know the world which they serve, nor God whom they should serve; they do not know that the world lies in wickedness, that it is a deceiver. A choice has to be made: "to go to Sohar, and to look back to Sodom; to travel to Canaan, and to look back to the flesh-pots of Egypt ... these are incompatible ..."[53] Indeed, much of what Van den Honert remarks sounds like the complaints and the warnings of the Pietists, although the differences in context and in background should not be overlooked.

As we noticed before, on a number of practical points all orthodox agreed. Of course, they were opposed to the theatre. In 1711 the liberally-minded Utrecht professor of history, literature and civics Petrus Burman gave a public lecture *Pro Comoedia*, in which he openly defended theatre-visiting. This was soon published in Latin and Dutch and created a stir in ecclesiastical circles.[54] The Utrecht ministers were unanimous in their protest, whereupon Burman ironically wrote, that he thought it a pleasure to be the peace-offering which brought together the parties, once deadly opposed to each other.[55] A theatre-visiting minister seems to have been so rare that it could be used as an additional point of reproach in a heresy-case.[56] And as late as 1772, the struggle around the theatre broke out anew after the terrible fire at the Amsterdam theatre, which according to at least a number of orthodox people was clearly an act of God's judgement.[57] In the same circles, dancing too was strictly prohibited. There is the notorious Groningen case of 1771-72, when an elder of the Reformed Church was attacked by his consistory because of the opportunity given to dance at his daughter's wedding-party.[58] The offended elder argued, that if it were true that the old rules forbade elders to dance, the ministers themselves were equally guilty because they wore periwigs. The whole affair inspired Elizabeth Wolff to write her satirical poem: "The Menuet and the Minister's Periwig".[59] In this case, too, ministers of various parties joined hands to defend the traditional way of life. A third point on which the orthodox were uncompromising was that of card-playing; in an early eighteenth-century sermon, which was reprinted several times, a Middelburg minister, De Frein, remarked that playing cards sprang from the devil himself and that it was a sin against all God's command-

---

[53] *Ibid.* 380ff.

[54] See H.C. Hazewinkel, "Professor Burman, de kerkeraad en het tooneel", *Jaarboekje ... van "Oud-Utrecht" 1927*, Utrecht 1927, 120-54.

[55] P. Burman, *Redevoering voor de Comedie*, Amsterdam ^{3}1772, 5.

[56] *Examen van het Ontwerp van Tolerantie* vol. X, XXXV.

[57] In a poem by J.C. Mohr, *Ontzaglijke doch nuttige Beschouwing van het akelig treurtooneel*, Amsterdam n.d., it appeared shortly after the fire, we read (3): "I sing, though trembling, Jehovah's majesty, manifested in the exercise of his justice." For this, see now J.W. Buisman, *Tussen vroomheid en Verlichting* I, Zwolle 1992, 157-187.

[58] See S.D. van Veen, *Historische Studiën en Schetsen*, Groningen 1905, 279-310.

[59] P. Minderaa (ed.), *De menuet en de domineespruik*, Amsterdam and Antwerpen 1954.

ments.[60] But of course there were still many other things, large and small, which were seen as manifestations of an attitude of conformity to this world. Those who wanted to know the strict orthodox rules regarding all matters of a practical nature could find them in alphabetical order in Hondius' *Black Register*, where under the heading "World" we read: "such people are sinning who, being members of the congregation, nevertheless are worldly minded, love the world above God and more attend to what belongs to the earth than to what appertains to heaven ..."[61]

We may ask how eighteenth-century Christians, who leaned towards rationalism, regarded the world, what expression they gave to the Christian ideal of sanctity, how they reacted to the secularising tendencies which revealed themselves in the age of Enlightenment. While orthodox Christians—and in particular the pietistically-minded—considered themselves involved in a dramatic struggle between God and Satan, and believed the devil to be ever personally present to ensnare them by the temptations of this dark and evil world, more enlightened Christians lived in a disenchanted world, in which the night of ignorance, disorder, intolerance and superstitution gradually gave way to the light of reason and virtue. In his work *The Enchanted World* the Amsterdam minister Balthasar Bekker, who because of the consistent use of the Cartesian method of reasoning had been led to a more rationalist attitude than we find with most contemporary theologians,[62] had blazed the trail for a more undramatic, almost secular understanding of the processes going on in this world: much of what formerly was ascribed to the devil could be explained in a rational way. According to Bekker, it was mostly common people, children and old women who were deeply impressed by the stories told about the devil's activities.[63] Stinstra, the Frisian Mennonite preacher mentioned earlier, also dealt with the problem of the devil and his work, although he approached it from a different angle. In his *Sermons on the Nature and Condition of the Kingdom of Christ*,[64] which made him the object of the dangerous charge of Socinianism,[65] he emphasised the spiritual character of the Kingdom of God, which can only be propagated by love of truth and virtue into the hearts of men.[66] In this, he followed the argument of Bishop Hoadly's well-known

---

[60] H. de Frein, *Het spelen met de kaart den Christenen ongeoorlooft*, Amsterdam ²1720 (1st ed. 1719), 32, 58ff.
[61] Hondius, *Swart Register*, 444.
[62] For Bekker (1634-98) see W.P.C. Knuttel, *Balthasar Bekker*, 's-Gravenhage 1906; for his philosophical emphasis see W. Reuning, "Balthasar Bekker", *Zeitschrift für Kirchengeschichte* 45 (1927) 562-96.
[63] *De Betoverde Weereld*, Deventer 1739 I, 137.
[64] J. Stinstra, *De Natuure en Gesteldheid van Christus Koningrijk*, Harlingen 1741.
[65] For the "Stinstra affair", see next to Sepp, *Stinstra* I, 238-68, II, 1-160, now also J. van Eynatten, *Mutua Christianorum Tolerantia. Irenicism and toleration in the Netherlands: the Stinstra affair 1740-1745*, Firenze 1998.
[66] Stinstra, *Christus Koningrijk*, 37.

sermon on *The Nature of the Kingdom or Church of Christ* (1717); no doubt, the spiritual element in his Mennonite heritage made him the more responsive to the much debated ideas of the Bishop of Bangor.[67] In accordance with the thinking of the English Latitudinarians, whom he so much admired, the Frisian preacher saw a close connection between truth and virtue. Truth is always combined with virtue, because it is moral truth, marked by moderation, justice and piety. It is a reasonable truth, "nothing else but pure and sound reason, and its knowledge and practice amongst men".[68] Christ has been manifested that he might destroy the works of the devil and might overcome the power of darkness. This must not come to pass by force, but through the light of truth, which expels the darkness and recommends true virtue in its natural beauty: as the kingdom of Satan exists in sin and injustice, its destruction takes place through truth and justice.[69] Stinstra sings the praises of freedom, equality and tolerance;[70] in this, he is the exponent of the spirit of a new age, which for obvious reasons was more readily accepted in the circle of Enlightened Dissenters than in that of orthodox members of the privileged Reformed Church; half a century later many of the more liberal Mennonites would find themselves in the vanguard of the Patriot movement, looking forward to the blessings of "liberty, equality and fraternity", sometimes even taking up arms in the defence of the ideals of the revolution.[71]

We should not attribute to Stinstra an undue optimism with regard to the state of affairs in this world. In a sermon on Psalm 90.12 he remarked that life is transient, uncertain and short and that therefore man has to be wary of the enjoyment of worldly and temporary pleasures and of the temptation of the benefits which life offers to us: these things could possibly turn him away from his highest and most excellent good. Without any delay man has to enter seriously upon the work of sanctification and the practice of virtue.[72] All this, however, should be seen against the background of an image of man and of God, which differs much from that which we find in orthodox, and especially in pietist circles. In his *Pastoral Letter* he writes:

> That which the Fanatick calls the *Work of Regeneration*, consists in sensible Alarms, cruel Agitations of the Soul, arising from a Consideration of the Misery and Corruption of our Nature, (which he supposes a great deal more dreadful than they really are) and in a kind of dreadful Amazement and Terror for God, (painting this adorable

[67] For his views, see G.R. Cragg, *Reason and Authority in the Eighteenth Century*, Cambridge 1946, 196.
[68] Stinstra, *Christus Koningrijk*, 56.
[69] *Christus Koningrijk*, 69.
[70] Especially in Sermon V, on Rom. 14.12, *Christus Koningrijk*, 162-206.
[71] Van der Zijpp, *Geschiedenis Doopsgezinden*, 177.
[72] Johannes Stinstra, *Bedenkingen over des menschen leeftijd*, Harlingen 1744.

> Master as a barbarous Tyrant) which sometimes throw the Soul into the greatest Horror.[73]

The way that Stinstra pointed out to his Frisian Mennonites was quite different from the arduous journey of Bunyan's Christian and the narrow road of the Pietists: it was the road of a religion, based on sound reason and demanding what is perfectly reasonable, honest and decent.[74] He knew that among the "enthusiasts", Antinomians excepted, there also were people who strongly insisted on moral virtues, but all too often their idea of virtue was defective; while pressing some duties too far, they were inclined to overlook other duties. Stinstra stood for "a manly Piety": "Let us make appear by our Conduct, that a reasonable Faith has no less Power and Influence over us, than Superstitions and chimerical Opinions have over others."[75]

How far these fundamental views affected Stinstra's attitude with regard to what the Pietists used to call "worldly pleasures" may be seen in the preface to his translation of the third and fourth volume of Richardson's *Clarissa.*[76] Stinstra sees the search for pleasure and recreation as in agreement with the loving intentions of our Creator. Naturally, that which induces to evil inclination and crimes has to be avoided, the right measure has to be respected and the useful advantage of pleasure has to be kept in view—but given all this, there is ample room for various forms of "gay pleasure and light relaxation". The reading of novels is one of them, but from Stinstra's line of argument it appears that he is not opposed to other forms of relaxation either, whose "essential usefulness" does not detract from the "sweet pleasure" they may offer. "If you dance, if you take a pleasant walk for relaxation or enjoyment, you would not say that the enjoyment loses something of its power to refresh you because at the same time you have in mind protecting or promoting the fresh and well-kept health of your body." Stinstra was far from being a libertine; he, too, shows a certain restraint with regard to the pleasures of this world; but still, how much more open, how much less grim is his attitude towards the world than that of so many of his orthodox contemporaries. And even when he, too is critical of some forms of relaxation he remains moderate and urbane: his slightly ironical treatment of the question of card-playing is strikingly different from the vehement denunciations of De Frein's sermon on the subject. In all this, the social factor may neither be overlooked nor unduly stressed: of course, Stinstra stands for much that was customary in the more prosperous and well-educated upper middle classes, although there, too, besides a more

---

[73] Stinstra, *A Pastoral Letter*, 18.
[74] *Ibid.*, 32.
[75] *Ibid.* 85, 88.
[76] *Clarissa of de Historie van eene Jonge Juffer* III, Harlingen 1753. I follow the translation, given by Slattery, 129-55.

liberal and latitudinarian attitude an almost Methodist strictness could be found, as John Wesley noticed when he visited Holland in 1783 and 1786.[77]

Stinstra is the almost perfect example of a Dutch moderate. Some, however, went just a bit further: their world-view was marked by an optimism which was in striking contrast to the often pessimistic world-view of the Pietists. Perhaps it is best summarised in a review, probably written by Van der Meersch, in the *Algemeene Bibliotheek* of a work by the abbot Jerusalem—

> Could we not, when we regard the gradual progress of arts and sciences in former times, and their amazing progress in this present century, deduce with rightful expectation, that this Enlightenment will spread further and further? Once this is realised it is highly probable that eventually it will have a salutary influence on human morality ... With civilisation spreading, society, virtue and sound morals will necessarily improve, although it is beyond doubt that there will always be people unable to overcome their corrupt nature. To this ever spreading civilisation and improvement of morals, Christian religion can be a strong impetus.[78]

Those, who looked at the world with such almost unbounded optimism, were fighters for a new society, in which freedom and tolerance would be dominant concepts. Amongst them was Van der Meersch, whose great ideal was a free and open society, in which there would be no privileged church and no infringements upon the great principle of religious liberty. Yet he did not stand for a secular society in the modern sense of the word: while he agreed with Hoadly and Stinstra that the Kingdom of God is not of this world, he, too, believed that the Christian religion would have a wholesome influence on life in civil society, which in its turn would advance the influence of religion as much as possible.[79]

It is a far cry from men like Lampe and Schortinghuis, who lived in the darkness of a world where Satan raged and sin abounded, and Van den Honert, who stood in the *clair-obscur* of a nostalgic longing for a better more godly past, to people like Stinstra and Van der Meersch, who rejoiced at the mild light of a morning full of promise. And yet, Lampe, Schortinghuis and Van den Honert also looked forward, each in his own way, to the coming day when the Kingdom of God would fill the whole world—while Stinstra and Van der Meersch were also conscious of the distance between this world and the Kingdom of Christ. There is much ambivalence—as there was in the men and women, who are described in the novels of Wolff and Deken. They lived in a

---

[77] See J. van den Berg, "John Wesley's contacten met Nederland", *Nederlands Archief voor Kerkgeschiedenis* 52 (1971), 82.

[78] *Algemeene Bibliotheek* 4 (Amsterdam 1784), 270-2. The review deals with Jerusalem's best-known work *Betrachtungen über die vornehmsten Wahrheiten der Religion*; the first vol. of a Dutch translation had appeared in Amsterdam in 1783.

[79] In his anonymously published work *De Vryheid van Godsdienst in de Burgerlyke Maatschappy betoogd en verdeedigd*, Amsterdam 1774, XXXIV ff.

small rather parochial world, as so many Dutchmen did:[80] it is strange that, apart from the small group of Moravians and a few others especially in the closing years of the century, eighteenth-century Dutch Christianity was almost completely unaware of the missionary dimension of the word "world", once so important in Dutch Protestantism. They lived in a world full of innocuous and dangerous pleasures, as the girl Sara Burgerhart did: religious, but rebelling against the fetters of a narrow orthodoxy and striving for a life of which the end would be free, gay and beautiful.[81] They wished each other a "heaven on earth",[82] but yet they knew that there was more than this present world—the world beyond the grave with which this generation was so much concerned.[83] They were children of their own age, full of a remarkable optimism with regard to this world, but they also knew their Bible and were sensitive to the tensions inherent in the word "world". And in the great spiritual struggles of the next century, which would so thoroughly plough the Dutch soil, it appeared how much the problems the eighteenth century had left behind were still unsolved.[84]

---

[80] For Dutch social life in the eighteenth century see J. Hartog, *De Spectatoriale Geschriften van 1741 tot 1800*, 2nd ed. Utrecht 1890, and L. Knappert, *Het zedelijk leven onzer vaderen in de achttiende eeuw*, Haarlem 1910.

[81] For the meaning of the word "gay" in this context see P.J. Buijnsters, *"Sara Burgerhart" en de ontwikkeling van de Nederlandse roman in de 18de eeuw*, Groningen 1971, 28, n. 70.

[82] E. Bekker and A. Deken, *Historie van Mejuffrouw Sara Burgerhart*, ed. L. Knappert, Amsterdam 1906, II, 269 letter 173.

[83] For the influence of English literature of death and the grave in the Netherlands see P.J. Buijnsters, *Tussen twee werelden*, Assen 1963.

[84] Dr. M. van Beek, Amstelveen (†), author of *An enquiry into Puritan vocabulary*, Groningen 1960, was so kind to advise me with regard to linguistic problems.

CHAPTER FIFTEEN

THE LEIDEN PROFESSORS OF THE SCHULTENS FAMILY AND THEIR CONTACTS WITH BRITISH SCHOLARS[1]

In a letter, sent on 24 April 1773 by the Prime Minister Lord North, then Chancellor of the University of Oxford, to the Vice-Chancellor, we read: "It has been represented to me, that at a meeting of the Vice-Chancellor and Heads of Houses it was proposed to confer the degree of Master of Arts by Diploma on Henry Albert Schultens Esquire Gentleman-Commoner of Wadham College, Grandson of the celebrated Albert Schultens, and son of the present Professor of Arabic and Divinity in the University of Leyden, on account of his great knowledge of the Eastern Languages ...".[2] The three Schultenses, mentioned here, together formed a kind of dynasty of oriental scholars in the University of Leiden; their scholarly activities, well known also outside the boundaries of the Netherlands, span a large part of the eighteenth century.

Albert Schultens, grandfather of the recipient of the Oxford degree, became Professor of Theology at the University of Franeker (Friesland) in 1713.[3] In 1729 he was entrusted with the honourable post of "regent" (director) of the "States College" at Leiden.[4] At the same time he was appointed "Doctor Linguarum Orientalium" (here, "doctor" is equivalent to "lecturer") and "Interpres Legati Warneriani"; the latter function made him the custodian of the collection of oriental manuscripts, bequeathed to the University by a seventeenth century Dutch ambassador in Constantinople.[5] In 1732 he became Professor of Oriental Languages and in 1740 also Professor of Hebrew Antiquities. He was an orientalist of international fame; in a lecture, given in the Schola Linguarum at Oxford in 1748, the newly appointed Regius Professor of Hebrew, Thomas Hunt, remarked that among the foreign scholars who exercised themselves in the

---

[1] This study originally served as a paper at the first Anglo-Dutch church history colloquium, Leiden, 17-20 April 1979. Professor P.S. van Koningsveld and Professor M.J. Mulder †, both of Leiden University gave valuable advice in the fields of Arabic and Hebrew studies.

[2] Oxford University Archives, Register of Convocation 1766-76, N.E.P. *Subtus*, Register B i, 273 (quoted by permission of the Keeper of the University Archives).

[3] A short biography, together with a bibliography of the three Schultenses, by J.C. de Bruïne in *Biografisch Lexicon voor de Geschiedenis van het Nederlandse Protestantisme* I, Kampen 1978, 330-335.

[4] A college for theological students, founded in 1592 by the States of Holland; the teaching, given in the college, was supplementary to university teaching. See G.D.J. Schotel, *De Academie te Leiden*, Haarlem 1875, 23-34.

[5] See G.J. Drewes, "The Legatum Warnerianum of the Lciden University Library", in: *Levinus Warner and his legacy*, Catalogue of the commemorative exhibition ..., Leiden 1970.

palaestra of the study of oriental languages, Schultens could claim the most prominent place.[6]

Hunt's deep respect for Schultens was primarily founded upon his acknowledgement of the latter's ability as an orientalist in general. But besides this, there was a special reason for Hunt's appreciation: the fact that the Leiden orientalist attached supreme importance to the study of Arabic as an aid to the right understanding of the language of the Old Testament; this, according to Hunt, was in line with the views of the seventeenth century English orientalist Edward Pococke. This stand was not generally appreciated, as it implied an infringement of the sacred character of the Hebrew language.[7] In his lecture, Hunt remarked that by some it was considered "infra *Hebraismi* majestatem" to acknowledge any affinity with the Arabic language or to seek help from that side in the study of the Old Testament.[8] Schultens was rather vehemently attacked on this point by some Dutch theologians. It is interesting that he defended his views by indicating that his philological method was the "vetus et regia via" of interpreting the Hebrew text, while on the contrary the "metaphysical" method of his opponents should be characterized as "modern".

It is difficult to establish which way in fact was a *via moderna*. Schultens saw his opponents as people who had exchanged the well-tried road of open-minded philological research for the road of an approach, not based upon linguistic arguments but upon the weak foundation of metaphysical speculations. In the margin of his personal copy of a work of the Leiden professor T.H. van den Honert, who tried to prove that the "sancta Hebraeo-Biblica lingua" by God's special providence had been preserved from all corruption and defects and thus had to be studied without the help of other languages, Schultens more than once jotted down the word "incertum", at one time even the word "absurdum".[9] Already a century earlier, other Leiden orientalists, such as Thomas Erpenius and Louis le Dieu, had stressed the importance of the study of Arabic for the knowledge of Hebrew. Erpenius had contacts with the English orientalist William Bedwell, who was the teacher of Pococke.[10] Seen

[6] T. Hunt, *De Usu Dialectorum Orientalium ac praecipue Arabicae in Hebraico Codice Interpretando*, Lugd. Bat. 1749, 30f.

[7] Thus J.C. de Bruïne, *Herman Venema. Een Nederlandse theoloog in de tijd der Verlichting*, Franeker 1973, 27.

[8] T. Hunt, *De Usu*, 29.

[9] T.H. van den Honert, "Dissertatio Historica de Lingua Primaeva ...", in: *Dissertationes Historicae*, Lugd. Bat. ed. alt 1739, Pars III, 145-281 (Un. Libr. Leiden 1166F9). *Cf.* J. Nat, *De Studie van de Oostersche talen in Nederland in de 18e en 19e eeuw*, Purmerend 1929, 52ff.

[10] See for this the studies of J.C.H. Lebram, "Ein Streit um die hebräische Bibel und die Septuaginta", H.J. de Jonge, "The Study of the New Testament" and J. Brugman, "Arabic Scholarship", in: Th.H. Lunsingh Scheurleer and G.H.M. Posthumus Meyjes, *Leiden University in the Seventeenth Century*, Leiden 1975. The relations between Bedwell and Erpenius are mentioned by G.J. Vossius, *Oratio in Obitum ... Thomae Erpenii*, Lugd. Bat. 1625, 10.

against the background of this tradition, to a certain extent the road of Schultens' opponents was indeed new.[11] When, in this context, Schultens used the word "modern", he made use of a polemical device which was legitimized by his conviction that the method of those who denied the necessity of the study of the "oriental dialects" in connection with the study of the Old Testament was a dangerous innovation. At the same time, however, it is clear that the motives behind this "innovation" were of a conservative nature: Schultens' opponents wanted to maintain at any cost the sanctity of the Hebrew language as a safeguard for the acknowledgement of the divine character of the Old Testament. Over against them, Schultens tried to show that his method by no means detracted from the majesty, authority and dignity of Scripture. In this, he was fundamentally orthodox; yet he was more modern than his opponents when he explicitly rejected metaphysical prejudices in the study of the Hebrew language. Is that language not human, but totally divine?, he asked indignantly; is it the sun of all languages, which makes the power of its own character known to us without the study of dialects, of rabbinic scholarship, of old and new translations? "Nunquam quicquam absurdius in Orbi Erudito auditum ...".[12] His approach towards the study of Hebrew, which to a certain extent was in line with a long tradition of humanistic philological scholarship, at the same time reflected something of the free and open attitude of the age of Enlightenment.

Early in the nineteenth century, a Dutch church historian, who saw Albert Schultens as the "torchbearer" of the interpreters of the Old Testament inside as well as outside the Netherlands, wrote: "Through the light he kindled everything received a different, more radiant aspect".[13] While he was no innovator in the field of theology, he was a man of an independent mind, whose thinking had outgrown the patterns of the seventeenth century division between the followers of Gisbertus Voetius and those of Johannes Coccejus. In this as in other things he followed the steps of his Franeker colleague Campegius Vitringa, of whom he declared in a "Laudatio Funebris": "His friend was Coccejus, his friend was Voetius, but above these his friend was the truth; and thus he did not sufficiently please one of the two parties, but he pleased God

---

[11] In his *Vetus et regia via Hebraizandi, asserta contra novam et metaphysicam hodiernam*, Lugd. Bat. 1738, A. Schultens sought the origins of the new methode in the teaching of the Groningen professor Jacques Gousset, "qui ex Philosophicis et Metaphysicis principiis Linguam Hebraeam, quam a reliquis omnibus Linguis Humanis toto coelo diversam ajebat, illustrandam esse sibi persuaserat", 6. J. Nat, however, points out that though for the Netherlands the ideas which Gousset propagated around 1700 were new, in the first half of the seventeenth century Samuel Bohle in Rostock had defended similar ideas: *op. cit.*, 7, 34-36; *cf.* F. Mühlau, "Albert Schultens und seine Bedeutung for die hebräische Sprachwissenschaft", *Zeitschrift für die gesammte lutherische Theologie und Kirche* 31 (1870), esp. 10f.

[12] *Vetus et regia via*, 22.

[13] A. Ypey, *Geschiedenis van de Kristlyke Kerk in de achttiende eeuw* VIII, Utrecht 1807, 56.

and he pleased those of a quiet and moderate mind, he pleased those who loved the peace of Zion ...".[14] Like other adherents of a moderate, irenic, biblical trend of thinking, Schultens somehow sympathized with contemporary pietist tendencies, while at the same time he objected to the contentious and intolerant spirit of the rigid conservatives. His son could characterize him as a man "du vrai pietisme", a man of an enlightened piety.[15] Schultens' attitude was the same as that of his friend, the medical professor Herman Boerhaave; in the famous funeral oration which he spoke in honour of his friend he pointed out that Boerhaave experienced the bitter dissensions among theologians as contrary to peace with God and men.[16] On his deathbed, Schultens gave his son Jan Jacob his blessing in his fight for tolerance, and he foretold that light would arise out of the darkness of the conflicts which harassed the church of his days.[17]

In almost all respects, the younger Schultens followed the footsteps of his revered, though very exacting, father.[18] He studied at the University of Leiden, where he qualified in the field of oriental studies as well as in theology. In 1744, he became Professor of Oriental Languages at the Academy of Herborn in Germany. Five years later, he returned to Leiden in order to teach oriental languages and theology. The German orientalist Johann Jacob Reiske, in this affair perhaps not quite unbiased, ascribed his nomination to his father's fame and protection: "wer den Pabst zum Freunde hat, kan leicht Cardinal werden".[19] After his father's death in 1750 Schultens was also appointed regent of the States' College and "Interpres Legati Warneriani". His appointment as regent did not come about without some difficulty. The post was considered important. Count Bentinck, "curator" of the University and one of

[14] A. Schultens, *Laudatio Funebris in memoriam ... Campegii Vitringa* ... Franequerac 1732, 82

[15] J.J. Schultens, *Omstandige brief aan den Heere Nikolaas Holtius*, Leiden 1755, LXXIX. Schultens no doubt derived the expression from the title of a work of the French minister in Basle Pierre Roques, *Le Vray Pietisme*, Basle 1731, which was in his possession (see *Bibliotheca Schultensiana* ... 1780, 157). The work of Roques is a defence of a "true pietism", *i.e.* a rational and tolerant form of piety, over against libertinism on the one hand and enthusiasm on the other: see J. van den Berg, "Le Vray piétisme, Die aufgeklärte Frömmigkeit des Basler Pfarrers Pierre Roques", *Zwingliana* 16 (1983) 35-53.

[16] A. Schultens, *Oratio Academica in memoriam Hermanni Boerhaave*, Lugd. Bat. 1738, 16; the passage in question is based on Boerhaave's autobiographical notes, used by Schultens.

[17] J.J. Schultens, *Hoognoodig Addres aan de Hoog Eerw. Fakulteit van Utrecht*. Leiden 1755, 6.

[18] On 18 May 1740 J.J. Reiske wrote to J.P. d'Orville about "the younger Schultens", who was then studying in Leiden under his father's supervision: "Neminem ipsi licet adire, neminem videre, nulli colloqui ... Adeo in arcto tenetur", R. Foerster, *Johann Jacob Reiske's Briefe*, Leipzig 1897, 52.

[19] Reiske went on: "Et bene facit pater filio prospiciens dum vivit, quem forte post ipsius excessum fortuna minus amico vultu respiciat", J.J. Reiske to J.S. Bernard, 4 Sept. 1749, *Briefe*, 350. For the conflict between Reiske and A. Schultens, which forms the background of this remark, see G. Strohmaier, "Johann Jacob Reiske, Byzantinist und Arabist der Aufklärung", *Klio* 58 (1976), 199-209.

the leading Dutch politicians of those days, wrote to his brother in connection with the States' College: "C'est une pépinière pour la République et pour toute l'Europe protestante".[20] For political reasons, Bentinck would have preferred a follower of the conservative seventeenth century theologian Voetius: the Voetian group formed a pillar of support for the Orangist party. Schultens could not be reckoned a Voetian. When in 1748 the post of vice-regent fell vacant, the Leiden philosopher Hemsterhuis had recommended young Schultens to Bentinck because the College needed "un théologien éclairé, modeste et modéré".[21] These qualities no doubt appealed to Bentinck's more enlightened attitude with regard to theological matters; moreover, Hemsterhuis had made him acquainted with the details of the discussion about the use of Arabic in the interpretation of the Hebrew text, which Bentinck thought highly interesting: "la matière est très curieuse et intéressante".[22] In 1748, young Schultens was not appointed, but in 1750 the fact that he continued the line of his father[23] settled the matter in his favour.[24]

During the first period of his professorship, Schultens became involved in the conflict around a former pupil of the University of Leiden, Antonius van der Os, who because of his enlightened views was ultimately deposed from his ministry in the Reformed Church.[25] According to Schultens, who as a champion of the cause of toleration defended the accused minister, there was a parallel between an action against a pietist author which took place some years earlier, and this new action against a more enlightened theologian: in both cases, the doctrine of the Holy Spirit was condemned; in 1745 as enthusiasm, in 1755 as Pelagianism or Remonstrantism.[26] Like his father, Schultens sympathized with certain aspects of the Pietist movement; at the same time, many of his utterances reveal an undeniable affinity with more enlightened ideas. He clearly saw the approach of new times; two years before his death, in 1776, he wrote to a friend: "The times will come, when *Arianism* and *Unitarianism* in our own Netherlands will become as much questions à la mode as has happened or still happens in England, Switzerland and Germany. Even rigid Scot-

---

[20] Willem Bentinck to Charles Bentinck, 12 Febr. 1750: C. Gerretson and P. Geyl, *Briefwisseling en aantekeningen van Willem Bentinck* II, 's-Gravenhage 1976, 358.

[21] F. Hemsterbuis to Willem Bentinck, 9 April 1748: *Briefwisseling* I, 428.

[22] *Briefwisseling* II, 357.

[23] For A. Schultens' relations with Bentinck, see *e.g.* his letter to Bentinck of 20 June 1748, in which he announced his intention to dedicate to him one of his works: "Mon livre aussi, tout glorieux de paraitre sous vos Auspices, me commande, de le recommander dans votre protection ...," Br. Libr. Add. Mss. Fr. Eg. 1745, f. 437.

[24] Bentinck's main consideration in this affair was "celle de retrancher la cagoterie et la superstition de l'étude des langues orientales"; it is interesting to see that he called the system of A. Schultens' opponents "l'ancien système": *Briefwisseling* II, *loc. cit.*

[25] For Schultens' stance in this conflict, see J. van den Berg, *Een Leids pleidooi voor verdraagzaamheid*, Leiden 1976.

[26] J.J. Schultens to A. van der Os, 5 May 1755, Un.Libr.Leiden MS BPL AD 3.

land has had to yield to the pressure of the break-through of Arian tendencies".[27] From this utterance we should not deduce that Schultens rejoiced in this development as such,[28] but he saw it as an inevitable result of the way the conservatives defended the old system. He himself was neither a conservative nor a radical, but a typical representative of an irenic and biblical trend in theology. In this, he stood near to Philip Doddridge, in whose works he recognized various traits of the "evangelical mind".[29]

No doubt, his involvement in ecclesiastical conflicts and theological discussions did not benefit his oriental studies. In 1754, at the height of the conflict we mentioned above, the Scotsman Robert Pollock wrote to Schultens that his opponents would be easily overcome "non scriptis et argumentis ... sed silentio et contemptu".[30] If Schultens had listened to this rather worldly-wise advice, he could have spent more time on his oriental studies. But that was not his way: in the course of the following year he published a work of not less than 972 pages on this conflict.[31] In practice, with Schultens the "connubium sapientiae Theologicae et scientiae philologicae", so highly praised in his Leiden inaugural oration,[32] was not always completely harmonious.

In spite of this, the fame of his erudition as an orientalist even spread outside the boundaries of the Netherlands; moreover, many of his pupils gratefully remembered his excellent gifts as a teacher. He left a number of studies on oriental topics in manuscript; among them materials for an Arabic lexicon, which was never finished.[33] Though for later generations he remained somewhat in the shadow of his father, according to contemporary opinion he was "the famous Schultens who inherited his father's ability and renown".[34] His son Hendrik Albert even declared that Jan Jacob's knowledge of Arabic literature surpassed that of Albert Schultens.[35]

---

[27] J.J. Schultens to R.M. van Goens, 25 March 1776, *Brieven aan R.M. van Goens* II, Utrecht 1886, 28.

[28] As J. Wille wrongly supposes in his *De literator R.M. van Goens en zijn kring* I, Zutphen 1937, 319.

[29] J.J. Schultens, *Nieuwjaarsgift, aan twee Heeren Voorstanderen der Formulieren*, Leiden 1754, 73. On 12 Dec. 1749 James Robertson, then at Lciden, wrote to Doddridge that "the Messrs. Schultcns, father and son ... have expressed a very great and sincere regard for the Reverend Dr. Doddridge", J.D. Humphreys (cd.), *The Correspondence and Diary of Philip Doddridge D.D.* V, London 1831, 145.

[30] R. Pollock to J.J. Schultens, 23 July 1754, MS BPL 245 XII.

[31] J.J. Schultens, *Uitvoerige Waarschuuwing op verscheide stukken der Kategismus Verklaaringe van ... Alexander Comrie*, Leiden 1755.

[32] J.J. Schultens, *Oratio inauguralis de fructibus in theologiam redundantibus ex penitiore linguarum orientalium cognitione*, Lugd. Bat. 1749, 27

[33] J. Nat, *Oostersche talen*, 68.

[34] Thus the German scholar Johann Beckmann in the journal of his travels through the Netherlands (1762), publ. by G.H. Kernkamp, *Bijdragen en Mededeelingen van het Historisch Genootschap* XXXIII (1912), 380.

[35] J. Kantelaar. *Lofreden op Hendrik Albert Schultens*, Amsterdam 1794, 74.

Hendrik Albert Schultens was reared as the crown-prince of the dynasty. While still a youth of about 15 years he received private tuition from one of his father's pupils, Everard Scheidius. In the letter to J.J. Schultens in which he applied for the post of tutor, Scheidius described his future pupil as "that gentleman who seems to have been born to sustain the glory of his grandfather and his father".[36] In 1765, Hendrik Albert followed his tutor when Scheidius became Professor of Oriental Languages in the University of Harderwijk in Gelderland. It must have been a difficult moment for Jan Jacob Schultens when he learned from Scheidius that his son "had fallen madly in love with the study of Medicine".[37] Soon, however, Hendrik Albert returned to what was, if not his first love, then still his first ambition: the study of oriental languages, which after his stay in Harderwijk he pursued in Leiden under his father's supervision.

In 1772 he went over to England, where he stayed in London, in Cambridge and for a longer time in Oxford. After his return he was nominated Professor of Oriental Languages and Hebrew Antiquities at the Amsterdam Athenaeum, where his lectures attracted much attention, not only because of their elegant style and delivery, but most of all because of their contents: he combined the philological, literary and philosophical aspects of his discipline in a way which fascinated his hearers. It is told that his pupils eagerly looked forward to his lectures as to a joyful feast.[38] For a broader public, he gave evening lectures in Dutch on oriental subjects, which were indeed popular in the best sense of the word. As an example may serve a passage from a dialogue between an Arab and an Englishman, taken from his lecture on blood-feud, and dealing with Pococke's Arabic translation of Grotius' *De Veritate Religionis Christianae* and of the *Book of Common Prayer*. In this dialogue, Schultens makes Ibrahim remark with regard to Pococke: "Twice he came over to us, and he applied himself so much to our language, that Phatallah, a well-known Mufti of Aleppo, on his departure gave him the following testimony: 'Go, Pococki! wherever you may come in the world, be assured that you speak Arabic as well as the Mufti of Aleppo'. Once returned to his fatherland, he [Pococke] wanted to win us over to his faith, and sent us the book of Hugo, with the prayers which are read in the mosques of England, both in Arabic".[39]

In 1778, he succeeded his beloved father as Professor of Oriental Languages and of Hebrew Antiquities and as "Interpres Legati Warneriani". He was not a theologian in the strict sense, and unlike his father he refrained from partici-

[36] E. Scheidius to J.J. Schultens, 30 April 1763, MS BPL 245 XII.
[37] E. Scheidius to J.J. Schultens, 11 March 1767, MS BPL 245 XII.
[38] J. Kantelaar, *Lofreden*, 26.
[39] H.A. Schultens, *Drie Redevoeringen*, Leeuwarden 1845, 56.

pation in theological and ecclesiastical disputes.[40] In his oriental studies, he followed in many respects the example of his father and grandfather. He shared their passion for these studies, and he fundamentally agreed with the method of explaining the Hebrew text of the Old Testament from its Arabic background. "To him remained the honour", said one of his pupils, "of making more generally useful his grandfather's discoveries, and of bringing over the right explanation of the sacred scriptures from the schools of the learned ... to the general use of all judicious readers in our country".[41]

On some points, however, he went further than his father and his grandfather. While they had been averse from the application of the critical method to the Old Testament text, Hendrik Albert took a different stand. In 1772 he corresponded about this matter with his friend Georgius Colonius, who advised him to listen more to the voice of reason than to that of authority, even the authority of his father and grandfather. In his answer Schultens declared that, though at the moment he still hesitated, yet he was inclined to accept textual criticism as an inevitable consequence of the rejection of a superstitious attitude towards the Hebrew text.[42] To James Robertson of Edinburgh he confessed he was not a strong believer in the integrity of the text.[43] Later, he wrote to the Glasgow scholar Robert Findlay: "Equidem, etsi ALBERTI SCHULTENSII nepos, a Critica me non alienum esse profiteor ..." Again, he averred that ultimately this stand was a result of the main thesis of his grandfather, who had rejected the ridiculous opinion of the sanctity of the Hebrew language.[44] He did not, however, approve of the temerity of some very radical critics, but tried to keep a middle way, in harmony with his character and his scholarly approach.

---

[40] While with his father and his grandfather their passion for theology sometimes overshadowed their orientalist interests, Hendrik Albert tried to keep both elements in a harmonious balance. In the "Dedicatio" of his *Anthologia Sententiarum Arabicarum cum Scholiis Zamachsjarii*, Lugd. Bat. 1772, f.** 1[ro,vo], he wrote: "Ex quo tempore de amplectendo studiorum genere serio cogitare coepi, literarum Orientalium praestantia, quae, tum in Sacra Seriptura rectius interpretanda, tum in omni liberaliore doctrina illustranda et amplificanda cernitur, ita animum affecit, ut regia, quae ad illarum scientiam ferret, via studio nunquam intermisso contendendum esse statuerem".

[41] J. Kantelaar, *Lofreden*, 32.

[42] G. Colonius to H.A. Schultens, 7 July 1772; H.A. Schultens to G. Colonius, undated, MS BPL 245 XIII. See for H.A. Schultens and biblical criticism also A. de Groot, *Leven en arbeid van J.H. van der Palm*, Wageningen 1960, 179.

[43] "To say the truth I am not a very strong believer of this integrity, and can't think but there must be several places, which, as they can't be explained neither by the help of dialects, nor versions, or any other of those means, we may safely suppose to be corrupted, tho'at the same time I know how much care and prudence there be required in not going too far, nor, indulging the pleasure of criticism too much", H.A. Schultens to J. Robertson, 29 May 1773, MS BPL 245 XIII.

[44] J. Kantelaar, *op. cit.*, 80; the letter from H.A. Schultens to R. Findlay, quoted by Kantelaar, probably should be dated 29 Dec. 1789.

Hendrik Albert Schultens has been called "a real representative of the Enlightenment in this country"; with equal right he can be characterized as "a connecting link between Enlightenment and Romanticism".[45] He admired Pope's *Essay on Man*,[46] he stimulated the translation into Dutch of Herder's *Vom Geiste der ebräischen Poesie*.[47] His fine literary taste enabled him to transcend the boundaries of a purely philological approach and to consider the objects of his studies also as works of art. His translation of Job, posthumously published, gives ample evidence of the aesthetic qualities of his scholarly work. At the same time, his approach towards the problems concerning the date of the first chapters and part of the last chapter of Job offers an interesting example of his enlightened views. Together with his grandfather, who had written a large commentary on Job,[48] he regarded these chapters as very late, as contrasted with the poetical part of the book. But while Albert Schultens' view was founded exclusively upon stylistic arguments, his grandson saw an additional argument for the post-exilic date of the first chapters in the fact that here Satan is mentioned, "which being does not occur in the books written before the Babylonian captivity".[49]

In respect of religion, according to those who knew him well he was a man of sincere piety, though not orthodox in the traditional sense. A German contemporary wrote that Schultens, while unshakable in his moral principles, was more liberal with regard to doctrine than many of his compatriots would have wished.[50] It seems that because of this liberal attitude he was sometimes attacked from the orthodox side; after his death, one of his pupils wrote about "the generation of vipers" which tried to cast suspicion on his religious sentiments.[51] Though living in politically turbulent times, he was not active in the field of politics, and while we may assume that he stood nearer to the "patriot" group, the party which stood for the ideals of liberty and of political reform, than to the more conservative Orangists, he seems to have been respected by both parties.[52] He died in 1793 at the age of 44, after a period of years of weak

[45] J. Nat, *Oostersche talen*, 94; J.C. de Bruïne, *BLGNP* I, 334. F. Schröder sees him as a figure who keeps the balance between an eighteenth century universalist attitude and a more romantic approach which stressed the specific character of peoples and languages, J. Brugman and F. Schröder, *Arabic Studies in the Netherlands*, Leiden 1979, 29.

[46] "He believed, with his beloved Pope, that the most worthy object of the study of mankind is man", J. Kantelaar, *Lofreden*, 43.

[47] See P.J. Buijnsters, *Tussen twee werelden*, Assen 1963, 8.

[48] A. Schultens, *Liber Jobi cum nova versione* ... I-II, Lugd. Bat. 1737. In the "Praefatio", Schultens strongly stresses the Arabic background of the book of Job.

[49] Hendrik Albert Schultens, *Het boek Job, uit het Hebreeuwsch vertaald, met aanmerkingen* (uitg. en voltooid door H. Muntinghe), Amsterdam 1794, XIX.

[50] F.Th.Rink (=Rinck), *Heinrich Albert Schultens*, Riga 1794, 39.

[51] J. Kantelaar, *Lofreden*, 63.

[52] Some of his pupils, such as J. Kantelaar and J.H. van der Palm, were outspoken patriots; so

health; this explains why the number of publications of this eminent scholar remained comparatively small.

Quite definitely, there existed a sense of continuity within the "gens Schultensia". If there were differences in outlook and opinion between the successive members of the Schultens family, they partly resulted from differences in character and personal circumstances, partly also from a natural progression in thought and approach within the compass of three generations. No doubt with Albert Schultens we find more of the Pietist spirit, with his grandson more of the Enlightenment mind, while we receive the impression that Jan Jacob moved from a more traditional to a more critical attitude. However this may be, all of them were men of an open and independent mind, who stood for tolerance and moderation; an according to the testimonies of those who knew them personally, all of them were men of a mild and undogmatic piety.

There were many contacts between the members of the Schultens family and a number of British scholars. Of these contacts, the traces are to be found in that part of the correspondence of Jan Jacob and Hendrik Albert which, together with the latter's journal of his stay in England, has been preserved in the archives of Leiden University Library. When we investigate these contacts, read the correspondence which was conducted across the North Sea and follow Hendrik Albert on his English journey, certain questions arise. How far does our knowledge of these contacts confirm and how far does it correct the image of the Schultens family we tried to give on the ground of the Dutch materials, and—more broadly—how far do the contacts between eighteenth century scholars in Britain and the Netherlands reflect something of the spirit we thought we recognized with the Schultens family, that of a moderate and religious form of enlightened thinking?

On Albert Schultens' contacts with Britain we can be brief. He never visited England or Scotland, and we have no proof of any correspondence with British scholars. His publications, however, carried his fame to Britain; Hunt was not the only one who was deeply impressed by Schultens' scholarship in the field of oriental studies.[53] No doubt, the way Hendrik Albert Schultens was received in English orientalist circles was at least partly due to the lustre of his grandfather's name. Albert Schultens had some British students: Robert Pollock,

was his widow, Catharina Elisabeth de Sitter, see H.T. Colenbrander, *Gedenkstukken der Algemeene Geschiedenis van Nederland* I (RGP I). 's-Gravenhage 1905, 399.

[53] Just after the death of Albert Schultens, one of his pupils, Johannes Guilelmus Kals, visited England. He was received by Hunt; in a letter of recommendation for Kals (quoted by Kals in his *Disquisitio Philologica*, 1753) Hunt mentioned him as "for some years scholar, and afterwards assistant to the famous Mr. Schultens ..." (communication by Prof. J.M. van der Linde †, Utrecht University, who later published a study on Kals: *Jan Willem Kals: leraar der Hervormden en advocaat van indiaan en neger*, Kampen 1987, see esp. 102f.).

later Professor of Divinity at Marischal College, Aberdeen;[54] the later Glasgow Professor of Divinity Robert Findlay, who remembered his teacher as a man "rarae tum probitatis, tum eruditionis";[55] James Robertson, later Professor of Hebrew at the University of Edinburgh, who in similar vein characterized Schultens as "a Gentleman and Scholar ... a Man of extraordinary abilities and profound erudition";[56] furthermore, Edward Wortley Montagu, a wellborn Englishman who, after an extraordinarily wild period, was "packed off" to the continent by his parents;[57] after having lived at Ysselstein near Utrecht, in 1741 he enrolled at the University of Leiden as "cultor Linguarum orientalium".[58]

Though, like his father, Jan Jacob Schultens never went over to England, he was much interested in English theology and English oriental studies. His "bibliotheca locupletissima"[59] (the auction catalogue has more than 600 pages) contained quite a number of English works, among them many by Doddridge. He carried on a rather irregular correspondence with British friends with whom he was acquainted since their studies together in Leiden, and with other British scholars. One of his correspondents was James Robertson, who in the summer of 1750 sent him the greetings of Doddridge, together with some information about a proposed German translation of Doddridge's *The Rise and Progress of Religion in the Soul*.[60] In 1753 Robertson visited his friend in Leiden; Schultens told Robertson about his plan to translate some of Doddridge's sermons.[61] About ten years later, he sent Schultens a letter in which he mentioned the sending of some of Doddridge's works, accompanied by an English grammar for Hendrik Albert; he also announced his intention to visit Leiden again.[62] With Robert Pollock, whose neglected advice we remember, he corresponded on the ecclesiastical troubles of those days, which, so Pollock thought, were caused by some furious zealots; in Britain, the common warfare against the Deists had silenced all these small questions. Pollock himself was an admirer of Leighton, "viri vere pacifici"; he

---

[54] For Pollock, see Hew Scott, *Fasti Ecclesiae Scoticanae* VII (1928), 359.

[55] R. Findlay to J.J. Schultens, 1 Febr. 1752, MS BPL 245 XII. For Findlay, see *DNB* XIX, 24.

[56] J. Robertson to H.A. Schultens, 26 April 1773, MS BPL 245 XIII. For Robertson, see *DNB* XLVIII, 409.

[57] *DNB* XXXVIII, 238,

[58] For Montagu's contacts with Holland, see also J. Curling, *Edward Wortley Montagu 1713-1776*, London etc. 1954, and R. Halsband (ed.), *The Complete Letters of Lady Mary Montagu* II (1721-1751), Oxford 1966. Apparently, when in Holland he gave the impression of being an "enthusiast"; his mother wrote to her husband (6 May 1742: *Letters* II, 277) she was convinced "that his pretended Enthusiasm is only to cheat those that can be impos'd on by it".

[59] Thus William Jones to H.A. Schultens, 22 May 1781, G. Cannon(ed.), *The Letters of Sir William Jones* II, Oxford 1970, 470.

[60] J. Robertson to J.J. Schultens, 15 July 1750, MS BPL 245 XII.

[61] J.J. Schultens, *Nieuwjaarsgift*, 78.

[62] J. Robertson to J.J. Schultens, 4 June 1764, MS BPL 245 XII.

sent a copy of Leighton's sermons to Schultens as a present.[63] Another former Leiden friend, Robert Findlay, sent him a copy of his *Two Letters to Dr. Kennicott of Oxford* in vindication of the Jews,[64] written against Kennicott's critical method. Schultens would have agreed with Findlay: his views of the integrity of the Hebrew text were contrary to those of Kennicott, and it seems he did not value him highly as a Hebraist. Still, there were some friendly contacts between the two scholars: on Kennicott's request, Schultens sent him some Hebrew manuscripts which Kennicott needed for his edition of the Hebrew Bible.[65]

A special case was that of Montagu. In the spring of 1761, Montagu was again in Leiden, where he sought contact with Jan Jacob Schultens, the son of his former teacher. From the correspondence which ensued we may deduce that at that time Montagu was engaged in the trade in oriental manuscripts. Schultens was a collector of manuscripts and as such of course interested, but apparently he had his doubts with regard to Montagu's trustworthiness. He tried to get some information from one of his former pupils, Louis de la Chaumette, a minister of the French Church at London. De la Chaumette replied in a large and charming letter, in which he wrote that according to his informations Montagu, "revenu de quelques folies de jeunesse ... menoit une vie aussi retirée que sage, sobre, réglée". In a postscript, however, he added: "Je ne suis pas fait sûr de ce qui regarde Mr. Montaigu. Rien n'est plus obscure que son histoire".[66] A letter, written by Montagu to Schultens shortly after his return to London, is also rather obscure. Montagu wrote about the dispatch of a chest of books for Schultens, but also about the sending of a Persian letter, which would bring to Schultens much profit if he could translate it and return it to Montagu as soon as possible; the whole affair would have to be transacted in deep secrecy. In a second letter, in which he announced a new visit to Leiden "pour y étudier sous vos auspices", he wrote that he worried about the fact that the manuscript had not yet been returned.[67] Some years later, Montagu wrote to Schultens from Venice and from Leghorn about the sale of the books he had left at Leiden and about the purchase of oriental manuscripts, and also about his adventures in Arabia; we do not know whether Schultens was aware of the fact that at that time Montagu had gone over to Islam.[68]

---

[63] R. Pollock to J.J. Schultens, 23 July 1754, MS BPL 245 XII.

[64] See the accompanying letter, R. Findlay to J.J. Schultens, 7 July 1762, MS BPL 245 XII.

[65] For Schultens' judgment of Kennicott, see Beckmann's Journal, *op. cit.*, 382; for the sending of the MSS, B. Kennicott to J.J. Schultens, 24 June 1763; 9 April 1764, MS BPL 245 XII.

[66] L. de la Chaumette to J.J. Schultens, 1 May 1761, MS BPL 245 XII. His mother remarked with regard to her son's character: "I expect nothing from him but going from one Species of Folly to another", *Letters* II, 249.

[67] E.W. Montagu to J.J. Schultens, 19 May 1761; 2 June 1761, MS BPL 245 XII.

[68] E.W. Montagu to J.J. Schultens, 5 Sept. 1765; 13 Oct. 1765, both from Venice; 6 Aug. 1766, from Leghorn. MS BPL 245 XII.

Some people turned to Schultens for help or advice; as did Lawrence Holden, a dissenting minister, suspected of Unitarian tendencies, who had visited Schultens in Leiden and asked for his help in the preparation of a paraphrase of some Old Testament books.[69] A former Swiss pupil, J.H. Ziegler, shared with Schultens his foreign experiences in an interesting letter, written from Paris in 1760. Ziegler had been to England, where "ceux qui voyagent pour l'amour des sciences et des arts, trouvent toujours de quoi satisfaire leur curiosité". In London, he saw the oriental manuscripts in the British Museum. A short visit to Oxford did not deeply impress him; about the professors and the students he wrote: "Il me semble que presque tous ensemble se reposent pendant la belle saison, et en hiver ils ne font rien". Back in London, he was introduced to the Archbishop of Canterbury, Thomas Secker, on the day of the death of King George II, of which at the time the Archbishop was still ignorant. Secker, who had studied medicine at Leiden University and who afterwards had acquired some fame as a Hebraist,[70] was much interested as well in Holland as in Switzerland. It must have flattered Schultens, when he read in his pupil's letter: "J'ai l'honneur de vous assurer, que l'Archeveque, quoique ignorant, comme il dit, dans l'Arabe, revere le nom de Schultens".[71]

Hendrik Albert Schultens went to England at his father's instigation. To his father's friend James Robertson he wrote in 1773; "... my father has sent me to England, chiefly to visit the treasures of the Bodl. Library and to make use of some curious MSS. wanting in our's; Amongst which I reckon that of the translation of Meidani's proverbs by the celebrated Dr. Pocock".[72] From that time onward, Al Maidani would play a large, if not a dominant part in Schultens' life as a scholar.[73] In the summer before his departure, he worked hard on the edition of another collection of Arab proverbs, the "Elnawabig", which was published in 1772;[74] to a friend he wrote he hoped it would make him more agreeable to Kennicott than if he came with empty hands.[75]

On 12 September 1772, he sailed from Hellevoetsluis.[76] First of all he went

---

[69] L. Holden to J.J. Schultens, 13 April 1761, MS BPL 245 XII. For Holden, see *DNB* XXVII, 120.

[70] See E. Carpenter, *Cantuar. The Archbishops in their Office*, London 1971, 250.

[71] J.H. Ziegler to J.J. Schultens, 19 Nov. 1760, MS BPL 245 XII.

[72] H.A. Schultens to J. Robertson, 29 March 1773, MS BPL 245 XII.

[73] Kantelaar wrote that Schultens "before all things deplored the fate of MEIDANI, whose excellent collection of more than 6000 proverbs in the last century in Edward Pococke seemed to find an able editor and translator, but who, first because of the English troubles of those times, and later because of the death of that great man, was deprived of that felicity", *op. cit.*, 19. For Al Maidani see: R.A. Nicholson, *A Literary History of the Arabs*, Cambridge 1930 (reprint 1966), 31.

[74] "Elnawabig" was published as *Anthologia Sententiarum Arabicarum;* see for full title etc. note 40.

[75] H.A. Schultens to G. Colonius (see note 42).

[76] If not indicated otherwise, the communications with regard to his stay in England are derived

to London, where Mr. and Mrs. H. Goodricke acted as his hosts. Henry Goodricke, the only son of the British ambassador in Sweden, was a lawyer who for a long period lived in the Netherlands, where he pleaded for a comparatively large measure of doctrinal freedom within the church.[77] His championship of the cause of toleration brought him into friendly relations with Jan Jacob Schultens.[78] The Goodrickes introduced Hendrik Albert to a number of people. Matthew Maty, of Dutch descent,[79] secretary of the Royal Society, showed him the treasures of the British Museum. De la Chaumette introduced him to a group of French ministers in London. A former pupil of his grandfather, Karl Gottfried Woide, of Polish Unitarian background,[80] no doubt helped him to find his way in the small world of British orientalists. He also made his acquaintance with William (later: Sir William) Jones, who had already written some oriental studies and now applied himself to the study of law.[81] Apparently, from the beginning the two young men got on very well; Jones described Schultens as "a young and agreeable man", a description which is similar to that which about the same time Woide gave of Jones.[82] A lasting friendship would connect them.

On the first Sunday of his stay in London Hendrik Albert attended a Dutch service "after the episcopal manner" in the chapel of St. James's Palace, with only four people present.[83] He more enjoyed the English evening service in the Savoy, where he was deeply impressed by the psalms, "sung in chorus". Next Sunday, he attended a service in Westminster Abbey, where again the music was "very beautiful". Being a lover of music[84] he much liked the musical

from his travelling journal: "Dagboek van Hendrik Albert Schultens nopens zijn verblijf in Engeland", MS BPL 245 VIII.

77 See J. van den Berg, "Tussen ideaal en realiteit. De Engelse jurist Goodricke in discussie met de Nederlandse theologen Bonnet en van der Kemp ...", *Gereformeerd Theologisch Tijdschrift* 81 (1981), 217-250.

78 This appears from the postscripts Goodricke added to some letters which Hendrik Albert wrote to his father from London.

79 For Maty, see *DNB* XXXVII, 76-79. He was a son of the theologian Paulus Mat(t)y, who as a "catechist" of the Walloon Church at The Hague was accused of heretical views and who subsequently went over to the Remonstrants: *Nieuw Nederlandsch Biografisch Woordenboek* X, c. 596f.; A.Ypey and I.J. Dermout, *Geschiedenis van de Nederlandsche Hervormde Kerk* III, Breda 1824, 210-215.

80 For Woide, see *DNB* LXII, 289f.

81 For Jones, see *DNB* XXX, 174-177; furthermore G. Cannon, *Letters*, I-II (with extensive bibliography).

82 Woide wrote to J.D. Michaelis on 13 Oct. 1774: "Herr Jones ist noch jung, leutselig und von vielen Gaben". *Litterarischer Briefwechsel von Johann David Michaelis* III, Leipzig 1796, 104.

83 For the services in the Dutch Chapel Royal, St. James's, held between 1689 and 1809, see J.S. Burn, *The History of the French, Walloon, Dutch and other Protestant Refugees settled in England* ..., London 1846, 232f.; cf. what Woide writes about these services in his letters to Michaelis of 21 April 1772 and 7 March 1777: *op. cit.*, 45, 135.

84 He could not appreciate, however, the "Beggar's Opera", to which the Goodrickes took him out; he thought it vulgar, though Maty tried to convince him of the contrary.

aspects of Anglican worship, so different from the bare form of worship in which he had been reared.

His first impressions of England were very favourable: to his father he wrote that the town, the country, the people, food and drink, in short everything particularly pleased him.[85] In London he only stayed for a few weeks; on the 10th of October he went to Oxford, provided with letters of recommendation to the leading Oxford orientalists. He took up his residence at the Angel Inn and visited a number of people. Joannes Uri, a Hungarian who had studied under his father, could render him valuable help, because he was engaged in the task of preparing a catalogue of the oriental manuscripts in the Bodleian Library, which according to a letter to J.J. Schultens he found "in a most confused and inordinate state".[86] Thomas Hunt, at an advanced age—Hendrik Albert thought him "extra venerable"—was much interested in the son and grandson of those Dutch orientalists he so sincerely admired.[87] Joseph White, only a little older than Hendrik Albert, would become his most intimate English friend.[88] At a later stage, he also visited Kennicott and Lowth. Kennicott, whom he respected more deeply as a scholar than his father had done,[89] received him very kindly and showed him various manuscripts; Hendrik Albert described him as "a right cheerful fellow, looking thick and fat and healthy". Of Robert Lowth, Bishop of Oxford, whom Schultens visited in Cuddesdon, we receive a slightly different description: "He is an extraordinarily kind and polite man, and he received us with extreme courtesy".

In the mean time, Schultens had been admitted to the Bodleian Library (he thought it was a solemn ceremony) and had become a member of Wadham College as a gentleman-commoner. On 27th October he appeared before the Vice-chancellor in order to be matriculated in the University. He signed the

---

[85] H.A. Schultens to J.J. Schultens, 22 Sept. 1772, MS BPL 245 VIII.

[86] J. Uri to J.J. Schultens, 8 Dec. 1766, MS BPL 245 XII: "... in Bibliothecam Bodl. ad inordinatissimum et confusissimum Manuscriptorum Orientalium statum lustrandum intravi ..."; in the same letter he speaks about the kind intervention of the Archbishop (Secker) on his behalf when the Harwich customs had seized his luggage. For Uri see *DNB* LVIII, 42; Christopher Wordsworth, *Scholae Academicae*. Some account of the Studies at the English Universities in the Eighteenth Century, Cambridge 1910 (first ed. 1877), 170.

[87] For Hunt, see *DNB* XXVIII, 279 I.; for Hendrik Albert's description of Hunt his letter of 31 Oct. 1772, MS BPL 245 VIII.

[88] For White, see *DNB* LXI, 62f., C. Wordsworth, *loc. cit.*

[89] For Kennicott, see *DNB* XXXI, 10 I; furthermore William McKane, "Benjamin Kennicott: An Eighteenth Century Researcher", *Journal of Theological Studies* NS 28 (1977), 445-464. In the *Bibliotheca Critica* 1 (1779), 79-115, appeared a review of Kennicott's *Vetus Testamentum Hebraicum*, by J. Kantelaar ascribed to H.A. Schultens, who was a regular contributor to the *B.C.* The review, though not uncritical, in general was appreciative: Kennicott's "opera ab omnibus grate agnoscenda, et omni laude celebranda est". C. Wordsworth observes in a passage, devoted to the Dutch philologist Daniel Wyttenbach and his *Bibliotheca Critica*: "... it is most instructive to observe the lively interest taken in Holland both in English Philology and philologers contrasted with some jealousy of the French Academy", *Scholae*, 96.

XXXIX Articles. Hunt had kindly asked him whether he would not have objections against subscription, but Schultens, who had read the Articles, replied he had found nothing in them which was contrary to the doctrine of the Dutch Church in which he had made his "confession of faith".

Hendrik Albert was quite happy with his stay in College, where he led a quiet and rather retired life. He regularly took part in College prayers, especially on Saturdays and Sundays; the communion service he thought dignified, though as a thorough Protestant he was amazed at the custom not to leave any bread or wine. Sometimes he was impressed, sometimes also amused, by University and College ceremonies. The ceremony of the election or continuation of the Fellows of Wadham College, which took place on 5 December, he thought "one of the most ridiculous things one can imagine, but here in general the ancient landmarks are not easily removed". During the day, he worked in the Bodleian, though in the cold season this created some problems: "In this town of ceremonies it is not allowed to sit without a gown in the Library, nor to put on a coat under the gown; but I can sit, in a coat, in the room of the professor of astronomy ...".[90] The main task he had set himself was the work on Maidani's proverbs; he corrected Pococke's translation and intended to have a specimen of a Maidani edition printed in England.

In January and February, young Schultens stayed again with the Goodrickes in London: the cold made it impossible to work in the Bodleian. He made the acquaintance of a number of leading Dissenters, among whom we mention Edward Harwood, a personal friend of the Goodrickes; in Schultens' opinion an extremely kind man, experienced in theology and with a broad erudition. Harwood was considered a semi-Arian; on the occasion of the appearance of his edition of the Greek New Testament, J.J. Schultens wrote to a friend: "How loudly our zealots will cry, when it becomes known that Harwood's Greek Testament comes into the hands of our students".[91] One gets the impression that Hendrik Albert particularly enjoyed the kind of sermons preached in enlightened dissenting circles. Once he heard a Methodist sermon, which reminded him of the type of preaching one could hear in Dutch pietist circles; it was his only acquaintance with Methodism.[92]

From London he went to Cambridge, where he stayed from 9 till 24 March. Of course he compared Cambridge with Oxford: the view from the backs "is enchantingly beautiful and surpasses any view in Oxford. But that is all ..." He was kindly received by the vice-chancellor, and more than once he met the four Cambridge orientalists: William Craven, Samuel Ogden, Samuel Hallifax and

---

[90] H.A. Schultens to J.J. Schultens, 31 Oct. 1772, MS BPL 245 VIII.

[91] J.J. Schultens to R.M. van Goens, 25 March 1776, *Brieven aan R.M. van Goens*, 27. For Harwood, see *DNB* XXV, 102.

[92] Apart from a short visit to a small Methodist meeting-house in Oxford, where the atmosphere apparently was not quite to his taste.

John Jebb.[93] At that time, the conflict between Hallifax and Jebb was at its height, and Schultens felt the tension, when he noticed they avoided meeting in the same room. Hallifax spoke in a rather bitter way about Jebb, whom he considered "quite a Socinian". No doubt the underlying reason for his anger was, that Mrs. Ann Jebb as "Priscilla" had written some articles in defence of the idea of toleration which contained an attack on Hallifax; according to Paley, the Lord had sold Sisera into the hand of a woman.[94] Ogden was considered by Schultens as the "chief" of the group; he was not as redoubtable as he seemed to be at first sight. The conversation between Hallifax, Craven and Ogden Hendrik Albert thought rather singular: "it seemed strange to me to hear three orientalists ... ridicule those languages over and over again ... Ars non habet osores nisi ignorantes". On closer acquaintance, however, he received a better impression, especially of Craven as an Arabic scholar. Much of his time he spent in the University Library, which rather disappointed him with regard to oriental manuscripts; to his father he wrote: "In the Library I did not find anything of the least interest which we do not possess ourselves". The detection of a number of discrepancies between the written and the printed catalogues of the oriental manuscripts, which made it clear how much he was an expert in this field, led to an offer, made to him by the Regius Professor of Divinity Richard Watson (later Bishop of Llandaff) to be engaged by the University for the composition of a new catalogue. This offer he declined "for more than one reason", though he gave some help by filling in the missing or incomplete titles of 50 to 60 manuscripts.[95] After a short stay in London, he returned to Oxford. The plan of a visit to Edinburgh had to be abandoned, "as some circumstances don't allow me to be abroad so long as I thought", he wrote to James Robertson.[96]

From Hendrik Albert's correspondence it becomes clear that at one time he had hoped to be able to find a post in England. Soon, however, he came to understand that this would be impossible in Oxford or Cambridge. Goodricke thought there might be a possibility if he became a "clergyman", but Hendrik Albert thought it wrong to take this step for the sake of material gain; his father praised him for his magnanimous attitude in this matter.[97] "The more I have a

---

[93] For Craven, see J. Venn and J.A. Venn, *Alumni Cantabrigienses* I (1922), 414; for Ogden *DNB* XLII, 13f.; for Hallifax *DNB* XXIV, 112 If.; for Jebb *DNB* XXIX, 258 f. J.J. Schultens mentions Jebb as a Unitarian in his letter to Van Goens of 25 March 1776 (see note 91). It was Harwood who had provided Hendrik Albert with a letter of introduction to Jebb. A not very favourable judgement of the contributions of Hallifax and Craven to Arabic studies is given by A.J. Arberry, *The Cambridge School of Arabic*, Cambridge 1948, 19.

[94] *DNB* s.v. Jebb.

[95] H.A. Schultens to J.J. Schultens, 5 April 1773, MS BPL 245 VIII. See also C. Wordsworth, *Scholae*, 164 note 2.

[96] H.A. Schultens to J. Robertson, 29 March 1773, MS BPL 245 XIII.

[97] H.A. Schultens to J.J. Schultens, 2 Dec. 1772; J.J. Schultens to H.A. Schultens, 11 Dec. 1772, MS BPL 245 VIII.

desire to stay in this fortunate country, the less becomes the hope to succeed. I am now sufficiently acquainted with the constitution of the Universities to know with sufficient and perfect certainty that there, in Oxford or Cambridge, it is impossible", he wrote to his father in January 1773.[98] His hope for a post at the British Museum was not fulfilled.[99] His father tried to hearten him: "The Lord will open a way".[100] Perhaps in the spring of 1773 Jan Jacob himself was already attempting to find a way for his son in Holland; that would explain why Hendrik Albert declined the Cambridge offer and what were the circumstances which withheld him from going to Edinburgh.

The most spectacular event of his stay in England was the fact of the reception of the degree of Master of Arts by Diploma, conferred on him "on account of his great knowledge in the Eastern Languages, which he has shewn in two Publications, the one entitled *Elnawabig* ... the other entitled *Specimen Proverbiorum Meidanii* ..."[101] The matter had been prepared by his Oxford friends; Lowth, who (not without Hendrik Albert's knowledge) had used his influence behind the scenes, wrote to him: "... a Degree in that form is the most honourable, which the University can confer; if I may be allowed to say so, who have received that honour myself".[102]

---

[98] H.A. Schultens to J.J. Schultens, 12 Jan. 1773, MS BPL 245 VIII. The expression "this fortunate country" reminds of an expression the German scholar G.C. Storr used in a letter to J.J. Schultens from Oxford, 12 Aug. 1770 (MS BPL 245 XII): "... progrediar ad enarranda ea, quae mihi in hac fortunata insula vel evenerunt vel innotueruunt", just as the expression used for Hunt, "extra venerable", reminds of Storr's characterization of Hunt as "venerabilis senex". It is not impossible that the reading of this letter, which apart from a passage about the conflict around Francis Blackburne's *The Confessional* contained some information about the leading Oxford orientalists, had made Hendrik Albert the more eager to follow his father's counsel with regard to a sojourn in Oxford.

[99] For the post at the British Museum, see M. Maty's letter to H.A. Schultens, 2 Jan. 1773, and those of H.A. Schultens to his father, 19 Jan. and 23 Febr. 1773; for J.J. Schultens' first reaction his letter of 19 Jan. 1773, MS BPL 245 VIII.

[100] In his letter of 23 Febr., Hendrik Albert had asked his father to take to heart his interests by trying to procure for him in Holland an extraordinary professorship in oriental languages. From what follows it appears that he did not think of Amsterdam, but of Leiden: he thought that the good grace in which his father stood with the Prince of Orange and the curators of the University would make possible the creation of such a post. Apparently, in April the matter was still unsettled; *cf.* a sentence in Hendrik Albert's letter to his father of 5 April: "I hope and trust I know my duty well enough to follow my father's will without any disinclination. But as long as this [his father's will] is still so vague it seems to me that I am allowed to make known my wishes in all honesty ...", MS BPL 245.

[101] From the Chancellor's letter, see note 2.

[102] R. Lowth to H.A. Schultens, 10 April 1773, MS BPL 245 VIII. According to Hendrik Albert's letter of 23 Febr., the subject came up "by chance" in a conversation with Kennicott and Hunt, who advised him to speak about it with the Warden of Wadham College, Dr. Wyndham. "He is strongly in favour of it, and in this case he can do much. as I am a member of his College ... But a great weight has been added by the favourable declaration of Bishop Lowth, with whom I spoke about it last week". For the degree as such, see L.H. Dudley Buxton and S.Gibson, *Oxford University Ceremonies*, Oxford 1935, 86 ff. The conferring of the degree was recorded in *Jackson's Oxford Journal* No 1045, Saturday May 18th, 1773 (I owe this information to Dr. J.E. Platt, Oxford).

On the 5th of May, the degree was awarded to him *in absentia*; on the advice of Hunt and others he stayed in London during the time the degree was discussed.[103] There were some difficulties. A number of Fellows sent around a printed "Query", in which they asked: "Whether the Convocation will not do more real honour to Mr. Schultens and to the University, if they admit him, for the present, by an Honorary Degree, to the Rank and Society of Master of Arts, and reserve the Diploma for some other opportunity which he probably will furnish them with, than if, by raising him, *prematurely* and *per saltum* to the highest Honours and Privileges: they preclude themselves from paying him, on future occasions, a compliment proportioned to his advanced Merit".[104] As already becomes clear from the charming form in which the protest was couched, it did not contain anything personal against Hendrik Albert. The young (and proud) Master himself explained the protest from the fact that the younger Masters were accustomed to thwart the Doctors and Heads of Houses, and that in this case they partly thought he was too young for the honour, and also were partly afraid that more foreigners would come to whom then the degree could not easily be refused.[105] However, the opinion of the Doctors and Heads of Houses prevailed. How highly the Oxford orientalists thought of Hendrik Albert appears from a letter, written by White to old Schultens shortly before the conferring of the degree: "... I dare venture to prophesy, Your son will one day make a conspicuous figure in Europe, and raise himself to as great an eminence in the Republic of Letters as his Father and Grandfather have done before him".[106]

The preparation of the *Specimen* had filled a large part of Hendrik Albert's time in Oxford. His father advised him to have it printed in London, where the Arabic script was better than in Oxford; also to dedicate the work to Lowth.[107] Hendrik Albert, however, was certain that Lowth would refuse: on the occasions he met Lowth they did not agree on the subject of Arabic, of which Lowth absolutely denied the great usefulness.[108] The work indeed appeared in London; it was dedicated to Hunt, "magni Pocockii dignissimo successori".[109] Alas, Hendrik Albert did not live long enough to see the publication of his great

---

[103] Apparently, Schultens had learned already some time beforehand that there might be opposition; *cf.* his letter to his father of 5 April: "But nothing is more uncertain than success. Though the situation is as favourable as it can be—if the Masters of Art get wind of the fact that I am strongly pushed by the Upper House, as it is called here, everything will fall to pieces just because of their desire to thwart them and to show their independence". Lowth, however, wrote in his letter of 10 April that he did not apprehend there would he any difficulty.

[104] A printed copy in BPL 245 VIII.

[105] H.A. Schultens to J.J. Schultens, 10 May 1773, MS BPL 245 VIII.

[106] J. White to J.J. Schultens, 11 April 1773, MS BPL 245 VIII.

[107] J.J. Schultens to H.A. Schultens, 11 Dec. 1772, MS BPL 245 VIII.

[108] H.A. Schultens to J.J. Schultens, 12 Jan. 1773, MS BPL 245 VIII.

[109] H.A. Schultens, *Specimen Proverbiorum Meidanii ex Versione Pocockiana*, Londoni 1773.

Maidani edition, of which the *Specimen* was a forerunner: it was published posthumously in 1795.[110]

After his return to Holland, Schultens stayed in correspondence with a number of his British connexions; he certainly was a more regular correspondent than his father had been. With Jones, he exchanged many letters, which bear witness to their friendship and affinity. In 1774, Schultens was somewhat disappointed at the fact that his friend had given up his oriental studies in order to make a career in public life;[111] a number of years later, however, Jones wrote to Schultens: "I have not wholly deserted Arabia".[112] How much Schultens belonged to his friend's "inner circle" appears from the fact that in 1780 Jones sent him a letter, in which he announced his intention to stand for Parliament and asked for his friends" exertions, good words and influence.[113] The Anglo-Dutch war brought no separation between the friends; Jones, who considered the war "most criminal", wrote to Schultens: "Perge me igitur, Batavus Anglum, ut facis, amare; quemadmodum ego te, Anglus Batavum, et amo et amabo".[114] It must have been a great pleasure to Schultens to receive an unexpected visit from his friend in 1782; in the letter, written "at the Golden Lion, Leyden", in which Jones announced his visit, he said: "I have a thousand things to tell you about Oxford and our Oxford friends".[115]

Kennicott wrote him a number of letters, partly on the publication and distribution of his *Vetus Testamentum Hebraicum*. One letter contains a critical note, with an interesting addition; thanking Schultens for his Amsterdam inaugural oration, Kennicott wrote that this oration "would have been read with still greater pleasure by some persons here, if you had said a little more of your connexion with this place. But, perhaps, it was a very delicate point; as some of your chief Friends must have disapproved, had you said much in favour of Oxford".[116] Did Kennicott suppose that Schultens' patriotic friends did not quite appreciate his Anglophile attitude? Hunt sent him a very kind letter on his appointment as professor at the Amsterdam Athenaeum, and stimulated him to continue his work on "that difficult author" Maidani.[117]

---

[110] H.A. Schultens, *Meidanii Proverbiorum Arabicorum pars* ... Opus Posthumum, Lugd. Bat. 1795.

[111] W. Jones to H.A. Schultens, 6 Oct. 1774, *Letters* I, 163: "... quod addis, amicissime tu quidem et humanissime, aegre te ferre, me politioris doctrinae desertorem esse, agnosco benevolentiam expostulationis tuae".

[112] W. Jones to H.A. Schultens, 14 Nov. 1780, *Letters* I, 445f.

[113] W. Jones to H.A. Schultens, 13 May 1780, *Letters* I, 367f.; an identical letter was sent to a number of other people.

[114] W. Jones to H.A. Schultens, 22 May 1781, *Letters* II, 470.

[115] W. Jones to H.A. Schultens, 25 August 1782, *Letters* II, 564f..

[116] B. Kennicott to H.A. Schultens, 28 Aug. 1775, MS BPL 245 XIII.

[117] "I am glad to hear that you intend to go on with Meidani this winter, and doubt not but you will, by pursueing the method you propose, soon become acquainted with that difficult author; especially if you shall be assisted by some good commentary, and have the opportunity of

White informed him of the College news and gossip; this kind of friendly correspondence will especially have reminded him of the good days spent in Oxford.[118] He always looked back on his stay in England with grateful pleasure. It broadened his outlook, and it made him acquainted with people whose scholarship won his deep respect. Hunt, "Musarum Arabicarum maximum in *Anglia* decus",[119] a representative of the school to which his father and his grandfather belonged, he loved and revered. Kennicott, "Critices ... Sacrae verae at genuinae instaurator",[120] confirmed him in his appreciation of a moderate form of textual criticism. Lowth and Jones, whose approach heralded the romantic era in literary studies, helped him to understand the literary qualities of the Old Testament. And in general, as a German pupil and admirer observed, his way of thinking and acting was marked by many specific traits of the English nation.[121] As late as 1790 he even tried to find employment in England, as he had tried many years ago. The reasons of this new attempt are unknown to us. That the attacks on his theological stance played a part is improbable. We are rather inclined to think of the burden of the political tensions in the Netherlands, which also made themselves felt in Leiden.[122] White, however, whom apparently he had asked to help him in this matter, wrote: "I am sorry, very sorry to inform you that it is wholly out of my power to procure you any establishment in England, even to the half of your present emoluments; as nothing can be lower than the state of Oriental literature in this country".[123]

The contacts between two Schultens generations and a number of British scholars confirm the image we had already formed of the Schultens family: that of eighteenth century enlightened Protestants, men of sound scholarship and of mild piety, who tried to combine a critical attitude with a biblical orientation. Most of their British connexions lived in the same spiritual climate: they, too, were enlightened Protestants, open to the challenge of a new

---

consulting other copies. The former of these advantages my predecessor, Dr. Pococke had, but, I think, it does not appear that he enjoyed the latter", T. Hunt to H.A. Schultens, 14 Oct. 1773, MS BPL 245 XIII.

[118] On 14 Nov. 1774 White sent a short note to Schultens: "White had the honour of being unanimously elected Professor of Arabic in the room of Dr. Hunt on Tuesday last". In a letter of 3 May 1775 he wrote: "I spoke my inaugural speech on the 17th of April ... I am at present applying very closely to the Arabic, and what I believe will surprise you, my whole view in so doing is to illustrate the Heb. Bible ...," MS BPL 245 XIII.

[119] From the dedication of the *Specimen* (see note 109).

[120] In his review of Kennicott's *Vetus Test. Hebr., Bibl. Critica* 1, 93.

[121] F.Th. Rink, *H.A. Schultens*, 23f.

[122] J.F. White to H.A. Schultens, 3 Aug. 1790, MS BPL 245 XIII.

[123] For his intervention in a conflict between Orangist townsmen and patriot students, see M. Siegenbeek, *Geschiedenis der Leidsche Hoogeschool in Leiden* 1829, 322. Rink, who was in Leiden as a pupil of Schultens in 1789-1790, observed a certain sadness in his teacher: "Im allgemeinen ... lächelte er selten; nie in zehen Monaten, und im täglichen Umgang mit ihm, habe ich ihn auch nor einmal eigentlich laut lachen gehört", *H.A. Schultens*, 64.

age and at the same time deeply rooted in the Christian tradition. Speaking of the Dutch oriental scholars of the eighteenth century, J. Willmet—himself an orientalist of the Schultensian school—remarked that with them the study of oriental languages and literature was made to serve, though not exclusively, "the advancement of an enlightened knowledge of the documents of religion".[124] In this, nothing divided them from their friends on the other side of the sea.

[124] J. Willmet, "Schets van den staat der Oostersche litteratuur in Holland in de achttiende eeuw", in *Gedenkschriften ... van de derde Klasse van het Kon. Ned. Instituut*, Amsterdam 1820, 149.

CHAPTER SIXTEEN

THEOLOGY IN FRANEKER AND LEIDEN IN THE EIGHTEENTH CENTURY

In general, Protestant theology as it was cultivated in the Netherlands in the eighteenth century was not what may be called exciting. There were no spectacular developments; rarely we meet with shocking or challenging propositions, and in the few cases when there was "rumor in casa" the matters in dispute more often than not were only of a marginal character. All this applies in particular to the study of theology within the circle of the "established" church. At least in formal respect the doctrines, confirmed or formulated by the Synod of Dort (1618-19), still held absolute sway. Of all those who held an ecclesiastical office it was expected that they subscribed to the "Three Formularies of Unity": consequently not only to the Belgic Confession and the Catechism of Heidelberg, but also to the Canons of Dort, sometimes called "the Five Articles against the Remonstrants". With regard to the Province of Friesland the latter point has been called in question or even denied. The church historians Ypey and Dermout declare in their "History of the Netherlands Reformed Church": "In that province, much as one was or remained opposed to the Remonstrants, the forementioned Canons of Dort have not been introduced nor received authority".[1] Their arguments, however, are not convincing; in more than one study it has been demonstrated that in Friesland, too, the Canons of Dort had official validity.[2]

The maintenance of the Canons of Dort had an ecclesiastical as well as a political aspect. In ecclesiastical respect the boundaries with regard to all groups and movements which deviated from the fundamental convictions of Calvinism were sharply marked; they maintained and protected the cohesion of a church which for the rest could hardly manifest itself as a unity in the context of a federally organized commonwealth. Furthermore, an abandoning of the standards set by Dort, and consequently of the confessional basis of the church, could have disturbed the precarious balance within a plural society which acknowledged the existence of an established church, but not of a state church in the full sense of the word. It was the church based on the confessional

[1] A. Ypey and I.J. Dermout, *Geschiedenis der Nederlandsche Hervormde Kerk* II, Breda 1822, 242, and the annotations at this volume, 169-175.

[2] The latest study is that by J. Hovius, "Zijn de Dordtse Leerregels van 1619 in Friesland aangenomen en ingevoerd?", in: *Uw knecht hoort* (Theologische opstellen aangeboden aan Prof. W. Kremer, Prof. dr. J. van Genderen en Prof. dr. B.J. Oosterhof), Amsterdam 1979, 11-44, where further literature.

standards of Dort which was recognized, protected and for the greater part materially maintained by public authority; what should happen to the church within the context of the Republic when this basis would be impaired? In this connection a passage from a letter of the Frisian Stadtholder (who later as William IV would be Stadtholder of the United Provinces) of 18 September 1740, directed to the Curators of the University of Franeker in Friesland, in illustrative: "Thus we are of opinion, that in particular in a republic it is dangerous to innovate anything in the accepted doctrine, and because of this we have no objection in declaring and testifying that we are much in favour of the maintenance of unity in doctrine ...".[3]

In view of all this it is not surprising that the ecclesiastical authorities exerted themselves in maintaining the confessional basis of the church. No doubt, especially in the second half of the eighteenth century there occurred some paltering with the subscription to the Canons of Dort,[4] and also when this was not the case the act of subscribing could be a very inadequate expression of inner conviction. This will have made, however, the "watchmen on the walls of Zion", as the orthodox leaders of the church considered themselves, all the more diligent. Of this, the Province of Friesland as well as that of Holland present quite a number of examples. Naturally in this matter the theological faculties received special attention: the publications of those professors of theology, who for some reason were under suspicion of being less pure in doctrine, were read with Argus-eyes, and their utterances, in particular those which dealt with ecclesiastical or theological controversies, were followed in a highly critical way. All this could trammel the study of theology: the margins for innovating opinions were narrow, and notably with regard to the very sensitive issue of the doctrine of predestination, the explicit point of difference with the Remonstrants, it was necessary to proceed with the greatest caution. It may be true that some controversies which had troubled the church in the second half of the seventeenth century had lost their relevance—Voetians no longer charged Coccejans as such with heresy—, but there existed a critical boundary which it was not allowed to overstep.

In the Dutch universities of the eighteenth century theology was still studied within the formal context of "Dort". This does not take away, however, that this study took place in what with a broad term may be called "the Age of Enlightenment". This produced an element of tension which, as we shall see,

[3] The letter of the Stadtholder is in large part quoted by W.B.S. Boeles, *Frieslands Hoogeschool en het Rijksatheneum te Franeker* II, Leeuwarden 1879, 479 ff. A probably contemporary copy is in the Provinciale Bibliotheek van Friesland, Collection-Eekhoff 1077 Hs., Inv. no. 81b-83, with some deviations. In my rendering of parts of the letter I follow Boeles.

[4] See Hovius, 28f.; *cf.* also for the attitude towards the "Formularies of Unity" in general in Friesland in the latter part of the eighteenth century S. Cuperus, *Kerkelijk leven der Hervormden in Friesland tijdens de Republiek* I, Leeuwarden 1916, 89.

manifested itself in the theological faculty of the University of Franeker as well as in that of her sister university in Leiden, the university of the Province of Holland. In this connection I would like to pose the question, to what extent Enlightenment thinking has influenced the study of theology at Franeker and at Leiden, and furthermore whether it is possible to ascertain a difference regarding this point between both universities. Or perhaps it is better, avoiding a generalizing approach, to formulate the question this way: is it possible to indicate elements in the way in which in the eighteenth century theology was studied at Franeker and at Leiden, to detect tendencies and to trace developments which reflect something of those innovating factors in eighteenth century culture which are summarized in the term "Enlightenment"?

When, for a moment, we take a glance at Protestantism outside the Netherlands, in order to avoid the danger that we take for typically Dutch what in fact is a more general phenomenon, we may perceive certain tendencies of theological renewal which one way or another are linked with the cultural climate of the Enlightenment period. In this connection sometimes the terms "Enlightenment within the circle of the Reformed tradition" (Dutch: "reformatorische Verlichting"), or "Protestant Enlightenment" are used[5]—terms which should be used with some caution because they may suggest more than contemporary reality warrants, but which yet may have an indicative function. In Germany, in England, in Switzerland—everywhere we find more or less parallel tendencies in regard to this point.[6] Elements and factors from the field of eighteenth century thinking which have a mutual coherence and which we bring together under the term "Enlightenment" also appear to have exercised their influence in the field of theology. Not all of those were new, but they functioned in a new way and within a new context. By way of example I mention the notion of emancipation ("Mündigkeit"), often—under the influence of Kant's famous definition—regarded as the most important characteristic of the Enlightenment.[7] Many eighteenth century theologians emancipated themselves from too rigid doctrinal bonds, and they started to read the Bible with new eyes, not overmuch restricted by traditional schemes of interpretation.[8]

---

[5] With regard to the Netherlands the term "reformatorische Verlichting" was introduced by F. Sassen in: *Johan Lulofs (1711-1768) en de Reformatorische Verlichting in de Nederlanden* (Mededelingen Kon. Ned. Ac. van Wetenschappen NR XXVIII, 7), Amsterdam 1965. For various reasons I have a preference for the term "Protestant Enlightenment".

[6] For the varieties and similarities, see R. Porter and M. Teich (eds.), *The Enlightenment in National Context*, Cambridge etc. 1981.

[7] For Kant, "Aufklärung" is man's liberation from his "selbstverschuldete Unmündigkeit": I. Kant, "Beantwortung der frage: Was ist Aufklärung?", in *Berlinische Monatsschrift* IV (1784), 481 (Facsimile in *Was ist Aufklärung?*, Darmstadt 1977, 452).

[8] See *inter alia* O. Merk, "Anfänge neutestamentlicher Wissenschaft im 18. Jahrhundert", in G. Schwaiger (ed.), *Historische Kritik in der Theologie*, Göttingen 1980, 37-59 (with a strong emphasis on the importance of the Swiss theologian J.A. Turrettini, to be mentioned below)

Closely connected with this is the idea of freedom: those who wanted to deal with tradition as emancipated theologians, naturally were led to turn down the sometimes oppressive authority of the confessions, and especially of those confessional statements which had been formulated in the period of Protestant orthodoxy.[9] And ever louder sounded the pleas for toleration—a toleration which should determine the relation between the various religious communities and their place within the commonwealth, but which also made its influence felt within the boundaries of one church.

That faith should be reasonably accountable was not a *novum*—that was also the case in the old Aristotelian-scholastic and the younger Cartesian tradition—, but more strongly than ever the rational character of the Christian faith was emphasized. There were shifts in the image of God as well as in that of man: in the image of God the idea of God's love, in the image of man the notion of man's responsibility became dominant. This implied a critical attitude towards the doctrine of a double predestination (to eternal life or to eternal death) and towards the connected doctrines of man's total depravity and spiritual impotence. Lastly, the practical attitude of the Christian, the "virtuous" life, received a heavy emphasis: here, the Protestant Enlightenment verged upon Pietism with its emphasis on the "praxis pietatis".[10]

An interesting "model" of a Protestant theology in which all these elements one way or another are recognizable is to be found in that form of theology which was dominant in Switzerland in the first half of the eighteenth century, a theology which is sometimes described rather paradoxically as "orthodoxie libérale".[11] It was developed by three theologians who closely cooperated and who, thanks to their leading position in the field of Swiss theology, were known as the "Swiss triumvirate": Samuel Werenfels, professor at Basel, Jean-Frédéric Ostervald, minister and professor at Neuchâtel, and Jean-Alphonse Turrettini, professor at Geneva. Next to them, I mention a fourth theologian: Pierre Roques, minister of the French church at Basel.[12] I refer to this theological "model" for two reasons. First of all it is interesting because this theology developed on a soil which bears a clear resemblance to that of mainstream Protestant life in the Netherlands: the soil of a Calvinism, marked in its later development by the spirit of a rigid Reformed orthodoxy, which tried to maintain the doctrine of Dort in all its consequences. Furthermore, it

---

[9] I think here particularly of *ad hoc* declarations with a confessional authority, such as the Canons of Dort (1619) and the Swiss "Formula Consensus" (1675).

[10] For this, see the fundamental article of K. Scholder, "Grundzüge der theologischen Aufklärung in Deutschland", in *Geist und Geschichte der Reformation* (Festgabe Hanns Rückert), Berlin 1966, 466-485.

[11] See H. Vuilleumier, *Histoire de l'"Eglise Réformée du Pays de Vaud* III, Lausanne 1930, 551f.

[12] See J. van den Berg, "Le Vrai Piétisme", *Zwingliana* 16(1983), 35-53.

is exactly this "model" which in the Netherlands ran up against the opposition of the orthodox, but awakened the sympathy of the more progressive, and thus may serve as a mark of recognition for a more or less enlightened attitude.[13]

Once again: how far did all this influence the theological faculties of Franeker and of Leiden? When we survey the "tableau de la troupe" in the theological faculty of Franeker University during the first decades of the eighteenth century we are struck by the ascendency of the Coccejan party. In general, in the appointments of town ministers and theological professors the authorities in the Dutch Republic (on the local as well as on the provincial level) tried to maintain a certain balance between Voetians and Coccejans as representatives of what was called the "old" and the "new study".[14] This policy had both an ecclesiastical and a political component: the parties in the church reflected in some measure the contrasts between the political tendencies in the Republic. While in general the Voetians were strong supporters of the House of Orange, the Coccejans (though not by definition anti-Orangists) were more inclined to sympathize with the republican tendencies of many representatives of the town patriciate. In Franeker, however, the scales clearly dipped towards one side: in 1700 three of the four professors of theology (Johannes van der Waeyen, Campegius Vitringa en Alexander Röell) were Coccejans, while the fourth one (Henri Philippe de Hautecour) was an outsider who somehow sympathized with Coccejan theology.[15] Also in the following period nomination policy was marked by a favourable disposition towards the Coccejan party: I mention here the names of the younger Johannes van der Waeyen, the younger Campegius Vitringa, Herman Venema and Albertus Wilhelmus Melchior(is). In 1704, Franeker University tried to attract Samuel Werenfels in the vacancy, caused by Röell's departure for Utrecht, though in vain;[16] one may wonder how he would have developed theologically if he had not made his further career in Basel but in Franeker, far from his "liberal orthodox" friends in Switzerland. In the end, Nicolaus Gürtler, also a Swiss, not an outspoken party-man, was appointed as Röell's successor. In his turn, he was succeeded by Ruardus Andala, a man of the "new study". Andala's successor, however, Petrus Laan, appointed in 1737, was an—albeit moderate—Voetian. Boeles, the historian of Franeker University, assumes that this representative of the "old study" was attracted for tactical reasons, "in order, if possible, to turn the tide of the increasing decline of the Frisian school".[17] When

[13] For the characterization of the Swiss "triumvirate" as "the remonstrant trio" and their defence by J.J. Schultens, see his *Omstandige brief aan den Heere Nikolaas Holtius* ..., Leiden 1755, CXXIII.

[14] For a general survey of the controversies within the Reformed Church between 1650 and 1750, see now J. van den Berg, "Het stroomlandschap ..." (full title, this vol. 271, bibliography, *sub* 1994).

[15] Boeles II, 326f.

[16] Boeles II, 367.

[17] Boeles II, 456.

in 1741 he was asked to give his opinion on a work of the Mennonite minister Johannes Stinstra, who was accused of Socinian tendencies, his advice was unfavourable, in line with his dogmatic presuppositions. As we shall see, the advice of Laan's colleague Venema showed a much more tolerant disposition.[18]

Melchior died in 1738. On the recommendation of the Curators of the University, the "Deputied States" (the daily government of the Province of Friesland) appointed Paul Ernst Jablonski, professor at the University of Frankfurt on the Oder, son of the well-known irenic court-preacher David Ernst Jablonski, as Melchior's successor; this without having previously submitted the recommendation to the Stadtholder, who as "curator magnificentissimus" should have been consulted, but who at that moment sojourned far away on the Dillenburg in Germany. On the list of three names from which Jablonski was chosen also occurred that of Pierre Roques. Everything points to an attempt of the Curators to strengthen the more liberal element in the faculty; also the fact that together with Jablonski they appointed the able and broad-minded theologian Petrus Conradi, a pupil and follower of Venema. For more than formal reasons, the appointment of Jablonski did not go down well with the Stadtholder. In his letter of 18 September 1740, from which we quoted already a short passage above, he remarked that both of them (Jablonski and Roques) are Universalists, and the first one not only has subscribed to that doctrine, but also openly teaches it.

> Much as we are of opinion that toleration and love are most in keeping with the spirit of the Gospel, and most behove a Christian, and while these also are our particular sentiments and we always have shown ourselves to be inclined and also in the future will be inclined to a proper toleration, and are averse from everything which savours of compulsion of conscience; yet it is our opinion that there is a great difference between compulsion of conscience and compulsion in matters of speech; between forcing someone to be of a certain opinion and not permitting someone to teach a certain matter. Because Mr. Jablonski adheres to the doctrine of general grace and has subsribed to it, and up till now teaches this doctrine, it cannot be surmised that, once he has come over to our academy, he would change his mind and teach the Doctrine of the Reformed Religion as it is at present openly taught in our country, and has received approbation in the National Synod, held at Dort, which doctrine ... we are bound to maintain and to defend ...[19]

Thereupon the Stadtholder highhandedly proposed to the Deputied States a list of three candidates, from whom the Leiden minister Petrus Couwenburg

[18] For the opinions of Laan and Venema, see C. Sepp, *Johannes Stinstra en zijn tijd* II, Amsterdam 1866, 34f.

[19] For this letter, see note 3; for Jablonski *Allgemeine Deutsche Biographie* XIII, 526. In 1724 Jablonski had already become the target of theological attacks because of his defence of the Nestorians.

du Bois, a Coccejan, was chosen. The Curators were outraged. In a letter of July 1741 to the States of Friesland they declared that Jablonski was "a most honest and renowned theologian", in testimony of which they submitted some theological propositions by Jablonski. They asked the States to declare the appointment of Du Bois and all the actions of the Stadtholder and of the Deputied States in this matter "informal, unlawful, null and void".[20] Understandably the Deputied States, to whom the request of the Curators had been transmitted by the States of Friesland, did not agree. They defended the Stadtholder's policy by pointing out that Venema and Conradi within and outside the province had the reputation "of not only much favouring the heresy of the Remonstrants, but even openly giving evidence of this to such a degree that in other provinces and particularly in Holland disciples of Franeker ... are no longer eligible for the ministry".[21] From this it becomes clear that the appointment policy was directed against more enlightened tendencies as they were represented by Venema and Conradi. No doubt, the background of this policy was the fear of a penetration of Remonstrant views into the established church. It is not clear who advised the Stadtholder (himself in his whole attitude a rather tolerant man) in this affair. One might think of the later Rotterdam minister Petrus Hofstede, then minister of Anjum in Friesland, a man of strict orthodoxy and an extreme Orangist, who had personal contacts with the Stadtholder.[22] It is also possible (though not very obvious) that Laan, afraid of "Remonstrant" infiltration into his own faculty, had warned the Stadtholder against Jablonski. Furthermore, the jurist and author of pamphlets Wybrand van Ytsma may have advised the Stadtholder in this matter.[23] However this may be, the ambivalence of the wordings of the Stadtholder's letter gives ground for the supposition that, contrary to his self-confessed toleration, he acted under rather strong pressure from outside.

When Laan died in 1743, at the personal request of the Stadtholder[24] the Voetian and Orangist Bernhardinus de Moor was appointed as his successor. Soon afterwards, however, he departed for Leiden, where in 1745 he gave his inaugural address. In his vacancy Aegidius Gillissen was appointed, probably also a Voetian, though rather colourless.[25] After some time, he, too, left Fra-

---

20 Boeles II, 481; a copy of the whole letter in Provinciale Bibliotheek Friesland, Coll.-Eekhoff 1077 Hs, Inv. no. 76-80.

21 Boeles I (1878), 72f.; the minute from which Boeles quotes is (like the original) untraceable.

22 For the relations between the Stadtholder and Hofstede during the latter's Frisian period, see J.P. de Bie, *Het leven en de werken van Petrus Hofstede*, Rotterdam 1899, 44f.

23 I owe this suggestion to Mr. S. van Tuinen (Hattem) †, who grounds his supposition on a letter of Ypma to the Prince d.d. 18 July 1741 (communication S. van Tuinen 16 Oct. 1985).

24 Boeles II, 553.

25 Sepp describes him as a Coccejan, *Stinstra* II, 41; the *Biographisch Woordenboek van Protestantsche Godgeleerden in Nederland* III, 252, however, as a Voetian. Given the fact that he succeeded De Moor the latter is more probable.

neker for Leiden. In 1765 he was succeeded by Johannes Ratelband, a man of the "old study", whose theology at that time was already out of date[26]—but apparently for tactical reasons the succession of the one Voetian chair had to be continued. His activities in the affair of Gerardus Theodorus de Cock, an outspoken advocate of toleration,[27] were intransigent and for the faculty to which he was just appointed but in which he did not yet possess the right to vote undoubtedly painful; they might make us surmise that he was rather an extremist. But in spite of his old-fashioned orthodoxy he did not prove himself an extremist: in his inaugural lecture, delivered two years later, in 1767, he appealed to the students to free themselves from all party spirit, and he exhorted them not to swear by the words of the masters, be it Voetius, Coccejus or Lampe.[28] In the second half of the eigthteenth century the old controversies had indeed faded.

Venema and Conradi were moderately enlightened theologians; to a certain degree representatives of a new time. Both of them were influenced by the theology of the elder Campegius Vitringa, who had put his mark upon his pupils and followers to such an extent that later his name served to indicate a new current in church and theology: that of the "Vitringians". The elder Vitringa, as he was called to distinguish him from his like-minded son of the same name,[29] stood (as we saw) in the Coccejan tradition. As such this was no warrant of theological openness and ecclesiastical moderation, but still there were elements in Coccejanism which at least with some Coccejans made for a more broadminded, or at least less rigid attitude. The theology of Coccejus no doubt was more modern and more directly "biblical" than that of Voetius, and thanks to the links between Coccejanism and Cartesianism, theologians of the "new study" more easily adapted themselves to new trends in the field of philosophy. The sociological and cultural factor should also be taken into account: we may safely assume that in general the higher, potentially more "progressive" strata of society sympathized with the Coccejans rather than with the Voetians. All this may serve to explain why the more enlightened theologians in the Reformed Church usually had their background in the Coccejan circle.

---

[26] Boeles II, 553.

[27] In 1765, De Cock (a pupil of Venema) had preached a sermon (on John 15.17) on christian love and toleration. On the ground of this sermon he was accused of unorthodoxy; the sermon received, however, the approbation of the theological faculty of Franeker, which maintained its point of view also against the objections of Ratelband. See, among others, E.J. Diest Lorgion, *Geschiedkundig Gedenkboek voor de Hervormden in Friesland*, Leeuwarden and Groningen 1848, 267-284.

[28] *Oratio inauguralis de pietate christiana theologo prorsus necessaria*, Franequerae 1767, 63. The German theologian Friedrich Adolph Lampe was an outspoken Pietist, who when he was professor at the University of Utrecht (1720-1727) exercised a rather large influence in the Netherlands.

[29] For the younger Vitringa, see *Biografisch Lexicon voor de Geschiedenis van het Nederlandse Protestantisme* II, 438f.

Vitringa was not a conspicuous innovator. He was loyally orthodox, though not in a narrow or fanatical way, and he was cautious in his scholarly approach. In general averse from polemics, he took up his pen when he feared such fundamental doctrines as that of the Trinity were in danger, as appears from his unneccessarily fierce discussion with his colleague Röell.[30] But though in some respects still a man of the seventeenth century he stimulated his pupils to find their way in the new cultural climate of the eighteenth century. In his exegetical work he moved along the lines set by Coccejus, though without slavishly following the great master. He taught his students to approach the text of the Bible with an open mind, and not to make their exegesis unduly dependent on dogmatic prejudices. This element was taken up by leading scholars such as Albert Schultens, Herman Venema and Joannes Alberti;[31] it did not directly result in a historical-critical approach of the Bible, but yet it created the condition for the loosening of the stringent bonds of a mechanical doctrine of inspiration.

Vitringa's scholarly approach was attended by a spiritual attitude that was marked by a conjunction between a more or less enlightened openness and an almost pietistic warmth and seriousness. Of his sermons it was said that they were characterized by a gentle and yet serious tone.[32] This tone also becomes audible in his inaugural oration of 1683 "de amore veritatis". To love the truth means: to know her in her beauty, friendliness and elegance. This point of view brings him to criticize the heresy-hunt in the Early Church, the condemnations of people such as Origen and Nestorius, the dissensions and strife between bishops in old and new Rome. With regret he observes, how similar phenomena present themselves in the church of his own country and his own time. Because of this, he appeals for humility, gentleness, dislike of partisanship, and he looks forward to better and kinder times ("meliora et melliora tempora"). His love of freedom manifests itself in the striking sentence: "I have never suffered to be led or to be led astray by the authority of any person whatsoever".[33] The same is implicit in one of his aphorisms on christian doctrine, to be found in his *Doctrina Christianae Religionis*: "It is a distinguishing mark of the dispensation of grace (the "economia gratiae"), that the last judgement is passed before the conscience of each believer"—a sentence by Jan Jacob Schultens firmly and empathically underlined in his personal copy.[34]

---

[30] See J. van Sluis, *Herman Alexander Röell*, Ljouwert (Leeuwarden) 1988, 86-98; *cf.* B. de Moor, *Commentarius perpetuus in Johannis Marckii Compendium* I, Lugd. Bat. 1761, 761-771.

[31] See, *e.g.*, H.W.M. van de Sandt, *Joan Alberti, een Nederlands theoloog en classicus in de achttiende eeuw*, Utrecht 1984, *sparsim*.

[32] Boeles II, 290.

[33] *Oratio de amore veritatis*, Franequerae 1683, 37, 42f.; *cf.* for Vitringa's dislike of ecclesiastical strife also A. Schultens' remark in his *Oratio funebris in memoriam Campegii Vitringa*, Fran. 1722, 82: "A studio partium, tanquam a scopulo, resiluit".

[34] C. Vitringa, *Doctrina christianae religionis in aphorismos summatim descripta*, Fran. [5]1714 (with marginal notes by J.J. Schultens, Universiteitsbibliotheek Leiden 154 C 30), 17 (Cap. II, 76).

Apart from his son, who died early, in 1723 (one year after his father), Vitringa's most gifted pupil was doubtless Herman Venema, who for a long period, between 1724 and 1774, was active as professor in Franeker.[35] He was perhaps the most outstanding Dutch theologian of the eighteenth century. Rightly, De Bruïne describes him as an enlightened theologian, though not without some reservation. Just like Vitringa, Venema stood in the Coccejan tradition, but Venema was further from Coccejus than his teacher was. In his works we still recognize the federal scheme of Coccejus, but he was too much of a level-headed exegete to be imprisoned in the Coccejan scheme. He expounded his hermeneutical principles in a preface to a work by Vitringa, which he edited in 1725. In this, he pleads for a careful, open-minded exegesis, free from dogmatic constraint. At the same time he proves himself heir to the Coccejan tradition, when by means of the idea of a double sense of Scripture he tries to make clear that the history of salvation, as described in the Old and New Testament, is also relevant for the interpretation of contemporary events. When Vitringa and Venema speak about the Reformation they emphasize the notions of "light" and "freedom". According to Vitringa, at the time of the Reformation the light of truth began to shine anew, and thus also "the light of other studies at that time broke out with force ...". According to Venema the church was set free by the Reformers just as Israël once was liberated through the struggle of the Maccabees.[36] For enligthened Protestants the Reformation meant that the church, liberated from the constraining bonds of coercion and superstition, could breathe the air of a new freedom.

Venema's feeling for toleration is doubtless closely connected with this view. He defended the idea of toleration in theory and also in practice (which at that time was more difficult), particularly in the position he took in the affair of Johannes Stinstra, who (as we saw) was accused of Socinianism. In the struggle around Antonius van der Os, Reformed minister at Zwolle, who in 1755 was deposed because of his enlightened views, he remained in the background, as he thought (perhaps rightly) that his intervention would harm rather than help the case. But from a distance he sympathized with Van der Os, as appears from his correspondence with Van der Os' defender J.J. Schultens, whose indignation with regard to the activities of the "zealots" he shared.[37] And certainly the Franeker faculty also spoke on his behalf, when in 1765 it cleared G.Th. de Cock from the blame of unorthodoxy.

---

[35] For him, see J.C. de Bruïne, *Herman Venema. Een Nederlands theoloog in de tijd der Verlichting*, Franeker 1973.

[36] C. Vitringa, *Verklaringen en heilige bedenkingen over de verborgene sin der miraculen van Jezus Christus ... Met een voorreden over de sin van de Heilige Schrift* by H. Venema, Franeker 1725, 346, 39.

[37] See Venema's letter to J.J. Schultens, 25 Febr. 1754, in which he thanks Schultens for his "cordial manly defence of such a good matter": UBL, BPL 127 AD 1.

How constraining was the framework of "Dort" for the broadminded Venema? As appears from his works he clearly was in sympathy with his Swiss contemporaries.[38] Just like them he had affinity with the theology, developed in the seventeenth century at the French Protestant academy of Saumur. Its leading representative, Moyse Amyraut, tried to soften the doctrine of predestination without quite abandoning it. In 1735 Venema, then already accused of unorthodoxy, saw himself in the necessity to give "a short defence of his honour and doctrine".[39] Various dogmatic questions are raised in this publication; last but not least the very sensitive point of the idea of predestination. In fact, adopting the emphasis Saumur and the Swiss theologians put on God's general will of love, he moves here, cautiously and sometimes even ambiguously, on the verge of the system of Dort; hence, we may assume, the accusation of Remonstrantism in 1741. The writing ends with a call to freedom: "I trust that there will be a man who will stand in the breaches against the breaking through of Antichristianity, that is, superstition and constraint of conscience, and who will not suffer that, together with a suitable freedom, wisdom and virtue will be banished from this country, which after so much strife and blood has picked and tasted the fruits of *freedom*".[40] As with the Swiss theologians—I think here in particular of Pierre Roques, who as we saw once was one of the candidates for a theological chair in Franeker—we find with Venema a strong emphasis on the "praxis pietatis". This comes to expression in a very personal way in his funeral oration on the professor of medicine Wijer Willem Muys. It is as if in the figure of Muys he wants to paint the ideal image of the pious enlightened Christian. Muys opposed the practice of partisanship, which he considered an illness, to be compared with melancholy. He read the Bible (as Venema also wanted to do) with open eyes, "sine ullo praejudicio". Valiantly he defended the liberty of conscience, and he was averse from everything which could hinder truth and virtue; from "inquisitio" and "persecutio". He was an advocate of freedom, though an enemy of licentiousness. He only sympathized with modest and peaceful theologians, not with such as let themselves ignite with partisanship.[41] His piety was "manly", "mascula"—the same term occurs in a similar context in England to denote openness, freedom,

---

[38] How much Venema felt at home with the theology of Saumur and its Swiss repercussions appears from his letter to J.J. Schultens of 1 March 1754: UBL, BPL 127 AD 1.

[39] The apology was necessitated by a strong attack on his orthodoxy by the Groninger professor Antonius Driessen: De Bruïne, *Venema*, 68-84.

[40] *Korte verdediging van syne eere en leere*, Leeuwarden 1735, 100.

[41] *Oratio funebris in memoriam viri clarissimi et celeberrimi Wyeri Gulielmi Muys,* Fran. 1754, 8, 72, 76f. and (for "mascula pietas") 84. There is a striking parallel with the description of the toleration of the Leiden medical professor Herman Boerhaave and his dislike of ecclesiastical and theological strife in A. Schultens' funeral oration on Boerhaave, which partly rests on Boerhaave's autobiographical communications: *Oratio academica in memoriam Hermanni Boerhaavii*, Lugd. Bat. 1738, 16f., 60f., 77.

courage and independence: qualities which at that time apparently were attributed pre-eminently to men.[42]

Together with Venema also his pupil and colleague Petrus Conradi was accused of Remonstrantism.[43] While Venema was more explicit than Vitringa, in his turn Conradi expressed his enlightened views still more unreservedly than his teacher did. In this context, his inaugural oration on the necessary virtues of the "theologus polemicus" is significant. In spite of the title, this oration is a plea for moderation and tolerance. He protests against the activities of the zealots, who make black white and white black. He, too, describes partisanship as an illness; those who are partisan are blinded by the haze of prejudice. It is foolish to think of oneself as possessing already all the truth, as if it could not be clarified through new light. There is progress in knowledge: the children see what the fathers have not seen. The peace in the church can only be maintained in two ways: either through absolute uniformity, or (this is what Conradi advocates) along the way of toleration. In all this he repeatedly and very explicitly appeals to the Swiss theologians.[44]

Conradi proves himself also a child of the period of Enlightenment, because he attaches a high importance to the function of reason in relation to religion. We should not see him as a consistent rationalist; in a oration delivered as rector magnificus in 1752, he warned against an overestimation of reason which would result in a subjection of all revealed truths to her supreme authority. But not less clear was his warning against a contempt of reason: without confirmation by reason our faith would be nothing but "Enthusiasmus". For him, reason is "eximium ... Divinae Benignitatis donum".[45]

The line of Vitringa, Venema and Conradi was continued by Samuel Hendrik Manger, professor of theology from 1764 till 1787.[46] He, too, was a warm advocate of the ideal of mutual toleration; thus in his *Oratio de diversis remediis ad tollenda Christianorum dissidia adhibitis* (1771), in which he appealed to irenic scholars such as Erasmus, Melanchthon and Cassander.[47] In 1785 he delivered the official lecture at the bicentenary of Franeker Univer-

---

[42] I think here of a sermon by the English Latitudinarian Bishop Benjamin Hoadly, *The Nature of the Kingdom or Church of Christ*, London 1717, 29: "The Peace of Christ's Kingdom is a manly and reasonable Peace". *The Oxford English Dictionary*, s.v., gives as meanings of "manly": "possessing the virtues of a man ...; chiefly, courageous, independent in spirit, frank, upright".

[43] See the letter of the Deputied States to the Curators, mentioned in nr. 21.

[44] P. Conradi, *Oratio inauguralis de necessariis theologi polemici virtutibus*, Fran. 1741, *inter alia* 12f., where S. Werenfels and J.A. Turrettini are quoted with approval.

[45] *Sermo academicus de necessario, sed probe administrando, rationis usu in religionis revelatae negotio*, Fran. 1752, 16, 4.

[46] For Manger, see K.M. Witteveen, "S.H. Manger, een Franeker theoloog in de achttiende eeuw", *Nederlands Archief voor Kerkgeschiedenis* 54(1974), 207-230.

[47] The oration was published by G.H.M. Delprat in *Nederlandsch Archief voor Kerkelijke Geschiedenis* 7(1847), 347-370.

sity; a lecture which in particular in its rejection of the spirit of partisanship and in the tone of its pleading for peace and love was characteristic of the Protestant Enlightenment.[48] It will have afforded much pleasure to Venema, then 87 years old, who was present and to whom high tribute was paid.[49] It may be doubted, however, whether Venema would have felt at home in the theology of some Franeker theologians from the next generation, such as Johannes Hendrik Regenbogen (from 1797 till 1811 in Franeker, after that professor of history at Leiden University), who has been described as "the first modernist professor".[50] That description goes too far: he was not a radical innovator, and (at least formally) he remained within the established confessional limits.[51] But still, with regard to the doctrines of inspiration and of satisfaction we notice in his theology a shift of emphasis which divided him from a former generation.[52] He was a typical exponent of the so-called "old-liberal" theology—by O. Noordmans described as a "faded Reformed doctrine"[53]—, which in the first decades would dominate the theological scene of the Netherlands; it paved the way for new, much more radical developments of which the first "old-liberals" could not even have dreamed.

How far is it possible to recognize developments, similar to those we noticed in the faculty of Franeker, in its Leiden sister faculty? As in Franeker, Coccejan theology was dominant in Leiden during a large part of the eighteenth century, but next to it Voetian orthodoxy had some outspoken representatives in Leiden, such as Johannes à Marck and Bernhardinus de Moor. In their appointment policy the Curators tried also to do justice to the Voetian party.[54] Yet it is clear that the theological approach which was characteristic of Franeker unde-

---

[48] *Oratio panegyrica in auspicium seculi tertii Academiae Frisiae*, Fran. 1785, in particular 17f.: "Amat haec (sc. disciplina theologica), si vera sit, si Christiana, doctores a partium studio remotos, unius Christi sectatores, veritatis simul ac pacis et caritatis studiosos ...".

[49] He remarked with regard to Venema (22): "Non sibi soli, sed scholae nostrae, ubi docuit, gloriam peperit nunquam intermorituram".

[50] Thus G.H.M. Delprat, "De stichting der Hoogeschool te Franeker. Blik op hare geschiedenis en latere lotgevallen", in *Geschiedenis der Christelijke Kerk in Nederland in tafereelen* II, Amsterdam 1869, 145.

[51] In a defence against his colleague J.A. Lotze, who had accused him of heretical opinions with regard to the doctrine of satisfaction, Regenbogen remarked that his views were more in conformity with the "Three Formularies of Unity" than those of Lotze; furthermore, that no one had the freedom to determine what was more or less essential in Reformed religion according to his personal views: *De leerrede van den Hoogleeraar J.A. Lotze getoetst* ..., Franeker 1807, 60.

[52] For Regenbogen's rejection of the doctrine of "mechanical inspiration", see *inter alia* his *Oratio de extremis in quae interpretes Sacri Codici passim prolapsi sunt sedulo cavendis*, Leovardiae 1799; for his views of satisfaction in particular his *De leerrede van ... Lotze*, 28f.

[53] O. Noordmans, "Twee kerkelijke richtingen", *Geestelijke perspectieven*, ^{2}1939, 90.

[54] For the third quarter of the eigtheenth century, see J. van den Berg, "Willem Bentinck (1704-1774) en de theologische faculteit te Leiden", in S. Groenveld and others, *Bestuurders en geleerden*, Amsterdam-Dieren, 169-177.

niably influenced the developments in Leiden. First of all I mention Albert Schultens, philologist and theologian, who in Franeker taught as professor of oriental languages and who in Leiden, where he taught from 1732 till 1750, also held the office of regent of the "States College", so important for the forming of future ministers. As a scholar he was as independent as Vitringa; in his Old Testament studies he took what was a new and dangerous road according to more conservative scholars, by strongly emphasizing the influence of Arabic on Hebrew—in the eyes of his opponents a desacralization of the holy language.[55] Also in his personal stand he showed himself congenial to Vitringa and Venema. In one of his publications his son Jan Jacob Schultens (professor of Old Testament in Leiden 1749-1778, and after his father's death also regent of the States College) reproduced some conversations with his father, from which appears the latter's irenic and tolerant attitude. Albert seriously warned against the tendency to accuse theological opponents such as the Remonstrants of Socinianism. He taught Jan Jacob to judge the Arminians with moderation. The way Venema was attacked aroused his indignation. He viewed the doctrinal controversies between Voetians and Coccejans "with impartiality of mind", and he admonished his son: "Truth is mild and conciliatory, and can never lose anything by the exercise of love and Christian goodwill".[56] The son followed the same track in his struggle for toleration; especially in the conflict around his friend Van der Os he exerted himself to the utmost, though to his great disappointment without any result. In dogmatic matters he was perhaps just a bit more traditional than Venema, and he did not fully share the Amyraldist inclinations of some of his Franeker colleagues, though he wholeheartedly defended their orthodoxy.[57]

A famous pupil of Vitringa was Joannes Alberti, one of the "stars" of the theological faculty of Leiden, where he taught from 1740 to 1762.[58] In his exegetical work he made use of Vitringa's method, though in a way which shows his independence. He was open-minded in his dogmatic views. Alberti did not mix in ecclesiastical or theological conflicts, not even when he became the target of fierce attacks from the side of two ultra-orthodox ministers, Alexander Comrie and Nicolaus Holtius; they saw in him an "Euruodius", a man who walked the broad way which, if not personally, then still with regard to church and doctrine would lead to destruction.[59] Alberti was succeeded by Manger's brother-in-law Ewald Hollebeek, who, though not a pupil of Vitringa, still was defined as a "Vitringian";[60] it shows to what extent this name

---

[55] See J. van den Berg, "The Leiden professors of the Schultens family and their contacts with British scholars", this volume Ch. 15.

[56] *Nieuwjaarsgift aan twee heeren voorstanderen der Formulieren*, Leiden 1754, 179f., 193f.

[57] *Nieuwjaarsgift*, 156f.; *Omstandige brief aan … N. Holtius*, Leiden 1755, LII.

[58] For him, see the biography by Van de Sandt (above, note 30).

[59] See J. van den Berg, *Een Leids pleidooi voor verdraagzaamheid*, Leiden 1976, 4.

[60] J. van den Berg, "Willem Bentinck", 173.

had become the name of a party. Hollebeek was of a mild and irenic disposition, an advocate of toleration and a promoter of the "praxis pietatis"—a man who embodied the ideal of a moderate theologian which Muys and Venema envisaged. Probably he was the likable Professor Maatig ("Moderate") from Betje Wolff and Aagje Deken's novel *Willem Leevend* (1784-85).[61]

The word "moderate" would be appropriate for characterizing the Protestant Enlightenment in the Netherlands. Like the Swiss theologians their colleagues in Franeker and Leiden who sympathized with them were essentially orthodox. Perhaps they even more strongly emphasized their orthodoxy than the Swiss because of the fact that their theological context was still strongly marked by the tradition of "Dort". In general, we find with them no provocative utterances, no radical ideas, no revolutionary views. But yet their orthodoxy, too, was an "orthodoxie libérale" which opened up a new way, which created the possibility of a new exegetical approach and which contributed to the advance of toleration in church and theology in the Netherlands.

Of this form of Protestant Enlightenment in the field of theology Franeker was perhaps the most important centre within the Dutch Republic. It may be that in Friesland the ecclesiastical and political pressure was a bit less strong than in Holland. No doubt in Franeker the conservative-orthodox reaction was less vigorous than in Leiden, where the protest which the traditionalist professor Didericus van der Kemp entered in the late sixties against the progress of toleration can be seen as a backlash against the growing influence of the Protestant Enlightenment.[62] The differences, however, are only gradual, and it is difficult to measure them exactly. Still, we may conclude that the presence of elements of the Protestant Enlightenment in the faculty of Leiden in the eighteenth century was largely due to her slightly younger sister at Franeker, which alas did not survive the first half of the nineteenth century. For Leiden, the closing down in 1843 of what was since 1815 the Franeker "Athenaeum" had at least one important effect: then, the first Dutch "modernist" theologian, Johannes Henricus Scholten, the "father" of the modernist school of theology in the Netherlands, moved to Leiden, where in his teaching he tried to connect in an idiosyncratic way the heritage of Dort with that of the Enlightenment.[63]

---

[61] See among others P. van der Vliet, *Wolff en Deken's Brieven van Abraham Blankaart*, Utrecht 1982, 336.

[62] For this, see: J. van den Berg, "Tussen ideaal en realiteit". De Engelse jurist Goodricke in discussie met de Nederlandse theologen Bonnet en Van der Kemp ...", *Gereformeerd Theologisch Tijdschrift* 81(1981), 217-250.

[63] This paper was originally read at a symposium which met in Franeker in commemoration of the founding of Franeker University in 1585.

BIBLIOGRAPHY (END 1987-1998)

To the list of publications in the bibliography in *Kerkhistorische Opstellen*, Kampen 1987, should be added:

1979

"Eighteenth century Dutch translations of the works of some British Latitudinarian and enlightened theologians", *Nederlands Archief voor Kerkgeschiedenis* 59 (1979), 194-212.

The publication "Kenterend getij", mentioned under 1987 did in fact appear in 1989. Below, it is mentioned again.

1987 (continued)

Dordt in de weegschaal. Kritische reacties op de synode van Dordrecht (1618-1619), Leiden 1987 (Farewell Lecture), Leiden 1987.

1988

"Between Platonism and Enlightenment. Simon Patrick (1625-1707) and his Place in the Latitudinarian Movement", *Nederlands Archief voor Kerkgeschiedenis* 68 (1988), 164-179.

"Continuity within a changing context": Henri More's millenarianism, seen against the background of the millenarian concepts of Joseph Mede", in: *Chiliasmus in Deutschland und England im 17. Jahrhundert*, Göttingen 1988 (*Pietismus und Neuzeit*, Bd 14), 185-202.

"Proto-Protestants? The Image of the Karaites as a Mirror of the Catholic-Protestant Controversy in the Seventeenth Century"; "John Covel's Letter on the Karaites (1677); "Latin Table of Contents from the Hebrew Work of Menasseh ben Israel, Nishmet Chajjim", and (together with R.H. Popkin) "Menasseh ben Israel, "Compendium Kabbalae"", in: J. van den Berg and E.G.E. van der Wall (eds.), *Jewish-Christian Relations in the Seventeenth Century*, Dordrecht 1988, 33-50, 135-144, 161-170, 171-186.

1989

"Menasseh ben Israel, Henry More and Johannes Hoornbeeck on the Pre-existence of the Soul", in: Y. Kaplan, H. Méchoulan and R.H. Popkin (eds.), *Menasseh ben Israel and his World* , Leiden etc, 1989, 98-116.

"Kenterend getij: Leidse theologen en remonstrantisme, met name in de achttiende eeuw", in: E.K. Grootes and J. de Haan (eds.), *Geschiedenis, godsdienst, letter-*

kunde (Opstellen aangeboden aan dr S.B.J. Zilverberg), Roden 1989, 178-185.
"The Synod of Dort in the Balance", *Nederlands Archief voor Kerkgeschiedenis* 69 (1989), 176-194.
The Idea of Tolerance and the Act of Toleration (Friends of Dr. William's Library Forty-third Lecture), London 1989.

1990

"Religion and Politics in the Life of William and Mary", in: P.G. Hoftijzer and C.C. Barfoot, *Fabrics and Fabrications. The Myth and Making of William and Mary*, Amsterdam 1990, 17-40.
"De 'Evangelical Revival' in Schotland en het Nederlandse Réveil", *Documentatieblad voor de Nederlandse Kerkgeschiedenis na 1800* 13 (1990), 48-73.
"Leiden, Universität", in: *Theologische Realenzyklopädie* 20 (1990), 711-713.

1991

"Glorious Revolution and Millennium: The 'Apocalyptical Thoughts' of Drue Cressener", in: J. van den Berg and P.G. Hoftijzer (eds.), *Church, Change and Revolution*, Leiden etc. 1991, 130-144.
"Samenwerking zonder 'subjectie': synode en theologische faculteit te Leiden tot 1878", in G. Ackermans, A. Davids and P.J.A. Nissen (eds.), *Kerk in beraad* (Opstellen aangeboden aan prof.dr. J.C.P.A. van Laarhoven), Nijmegen 1991, 207-220.
"Een achttiende-eeuwse Coccejaan over de kerk van zijn tijd: Johan van den Honerts *De Kerk in Nederland*", in: C.G.F. de Jong en J. van Sluis (eds.), *Gericht verleden* (Kerkhistorische opstellen aangeboden aand prof.dr. W. Nijenhuis), Leiden 1991, 159-180.
"Honderd jaar Gereformeerde Kerk te Ottoland", in: *Kwartaalblad Historische Vereniging Binnenwaard* 8 (1991), 34-41, 76-83.

1992

"'De vrijheid der Godgeleerde Wetenschap': Kerk en theologische faculteit in de middenjaren van de negentiende eeuw", in: *Kerkhistorische Studiën* (Feestbundel 90-jarig bestaan S.S.S.), Leiden 1992, 7-24.

1993

"Creatieve vriendschap. John Locke en Philippus van Limborch", in: *Voorbeeldige vriendschap. Vrienden en vriendinnen in theologie en cultuur* (aangeboden aan prof.dr. E.J. Kuiper), Groningen 1993, 57-66.

"William Carey's Enquiry", in: *Wereld en zending* 22 (1993), 78-89.

"Die Frömmigkeitsbestrebungen in der Niederlanden", in: M. Brecht (ed.), *Geschichte des Pietismus* (Der Pietismus vom siebzehnten bis zum frühen achtzehnten Jahrhundert), Göttingen 1993, 57-112.

1994

"Dutch Calvinism and the Church of England in the Period of the Glorious Revolution", in: S. Groenveld and M.J. Wintle (eds.), *The Exchange of Ideas: Religion, Scholarship and Art in Anglo-Dutch Relations in the 17th Century (Britain and the Netherlands* XI), Zutphen 1994, 84-99.

"Grotius' Views on Antichrist and Apocalyptic Thought in England", in: H.J.M. Nellen and E. Rabbie (eds.), *Hugo Grotius Theologian.* Essays in honour of G.H.M. Posthumus Meyjes, Leiden 1994, 169-183.

"The Evangelical Revival in Scotland and the nineteenth-century "Réveil" in the Netherlands", in: *Records of the Scottish Church History Society* 25 (1994), 309-337.

"Joseph Mede and the Dutch Millenarian Daniel van Laren", in: M. Wilks (ed.), *Prophecy and Eschatology* (*Studies in Church History,* Subsidia 10), Oxford 1994, 111-122.

"In memoriam D. Nauta", in: *Nederlands Archief voor Kerkgeschiedenis* 74 (1994), 139-142.

"Het stroomlandschap van de Gereformeerde Kerk in Nederland tussen 1650 en 1750", in: F.G.M. Broeyer and E.G.E. van der Wall (eds.), *Een richtingenstrijd in de Gereformeerde Kerk*, Zoetermeer 1994, 9-27.

1995

"'Blijve hun werk': de oude ethischen in historische context", in: J. Vlasblom and J. van der Windt (eds.), *Heel de kerk. Enkele visies op de kerk binnen de Ethische Richting*, Zoetermeer 1995, 13-28.

"Die Frömmigkeitsbestrebungen in den Niederlanden", in: M. Brecht and K. Deppermann (eds.), *Geschichte des Pietismus* 2 (Der Pietismus im achtzehnten Jahrhundert), Göttingen 1995, 542-587.

1996

"Toch een wegbereider? Salomon van Til (1643-1713)" in: K. Fens (ed.), *Verlichte geesten. Een portrettengalerij voor Piet Buijnsters*, Amsterdam 1996, 107-120.

"Het Réveil" and "De moderne theologie", in: C. Augustijn, F.G.M. Broeyer, P. Visser, E.G.E. van der Wall (eds.), *Reformatorica—Teksten uit de geschiedenis van het Nederlandse protestantisme*, Zoetermeer 1996, 229-238, 246-255.

1997

"Puritanismus, II", in : *Theologische Realenzyklopädie* 27 (1997), 26-30.

"Le protestantisme réformé en Europe au XVIe et au XVIIe siècles" and "Radicaux, millénaristes et spiritualistes", in: John Miller (ed.), *L'Europe protestante aux XVIe et XVIIe siècles*, Paris 1997, 193-208, 271-289.

1998

"Salomon van Til", in: *Biografisch Lexicon voor de geschiedenis van het Nederlandse Protestantisme*, IV, Kampen 1998, 424-428.

"Feestelijke ontvangst van Koning-Stadhouder Willem III in Den Haag"; "De tragiek in het korte leven van de 'negerpredikant' Jacobus Elisa Joannes Capitein"; "Abraham Kuenen, de vader van de historische kritiek in Nederland, als predikant bevestigd", in A.B. Vaandrager (ed.), *Flitsen uit zes eeuwen Kloosterkerk*, Den Haag 1998, 49-53, 59-64, 73-77.

Moreover

Book reviews in: *Journal of the History of Philosophy* 29 (1991), 312-314. *Nederlands Archief voor Kerkgeschiedenis* 71 (1991), 116-120; 72 (1992), 116-118, 233-234; 73 (1993), 128-130; 74 (1994), 129-131; 75 (1995), 135-137; 76 (1996), 94-96, 263-265; 77 (1997), 110-114, 277-280, 282-283. *Kerknieuws* 46 (1989), 12-13; *Centraal Weekblad* 45 (1997), 12, 9; *The Journal of Theological Studies* 49(1998), 460-463.

In Memoriam C.C. de Bruin, in: *Trouw*, 13 oktober 1988.

"Traditie, geschiedenis, continuïteit en SoW", in: *Woord en Dienst* 42 (1993), 301.

Interview "Nadere Reformatie en Piëtisme" (by E.H. Cossee and A. de Groot), in: *Kerktijd* 6 (1994), 1-8.

INDEX OF NAMES AND PLACES

SELECT INDEX OF SUBJECTS

Studies in the History of Christian Thought

EDITED BY HEIKO A. OBERMAN

3. BAUMAN, Cl. *Gewaltlosigkeit im Täufertum.* 1968. ISBN 90 04 02181 7
6. TIERNEY, B. *Origins of Papal Infallibility, 1150-1350.* 2nd ed. 1988. ISBN 90 04 08884 9
10. FARR, W. *John Wyclif as Legal Reformer.* 1974. ISBN 90 04 04027 7
12. BALL, B. W. *A Great Expectation.* Eschatological Thought in English Protestantism. 1975. ISBN 90 04 04315 2
21. NIJENHUIS, W. *Adrianus Saravia (c. 1532-1613).* Dutch Calvinist. 1980. ISBN 90 04 06194 0
22. PARKER, T. H. L. (ed.). *Iohannis Calvini Commentarius in Epistolam Pauli ad Romanos.* 1981. ISBN 90 04 06408 7
25. LOCHER, G. W. *Zwingli's Thought.* New Perspectives. 1981. ISBN 90 04 06420 6
26. GOGAN, B. *The Common Corps of Christendom.* Ecclesiological Themes in Thomas More. 1982. ISBN 90 04 06508 3
27. STOCK, U. *Die Bedeutung der Sakramente in Luthers Sermonen von 1519.* 1982. ISBN 90 04 06536 9
28. YARDENI, M. (ed.). *Modernité et nonconformisme en France à travers les âges.* 1983. ISBN 90 04 07087 7
29. PLATT, J. *Reformed Thought and Scholasticism.* 1982. ISBN 90 04 06593 8
31. SPRUNGER, K. L. *Dutch Puritanism.* 1982. ISBN 90 04 06793 0
32. MEIJERING, E. P. *Melanchthon and Patristic Thought.* 1983. ISBN 90 04 06974 7

34-35. COLISH, M. L. *The Stoic Tradition from Antiquity to the Early Middle Ages.* Vols. 1-2. 2nd ed. 1991. ISBN 90 04 09330 3

36. GUY, B. *Domestic Correspondence of Dominique-Marie Varlet, Bishop of Babylon, 1678-1742.* 1986. ISBN 90 04 07671 9

37-38. CLARK, F. *The Pseudo-Gregorian Dialogues.* 2 pts. 1987. ISBN 90 04 07773 1

39. PARENTE, Jr. J. A. *Religious Drama and the Humanist Tradition.* 1987. ISBN 90 04 08094 5
40. POSTHUMUS MEYJES, G. H. M. *Hugo Grotius, Meletius.* 1988. ISBN 90 04 08356 1
41. FELD, H. *Der Ikonoklasmus des Westens.* 1990. ISBN 90 04 09243 9
42. REEVE, A. and SCREECH, M. A. (eds.). *Erasmus' Annotations on the New Testament.* Acts —Romans — I and II Corinthians. 1990. ISBN 90 04 09124 6
43. KIRBY, W.J.T. *Richard Hooker's Doctrine of the Royal Supremacy.* 1990. ISBN 90 04 08851 2
44. GERSTNER, J.N. *The Thousand Generation Covenant.* Reformed Covenant Theology. 1990. ISBN 90 04 09361 3
46. GARSTEIN, O. *Rome and the Counter-Reformation in Scandinavia.* 1553-1622. 1992. ISBN 90 04 09393 1
47. GARSTEIN, O. *Rome and the Counter-Reformation in Scandinavia.* 1622-1656. 1992. ISBN 90 04 09395 8
48. PERRONE COMPAGNI, V. (ed.). *Cornelius Agrippa, De occulta philosophia Libri tres.* 1992. ISBN 90 04 09421 0
49. MARTIN, D. D. *Fifteenth-Century Carthusian Reform.* The World of Nicholas Kempf. 1992. ISBN 90 04 09636 1
50. HOENEN, M. J. F. M. *Marsilius of Inghen.* Divine Knowledge in Late Medieval Thought. 1993. ISBN 90 04 09563 2
51. O'MALLEY, J. W., IZBICKI, T. M. and CHRISTIANSON, G. (eds.). *Humanity and Divinity in Renaissance and Reformation.* Essays in Honor of Charles Trinkaus. 1993. ISBN 90 04 09804 6
52. REEVE, A. (ed.) and SCREECH, M. A. (introd.). *Erasmus' Annotations on the New Testament.* Galatians to the Apocalypse. 1993. ISBN 90 04 09906 9
53. STUMP, Ph. H. *The Reforms of the Council of Constance (1414-1418).* 1994. ISBN 90 04 09930 1

54. GIAKALIS, A. *Images of the Divine.* The Theology of Icons at the Seventh Ecumenical Council. With a Foreword by Henry Chadwick. 1994. ISBN 90 04 09946 8
55. NELLEN, H. J. M. and RABBIE, E. (eds.). *Hugo Grotius – Theologian.* Essays in Honour of G. H. M. Posthumus Meyjes. 1994. ISBN 90 04 10000 8
56. TRIGG, J. D. *Baptism in the Theology of Martin Luther.* 1994. ISBN 90 04 10016 4
57. JANSE, W. *Albert Hardenberg als Theologe.* Profil eines Bucer-Schülers. 1994. ISBN 90 04 10071 7
59. SCHOOR, R.J.M. VAN DE. *The Irenical Theology of Théophile Brachet de La Milletière (1588-1665).* 1995. ISBN 90 04 09961 1
60. STREHLE, S. *The Catholic Roots of the Protestant Gospel.* Encounter between the Middle Ages and the Reformation. 1995. ISBN 90 04 10203 5
61. BROWN, M.L. *Donne and the Politics of Conscience in Early Modern England.* 1995. ISBN 90 04 10157 8
62. SCREECH, M.A. (ed.). *Richard Mocket, Warden of All Souls College, Oxford, Doctrina et Politia Ecclesiae Anglicanae.* An Anglican Summa. Facsimile with Variants of the Text of 1617. Edited with an Introduction. 1995. ISBN 90 04 10040 7
63. SNOEK, G.J.C. *Medieval Piety from Relics to the Eucharist.* A Process of Mutual Interaction. 1995. ISBN 90 04 10263 9
64. PIXTON, P.B. *The German Episcopacy and the Implementation of the Decrees of the Fourth Lateran Council, 1216-1245.* Watchmen on the Tower. 1995. ISBN 90 04 10262 0
65. DOLNIKOWSKI, E.W. *Thomas Bradwardine: A View of Time and a Vision of Eternity in Fourteenth-Century Thought.* 1995. ISBN 90 04 10226 4
66. RABBIE, E. (ed.). *Hugo Grotius, Ordinum Hollandiae ac Westfrisiae Pietas (1613).* Critical Edition with Translation and Commentary. 1995. ISBN 90 04 10385 6
67. HIRSH, J.C. *The Boundaries of Faith.* The Development and Transmission of Medieval Spirituality. 1996. ISBN 90 04 10428 3
68. BURNETT, S.G. *From Christian Hebraism to Jewish Studies.* Johannes Buxtorf (1564-1629) and Hebrew Learning in the Seventeenth Century. 1996. ISBN 90 04 10346 5
69. BOLAND O.P., V. *Ideas in God according to Saint Thomas Aquinas.* Sources and Synthesis. 1996. ISBN 90 04 10392 9
70. LANGE, M.E. *Telling Tears in the English Renaissance.* 1996. ISBN 90 04 10517 4
71. CHRISTIANSON, G. and T.M. IZBICKI (eds.). *Nicholas of Cusa on Christ and the Church.* Essays in Memory of Chandler McCuskey Brooks for the American Cusanus Society. 1996. ISBN 90 04 10519 0
72. MALI, A. *Mystic in the New World.* Marie de l'Incarnation (1599-1672). 1996. ISBN 90 04 10606 5
73. VISSER, D. *Apocalypse as Utopian Expectation (800-1500).* The Apocalypse Commentary of Berengaudus of Ferrières and the Relationship between Exegesis, Liturgy and Iconography. 1996. ISBN 90 04 10621 9
74. O'ROURKE BOYLE, M. *Divine Domesticity.* Augustine of Thagaste to Teresa of Avila. 1997. ISBN 90 04 10675 8
75. PFIZENMAIER, T.C. *The Trinitarian Theology of Dr. Samuel Clarke (1675-1729).* Context, Sources, and Controversy. 1997. ISBN 90 04 10719 3
76. BERKVENS-STEVELINCK, C., J. ISRAEL and G.H.M. POSTHUMUS MEYJES (eds.). *The Emergence of Tolerance in the Dutch Republic.* 1997. ISBN 90 04 10768 1
77. HAYKIN, M.A.G. (ed.). *The Life and Thought of John Gill (1697-1771).* A Tercentennial Appreciation. 1997. ISBN 90 04 10744 4
78. KAISER, C.B. *Creational Theology and the History of Physical Science.* The Creationist Tradition from Basil to Bohr. 1997. ISBN 90 04 10669 3
79. LEES, J.T. *Anselm of Havelberg.* Deeds into Words in the Twelfth Century. 1997. ISBN 90 04 10906 4
80. WINTER, J.M. VAN. *Sources Concerning the Hospitallers of St John in the Netherlands, 14th-18th Centuries.* 1998. ISBN 90 04 10803 3
81. TIERNEY, B. *Foundations of the Conciliar Theory.* The Contribution of the Medieval Canonists from Gratian to the Great Schism. Enlarged New Edition. 1998. ISBN 90 04 10924 2
82. MIERNOWSKI, J. *Le Dieu Néant.* Théologies négatives à l'aube des temps modernes. 1998. ISBN 90 04 10915 3

83. HALVERSON, J.L. *Peter Aureol on Predestination.* A Challenge to Late Medieval Thought. 1998. ISBN 90 04 10945 5
84. HOULISTON, V. (ed.). *Robert Persons, S.J.: The Christian Directory (1582).* The First Booke of the Christian Exercise, appertayning to Resolution. 1998. ISBN 90 04 11009 7
85. GRELL, O.P. (ed.). *Paracelsus.* The Man and His Reputation, His Ideas and Their Reputation. 1998. ISBN 90 04 11177 8
86. MAZZOLA, E. *The Pathology of the English Renaissance.* Sacred Remains and Holy Ghosts. 1998. ISBN 90 04 11195 6

Prospectus available on request

BRILL — P.O.B. 9000 — 2300 PA LEIDEN — THE NETHERLANDS